U.S. CORPORATE GOVERNANCE

U.S. CORPORATE GOVERNANCE

Edited by Donald H. Chew
and Stuart L. Gillan

Columbia University Press

NEW YORK

Columbia University Press
Publishers Since 1893
New York   Chichester, West Sussex
Copyright © 2009 Morgan Stanley Content Corporation
All rights reserved

Library of Congress Cataloging-in-Publication Data

U.S. corporate governance / edited by Donald H. Chew and Stuart L. Gillan.
    p.   cm.
    Includes index.
    ISBN 978-0-231-14856-6 (cloth : alk. paper)—ISBN 978-0-231-14857-3 (pbk. : alk. paper)—ISBN 978-0-231-51998-4 (e-book)
    1. Corporate governance—United States.   I. Chew, Donald H.   II. Gillan, Stuart L.   III. Title: US corporate governance.

    HD2741.U22   2009
    338.60973—dc22   2009016800

Columbia University Press books are printed on permanent and durable acid-free paper.

This book is printed on paper with recycled content.

Printed in the United States of America

c 10 9 8 7 6 5 4 3 2 1
p 10 9 8 7 6 5 4 3 2 1

References to Internet Web sites (URLs) were accurate at the time of writing. Neither the author nor Columbia University Press is responsible for URLs that may have expired or changed since the manuscript was prepared.

To our wives: Susan Emerson and Laura Gillan

Contents

Introduction / ix

Part I: Broad Perspectives on Corporate Governance

1. Value Maximization, Stakeholder Theory, and the Corporate Objective Function / 3
   Michael C. Jensen

2. The State of U.S. Corporate Governance: What's Right and What's Wrong? / 26
   Bengt Holmstrom and Steven N. Kaplan

3. U.S. Corporate Governance: Accomplishments and Failings: A Discussion with Michael Jensen and Robert Monks / 48

Part II: Internal Governance: Boards and Executive Compensation

4. The Director's New Clothes (or, The Myth of Corporate Accountability) / 79
   Robert Monks and Nell Minow

5. Best Practices in Corporate Governance: What Two Decades of Research Reveals / 90
   Anil Shivdasani and Marc Zenner

6. Pay without Performance: Overview of the Issues / 113
   Lucian A. Bebchuk and Jesse M. Fried

7. Is U.S. CEO Compensation Broken? / 144
   John E. Core, Wayne R. Guay, and Randall S. Thomas

Part III: External Governance: Ownership Structure

8. Just Say No to Wall Street: Putting a Stop to the Earnings Game / 161
   Joseph Fuller and Michael C. Jensen

9. Identifying and Attracting the "Right" Investors:
   Evidence on the Behavior of Institutional Investors / 170
   Brian Bushee

10. U.S. Family-Run Companies—They May Be Better Than You Think / 184
    Henry McVey and Jason Draho

11. The Evolution of Shareholder Activism in the United States / 202
    Stuart L. Gillan and Laura T. Starks

Part IV: External Governance: The Market for Corporate Control

12. Corporate Control and the Politics of Finance / 243
    Michael C. Jensen

13. Where M&A Pays and Where It Strays: Survey of the Research / 280
    Robert Bruner

14. Private Equity, Corporate Governance, and the Reinvention
    of the Market for Corporate Control / 307
    Karen H. Wruck

About the Contributors / 337

Index / 339

Introduction

WRITING IN *THE WEALTH OF NATIONS* IN 1776, Adam Smith was skeptical about the future of the publicly traded corporation, or what back then was called the "joint stock company." Given the role of self-interest in human affairs, the proposition that a faceless and uncoordinated group of outside investors could be brought to entrust their savings to professional corporate managers—people whose interests were almost sure to diverge from their own—was doubtful at best. Faced with the challenge of controlling this divergence of interests, Smith argued that joint stock companies would end up being well suited only to "turnkey operations"—enterprises like banks, canal operators, and water suppliers—that did not require much managerial discretion or initiative, mainly just the ability to administer a preestablished and well-understood set of rules.

But Smith turned out to be wrong. During the past two centuries, publicly traded corporations with dispersed ownership have come to dominate business activity in the United States and the United Kingdom. And in continental Europe and Asia, where private and closely held corporations have long been the rule, listed companies are beginning to account for an expanding share of GDP.

What Smith failed to foresee was the development of effective corporate governance systems. Critical to this development have been innovations in regulation and law, including the enactment of limited liability for shareholders, that offer protection to minority stockholders. But in addition to such legal and regulatory changes, the emergence of effective corporate governance systems has also required the evolution of corporate procedures and financial institutions that work together to assure investors that professional managers will make efficient use of their capital.

In the United States, and indeed around the world, corporate governance mechanisms can be seen as falling into two main categories, internal and external. Internal governance mechanisms include the board of directors, sub-committees of the board (including audit, compensation, and nominating committees), compensation programs designed to align the interests of managers and shareholders, and other corporate control systems. External governance mechanisms include accounting rules and regulatory reporting requirements, external auditors, investment bankers (who help companies raise capital), securities analysts (who issue buy-sell recommendations), credit analysts (who issue credit ratings), local laws (based on where the company is incorporated), and the shareholders themselves (through their willingness to buy and sell shares). Other forces with potential for disciplining corporate managers are product markets (in the sense that consumer dissatisfaction will soon show up in declining profits and stock prices) and the market for executive labor (since a high-level manager's reputation for building shareholder value is likely to be a key determinant of his or her next job). If all of these different mechanisms fail to get managers to work to increase shareholder value, the "market for corporate control"—in its most extreme forms, hostile takeovers and leveraged buyouts (LBOs)—is available as a last resort.

In the past, criticism has been directed mainly at *external* corporate governance mechanisms—at U.S. capital markets and their relentless pressuring of U.S. companies to increase profits. In the 1980s, for example, the popular story was that the threat of takeover by corporate "raiders" was forcing managers to lay off productive employees and cut back on promising investment to meet near-term earnings targets. And in a claim that has been proven wrong by time (and by an impressive body of research documenting the shareholder gains of the 1980s), such cutbacks were in turn said to be weakening the competitive position of American companies relative to their Japanese and European counterparts.

In more recent attacks on U.S. corporate governance, although public accountants and securities analysts and ratings agencies have certainly come in for their share of the blame, the main focus has shifted to *internal* corporate governance. In particular, U.S. boards and managers (particularly those in banks and other financial institutions) are now being subjected to intense criticism and scrutiny. The principal charge appears to be this: many executives of U.S. companies, having received large awards of stock options, took outsized risks and, when given the opportunity, cashed out their holdings when their stock prices proved to be unsustainably high. In a number of cases at the beginning of this decade, notably, Enron and WorldCom, the stock price run-ups were fueled in part by accounting manipulation or outright falsification of reported earnings. In the more recent case of banks and other financial institutions, fair value accounting also enabled the reporting of profits that failed to materialize. But whether achieved by accident or design, the resulting transfers of wealth from "long-term" shareholders to top management have aroused increased skepticism about U.S. financial reporting and executive pay practices—so much so that the U.S. corporate governance system is now once again said to be suffering a crisis of confidence.

But are things as bad as they seem? Although written before the current financial crisis, the chapter in this book by Bengt Holmstrom and Steven Kaplan offers a number of reasons to be optimistic about the future. After pointing to the superior performance of the U.S. economy and stock market (again, until recently), Holmstrom and Kaplan argue that the most important changes in U.S. corporate governance during the 1980s and 1990s—especially the increased ownership of U.S. companies by institutional shareholders and the dramatic increase in equity-based executive pay—have been positive developments on the whole, serving mainly to strengthen the accountability of U.S. managers to their shareholders and to reinforce the bond of common interest between them. The growth of institutional share ownership that accelerated in the 1980s helped corporate raiders to launch the highly productive restructuring of U.S. companies that took place during that decade. And after the shutdown of the leveraged restructuring movement at the end of the 1980s, an explosion of equity-based pay motivated U.S. managers to initiate their own value-increasing restructurings—particularly mergers and acquisitions (M&A) and divestitures—throughout the 1990s.

But if equity incentives played an important role in the corporate value creation of the 1990s, they have also been implicated in the recent scandals, where fraudulent behavior or excessive risk taking have been linked to significant holdings of stock or options. As Holmstrom and Kaplan see it, however, the problem here is not the use of stock or options per se, but rather a serious flaw in the design of equity pay plans. The extraordinary growth of executive stock option grants by U.S. public companies that began in the early 1990s was premised in large part on the accomplishments (also well documented by academic research) of the LBO movement in the 1980s. But while achieving their goal of getting significant equity ownership into the hands of top management, the corporate boards of U.S. public companies failed to recognize a critical feature of the equity typically provided to the key managers of LBO firms—namely, its "illiquidity," resulting from the lack of a public market and extensive restrictions on selling. Without such restrictions, and in the midst of the bull market of the late 1990s, the top managers of U.S. public companies found themselves not only with the opportunity to unload stock during price run-ups, but also under considerable pressure to sustain or propel such run-ups by putting the best face on quarterly accounting results.

As a consequence, all aspects of the U.S. corporate governance system are now being reexamined. (And, given the recent fates of companies like Bear Stearns and Lehman Brothers, even the value of significant employee stock ownership is being questioned.) Indeed, U.S. corporate governance now appears to be at a critical point in its evolutionary course, with major accomplishments behind it and challenges ahead. And to the extent that the U.S. system serves as a model for other national governance systems, the concerns about U.S. corporate governance have become a global preoccupation.

Part I: Broad Perspectives on Corporate Governance

Part I of this book consists of chapters that provide general perspectives on corporate governance and incentives. In "Value Maximization, Stakeholder Theory, and the Corporate Objective Function," Michael Jensen tries to clear up a major source of confusion in corporate governance debates—the continuing disagreement about the fundamental purpose of the corporation. As Jensen notes, there are two main views of the corporate "objective function" that are contending for the minds and hearts of social scientists and policymakers not just in the United States but in all nations with industrialized economies. The first is what Jensen refers to as "the value maximization proposition," which is rooted in 200 years of economic theory and research—which takes the form of "maximization of the long-run market value of the firm"—a value that is determined mainly, though not entirely, by a company's stock price.

The main rival to value maximization is called "stakeholder theory." Stakeholder theory, in brief, says that corporations should attempt to maximize not the value of their shares (or financial claims) but rather the total value that is distributed among all corporate "stakeholders," including employees, customers, suppliers, local communities, and tax collectors. What is perhaps most remarkable about the theory, at least to an economist like Jensen, is its extraordinary popularity. The language and concepts of stakeholder theory have been adopted by many professional organizations, politicians, and special interest groups—and the theory itself has even received formal endorsement by the current British government. And as Jensen goes on to note, stakeholder theory has also received implicit support from many U.S. corporate managers, as reflected in the widespread use of the Balanced Scorecard—a multidimensional performance measurement system that Jensen describes as the "managerial equivalent" of stakeholder theory.

Jensen's verdict on stakeholder theory is as follows: those nations and companies that embrace its principles will find themselves handicapped in the global race for competitive advantage. In Jensen's words, "Without the clarity of mission provided by a single-valued objective function, companies embracing stakeholder theory will experience managerial confusion, conflict, inefficiency, and perhaps even competitive failure. And the same fate is likely to be visited on those companies that use the so-called Balanced Scorecard approach—the managerial equivalent of stakeholder theory—as a performance measurement system."

Jensen goes on to propose a "somewhat new" version that he calls *"enlightened* value maximization." As Jensen describes it, "Enlightened value maximization uses much of the structure of stakeholder theory but accepts maximization of the long-run value of the firm as the criterion for making the requisite tradeoffs among its stakeholders." He also ends with a strongly qualified endorsement of the Balanced Scorecard: although likely to be disastrous as the basis of a performance measurement system with its dozen or so measures (it is more a "dashboard" or "instrument panel" than it is a scorecard), it can nevertheless play a valuable role in helping managers and employees understand the different drivers of value in their business.

Following Jensen's attempt to clarify the corporate mission, Bengt Holmstrom and Steven Kaplan offer their fundamentally optimistic assessment of "The State of U.S. Corporate Governance." As already discussed, Holmstrom and Kaplan argue that the most notable changes in U.S. corporate governance in the 1980s and 1990s—including the institutionalization of U.S. shareholders and the dramatic increase in equity-based pay—have served mainly (though not always) to strengthen the accountability of U.S. managers to their shareholders. The authors' message, then, is that while parts of the U.S. corporate governance system gave way under the exceptional strain created by the bull market of the 1990s, the overall system—which includes oversight by the public and government and the corrective market forces that Miller had so much faith in—reacted quickly and decisively in the first part of this decade to address its weaknesses. Holmstrom and Kaplan also conclude that "the net effect" of such legislative and regulatory changes was "to make a good U.S. system a better one." But, as the authors also cautioned, perhaps the greatest risk then facing the U.S. financial market system (of which corporate governance is a critical part) was that of overregulation. And, as we look forward from the vantage point of today's crisis, the same caution needs to be exercised when attempting to rein in the risk taking of our financial institutions.

In the roundtable with which the section closes, two of America's most prominent shareholder activists, Robert Monks and Michael Jensen, discuss three current controversies surrounding the U.S. corporate governance system: (1) the case for increasing shareholder "democracy" by expanding investor access to the corporate proxy; (2) lessons for public companies in the success of private equity; and (3) the current level and design of CEO pay.

On the first of the three subjects, Robert Monks suggests that the U.S. should adopt the British convention of the "extraordinary general meeting," or "EGM," which gives a majority of shareholders who attend the meeting the right to remove any or all of a company's directors "with or without cause." Such shareholder meetings are permitted in virtually all developed economies outside the U.S. because, as Monks goes on to say, they represent "a far more efficient and effective solution than the idea of having shareholders nominate people for the simple reason that even very involved, financially sophisticated fiduciaries are not the best people to nominate directors."

Moreover, according to both Jensen and Monks, corporate boards in the U.K. do a better job than their U.S. counterparts of monitoring top management on behalf of shareholders. In contrast to the U.S., where the majority of companies continue to be run by CEO/Chairmen, over 90% of English companies are now chaired by outside directors, contributing to "a culture of independent-minded chairmen capable of providing a high level of oversight." In the U.S., by contrast, most corporate directors continue to view themselves as "employees of the CEO." And, as a result, U.S. boards generally fail to exercise effective oversight and control until outside forces—often in the form of activist investors such as hedge funds and private equity—bring about a "crisis."

In companies owned and run by private equity firms, by contrast, top management is vigorously monitored and controlled by a board made up of the firm's largest investors. And the fact that the rewards to the operating heads of successful private equity-controlled firms are typically multiples of those received by comparably effective public company CEOs suggests that the problem with U.S. CEO pay is not its level, but its lack of correlation with performance.

Part II: Internal Governance: Boards and Executive Compensation

Part II contains four chapters that each address important aspects of internal corporate governance. The first examines the role of the corporate board of directors. As the shareholders' representatives, corporate boards are charged with hiring, firing, and compensating the senior management team. Yet many contend that boards have failed in their duties and that boards function mainly as puppets of management. Nevertheless, the chapters do furnish some evidence that some boards have become more independent and effective and that boards can make a difference for shareholders.

Corporate boards of directors can be viewed as the linchpin of internal corporate governance. As the representatives of shareholders, boards are charged with hiring, firing, and compensating the senior management team. But in "The Director's New Clothes (or, The Myth of Corporate Accountability)," Robert Monks and Nell Minow suggest that since the board is "selected by management, paid by management, and—perhaps most important—informed by management, it is easy for directors to become captive to management's perspective." The authors contend that the idea of boards being accountable to shareholders is a myth—in reality, boards are beholden to management.

Moreover, a theme throughout the chapter is that management control of the director nominations process implies that current board structures are self-perpetuating. Consequently, shareholders' ability to seek genuine board representation is severely restricted. This observation is quite pertinent in today's environment with reports that the Securities and Exchange Commission is exploring whether the director nominations process should be more accessible to shareholders.

At the same time, there is evidence that some board characteristics are beneficial. Drawing on a broad range of academic studies in "Best Practices in Corporate Governance: What Two Decades of Research Reveals," Anil Shivdasani and Marc Zenner provide insights into key questions about optimal board structure, including the following: What makes directors independent? What is the right mix of inside, independent, and nonindependent outside directors on the board? How large should boards be? What are the desirable skill sets for board members? And how should board members be compensated? While Shivdasani and Zenner note that the evidence supports the conventional wisdom that independence on the board and nominating and compensation committees, along with incentive-based compensation for directors, are beneficial, the evidence for separating the positions of CEO and board chair is less clear. Nonetheless, it is apparent that context is important—that is, while there are some basic tenets of good governance when it comes to board structure, firm-specific needs must also be considered.

Compensation structures are also key aspects of internal governance. Indeed, since the early 1990s, the level of equity-based compensation has increased dramatically at U.S. companies. As most financial economists would verify, this dramatic increase has been a positive development on the whole, serving mainly to strengthen the bond of common interest between U.S. managers and their shareholders. But there have also been unfortunate side effects. The top executives of many U.S. companies took advantage of the bull market of the late 1990s to cash in significant portions of their stock and options. Making things worse, in a number of cases like Enron and WorldCom, stock price run-ups were fueled in part by manipulation of reported earnings. And whether accidental or deliberate, the resulting transfers of wealth from "long-term" shareholders to selling executives have aroused widespread skepticism about U.S. pay practices and corporate governance in general.

Perhaps the most forceful and credible statement of this skepticism is a recent book by two law professors, Lucian Bebchuk of Harvard and Jesse Fried of Berkeley. In "Pay without Performance: Overview of the Issues," Bebchuk and Fried argue that the pay-setting process in U.S. public companies is inconsistent with the economists' model of "arm's-length contracting" between executives and boards in a competitive labor market. In place of this model, the authors argue that managerial power and influence play a major role in shaping executive pay, distorting pay plans in ways that impose significant costs on investors and the economy.

Bebchuk and Fried also marshal evidence of a correlation between "power and pay." Studies have shown, for example, that CEO pay is higher when boards are larger, outside directors serve on three or more boards, more of the outside directors have been appointed by the CEO, and the CEO is chairman of the board. Other studies show that CEO pay is negatively correlated with such variables as the stock ownership of compensation committee members, the presence and percentage ownership of large outside blockholders, and the degree of concentration of institutional shareholders, all of which are expected to have disciplining effects. Also telling, studies report that CEOs of companies with antitakeover provisions have "above-market" pay before adopting the provisions and that they get further increases after the provisions are put in place.

The authors' main concern, however, is not the levels of executive pay but the distortion of incentives caused by practices that fail to tie pay to performance (including the widespread use of "stealth compensation," such as pensions and other deferred benefits, and "gratuitous goodbye payments") and to impose strict limits on executives' ability to sell their shares.

John Core, Wayne Guay, and Randall Thomas offer a different perspective in "Is U.S. CEO Compensation Broken?" The authors note that U.S. pay practices have not prevented the productivity and stock returns of U.S. companies from exceeding those of their international competitors over the past twenty-five years. And as the authors also show, the public debate over pay continues to be fueled by a misconception that is reinforced by media stories each March that, in focusing on annual pay and stock sales, are bound to miss the link between pay and performance. To see the extent to which CEOs' fortunes are really tied to those of their shareholders, you need to know not just how much they got paid last year but the change in the value of their accumulated stock and option holdings. In doing this analysis, the authors find that the pay-performance relationship is very much in evidence in large U.S. companies.

Part III: External Governance: Ownership Structure

One aspect of U.S. corporate governance that continues to receive criticism are the corporate practices of earnings guidance and earnings management. In "Just Say No to Wall Street: Putting a Stop to the Earnings Game," Jensen joins with Joe Fuller in arguing that CEOs are in a bind with Wall Street. Managers up and down the hierarchy work hard at putting together plans and budgets for the next year only to discover that the bottom line falls far short of Wall Street's expectations. CEOs and CFOs are therefore left in a difficult situation; they can stretch to try to meet Wall Street's projections or prepare to suffer the consequences if they fail. All too often top managers react by encouraging or requiring middle-and lower-level managers to redo their forecasts and budgets to get them in line with external expectations. In some cases, managers simply acquiesce to increasingly unrealistic analyst forecasts and adopt them as the basis for setting organizational goals and developing internal budgets. But either approach sets up the firm and its managers for failure if external expectations are impossible to meet.

Using the experiences of Enron and Nortel—experiences that were to be repeated by companies like Merrill Lynch and much of the U.S. financial sector—the authors illustrate the dangers of conforming to market pressures for unrealistic growth targets. They emphasize that an overvalued stock, by encouraging overpriced acquisitions and other value-destroying forms of overinvestment, can be as damaging to the long-run health of a company as an undervalued stock. Ending the "expectations game" requires that CEOs reclaim the initiative in setting expectations and forecasts so that stocks can trade at close to their intrinsic value. Managers must make their organizations more transparent to investors; they must promise only those results that they have a legitimate prospect of delivering and be willing to inform the market when they believe their stock is overvalued.

In so doing, moreover, corporate managers may end up influencing the kinds of investors who choose to own their shares. In "Identifying and Attracting the 'Right' Investors: Evidence on the Behavior of Institutional Investors," Brian Bushee summarizes the findings of research conducted with the aim of answering a number of questions about institutional investors: Are there significant differences among institutional investors in time horizon and other trading practices that would enable such investors to be classified into types on the basis of their observable behavior? Assuming the answer is yes, do corporate managers respond differently to the pressures created by different types of investors—and, by implication, are certain kinds of investors more desirable from corporate management's point of view? What kinds of companies tend to attract each type of investor, and how does a company's disclosure policy affect that process? The author's approach identifies three categories of institutional investors: (1) "transient" institutions, which exhibit high portfolio turnover and own small stakes in portfolio companies; (2) "dedicated" holders, which provide stable ownership and take large positions in individual firms; and (3) "quasi-indexers," which also trade infrequently but own small stakes (similar to an index strategy).

As might be expected, the disproportionate presence of transient institutions in a company's investor base appears to intensify pressure for short-term performance while also resulting in excess volatility in the stock price. Also not surprising, transient investors are attracted to companies with investor relations activities geared toward forward-looking information and "news events"—such as management earnings forecasts—that constitute trading opportunities for such investors. By contrast, quasi-indexers and dedicated institutions are largely insensitive to short-term performance, and their presence is associated with lower stock price volatility. The research also suggests that companies that focus their disclosure activities on historical information as opposed to earnings forecasts tend to attract quasi-indexers instead of transient investors.

In sum, the author's research suggests that changes in disclosure practices have the potential to shift the composition of a firm's investor base away from transient investors and toward more patient capital. By removing some of the external pressures for short-term performance, such a shift could encourage managers to establish a culture based on long-run value maximization.

In "U.S. Family-Run Companies—They May Be Better Than You Think," Henry McVey and Jason Draho discuss another kind of dedicated holder that continues to play a role in many U.S. companies—the founding family. Contrary to the common perception that family-run businesses are inefficient, the evidence on public family-run companies reported in this chapter suggests that they perform quite well. And there may be some good reasons for this: a family that both owns and controls a company avoids the classic agency problem—the natural tendency of professional managers to pursue some private interests at the expense of their shareholders—that confronts most publicly traded companies. The family's concentrated, long-term investment in the company and knowledge of the business make them potentially effective and highly motivated monitors.

Using a sample of "true" family firms from the S&P 500 (one that deliberately excludes "founder companies" like Microsoft and Dell), the authors show that these companies have in recent years produced considerably higher stock returns than their nonfamily counterparts. At the same time, family companies with dual-class share structures produced lower returns than did those with a single class of shares, and the returns to dual-class firms with insider-dominated boards were lower still. Specific examples highlight the different ways that families maintain control, the consequences of the CEO choice (family member versus professional manager), and the potential benefits of the family's permanent presence, including a long-term investment focus and reputation for fair dealing with corporate stakeholders.

Although institutional investors now occupy an important position in U.S. governance, this has not always been the case, as discussed by Stuart Gillan and Laura Starks in "The Evolution of Shareholder Activism in the United States." In the early 1900s, American financial institutions were active participants in U.S. corporate governance. But during the next few decades, laws were passed that limited the power of financial intermediaries and prevented them from having an active role in corporate governance. The consequence of such laws and regulations was a progressive widening of the gap between ownership and control in large U.S. public companies.

In 1942, SEC rule changes allowed shareholders to submit proposals for inclusion on corporate ballots. Since that time, shareholder activists have used the proxy process, along with other approaches, to pressure corporate boards and managers for change. In particular, the involvement of large institutional shareholders increased dramatically in the mid-1980s with the advent of public pension fund activism.

Although the aim of most shareholder activism is to increase corporate value, the empirical evidence on the effects of such activism is at best mixed. Studies have reported positive short-term market reactions to announcements of certain kinds of activism, as well as value-increasing changes in corporate investment and financing decisions in response to private shareholder activism. However, there is little evidence of improvement in the long-term operating or stock market performance of the targeted companies. The recent increase in hedge fund activism appears to be associated with dramatic corporate changes and increases in share values. But the research in this area, although suggestive, is still somewhat preliminary and the longer-term effects of such activism will become clear only with time.

Part IV: External Governance: The Market for Corporate Control

In "Corporate Control and the Politics of Finance," Michael Jensen provides a comprehensive perspective on the market for corporate control, the role of active investors and LBO groups in this marketplace, and how the resulting restructuring can translate into increased economic efficiency (and thus social welfare gains). At the same time, Jensen argues that law and regulation, including aspects of the bankruptcy code, can interfere with incentives for the restructuring of financially distressed firms, thus increasing agency costs and destroying economic value.

Although more than seventeen years have elapsed since this piece was written, the issues discussed shed light on events that we have witnessed in the United States during the past few years—a wave of LBO activity; increasingly active shareholders; and now, with the economic downturn and financial crisis, corporate downsizing and failure. A central question in today's environment is the extent to which this reflects failed corporate governance. While there are clearly governance concerns in today's economic environment, Jensen's discussion of "contract failure" in venture markets also seems quite relevant to today's crisis in real estate and financial markets. Jensen argues that the main problem with the LBO and highly leveraged transaction markets in the 1980s was their failure to require deal-makers to put significant equity (net of their fees) into their own deals, thereby providing them with incentives to do economically viable deals. Because deal-makers collected their fees up front and had no (or a residual) economic interest thereafter, too many deals were done—an argument that has remarkable parallels in the context of our current real estate and financial problems.

The business press has also featured stories of value destruction in mergers and acquisitions. In "Where M&A Pays and Where It Strays," Robert Bruner reviews the large and growing body of academic studies to refute the popular notion that corporate mergers and acquisitions generally fail to increase productivity and end up reducing shareholder value. A careful review of the evidence starts by confirming the obvious—namely, that the shareholders of selling firms earn large returns from M&A—and goes on to demonstrate an economic reality that is not widely understood: shareholders of acquirers generally earn about the required rate of return on investment, and hence M&A is at least a value-maintaining proposition.

Of greatest interest to corporate practitioners, however, is the very large dispersion of outcomes that underlies the average returns. Closer inspection of this variability shows that certain circumstances and company characteristics are reliably associated with value-increasing M&A. In particular, acquisitions of related companies tend to be better received by the market and to produce higher post-merger operating returns than do diversifying transactions (though there are a number of successful instances of the latter). Other fairly reliable indicators of value-increasing M&A are transactions involving mergers of equals or of smaller private targets (where the bidding competition is less intense) and deals structured as earn-outs and financed primarily with cash rather than with stock.

But what of the growing role in U.S. M&A played by private equity? Until credit markets began their sharp contraction in July 2007, U.S. private equity firms were consistently winning the competition for deals with corporate (or "strategic") buyers. In "Private Equity, Corporate Governance, and the Reinvention of the Market for Corporate Control," Karen Wruck argues that the effects of private equity on the behavior of companies both public and private have been important enough to warrant a new definition of the market for corporate control—one that emphasizes corporate governance and the benefits of the competition for deals between private equity firms and public acquirers. Along with their more effective governance systems, top buyout firms have developed a distinctive approach to reorganizing companies for efficiency and value. The author's research on private equity, comprising over 20 years of interviews and case studies as well as large-sample analysis, has led her to identify four principles of reorganization that help explain the success of these buyout firms. Besides providing a source of competitive advantage to private equity firms, the management practices that derive from these four principles are now being adopted by many *public* companies. And, in the author's words, "private equity's most important and lasting contribution to the global economy may well be its effect on the world's public corporations—those companies that will continue to carry out the lion's share of the world's growth opportunities."

PART I

Broad Perspectives on Corporate Governance

CHAPTER 1

Value Maximization, Stakeholder Theory, and the Corporate Objective Function

MICHAEL C. JENSEN

IN MOST INDUSTRIALIZED NATIONS TODAY, economists, management scholars, policymakers, corporate executives, and special interest groups are engaged in a high-stakes debate over corporate governance. In some scholarly and business circles, the discussion focuses mainly on questions of policies and procedures designed to improve oversight of corporate managers by boards of directors. But at the heart of the current global corporate governance debate is a remarkable division of opinion about the fundamental purpose of the corporation. Much of the discord can be traced to the complexity of the issues and to the strength of the conflicting interests that are likely to be affected by the outcome. But also fueling the controversy are political, social, evolutionary, and emotional forces that we don't usually think of as operating in the domain of business and economics. These forces serve to reinforce a model of corporate behavior that draws on concepts of "family" and "tribe." And as I argue in this chapter, this model is an anachronism—a holdover from an earlier period of human development that nevertheless continues to cause much confusion among corporate managers about what it is that they and their organizations are supposed to do.

At the level of the individual organization, the most basic issue of governance is the following. Every organization has to ask and answer the question: What are we trying to accomplish? Or, to put the same question in more concrete terms: How do we keep score? When all is said and done, how do we measure better versus worse?

At the economy-wide or social level, the issue is this: If we could dictate the criterion or objective function to be maximized by firms (and thus the performance criterion by which corporate executives choose among alternative policy options), what would it be? Or, to put the issue even more simply: How do we want the firms in our economy to measure their own performance? How do we want them to determine what is better versus worse?

Most economists would answer simply that managers must have a criterion for evaluating performance and deciding between alternative courses of action, and that the criterion should be maximization of the long-term market value of the firm. (And "firm value," by the way, means not just the value of the equity, but the sum of the values of *all* financial claims on the firm—debt, warrants, and preferred stock, as well as equity.) This Value Maximization proposition has its roots in two hundred years of research in economics and finance.

The main contender to value maximization as the corporate objective is called "stakeholder theory." Stakeholder theory says that managers should make decisions that take account of the interests of *all* the stakeholders in a firm. Stakeholders include all individuals or groups who can substantially affect, or be affected by, the welfare of the firm—a category that includes not only the financial claimholders, but also employees, customers, communities, and government officials.[1] In contrast to the grounding of value maximization in economics, stakeholder theory has its roots in sociology, organizational behavior, the politics of special interests, and, as I will discuss below, managerial self-interest. The theory is now popular and has received the formal endorsement of many professional organizations, special interest groups, and governmental bodies, including the current British government.[2]

But, as I argue in this chapter, stakeholder theory should not be viewed as a legitimate contender to value maximization because it fails to provide a *complete* specification of the corporate purpose or objective function. To put the matter more concretely, whereas value maximization provides corporate managers with a single objective, stakeholder theory directs corporate managers to serve "many masters." And, to paraphrase the old adage, when there are many masters, all end up being shortchanged. Without the clarity of mission provided by a single-valued objective function, companies embracing stakeholder theory will experience managerial confusion, conflict, inefficiency, and perhaps even competitive failure. And the same fate is likely to be visited on those companies that use the so-called Balanced Scorecard approach—the managerial equivalent of stakeholder theory—as a performance measurement system.

But if stakeholder theory and the Balanced Scorecard can destroy value by obscuring the overriding corporate goal, does that mean they have no legitimate corporate uses? And can corporate managers succeed by simply holding up value maximization as the goal and ignoring their stakeholders? The answer to both is an emphatic no. In order to maximize value, corporate managers must not only satisfy but enlist the support of all corporate stakeholders—customers, employees, managers, suppliers, local communities. Top management plays a critical role in this function through its leadership and effectiveness in creating, projecting, and sustaining the company's strategic vision. And even if the Balanced Scorecard is likely to be counterproductive as a performance evaluation and reward system, the *process* of creating the scorecard can add significant value by helping managers understand both the company's strategy and the drivers of value in their businesses.

With this in mind, I clarify what I believe is the proper relation between value maximization and stakeholder theory by proposing a (somewhat) new corporate objective function. I call it *enlightened* value maximization, and it is identical to what I call *enlightened* stakeholder theory. Enlightened value maximization uses much of the structure of stakeholder theory but accepts maximization of the long-run value of the firm as the criterion for making the requisite tradeoffs among its stakeholders. Enlightened stakeholder theory, while focusing attention on meeting the demands of all important corporate constituencies, specifies long-term value maximization as the firm's objective. In so doing, it solves the problems arising from the multiple objectives that accompany traditional stakeholder theory by giving managers a clear way to think about and make the tradeoffs among corporate stakeholders.

The answers to the questions of how managers should define better versus worse, and how managers in fact do define it, have important implications for social welfare. Indeed, the answers provide the business equivalent of the medical profession's Hippocratic oath. It is an indication of the infancy of the science of management that so many in the world's business schools, as well as in professional business organizations, seem to understand so little of the fundamental issues in contention.

With this introduction of the issues, let me now move to a detailed examination of value maximization and stakeholder theory.

The Logical Structure of the Problem

In discussing whether firms should maximize value, we must separate out two distinct issues:

1. Should the firm have a single-valued objective?

2. And, if so, should that objective be value maximization or something else (e.g., maintaining employment or improving the environment)?

The debate over whether corporations should maximize value or act in the interests of their stakeholders is generally couched in terms of the second issue, and is often mistakenly framed as stockholders *versus* stakeholders. The real conflict here, though this is rarely stated or even recognized, is over the first issue—that is, whether the firm should have a single-valued objective function or scorecard. The failure to frame the problem in this way has contributed greatly to widespread misunderstanding and contentiousness.

What is commonly known as stakeholder theory, while not totally without content, is fundamentally flawed because it violates the proposition that a single-valued objective is a prerequisite for purposeful or rational behavior by any organization. In particular, a firm that adopts stakeholder theory will be handicapped in the competition for survival because, as a basis for action, stakeholder theory politicizes the corporation and leaves its managers empowered to exercise their own preferences in spending the firm's resources.

Issue 1: Purposeful Behavior Requires the Existence of a Single-Valued Objective Function

Consider a firm that wishes to increase both its current-year profits and its market share. Assume, as shown in figure 1.1, that over some range of values of market share, profits increase. But, at some point, increases in market share come only at the expense of reduced current-year profits—say, because increased expenditures on R&D and advertising, or price reductions to increase market share, reduce this year's profit. Therefore, it is not logically possible to speak of maximizing both market share and profits.

In this situation, it is impossible for a manager to decide on the level of R&D, advertising, or price reductions because he or she is faced with the need to make tradeoffs between the two "goods"—profits and market share—but has no way to do so. While the manager knows that the firm should be at the point of maximum profits or maximum market share (or somewhere between them),

FIGURE 1.1

Tradeoff between Profits and Market Share

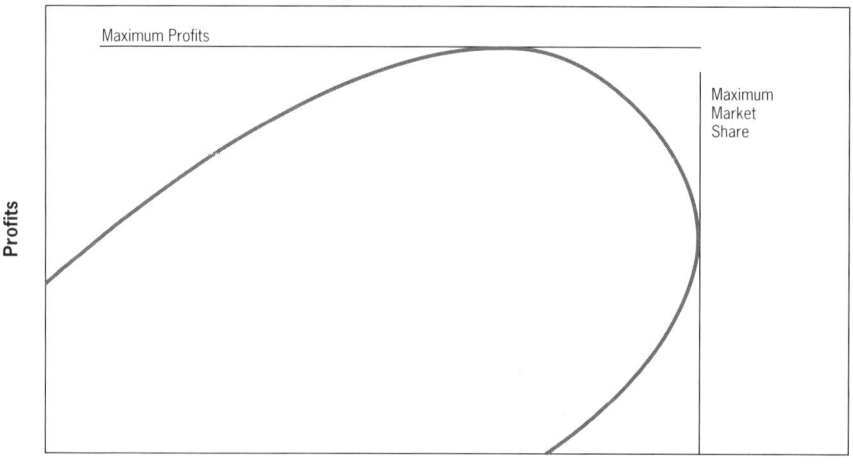

there is no purposeful way to decide where to be in the area in which the firm can obtain more of one good only by giving up some of the other.

Multiple Objectives Is No Objective

It is logically impossible to maximize in more than one dimension at the same time unless the dimensions are what are known as "monotonic transformations" of one another. Thus, telling a manager to maximize current profits, market share, future growth in profits, and anything else one pleases will leave that manager with no way to make a reasoned decision. In effect, it leaves the manager with *no* objective. The result will be confusion and a lack of purpose that will handicap the firm in its competition for survival.[3]

A company can resolve this ambiguity by specifying the tradeoffs among the various dimensions, and doing so amounts to specifying an overall objective such as $V=f(x, y, \ldots)$ that explicitly incorporates the effects of decisions on *all* the performance criteria—all the goods or bads (denoted by $(x, y, \ldots)$) that can affect the firm (such as cash flow, risk, and so on). At this point, the logic above does not specify what V is. It could be anything the board of directors chooses, such as employment, sales, or growth in output. But, as I argue below, social welfare and survival will severely constrain the boards' choices.

Nothing in the analysis so far has said that the objective function f must be well behaved and easy to maximize. If the function is non-monotonic, or even chaotic, it makes it more difficult for managers to find the overall maximum. (For example, as I discuss later, the relationship between the value of the firm and a company's current earnings and investors' expectations about its future earnings and investment expenditures will often be difficult to formulate with much precision.) But even in these situations, the meaning of "better" or "worse" is defined, and managers and their monitors have a "principled"—that is, an objective and theoretically consistent—basis for choosing and auditing decisions. Their choices are not just a matter of their own personal preferences among various goods and bads.

Given managers' uncertainty about the exact specification of the objective function f, it is perhaps better to call the objective function "value seeking" rather than value maximization. This way one avoids the confusion that arises when some argue that maximizing is difficult or impossible if the world is structured in sufficiently complicated ways.[4] It is not necessary that we be able to maximize, only that we can tell when we are getting better—that is, moving in the right direction.

Issue 2: Total Firm Value Maximization Makes Society Better Off

Given that a firm must have a single objective that tells us what is better and what is worse, we then must face the issue of what that definition of "better" is.

Even though the single objective will always be a complicated function of many different goods or bads, the short answer to the question is that two hundred years' worth of work in economics and finance indicate that social welfare is maximized when all firms in an economy attempt to maximize their own total firm value. The intuition behind this criterion is simple: that value is created—and when I say "value" I mean "social" value—whenever a firm produces an output, or set of outputs, that is valued by its customers at more than the value of the inputs it consumes (as valued by their suppliers) in the production of the outputs. Firm value is simply the long-term market value of this expected stream of benefits.

To be sure, there are circumstances when the value-maximizing criterion does not maximize social welfare—notably, when there are monopolies or "externalities." Monopolies tend to charge prices that are too high, resulting in less than the socially optimal levels of production. By "externalities," economists mean situations in which decision-makers do not bear the full cost or benefit consequences of their choices or actions. Examples are cases of air or water pollution in which a firm adds pollution to the environment without having to purchase the right to do so from the parties giving up the clean air or water. There can be no externalities as long as alienable property rights in all physical assets are defined and assigned to some private individual or firm. Thus, the solution to these problems lies not in telling firms to maximize something other than profits, but in defining and then assigning to some private entity the alienable decision rights necessary to eliminate the externalities.[5] In any case, resolving externality and monopoly problems, as I will discuss later, is the legitimate domain of the government in its rule-setting function.[6]

Maximizing the total market value of the firm—that is, the sum of the market values of the equity, debt, and any other contingent claims outstanding on the firm—is the objective function that will guide managers in making the optimal tradeoffs among multiple constituencies (or stakeholders). It tells the firm to spend an additional dollar of resources to satisfy the desires of each constituency as long as that constituency values the result at more than a dollar. In this case, the payoff to the firm from that investment of resources is at least a dollar (in terms of market value). Although there are many single-valued objective functions that could guide a firm's managers in their decisions, value maximization is an important one because it leads under most conditions to the maximization of social welfare. But let's look more closely at this.

Value Maximizing and Social Welfare

Much of the discussion in policy circles about the proper corporate objective casts the issue in terms of the conflict among various constituencies, or "stakeholders," in the corporation. The question then becomes whether shareholders should be held in higher regard than other constituencies, such as employees, customers, creditors, and so on. But it is both unproductive and incorrect to frame the issue in this manner. The real issue is what corporate behavior will get the most out of society's limited resources—or equivalently, what behavior will result in the least social waste—not whether one group is or should be more privileged than another.

Profit Maximization: A Simplified Case

To see how value maximization leads to a socially efficient solution, let's first consider an objective function, profit maximization, in a world in which all production runs are infinite and cash flow streams are level and perpetual. This scenario with level and perpetual streams allows us to ignore the complexity introduced by the tradeoffs between current- and future-year profits (or, more accurately, cash flows). Consider now the social welfare effects of a firm's decision to take resources out of the economy in the form of labor hours, capital, or materials purchased voluntarily from their owners in single-price markets. The firm uses these inputs to produce outputs of goods or services that are then sold to consumers through voluntary transactions in single-price markets.

In this simple situation, a company that takes inputs out of the economy and puts its output of goods and services back into the economy increases aggregate welfare if the prices at which it sells the goods more than cover the costs it incurs in purchasing the inputs (including, of course, the cost of the capital the firm is using). Clearly the firm should expand its output as long as an additional dollar of resources taken out of the economy is valued by the consumers of the incremental product at more than a dollar. Note that it is precisely because profit is the amount by which revenues exceed costs—by which the value of output exceeds the value of inputs—that profit maximization[7] leads to an efficient social outcome.[8]

Because the transactions are voluntary, we know that the owners of the inputs value them at a level less than or equal to the price the firm pays—otherwise they wouldn't sell them. Therefore, as long as there are no negative externalities in the input factor markets,[9] the opportunity cost to society of those inputs is no higher than the total cost to the firm of acquiring them. I say "no higher" because some suppliers of inputs to the firm are able to earn "rents" by obtaining prices higher than the value of the goods to them. But such rents do not represent social costs, only transfers of wealth to those suppliers. Likewise, as long as there are no externalities in the output markets, the value to society of the goods and services produced by the firm is at least as great as the price the firm receives for the sale of those goods and services. If this were not true, the individuals purchasing them would not do so. Again, as in the case of producer surplus on inputs, the benefit to society is higher to the extent that consumer surplus exists (that is, to the extent that some consumers are able to purchase the output at prices lower than the value to them).

In sum, when a company acquires an additional unit of any input(s) to produce an additional unit of any output, it increases social welfare by at least the amount of its profit—the difference between the value of the output and the cost of the input(s) required in producing it.[10] And thus the signals to the management are clear: Continue to expand purchases of inputs and sell the resulting outputs as long as an additional dollar of inputs generates sales of at least a dollar.

Value and Tradeoffs through Time

In a world in which cash flows, profits, and costs are not uniform over time, managers must deal with the tradeoffs of these items through time. A common case is when a company's capital investment comes in lumps that have to be funded up front, while production and revenue occurs in the future. Knowing whether society will be benefited or harmed requires knowing whether the future output will be valuable enough to offset the cost of having people give up their labor, capital, and material inputs in the present. Interest rates help us make this decision by telling us the cost of giving up a unit of a good today for receipt at some time in the future. So long as people take advantage of the opportunity to borrow or lend at a given interest rate, that rate determines the value of moving a marginal dollar of resources (inputs or consumption goods) forward or backward in time.[11] In this world, individuals are as well off as possible if they maximize their wealth as measured by the discounted present value of all future claims. In addition to interest rates, managers also need to take into account the risk of their investments and the premium the market charges for bearing such risk. But, when we add uncertainty and risk into the equation, nothing of major importance is changed in this proposition as long as there are capital markets in which the individual can buy and sell risk at a given price. In this case, it is the risk-adjusted interest rate that is used in calculating the market value of risky claims. The corporate objective function that maximizes social welfare thus becomes "maximize current total firm market value." It tells firms to expand output and investment to the point where the present market value of the firm is at a maximum.[12]

Stakeholder Theory

To the extent that stakeholder theory says that firms should pay attention to all their constituencies, the theory is unassailable. Taken this far, stakeholder theory is completely consistent with value maximization or value-seeking behavior, which implies that managers must pay attention to all constituencies that can affect the value of the firm.

But there is more to the stakeholder story than this. Any theory of corporate decision-making must tell the decision-makers—in this case, managers and boards of directors—how to choose among multiple constituencies with competing and, in some cases, conflicting interests. Customers want low prices, high quality, and full service. Employees want high wages, high-quality working conditions, and fringe benefits, including vacations, medical benefits, and pensions. Suppliers of capital want low risk and high returns. Communities want high charitable contributions, social expenditures by companies to benefit the community at large, increased local investment, and stable employment. And so it goes with every conceivable constituency. Obviously any decision criterion—and the objective function is at the core of any decision criterion—must specify how to make the tradeoffs between these demands.

The Specification of Tradeoffs and the Incompleteness of Stakeholder Theory

Value maximization (or value seeking) provides the following answer to the tradeoff question: Spend an additional dollar on any constituency provided the long-term value added to the firm from such expenditure is a dollar or more. Stakeholder theory, by contrast,[13] contains no conceptual specification of how to make the tradeoffs among stakeholders. And as I argue below, it is this failure to provide a criterion for making such tradeoffs, or even to acknowledge the need for them, that makes stakeholder theory a prescription for destroying firm value and reducing social welfare. This failure also helps explain the theory's remarkable popularity.

Implications for Managers and Directors

Because stakeholder theory leaves boards of directors and executives in firms with no principled criterion for decision-making, companies that try to follow the dictates of stakeholder theory will eventually fail if they are competing with firms that are aiming to maximize value. If this is true, why do so many managers and directors of corporations embrace stakeholder theory?

One answer lies in their personal short-run interests. By failing to provide a definition of "better," stakeholder theory effectively leaves managers and directors unaccountable for their stewardship of the firm's resources. Without criteria for performance, managers cannot be evaluated in any principled way. Therefore, stakeholder theory plays into the hands of managers by allowing them to pursue their own interests at the expense of the firm's financial claimants and society at large. It allows managers and directors to devote the firm's resources to their own favorite causes—the environment, art, cities, medical research—without being held accountable for the effect of such expenditures on firm value. (And this can be true even though managers may not consciously recognize that adopting stakeholder theory leaves them unaccountable—especially, for example, when such managers have a strong personal interest in social issues.) By expanding the power of managers in this unproductive way, stakeholder theory increases agency costs in the economic system. And since it expands the power of managers, it is not surprising that stakeholder theory receives substantial support from them.

In this sense, then, stakeholder theory can be seen as gutting the foundations of the firm's internal control systems. By "internal control systems," I mean mainly the corporate performance measurement and evaluation systems that, when properly designed, provide strong incentives for value-increasing behavior. There is simply no principled way within the stakeholder construct (which fails to specify what "better" is) that anyone could say that a manager has done a good or bad job. Stakeholder theory supplants or weakens the power of such control systems by giving managers more power to do whatever they want, subject only to constraints that are imposed by forces *outside* the firm—by the financial markets, the market for corporate control (e.g., the market for hostile takeovers), and, when all else fails, the product markets.

Thus, having observed that the efforts of stakeholder theory advocate weakening internal control systems, it is not surprising to see the theory being used to argue for government restrictions, such as state antitakeover provisions, on financial markets and the market for corporate control. These markets are driven by value maximization and will limit the damage that can be done by managers who adopt stakeholder theory. And, as illustrated by the 1990s campaigns against globalization and free trade, the stakeholder argument is also being used to restrict product-market competition as well.

But there is something deeper than self-interest—something rooted in the evolution of the human psyche—that is driving our attraction to stakeholder theory.

Families versus Markets: The Roots of Stakeholder Theory

Stakeholder theory taps into the deep emotional commitment of most individuals to the family and tribe. For tens of thousands of years, those of our ancestors who had little respect for or loyalty to the family, band, or tribe were much less likely to survive than those who did. In the last few hundred years, we have experienced the emergence of a market exchange system of prices and the private property rights on which they are based. This system of voluntary and decentralized coordination of human action has brought huge increases in human welfare and freedom of action.

As Friedrich von Hayek points out, we are generally unaware of the functioning of these market systems because no single mind invented or designed them—and because they work in very complicated and subtle ways. In Hayek's words:

We are led—for example, by the pricing system in market exchange—to do things by circumstances of which we are largely unaware and which produce results that we do not intend. In our economic activities we do not know the needs which we satisfy nor the sources of the things which we get. Almost all of us serve people whom we do not know, and even of whose existence we are ignorant; and we in turn constantly live on the services of other people of whom we know nothing. All this is possible because we stand in a great framework of institutions and traditions—economic, legal, moral—into which we fit ourselves by obeying certain rules of conduct that we never made, and which we have never understood in the sense in which we understand how the things that we manufacture function.[14]

Moreover, these systems operate in ways that limit the options of the small group or family, and these constraints are neither well understood nor instinctively welcomed by individuals. Many people are drawn to stakeholder theory through their evolutionary attachment to the small group and the family. As Hayek puts it:

Constraints on the practices of the small group, it must be emphasized and repeated, are *hated.* For, as we shall see, the individual following them, even though he depends on them for life, does not and usually cannot understand how they function or how they benefit him. He knows so many objects that seem desirable but for which he is not permitted to grasp, and he cannot see how other beneficial features of his environment depend on the discipline to which he is forced to submit—a discipline forbidding him to reach out for these same appealing objects. Disliking these constraints so much, we hardly can be said to have selected them; rather, these constraints selected us: they enabled us to survive.[15]

Thus we have a system in which human beings must simultaneously exist in two orders, what Hayek calls the "micro-cosmos" and the "macro-cosmos":

Moreover, the structures of the extended order are made up not only of individuals but also of many, often overlapping, suborders within which old instinctual responses, such as solidarity and altruism, continue to retain some importance by assisting voluntary collaboration, even though they are incapable, by themselves, of creating a basis for the more extended order. Part of our present difficulty is that we must constantly adjust our lives, our thoughts and our emotions, in order to live simultaneously within different kinds of orders according to different rules. If we were to apply the unmodified, uncurbed rules of the micro-cosmos (i.e., of the small band or troop, or of, say, our families) to the macro-cosmos (our wider civilization), as our instincts and sentimental yearnings often make us wish to do, we would destroy it. Yet if we were always to apply the rules of the extended order to our more intimate groupings, we would crush them. So we must learn to live in two sorts of worlds at once. To apply the name "society" to both, or even to either, is hardly of any use, and can be most misleading.[16]

Stakeholder theory taps into this confusion and antagonism toward markets and relaxes constraints on the small group in ways that are damaging to society as a whole and (in the long run) to the small group itself. Such deeply rooted and generally unrecognized conflict between allegiances to family and tribe and what is good for society as a whole has had a major impact on our evolution. And in this case, the conflict does not end up serving our long-run collective interests.[17]

Enlightened Value Maximization and Enlightened Stakeholder Theory

For those intent on improving management, organizational governance, and performance, there is a way out of the conflict between value maximizing and stakeholder theory. It lies in the melding together of what I call "enlightened value maximization" and "enlightened stakeholder theory."

Enlightened Value Maximization

Enlightened value maximization recognizes that communication with and motivation of an organization's managers, employees, and partners is extremely difficult. What this means in practice is that if we simply tell all participants in an organization that its sole purpose is to maximize value, we will not get maximum value for the organization. Value maximization is not a vision or a strategy or even a purpose; it is the scorecard for the organization. We must give people enough structure to understand what maximizing value means so that they can be guided by it and therefore have a chance to actually achieve it. They must be turned on by the vision or the strategy in the sense that it taps into some human desire or passion of their own—for example, a desire to build the world's best automobile or to create a film or play that will move people for centuries. All this can be not only consistent with value seeking, but a major contributor to it.

And this brings us up against the limits of value maximization per se. Value seeking tells an organization and its participants how their success in achieving a vision or in implementing a strategy will be assessed. But value maximizing or value seeking says nothing about how to create a superior vision or strategy. Nor does it tell employees or managers how to find or establish initiatives or ventures that create value. It tells them only how we will measure success in their activity.

Defining what it means to score a goal in football or soccer, for example, tells the players nothing about how to win the game; it just tells them how the score will be kept. That is the role of value maximization in organizational life. It doesn't tell us how to have a great defense or offense, or what kind of plays to create, or how much to train and practice, or whom to hire, and so on. All of these critical functions are part of the competitive and organizational strategy of any team or organization. Adopting value creation as the scorekeeping measure does nothing to relieve us of the responsibility to do all these things and more in order to survive and dominate our sector of the competitive landscape.

This means, for example, that we must give employees and managers a structure that will help them resist the temptation to maximize short-term financial performance (as typically measured by accounting profits or, even worse, earnings per share). Short-term profit maximization at the expense of long-term value creation is a sure way to destroy value. This is where enlightened stakeholder theory can play an important role. We can learn from stakeholder theorists how to lead managers and participants in an organization to think more generally and creatively about how the organization's policies treat all important constituencies of the firm. This includes not just the stockholders and financial markets, but employees, customers, suppliers, and the community in which the organization exists.

Indeed, it is a basic principle of enlightened value maximization that *we cannot maximize the long-term market value of an organization if we ignore or mistreat any important constituency*. We cannot create value without good relations with customers, employees, financial backers, suppliers, regulators, and communities. But having said that, we can now use the value criterion for choosing among those competing interests. I say "competing" interests because no constituency can be given full satisfaction if the firm is to flourish and survive. Moreover, we can be sure—again, apart from the possibility of externalities and monopoly power—that using this value criterion will result in making society as well off as it can be.

As stated earlier, resolving externality and monopoly problems is the legitimate domain of the government in its rule-setting function. Those who care about resolving monopoly and externality issues will not succeed if they look to corporations to resolve these issues voluntarily. Companies that try to do so either will be eliminated by competitors who choose not to be so civic minded, or will survive only by consuming their economic rents in this manner.

Enlightened Stakeholder Theory

Enlightened stakeholder theory is easy to explain. It can make use of most of what stakeholder theorists offer in the way of processes and audits to measure and evaluate the firm's management of its relations with all important constituencies. Enlightened stakeholder theory adds the simple specification that the objective function—the overriding goal—of the firm is to maximize total long-term firm market value. In short, the change in the total long-term market value of the firm is the scorecard by which success is measured.

I say "long-term" market value to recognize the possibility that financial markets, although forward looking, may not understand the full implications of a company's policies until they begin to show up in cash flows over time. In such cases, management must communicate to investors the policies' anticipated effect on value, and then wait for the market to catch up and recognize the real value of its decisions as reflected in increases in market share, customer and employee loyalty, and, finally, cash flows. Value creation does not mean responding to the day-to-day fluctuations in a firm's value. The market is inevitably ignorant of many managerial actions and opportunities, at least in the short run. In those situations where the financial markets clearly do not have this private competitive information, directors and managers must resist the pressures of those markets while making every effort to communicate their expectations to investors.

In this way, enlightened stakeholder theorists can see that although stockholders are not some special constituency that ranks above all others, long-term stock value is an important determinant (along with the value of debt and other instruments) of total long-term firm value. They would recognize that value creation gives management a way to assess the tradeoffs that must be made among competing constituencies, and that it allows for principled decision-making independent of the personal preferences of managers and directors. Also important, managers and directors become accountable for the assets under their control because the value scorecard provides an objective yardstick against which their performance can be evaluated.

Measurability and Imperfect Knowledge

It is important to recognize that none of the above arguments depend on value being easily observable. Nor do they depend on perfect knowledge of the effects on value of decisions regarding any of a firm's constituencies. The world may be complex and difficult to understand. It may leave us in deep uncertainty about the effects of any decisions we may make. It may be governed by complex dynamic systems that are difficult to optimize in the usual sense. But that does not remove the necessity of making choices on a day-to-day basis. And to do this in a purposeful way we must have a scorecard.

The absence of a scorecard makes it easier for people to engage in value-claiming activities that satisfy one or more group of stakeholders at the expense of value creation. We can take random actions, and we can devise decision rules that depend on superstitions. But none of these are likely to serve us well in the competition for survival.

We must not confuse optimization with value creation or value seeking. To create value we need not know exactly what maximum value is and precisely how it can be achieved. What we must do, however, is to set up our organizations so that managers and employees are clearly motivated to seek value—to institute those changes and strategies that are most likely to cause value to rise. To navigate in such a world in anything close to a purposeful way, we must have a notion of "better," and value seeking is such a notion. I know of no other scorecard that will score the game as well as this one. Under most circumstances and conditions, it tells us when we are getting better and when we are getting worse. It is not perfect, but that is the nature of the world.

The Balanced Scorecard

The Balanced Scorecard is the managerial equivalent of stakeholder theory. Like stakeholder theory, the notion of a "balanced" scorecard appeals to many, but it suffers from many of the same flaws. When we use multiple measures on the Balanced Scorecard to evaluate the performance of people or business units, we put managers in the same impossible position as managers trying to manage under stakeholder theory. We are asking them to maximize in more than one dimension at a time with no idea of the tradeoffs between the measures. As a result, purposeful decisions cannot be made.

The Balanced Scorecard arose from the belief of its originators, Robert Kaplan and David Norton, that purely financial measures of performance are not sufficient to yield effective management decisions.[18] I agree with this conclusion, though, as I suggest below, Kaplan and Norton have inadvertently confused this with the unstated but implicit conclusion that there should never be a *single* measure of performance. Moreover, especially *at lower levels of an organization,* a single pure financial measure of performance is unlikely to properly measure a person's or even a business unit's contribution to a company. In the words of Kaplan and Norton:

> The Balanced Scorecard complements financial measures of past performance with measures of the drivers of future performance. The objectives and measures of the scorecard are derived from an organization's vision and strategy. The objectives and measures view organizational performance from four perspectives: financial, customer, internal business process, and learning and growth. . . .
>
> The Balanced Scorecard expands the set of business unit objectives beyond summary financial measures. Corporate executives can now measure how their business units create value for current and

future customers and how they must enhance internal capabilities and the investment in people, systems, and procedures necessary to improve future performance. The Balanced Scorecard captures the critical value-creation activities created by skilled, motivated organizational participants. While retaining, via the financial perspective, an interest in short-term performance, the Balanced Scorecard clearly reveals the value drivers for superior long-term financial and competitive performance.[19]

As Kaplan and Norton go on to say,

> The measures are *balanced* between the outcome measures—the results of past efforts—and the measures that drive future performance. And the scorecard is *balanced* between objective easily quantified outcome measures and subjective, somewhat judgmental performance drivers of the outcome measures. . . .
>
> A good balanced scorecard should have an appropriate mix of outcomes (lagging indicators) and performance drivers (leading indicators) that have been customized to the business unit's strategy.[20]

The aim of Kaplan and Norton, then, is to capture both past performance and expected future performance in scorecards with multiple measures—in fact, as many as two dozen of them—that are intimately related to the organization's strategy.[21] And this is where my misgivings about the Balanced Scorecard lie. For an organization's strategy to be implemented effectively, each person in the organization must clearly understand what he or she has to do, how their performance measures will be constructed, and how their rewards and punishments are related to those measures.

But, as we saw earlier in the case of multiple constituencies (or the multiple goals represented in figure 1.1), decision makers cannot make rational choices without some overall single dimensional objective to be maximized. Given a dozen or two dozen measures and no sense of the tradeoffs between them, the typical manager will be unable to behave purposefully, and the result will be confusion.

Kaplan and Norton generally do not deal with the critical issue of how to weight the multiple dimensions represented by the two dozen measures on their scorecards. And this is where problems with the Balanced Scorecard are sure to arise: Without specifying what the tradeoffs are among these two dozen or so different measures, there is no "balance" in their scorecard. Adding to the potential for confusion, Kaplan and Norton also offer almost no guidance on the critical issue of how to tie the performance measurement system to managerial incentives and rewards. Here is their concluding statement on this important matter:

Several approaches may be attractive to pursue. In the short term, tying incentive compensation of all senior managers to a balanced set of business unit scorecard measures will foster commitment to overall organizational goals, rather than suboptimization within functional departments.... Whether such linkages should be explicit... or applied judgmentally... will likely vary from company to company. More knowledge about the benefits and costs of explicit linkages will undoubtedly continue to be accumulated in the years ahead.[22]

What the Balanced Scorecard fails to provide, then, is a clear linkage (and a rationale for that linkage) between the performance measures and the corporate system of rewards and punishments. Indeed, the Balanced Scorecard does not provide a scorecard in the traditional sense of the word. And, to make my point, let me push the sports analogy a little further. A scorecard in any sport yields a single number that determines the winner among all contestants. In most sports, the person or team with the highest score wins. Very simply, a scorecard yields a score, not multiple measures of different dimensions like yards rushing and passing. These latter drivers of performance affect who wins and who loses, but they do not themselves distinguish the winner.

To reiterate, the Balanced Scorecard does not yield a score that would allow us to distinguish winners from losers. For this reason, the system is best described not as a scorecard, but as a dashboard or instrument panel. It can tell managers many interesting things about their business, but it does not give a score for the organization's performance, or even for the performance of its business units. As a senior manager of a large financial institution that spent considerable time implementing a Balanced Scorecard system explained to me: "We never figured out how to use the scorecard to measure performance. We used it to transfer information, a lot of information, from the divisions to the senior management team. At the end of the day, however, your performance depended on your ability to meet your targets for contribution to bottom-line profits."

Thus, because of the lack of a way for managers to think through the difficult task of determining an unambiguous performance measure in the Balanced Scorecard system, the result in this case was a fallback to a single and inadequate financial measure of performance (in this case, accounting profits)—the very approach that Kaplan and Norton properly wish to change. The lack of a single one-dimensional measure by which an organization or department or person will score their performance means these units or people cannot make purposeful decisions. They cannot do so because if they do not understand the tradeoffs between the multiple measures, they cannot know whether they are becoming better off (except in those rare cases when all measures are increasing in some decision).

In sum, the appropriate measure for the organization is value creation, the change in the market value of all claims on the firm. And for those organizations that wish a "flow" measure of value creation on a quarterly or yearly basis, I recommend Economic Value Added (EVA). But I hasten to add that, as the performance measures are cascaded down through the organization, neither value creation nor the year-to-year measure, EVA, is likely to be the proper performance measure at all levels. To illustrate this point, let's now look briefly at performance measurement for business units.

Measuring Divisional Performance

The proper measure for any person or business unit in a multidivisional company will be determined mainly by two factors: the company's strategy and the actions that the person or division being evaluated can take to contribute to the success of the strategy. There are two general ways in principle that this score or objective can be determined: a centralized way and a decentralized way.

To see this let us begin by distinguishing clearly between the measure of performance (single dimensional) for a unit or person and the drivers that the unit or person can use to affect the performance measure. In the decentralized solution, the organization determines the appropriate performance measure for the unit, and it is the person or unit's responsibility to figure out what the performance drivers are, how they influence performance, and how to manage them. The distinction here is the difference between an outcome (the performance measure) and the inputs or decision variables (the management of the performance drivers). And managers at higher levels in the hierarchy may be able to help the person or unit to understand what the drivers are and how to manage them. But this help can only go so far because the specific knowledge regarding the drivers will generally lie not in headquarters, but in the operating units. Therefore, in the end, it is the accountable party, not headquarters, who will generally have the relevant specific knowledge and therefore must determine the drivers, their changing relation to results, and how to manage them.

At the opposite extreme is the completely centralized solution, in which headquarters will determine the performance measure by giving the functional form to the unit that lists the drivers and describes the weight that each driver receives in the determination of the performance measure. The performance for a period is then determined by calculating the weighted average of the measures of the drivers for the period.[23] This solution effectively transfers the job of learning how to create value at all levels in the organization to the top managers, and leaves the operating managers only the job of managing the performance drivers that have been dictated to them by top management. The problem with this approach, however, is that it is likely to work only in a fairly narrow range of circumstances—those cases where the specific knowledge necessary to understand the details of the relation between changes in each driver and changes in the performance measure lies higher in the hierarchy. Although this category may include a number of very small firms, it will rule out most larger multidivisional companies, especially in today's rapidly changing business environment.

Closing Thoughts on the Balanced Scorecard and Value Maximization

In summary, the Kaplan–Norton Balanced Scorecard is a tool to help managers understand what creates value in their business. As such, it is a useful analytical tool, and I join with Kaplan and Norton in urging managers to do the hard work necessary to understand what creates value in their organization and how to manage those value drivers. As they put it:

> [A] properly constructed Balanced Scorecard should tell the story of the business unit's strategy. It should identify and make explicit the sequence of hypotheses about the cause-and-effect relationships between outcome measures and the performance drivers of those outcomes. Every measure selected for a Balanced Scorecard should be an element in a chain of cause-and-effect relationships that communicates the meaning of the business unit's strategy to the organization.[24]

But managers are almost inevitably led to try to use the multiple measures of the Balanced Scorecard as a performance measurement system. And as a performance measurement system, the Balanced Scorecard will lead to confusion, conflict, inefficiency, and lack of focus. This is bound to happen as operating managers guess at what the tradeoffs might be between each of the dimensions of performance. And this uncertainty will generally lead to conflicts with managers at headquarters, who are likely to have different assessments of the tradeoffs. Such conflicts, besides causing disappointments and confusion about operating decisions, could also lead to attempts by operating managers to game the system—by, say, performing well on financial measures while sacrificing nonfinancial ones. Moreover, there is no logical or principled resolution of the resulting conflicts unless all the parties come to agreement about what they are trying to accomplish; and this means specifying how the score is calculated—in effect, figuring out how the balance in the Balanced Scorecard is actually attained.

As we saw earlier, even if it were possible to come up with a truly "optimizing" system where all the weights and the tradeoffs among the multiple measures and drivers were specified—a highly doubtful proposition—reaching agreement between headquarters and line management over the proper weighting of the measures and their linkage to the corporate reward system would be an enormously difficult, if not an impossible, undertaking. In addition, it would surely be impossible to keep the system continuously updated so as to reflect all the changes in a dynamic local and worldwide competitive landscape.

A 1996 survey of Balanced Scorecard implementations by Towers Perrin gives a fairly clear indication of the problems that are likely to arise with it.[25] Perhaps most troubling, 70 percent of the companies using a scorecard also reported using it for compensation—and an additional 17 percent were considering doing so. And, not surprisingly, 40 percent of the respondents said they believed that the large number of measures weakened the effectiveness of the measurement system. What's more, in their empirical test of the effects of the Balanced Scorecard implementation in a global financial services firm, a 1997 study by Christopher Ittner, David Larcker, and Marshall Meyer concluded that the first issue their study raised for future research was "defining precisely what 'balance' is and the mechanisms through which 'balance' promotes performance."[26] As I have argued in this chapter, this question cannot be answered because "balance" is a term used by Balanced Scorecard advocates as a substitute for thorough analysis of one of the more difficult parts of the performance measurement system—the necessity to evaluate and make tradeoffs. Advocates of the Balanced Scorecard and others have been seduced by this hurrah word (who can argue for "unbalanced"?) into avoiding careful thought on the issues.

In fact, the sooner we get rid of the word "balance" in these discussions, the better we will be able to sort out the solutions. Balance cannot ever substitute for having to deal with the difficult issues associated with specifying the tradeoffs among multiple goods and bads that determine the overall score for an organization's success. We must do this to stand a chance of creating an organizational scoreboard that actually gives a score—which is something every good scoreboard must do.

Closing Thoughts on Stakeholder Theory

Stakeholder theory plays into the hands of special interests that wish to use the resources of corporations for their own ends. With the widespread failure of centrally planned socialist and communist economies, those who wish to use non-market forces to reallocate wealth now see great opportunity in the playing field that stakeholder theory opens to them. Stakeholder theory gives them the appearance of legitimate political access to the sources of decision-making power in organizations, and it deprives those organizations of a principled basis for rejecting those claims. The result is to undermine the foundations of value-seeking behavior that have enabled markets and capitalism to generate wealth and high standards of living worldwide.

If widely adopted, stakeholder theory will reduce social welfare even as its advocates claim to increase it—much as happened in the failed communist and socialist experiments of the last century. And, as I pointed out earlier, stakeholder theorists will often have the active support of managers who wish to throw off the constraints on their power provided by the value-seeking criterion and its enforcement by capital markets, the market for corporate control, and product markets. For example, stakeholder arguments played an important role in persuading the U.S. courts and legislatures to limit hostile takeovers through legalization of poison pills and state control shareholder acts. And we will continue to see more political action limiting the power of these markets to constrain managers. In sum, special interest groups will continue to use the arguments of stakeholder theory to legitimize their positions, and it is in our collective interest to expose the logical fallacy of these arguments.

Notes

© 2001 Michael C. Jensen. An earlier version of this chapter appears in *Breaking the Code of Change,* Michael Beer and Nithan Norhia, eds., Harvard Business School Press, 2000. This research has been supported by The Monitor Group and Harvard Business School Division of Research. I am indebted to Nancy Nichols, Pat Meredith, Don Chew, and Janice Willett for many valuable suggestions.

1. Under some interpretations, stakeholders also include the environment, terrorists, blackmailers, and thieves. Edward Freeman, for example, writes: "The ... definition of 'stakeholder' [is] any group or individual who can affect or is affected by the achievement of an organization's purpose. ... For instance, some corporations must count 'terrorist groups' as stakeholders." Edward R. Freeman, *Strategic Management: A Stakeholder Approach* (Boston: Pitman Books, 1984), p. 53.
2. See, for example, *Principles of Stakeholder Management: The Clarkson Principles.* The Clarkson Centre for Business Ethics, Joseph L. Rotman School of Management, Univ. of Toronto, Canada. For a critical analysis of stakeholder theory, I especially recommend the following articles by Elaine Sternberg: "Stakeholder Theory Exposed," *The Corporate Governance Quarterly* 2, no. 1 (1996); "The Stakeholder Concept: A Mistaken Doctrine," London: Foundation for Business Responsibilities, Issue Paper No. 4 (Nov. 1999) (also available from the Social Science Research Network at http://papers.ssrn.com/paper=263144). See also Sternberg's recent book, *Just Business: Business Ethics in Action* (Oxford: Oxford University Press, 2000), which surveys the acceptance of stakeholder theory by the Business Roundtable and the *Financial Times,* and its recognition by law in thirty-eight American states. On the latter issue, see also James L. Hanks, "From the Hustings: The Role of States with Takeover Control Laws," *Mergers & Acquisitions* 29, no. 2 (Sept.–Oct. 1994).
3. For a case study of a small nonprofit firm that almost destroyed itself while trying to maximize over a dozen dimensions at the same time, see Michael Jensen, Karen H. Wruck, and Brian Barry, "Fighton, Inc. (A) and (B)," Harvard Business School Case #9-391-056, March 20, 1991; and Karen Wruck, Michael Jensen, and Brian Barry, "Fighton, Inc., (A) and (B) Teaching Note," Harvard Business School Case #5-491-111, 1991. For an interesting empirical paper that formally tests the proposition that multiple objectives handicap firms, see Kees Cools and Mirjam van Praag (2000), "The Value Relevance of a Single-Valued Corporate Target: An Empirical Analysis." Available from the Social Science Research Network eLibrary at http://papers.ssrn.com/

paper=244788. In their test using eighty Dutch firms in the 1993–1997 period, the authors conclude: "Our findings show the importance of setting *one* single target for value creation" (emphasis in original).
4. I'd like to thank David Rose for suggesting this simple and more descriptive term for value maximizing. See David C. Rose, "Teams, Firms, and the Evolution of Profit Seeking Behavior," May 1999, Dept. of Economics, University of Missouri—St. Louis, Unpublished manuscript, available from the Social Science Research Network eLibrary at http://papers.ssrn.com/paper=224438.
5. See Ronald H. Coase, "The Problem of Social Cost," *Journal of Law and Economics* 3 (Oct. 1960): 1–44; and Michael C. Jensen and William H. Meckling, "Specific and General Knowledge, and Organization Structure," in Lars Werin and Hans Wijkander (Eds.), *Contract Economics* (Oxford: Basil Blackwell, 1992), pp. 251–274. Available from the Social Science Research Network eLibrary at http://papers.ssrn.com/paper=6658.
6. In the case of a monopoly, profit maximization leads to a loss of social product because the firm expands production only to the point where an additional dollar's worth of inputs generates incremental revenues equal to a dollar, not where consumers value the incremental product at a dollar. In this case the firm produces less of a commodity than that which would result in maximum social welfare. In addition, we should recognize that when a complete set of claims for all goods for each possible time and state of the world do not exist, the social maximum will be constrained; but this is just another recognition of the fact that we must take into account the costs of creating additional claims and markets in time/state delineated claims. See Kenneth J. Arrow, "The Role of Securities in the Optimal Allocation of Risk Bearing," *Review of Economic Studies* 31, no. 86 (1964): 91–96; and Gerard Debreu, *Theory of Value* (New York: Wiley, 1959).
7. Again, provided there are no externalities.
8. I am indebted to my colleague George Baker for this simple way of expressing the social optimality of profit maximization.
9. An example would be a case where the supplier of an input was imposing negative externalities on others by polluting water or air.
10. Equality holds only in the special case where consumer and producer surpluses are zero, and there are no externalities or monopoly.
11. For those unfamiliar with finance and present values, the value one year from now of a dollar today saved for use one year from now is thus $\$1 \times (1+r)$, where r is the interest rate. Alternatively, the value today of a dollar of resources to be received one year from now is its present value of $\$1/(1+r)$.
12. Without going into the details here, the same criterion applies to all organizations whether they are public corporations or not. Obviously, even if the financial claims are not explicitly valued by the market, social welfare will be increased as long as managers of partnerships or nonprofits increase output so long as the imputed market value of claims on the firm continues to increase.
13. At least as advocated by Freeman (1984), Clarkson Principles (1999), and others.
14. F. A. Hayek, "The Fatal Conceit," in *The Collected Works of F. A. Hayek*, ed. W. W. Bartley (Chicago: University of Chicago Press, 1988), p. 14.
15. Ibid., pp. 13, 14; emphasis in original.
16. Ibid., p. 18; emphasis in original.
17. It is useful here to briefly summarize the positive arguments (those refutable by empirical data) and normative arguments (those propositions that say what should be rather than what is in the world) I have made thus far. I have argued positively that

firms that follow stakeholder theory as it is generally advocated will do less well in the competition for survival than those who follow a well-defined single-valued objective such as value creation. I have also argued positively that if firms follow value creation, social welfare will be greater and normatively that this is desirable. I have also argued positively that the self-interests of managers and directors will lead them to prefer stakeholder theory because it increases their power and means they cannot be held accountable for their actions. I have also argued positively that the self-interest of special interest groups who wish to acquire legitimacy in corporate governance circles to enhance their influence over the allocation of corporate resources will advocate the use of stakeholder theory by managers and directors. This leads to the positive prediction that society will be poorer if they are successful, and to the normative conclusion that this is undesirable. For a discussion of the role of normative, positive (or instrumental), and descriptive theory in the literature on stakeholder theory, see Thomas Donaldson and Lee E. Preston, "The Stakeholder Theory of the Corporation: Concepts, Evidence, and Implications," *Academy of Management Review* 20, no. 1 (1995): 65–91.
18. See Robert S. Kaplan and David P. Norton, "The Balanced Scorecard—Measures That Drive Performance," *Harvard Business Review,* Jan.–Feb. 1992, pp. 71–79; and Robert Kaplan and David P. Norton, *The Balanced Scorecard* (Boston: Harvard Business School Press, 1996).
19. Kaplan and Norton (1996), p. 8.
20. Ibid., pp. 10 and 150, emphasis in original.
21. Ibid., p. 162.
22. Ibid., p. 222
23. And of course I do not mean to imply that the functional relationship between the value drivers and the performance measure will always be a simple weighted average. Indeed, in general it will be more complicated than this.
24. Kaplan and Norton (1996), p. 31.
25. Towers Perrin, "Inside 'the Balanced Scorecard,'" *Compuscan Report,* Jan. 1996, pp. 1–5.
26. Christopher Ittner, David F. Larcker, and Marshal W. Meyer, "Performance, Compensation, and the Balanced Scorecard," Unpublished manuscript, Wharton School, Univ. of Pennsylvania, Nov. 1, 1997.

CHAPTER 2

The State of U.S. Corporate Governance: What's Right and What's Wrong?

BENGT HOLMSTROM AND STEVEN N. KAPLAN

TO A CASUAL OBSERVER, the United States corporate governance system must seem to be in terrible shape. The business press has focused relentlessly on the corporate board and governance failures at Enron, WorldCom, Tyco, Adelphia, Global Crossing, and others. Top executive compensation is also routinely criticized as excessive by the press, academics, and even top Federal Reserve officials.[1] These failures and concerns in turn have served as catalysts for legislative change—in the form of the Sarbanes-Oxley Act of 2002—and regulatory change, including new governance guidelines from the NYSE and NASDAQ.

The turmoil and the responses to it suggest two important questions that we attempt to answer in this chapter. First, has the U.S. corporate governance system performed that poorly—is it really that bad? Second, will the proposed changes lead to a more effective system?

In addressing the first question, we begin by examining two broad measures of economic performance for evidence of failure of the U.S. system. Despite the alleged flaws in its governance system, the U.S. economy has performed very well, both on an absolute basis and particularly relative to other countries. U.S. productivity gains in the past decade have been exceptional, and the U.S. stock market has consistently outperformed other world indices over the last two decades, including in the period since the scandals broke. In other words, the broad evidence is not consistent with a failed U.S. system. If anything, it suggests a system that is well above average.

Next, we discuss how important aspects of the U.S. corporate governance system have evolved over the last two decades and the implications of those changes. Again, contrary to the popular impression, the major changes in U.S. corporate governance in the past twenty years—notably, the dramatic increase in equity-based pay and the institutionalization of U.S. shareholders—appear to have been positive overall. As we discuss below, such changes played a central role in the highly productive restructuring of U.S. corporations that took place during the 1980s and 1990s. But the changes did have an unfortunate side effect. Besides spurring productivity improvements, the rise of equity-based pay—particularly the explosion of stock options—and the run-up in stock prices in the late 1990s created incentives for the shortsighted and at times illegal managerial behavior that has attracted so much criticism. Our view, however, is that the costs associated with such incentives and behavior have been far outweighed by the benefits.

Having addressed where the U.S. system is today and how it got there, we finally consider the probable near-term effects of the legislative, regulatory, and market responses to the perceived governance "problem." We conclude that the current changes are likely to make a good U.S. system a better one, although not without imposing some unnecessary costs. In fact, the greatest risk now facing the U.S. corporate governance system is the possibility of overregulation.

Given the volume and intensity of criticism of U.S. corporate governance, one would think that the U.S. stock market must have performed quite badly, particularly since the scandals broke in 2001. But the data summarized in table 2.1 indicate otherwise. Table 2.1 reports the total returns (measured in dollars) to the Morgan Stanley Capital International indices for the aggregate

TABLE 2.1

Stock Market Performance

	U.S.	Europe	Pacific
From 1982 (January)	1,222%	1,145%	276%
From 1987	436%	266%	3%
From 1992	164%	113%	−27%
From 1997	28%	13%	−39%
From 2001	−32%	−34%	−32%

	U.S.	Great Britain	France	Germany	Japan
From 1982	1,222%	1,223%	1,567%	595%	90%
From 1987	436%	290%	236%	93%	−37%
From 1992	164%	121%	147%	84%	−42%
From 1997	28%	11%	47%	5%	−39%
From 2001	−32%	−32%	−45%	−53%	−34%

Note: Stock returns reported by Ibbotson Associates for total return on Morgan Stanley Capital International (MSCI) Indices for the United States, Europe, Pacific, Great Britain, France, Germany, and Japan from January 1 of the given year through the end of December 2002.

U.S., European, and Pacific stock markets over five different time periods through the end of 2002. Although the U.S. stock market has had negative returns over the last several years, it has performed well relative to other stock markets, both recently and over the longer term. In fact, the U.S. market has generated returns at least as high as those of the European and Pacific markets during each of the five time periods considered—since 2001, since 1997, since 1992, since 1987, and since 1982. The returns to the U.S. stock market also compare favorably with the returns to the stock markets of the larger individual countries (including France, Germany, Great Britain, and Japan) that make up the indices.

How Bad Is U.S. Corporate Governance?

Because many factors affect stock returns, it would be inappropriate to claim that superior U.S. corporate governance explains the differences in returns. We can conclude, however, that whatever the shortcomings of the U.S. system, they have not been sufficiently great to prevent the stock returns of U.S. companies from outperforming those of the rest of the world.

It is worth pointing out two additional implications of the stock performance results. First, the returns to U.S. stocks have been at least as large as the returns to European and Pacific stocks since 2001, the period in which the U.S. corporate governance scandals first emerged. One possible explanation is that the effects of the governance scandals on U.S. stock values have not been particularly large relative to other factors that have weighed on most national economies. Another possibility is that while there may be some problems with the U.S. corporate governance system, the problems confronting the governance systems of other nations are even worse. But in our view, the most plausible explanation is that while parts of the U.S. system failed under the exceptional strain of the 1990s boom market, the damage was limited because the overall system reacted quickly to address the problems.

The second important point to keep in mind about stock returns is that they reflect publicly available information about executive compensation. Returns, therefore, are measured *net* of executive compensation payments. The fact that the shareholders of U.S. companies earned higher returns *even after* payments to management does not support the claim that the U.S. executive pay system is designed inefficiently; if anything, shareholders appear better off with the U.S. system of executive pay than with the systems that prevail in other countries. As we discuss later, however, the higher U.S. returns do not rule out the possibility that some top U.S. executives are paid more than is necessary for incentive purposes and that our incentive pay system can be improved.

Overall country productivity provides another broad measure of performance. Again, one might expect a less effective corporate governance system to

TABLE 2.2

Changes in Real GDP per Capita

	U.S.	Great Britain	France	Germany	Japan
From 1982 (beginning) to 2000	54%	58%	37%	44%	55%
From 1987 to 2000	38%	36%	28%	29%	36%
From 1992 to 2000	29%	24%	12%	12%	8%
From 1997 to 2000	14%	11%	11%	8%	3%

Note: Changes in real GDP per capita for the United States, Great Britain, France, Germany, and Japan. Calculated using the Penn World Tables.

lead to lower productivity growth. Table 2.2 presents calculations of the percentage change in gross domestic product (GDP) per capita for developed countries since 1982. The results do not suggest the presence of an ineffective U.S. governance system. From the beginning of 1992 to the end of 2000,[2] growth in GDP per capita was greater in the United States than in France, Germany, Great Britain, or Japan. And given the strong U.S. productivity numbers through the recent downturn, this gap has probably widened since then.

Again, these results do not necessarily demonstrate that the U.S. corporate governance system is the principal cause of the larger productivity improvements. Many other forces operate at the same time. The results do suggest, however, that any deficiencies in the U.S. corporate governance system have not prevented the U.S. economy from outperforming its global competitors.

Changes in U.S. Corporate Governance over the Last Twenty Years

Corporate governance in the United States has changed dramatically since 1980.[3] As a number of business and finance scholars have pointed out, the corporate governance structures in place before the 1980s gave the managers of large public U.S. corporations little reason to make shareholder interests their primary focus. Before 1980, corporate managements tended to think of themselves as representing not the shareholders, but rather "the corporation." In this view, the goal of the firm was not to maximize shareholder wealth, but to ensure the growth (or at least the stability) of the enterprise by "balancing" the claims of all important corporate "stakeholders"—employees, suppliers, and local communities, as well as shareholders.[4]

The external governance mechanisms available to dissatisfied shareholders were seldom used. Raiders and hostile takeovers were relatively uncommon.

Proxy fights were rare and didn't have much chance of succeeding. And corporate boards tended to be cozy with and dominated by management, making board oversight weak.

Internal incentives from management ownership of stock and options were also modest. For example, in 1980 only 20 percent of the compensation of U.S. CEOs was tied to stock market performance.[5] Long-term performance plans were widely used, but they were typically based on accounting measures like sales growth and earnings per share that tied managerial incentives less directly, and sometimes not at all, to shareholder value.

Partly in response to the neglect of shareholders, the 1980s ushered in a large wave of takeover and restructuring activity. This activity was distinguished by its use of hostility and aggressive leverage. The 1980s saw the emergence of the corporate raider and hostile takeovers. Raiders like Carl Icahn and T. Boone Pickens became household names. Nearly half of all major U.S. corporations received a takeover offer in the 1980s—and many companies that were not taken over responded to hostile pressure with internal restructurings that made themselves less attractive targets.[6]

The use of debt financing by U.S. companies was so extensive that, from 1984 to 1990, more than $500 billion of equity was retired (net of new equity issuances), as many firms repurchased their own shares, borrowed to finance takeovers, or were taken private in leveraged buyouts (LBOs). As a result, corporate leverage ratios increased substantially. LBOs were extreme in this respect, with debt levels typically exceeding 80 percent of total capital.

In the 1990s, the pattern of corporate governance activity changed again. After a steep but brief drop in merger activity around 1990, takeovers rebounded to the levels of the 1980s. Hostility and leverage, however, declined substantially. At the same time, other corporate governance mechanisms began to play a larger role, particularly executive stock options and the greater involvement of boards of directors and shareholders.

The preponderance of the evidence is consistent with an overall explanation as follows: In the early 1980s, the wedge between actual and potential corporate performance became increasingly apparent. In some cases, changes in markets, technology, or regulation led to a large amount of excess capacity—for example, in the oil and tire industries. In others, it became apparent that diversification strategies carried out in the late 1960s and 1970s were underperforming.[7] The top managers of such companies, however, were slow to respond to opportunities to increase value. As mentioned above, limited ownership of stock and options gave managers little monetary incentive to make major changes that might weaken their "partnership" with other corporate stakeholders. But perhaps equally important, some corporate leaders persisted in their conviction that growth and stability were the "right" corporate goals, and they simply refused to believe what the capital markets were telling them. This appears to have been true, for example, of the U.S. oil industry in the early 1980s, when oil companies traded below the value of their oil holdings because of industry-wide overinvestment in exploration.

At the same time that many U.S. companies were failing to maximize value, the U.S. capital markets were becoming more powerful because of increased stock ownership by large institutions. It was the potential for improved corporate performance, combined with the increased ownership of institutional investors, that gave birth to the takeovers, junk bonds, and LBOs of the 1980s. In some cases, the capital markets reversed ill-advised diversification through "bust-up" transactions (such as KKR's acquisition of Beatrice Foods in 1986). In other cases, the financial markets effectively forced managers to eliminate excess capacity (as in Chevron's leveraged acquisition of Gulf Oil in 1984). More generally, the capital markets disciplined managers who had ignored shareholders for the benefit of themselves and other stakeholders. As we discuss below, the incentive and governance features of LBOs are particularly representative of the discipline that the capital markets imposed.

The initial response of U.S. executives was to fight takeovers with legal maneuvers and to attempt to enlist political and popular support against corporate raiders. Over time, these efforts met with some legislative, regulatory, and judicial success. As a result, hostile takeovers became far more costly in the 1990s than in the previous decade.

But the accomplishments of the 1980s were by no means forgotten. By the 1990s, U.S. managers, boards, and institutional shareholders had seen what LBOs and other market-driven restructurings could do. With the implicit assent of institutional investors, boards substantially increased the use of stock option plans that allowed managers to share in the value created by restructuring their own companies. Shareholder value thus became an ally rather than a threat.

This general embrace of shareholder value helps to explain why restructurings continued at a high rate in the 1990s, but for the most part on amicable terms. There was also less of a need for high leverage because deals could now be paid for with stock without raising investors' concerns that managers would pursue their own objectives at the expense of shareholders.

The merger wave of the 1990s also appears to have had a somewhat different purpose than the wave of the 1980s, representing a different stage in the overall restructuring process. The deals of the 1980s were more of a bust-up wave whose main effect was to force corporate assets out of the hands of managers who could not or would not use them efficiently. The transactions of the 1990s, by contrast, had more of a "build-up" effect in which assets were reconfigured to take advantage of growth opportunities in new technologies and markets. This logic also fits with the increased use of equity rather than debt in funding the deals of the 1990s.

The move toward shareholder value and increased capital market influence has also been apparent in the way corporations have reorganized themselves. For example, there has been a broad trend toward decentralization. Large companies have been working hard to become more nimble and to find ways to offer employees higher-powered incentives. At the same time, external capital markets have taken on a larger role in capital reallocation, as evidenced by the large volume of mergers and divestitures throughout the 1990s. During the same period, the amounts of funds raised and invested by U.S. venture capitalists—who help perform the key economic function of transferring funds from mature to new high-growth industries—also increased by an order of magnitude over the 1990s.[8]

In sum, while corporate managers still reallocate vast amounts of resources in the economy through internal capital and labor markets, the boundary between markets and managers appears to have shifted. As managers have ceded authority to the markets, the scope and independence of their decision-making have narrowed.

We now focus more specifically on changes in three key elements of the U.S. (and indeed any) corporate governance system: executive compensation, shareholders, and boards of directors.

Changes in Executive Compensation

The total pay of top U.S. executives, particularly option-based compensation, has increased substantially over the last two decades. For example, a study published in the late 1990s reported that during the fifteen-year period from 1980 to 1994, the average compensation of CEOs of large U.S. companies tripled in real terms. The study also concluded that the average annual CEO option grant (valued at issuance) increased roughly sevenfold, and as a result, equity-based compensation in 1994 made up almost 50 percent of total CEO compensation (up from less than 20 percent in 1980).[9] Moreover, as reported in a more recent study, this trend continued from 1994 to 2001, with CEO pay more than doubling and option-based compensation increasing at an even faster rate.[10]

Overall, then, CEO compensation appears to have increased by a factor of six over the last two decades, with a disproportionate increase in equity-based compensation. The effect of the increase in equity-based compensation has been to increase CEO pay-to-performance sensitivities by a factor of more than ten times from 1980 to 1999.[11]

These increases in executive compensation, particularly options, have generated enormous controversy. The recent scandals and stock market declines have led some observers to argue that such increases represent unmerited transfers of shareholder wealth to top executives with limited, if any, beneficial incentive effects. For example, one recent survey of corporate governance concludes: "It is widely recognized . . . that these options are at best an inefficient financial incentive and at worst create new incentive or conflict-of-interest problems of their own."[12]

There are several reasons to be skeptical of these conclusions. First, as we have already pointed out, the performance of the U.S. stock market and the strong growth in U.S. productivity provide no support for such arguments.

Second, the primary effect of the large shift to equity-based compensation has been to align the interests of CEOs and their management teams with shareholders' interests to a much greater extent than in the past. Large stock option grants fundamentally changed the mind-set of CEOs and made them much more receptive to value-increasing transactions. The tenfold increase in pay-for-performance sensitivities implies that a one dollar increase in a company's stock price was ten times more valuable to a CEO at the end of the 1990s than at the beginning of the 1980s. As we noted earlier, this shift played a significant role in the continued restructuring of corporations in the 1990s.[13] It also helps explain the 1997 decision of the Business Roundtable—a group of two hundred CEOs of the largest American companies—to change its position on business objectives (after years of opposition and ambivalence to shareholder value) to hold that "the paramount duty of management and the board is to the shareholder and not to . . . other stakeholders."

A third reason to be skeptical of the criticism of U.S. top executive pay practices is that both buyout investors and venture capital investors have made, and continue to make, substantial use of equity-based and option compensation in the firms they invest in. A 1989 study by one of the authors reported that the CEOs of companies taken private in LBOs increased their ownership stake by more than a factor of four, from an average of 1.4 percent before the LBO to 6.4 percent after. The study also found that management teams as a whole typically obtained 10 percent to 20 percent of the post-buyout equity.[14] More recent research and anecdotal evidence suggest that such levels of managerial equity ownership are still typical in today's buyout transactions.[15]

This feature of LBOs is particularly notable. LBO sponsor firms such as KKR, Texas Pacific Group, and Thomas Lee typically buy majority control of the companies they invest in through the partnerships that the sponsors manage. The individual partners of the LBO sponsors have strong incentives to make profitable investments since the sponsors typically receive 20 percent of the profits of a particular buyout partnership, and the sponsors' ability to raise other funds is strongly related to the performance of their existing investments.[16] And the fact that such sponsors also insist on providing the managers of their companies with high-powered incentives suggests that incentives have been a critical ingredient in the success of LBOs.

Two other aspects of compensation contracts designed by LBO sponsors for the top executives of their portfolio companies are worth mentioning. First, the equity and options held by those top executives are typically illiquid—usually by necessity because most of the companies are private—unless and until the company has clearly succeeded through an IPO or a sale to another company. This means that top management cannot trade in and out of the stock (nor can it easily hedge its positions). Second, neither LBO sponsors nor venture capitalists typically index the executive compensation contracts they employ to industry performance or market performance. If non-indexed options and equity grants were so inefficient, as critics of executive compensation have argued, we would expect to see more indexing of private equity contracts.

Unfortunately, while the greater use of stock-based compensation has likely been a positive development overall, critics of the U.S. governance system are correct in pointing out that higher-powered incentives have not come without costs.[17] First, as executive stock and option ownership has increased, so has the incentive to manage and manipulate accounting numbers in order to inflate stock market values and sell shares at those inflated values.[18] This arguably was important in the cases of Global Crossing and WorldCom, among others.

Second, and related to the first, much of the compensation of top U.S. executives is fairly liquid—and, as we argue below, considerably more liquid than shareholders would like it to be. Unlike LBO sponsors, boards do not put strong restrictions on the ability of top executives to unwind their equity-based compensation by exercising options, selling shares, or using derivatives to hedge their positions. And finding a workable solution to the problem of optimal liquidity for top executive compensation is an important challenge faced by today's boards.

Third, most options are issued at the money because accounting rules do not require the cost of such options to be expensed. It is plausible that because the cost of the options does not appear as an expense, some boards of directors underestimate the cost of an option grant. It is undeniable that the size of some of the option grants has been far greater than what is necessary to retain and motivate the CEOs. In 2001, for example, the ten most highly rewarded CEOs in the S&P 500 were granted option packages with an estimated average value (at time of grant) of $170 million per person. Even if some of these grants represent multiyear awards, the amounts are still staggering. It is particularly disconcerting that among the executives receiving the largest grants in the past three years, several already owned large amounts of stock, including Larry Ellison of Oracle, Tom Siebel of Siebel Systems, and Steve Jobs of Apple. It is hard to argue that these people need stronger shareholder incentives. An obvious explanation is that they have been able to use their positions of power to command excessive awards.

Even so, it would be a mistake to condemn the entire system based on a few cases. That such cases are far from representative can be seen from the pronounced skew in the distribution of CEO incomes. In 2001, for example, the same year the top ten U.S. CEOs received average option grants of $170 million, the median value of total compensation for CEOs of S&P 500 companies was about $7 million. Thus, U.S. executive pay may not be quite the runaway train that has been portrayed in the press.[19]

Changes in Shareholders

As mentioned above, the composition of U.S. shareholders also has changed significantly over the past two decades. Large institutional investors own an increasingly large share of the overall stock market. For example, from 1980 to 1996, large institutional investors nearly doubled their share of ownership of U.S. corporations from less than 30 percent to more than 50 percent. (Conversely, individual ownership declined from 70 percent in 1970 to 60 percent in 1980 and to 48 percent in 1994.)[20]

There are at least two reasons public company shareholders are likely to monitor management more effectively today than in the 1980s. First, the large increase in the shareholdings of institutional investors means that professional investors—who have strong incentives to generate greater stock returns and are presumably more sophisticated—own an increasingly large fraction of U.S. corporations.

Second, in 1992 the SEC substantially reduced the costs to shareholders of challenging management teams. Under the old rules, a shareholder had to file a detailed proxy statement with the SEC before talking to more than ten other shareholders. Under the new rules, shareholders can essentially communicate at any time and in any way as long as they send a copy of the substance of the communication to the SEC afterward. The rule change has lowered the cost of coordinating shareholder actions and blocking management proposals. (Not surprisingly, the Business Roundtable and other management organizations were extremely hostile to this rule change when it was proposed.)

Consistent with these two changes, shareholder activism has increased in the United States since the late 1980s. The evidence on the impact of such activism, however, is mixed. For example, a 1998 summary of the results of twenty empirical studies of the effects of formal shareholder proposals and private negotiations with managements reported evidence of small or no effects on shareholder value.[21] When interpreting such evidence, however, it is important to keep in mind the difficulty of measuring the extent and effects of shareholder activity, in part because so much of this activity takes place behind the scenes and is not reported. And the fact that a recent study reported that stock returns over the period 1980–1996 were higher for companies with greater institutional ownership suggests that our large institutions may indeed be playing a valuable monitoring role—one that translates into higher stock prices.[22]

Changes in Boards of Directors

In an influential study of U.S. corporate boards in the second half of the 1980s, Jay Lorsch and Elizabeth MacIver pointed out a number of deficiencies and offered several recommendations. Chief among them were the following: (1) board selection by a nominating committee rather than the CEO; (2) more equity compensation for directors; and (3) more director control of board meetings through appointment of a lead director or outside chairman, annual CEO reviews, and regular sessions with outside directors only ("executive sessions").[23]

Since the publication of that study in 1989, the boards of U.S. companies have made progress in implementing all three of these recommendations. U.S. companies have significantly expanded the use of nominating committees and lead directors. Executive sessions are increasingly common (although, as suggested below, not as common as directors would like). Boards of U.S. companies now include a larger percentage of independent and outside directors and have become somewhat smaller over time (smaller boards are thought to be more effective in disciplining CEOs and tend to be associated with higher valuations).[24] Also encouraging, directors today receive a significantly larger amount of their total compensation in the form of stock or options. For example, one study reported that stock-based directors' compensation increased from 25 percent in 1992 to 39 percent in 1995, and that trend has since continued.[25]

The CEO turnover process—one of the most widely used measures of the effectiveness of a governance system—suggests that the CEO labor market has become broader and, arguably, more efficient. One recent study of CEO turnover for large companies from 1971 to 1994 found a marked increase in both forced CEO departures and the hiring of new CEOs from outside the company. Within the study, the incidence of forced turnovers and outside succession was highest from 1989 to 1994,[26] a trend that also appears to have continued. The same study reported that CEO turnover was more sensitive to poor performance—as measured by reductions in operating income—during the 1989–1994 period than in earlier years.[27]

On the negative side, however, antitakeover measures such as poison pills and staggered boards have increased substantially in the past two decades. And recent research finds that during the 1990s, companies with a high level of antishareholder provisions experienced substantially lower returns than firms with a low level of such provisions.[28]

Despite the improvements noted above, the recent events at companies like Enron, Tyco, and WorldCom suggest that the boards of U.S. companies continue to exhibit less than the optimal amount of independence and oversight. The Senate report on Enron's board is particularly critical in this respect. When a company is not doing well, everyone pays close attention—lenders and investors as well as board members. But when a company appears to be doing well, as was the case with both Enron and Tyco, investors and the board are likely to be less critical.

A recent survey of more than two thousand directors by Korn Ferry in early 2002 (and thus before the passage of Sarbanes–Oxley and the issuance of the new NYSE and NASDAQ regulations) is very interesting in this regard. The directors who responded to the survey consistently favored more monitoring than was the practice on the boards on which they served. For example, although 71 percent of the directors said they believed boards should hold executive sessions without the CEO, only 45 percent said their boards actually did so. And whereas almost 60 percent felt that their boards should have a lead director, only 37 percent reported that their boards had one.

Our bottom line on boards, then, is that the structure and operating procedures of U.S. corporate boards have improved since the 1980s, but they are still far from perfect.

International Developments

Indirect evidence of the effectiveness of the U.S. governance system is provided by changes in corporate governance in other countries. In recent years, as the forces of deregulation, globalization, and information technology have continued to sweep across the world economy, other countries have begun to move toward the U.S. model. Traditionally, European and Japanese firms have reallocated capital from sunset industries to sunrise industries mainly through internal diversification. External market interventions of the sort seen in the United States were almost unheard of. In the late 1990s, however, Europe experienced a sudden rise in hostile takeovers. In 1999 alone, thirty-four listed companies in continental Europe received hostile bids, representing a total value of $406 billion (as compared with fifty-two bids for just $69 billion over the entire period of 1990–1998).[29] These transactions included Vodafone's bid for Mannesmann, TotalFina's bid for Elf Aquitaine, and Olivetti's bid for Telecom Italia.

Shareholder activism has also been on the rise, with strong support from American institutional investors. For example, Telecom Italia's attempt to split off its wireless unit (at an unacceptable price) was blocked when TIAA-CREF put pressure on the Italian government. In France, shareholder activists managed to defeat a poison-pill proposal by Rhone-Poulenc. European universal banks also have begun to pay more attention to the value of their financial stakes than to their positions of power. These actions appear to have been very much influenced by the U.S. model of market intervention and by the fact that more than $1 trillion of U.S. funds was invested in Western Europe in the 1980s and 1990s.

Another way in which companies can make use of the market to reallocate capital more effectively is to repurchase their own shares. In the last several years, Japan, France, Germany, and several other countries have relaxed prohibitions or restrictions on share repurchases, and companies in those countries have responded by buying back increasing numbers of shares. Finally, the use of stock options for executives and boards is increasing around the world. Japan recently eliminated a substantial tax penalty on executive stock options, and a 2002 study based on Towers Perrin's yearly surveys reported that the rate of adoption of stock options in Europe has matched that of the United States in the 1990s.[30]

In sum, the conventional wisdom on corporate governance has changed dramatically since the 1970s and early 1980s, when the U.S. market-based system was subjected to heavy criticism and the bank-centered systems of Japan and Germany were held up as models.[31] Since the mid-1980s, the American style of corporate governance has reinvented itself, and the rest of the world seems to be following the U.S. lead.

Recent Regulatory Changes

The Sarbanes–Oxley Act (SOX), which was enacted in the summer of 2002, mandated a number of changes in corporate governance for publicly traded companies. The NYSE and NASDAQ also mandated corporate governance changes for firms listed on their respective exchanges. In this section, we discuss the likely effect of these changes on U.S. corporate governance.

Sarbanes–Oxley

SOX mandated changes that will affect executive compensation, shareholder monitoring, and, particularly, board monitoring. One provision requires the CEO and CFO to disgorge any profits from bonuses and stock sales during the twelve-month period that follows a financial report that is subsequently restated because of "misconduct." (We assume this provision also covers any hedging transactions the CEO or CFO undertakes.) Until "misconduct" is clearly defined, this provision increases the risk to a CEO or CFO of selling a large amount of stock or options in any one year while still in office. Some CEOs and CFOs will choose to wait until they are no longer in those positions before selling equity or exercising options. To the extent CEOs and CFOs behave this way, their equity holdings become less liquid and they will care less about short-term stock price movements. This would be a positive change. In addition, the rule will act as a deterrent to negligent or deliberate misreporting.[32]

Shareholder-related provisions include changes in restrictions on insider trading regulation and enhanced financial disclosure. Executives will now have to report sales or purchases of company stock within two days rather than the current ten days, which will have the effect of making executive shares somewhat less liquid. SOX also requires more detailed disclosure of off-balance-sheet financings and special purpose entities, which should make it more difficult for companies to manipulate their financial statements in a way that boosts the current stock price.

SOX also includes a number of provisions meant to improve board monitoring. These focus largely on increasing the power, responsibility, and independence of the audit committee. SOX requires that the audit committee hire the outside auditor and that the committee consist entirely of directors with no other financial relationship with the company.

Finally, SOX increases management's and the board's responsibility for financial reporting and the criminal penalties for misreporting. The increased responsibility and penalties have clearly increased the amount of time that executives of all companies must spend on accounting matters. For companies that are already well governed, that extra time is unnecessary and therefore costly. At least initially, some of the extra time meeting SOX's requirements will be time that could have been devoted to discussing strategy or managing the business. SOX has also caused companies to increase their use of outside accountants and lawyers. But part of the resulting increase in costs is likely to be recouped in the form of valuable new information not previously available to some CEOs, CFOs, and boards. Furthermore, the additional time and costs should decline as companies become more efficient at complying with SOX.

So, what has the new legislation really accomplished? The provisions of SOX deal both directly and indirectly with some of the deficiencies of U.S. corporate governance. But many U.S. companies would have instituted some of these changes anyway. The law already punished fraudulent reporting, including the misreporting uncovered in Enron, Tyco, and WorldCom. Furthermore, the Enron scandal brought the costs of such misreporting into sharp focus before the passage of SOX. No CEO wants to be the CEO of the next Enron. And no board member wants to be on the board of the next Enron.

There are two potentially significant dangers associated with SOX. First, the ambiguity in some of the provisions, particularly those that overlap with and even contradict aspects of state corporate law, will almost certainly invite aggressive litigation. The fear of such litigation will lead CEOs and CFOs to direct corporate resources to protect themselves against potential lawsuits. Fear of litigation is also making it harder to attract qualified board members—certainly an unintended consequence of all the effort to improve board effectiveness. The second, broader concern is that SOX represents a shift to more rigid federal regulation and legislation of corporate governance, as distinguished from the more flexible corporate governance that has evolved from state law, particularly Delaware law.[33]

At this point, SOX has probably helped to restore confidence in the U.S. corporate governance system. Apart from that, the act's expected overall effect is as yet unclear. Our guess is that the effects will be positive for companies with poor governance practices and negative for companies with good governance practices. Because some of the additional costs of complying with SOX are fixed rather than variable, the effects will be more negative for smaller companies than for larger ones. At the margin, this may lead some public companies to go private and deter some private companies from going public. And because of companies' initial uncertainty about how to comply with the act, we expect the effects of SOX to be somewhat negative in the short term, with compliance costs declining over time.

NYSE and NASDAQ Corporate Governance Proposals

In 2002, both the NYSE and NASDAQ submitted proposals designed to strengthen the corporate governance of their listed firms. Both exchanges will require the following:

1. shareholder approval of most equity compensation plans;
2. a majority of independent directors with no material relationships with the company;
3. a larger role for independent directors in the compensation and nominating committees; and
4. regular meetings of only nonmanagement directors.

Compared with SOX, these proposals address U.S. corporate governance deficiencies both more directly and with lower costs. The three provisions relating to board monitoring are particularly noteworthy in that they directly address some of the concerns mentioned by Lorsch and MacIver in 1989 and by outside directors in the recent Korn Ferry survey.

The closest historical parallel to these proposals is the Code of Best Practices (based on the recommendations of the Cadbury Committee) that was adopted by the London Stock Exchange (LSE) in 1992. The Code included recommendations that boards have at least three outside directors and a nonexecutive chairperson. Although the Code is voluntary, the LSE requires companies to state whether they are in compliance.

There is evidence that the Code can make a difference. A recent study of all LSE companies reported that both CEO turnover and the sensitivity of CEO turnover to performance increased following the adoption of the Code—and that such increases were concentrated among those firms that had adopted the recommendations. Furthermore, the changes in turnover appear to have been driven by the increase in the fraction of outsiders on the board rather than the separation of the chairperson and CEO.[34]

Overall, then, the NYSE and NASDAQ changes should prove to be unambiguously positive.

The Conference Board Recommendations

In response to the recent scandals, the Conference Board—an association of prominent U.S. companies—put together a Commission on Public Trust and Private Enterprise with the aim of advising companies on best practices in corporate governance. The first report by the Commission, released in September 2002, provides a set of principles to guide boards in designing top executive compensation. The report begins by noting the exceptional circumstances that led to the abuse of stock options—the equivalent of a "Perfect Storm"—and then makes the following recommendations:

1. compensation committees should be independent and should avoid benchmarking;
2. performance-based compensation should correspond to the corporation's long-term goals—"cost of capital, return on equity, economic value added, market share, environment goals, etc."—and should avoid windfalls related to stock market volatility;
3. equity-based compensation should be "reasonable and cost effective";
4. key executives and directors should "acquire and hold" a meaningful amount of company stock; and
5. compensation disclosure should be transparent and accounting neutral—that is, stock options should be expensed.[35]

Overall, we have a mixed reaction to these recommendations. Several are clearly beneficial. In particular, greater transparency and appropriate expensing of options will make the costs of options more clear not only to shareholders but also to boards. It also will "level the playing field" for options versus other forms of equity-based compensation.

Requiring key executives to hold a meaningful amount of company stock will reduce the temptation to manipulate earnings and stock prices in the short term by making executive stock holdings less liquid. Typically, stock options vest in one to four years, which is short given that most options are exercised and sold fairly soon after vesting. Economic logic suggests that boards should encourage longer-term holdings and a build-up of sizable executive stakes.

The Commission also endorses indexation of some kind to eliminate windfall gains. Indexation has been recommended by economists for a long time, yet practitioners have not adopted it. It is true that there has been an important accounting disadvantage to indexation in that indexed options must be expensed. But the fact that indexed options are rarely used by LBO investors and venture capitalists also suggests that there are hidden costs to indexation or that the benefits are low.

While it may be useful to experiment with some forms of indexation, we think it would probably be just as effective and more transparent to index implicitly by granting stock-based incentives more frequently and in smaller amounts. Mega-grants covering several years at a fixed price have proved too unstable; the options may go underwater and then need to be bailed out (to maintain incentives), making it hard initially to determine the true expected cost of the incentive plans. In general, the incentives from stock options are more fragile than those provided by restricted stock, a problem that more frequent, smaller awards would help alleviate.[36]

We are also skeptical of the recommendation to use performance-based compensation tied to a long list of potential long-term goals, including cost of capital, return on equity, market share, revenue growth, and compliance and environmental protection goals. Such performance plans would appear to take us back to the 1970s, an era that few incentive experts remember fondly. If the problem is windfall gains, then indexed stock options or, more simply, frequent (quarterly) issues of stock options are much preferred. If the problem is manipulation of the market, it should be evident that accounting measures of the kind endorsed by the Conference Board are very problematic. It was in large part because of their vulnerability to manipulation that standard performance plans were replaced by stock-based incentives in the 1980s. This is not to say that accounting-based incentives should never be used, just that they should not form the core of a CEO's incentive plan.

We are also somewhat skeptical of the recommendation that the compensation committee "act independently of management...and avoid benchmarking that keeps continually raising the compensation levels for executives." First, dictating terms without consulting with the executives about their preferences goes against efficient contracting principles; contracting is a two-sided affair. Second, the intent seems to be to give individual compensation committees the responsibility for the overall level of executive compensation. But it is hard to see how pay levels can be set in a fair and efficient way without benchmarking. Prices, including wages, are ultimately set by supply and demand, and benchmarking is nothing more than looking at market prices. The main problem with executive pay levels is not the overall level but the extreme skew in the awards, as we noted earlier. To deal with this problem, we need more effective benchmarking, not less of it.

Despite good intentions, then, we see potentially serious flaws in the recommendations of the Conference Board. It is also important to keep in mind that good incentive designs are sensitive to economic circumstances and to the desired performance. One size does not fit all. And because each situation requires its own compensation plan, the need to customize that plan will often conflict with the goals of benchmarking and transparency.

What Will the Future Bring?

Working together with normal market forces, SOX, the new NYSE and NASDAQ regulations, and the guidelines offered by groups like the Conference Board will significantly influence U.S. corporate governance.

Board behavior will be most strongly affected by these measures. External pressure will lead most boards to monitor top management more aggressively. Yet the relationship between boards and directors need not become more adversarial. The new regulatory requirements provide cover for a more independent and inquisitive board. Actions that in the past might have been construed as hostile will now be interpreted as following best practice. The mandated changes may in fact help reduce the tension inherent in the dual role boards play as monitors of management, on the one hand, and as advisors and sounding boards, on the other.

In addition to the changes in oversight and monitoring, boards also are likely to change their approaches to executive compensation (even though SOX and the exchanges did not address executive compensation directly). In particular, boards will increasingly restrict top executives' movements in exercising options, selling stock, and hedging their positions. As noted earlier, some of the incentives for the executives at Global Crossing, Tyco, and WorldCom to manage earnings came from their ability to sell shares when their stock prices were overvalued. Restrictions on such selling reduce the incentive to manage short-term earnings. While such restrictions have costs, particularly in the form of lack of diversification, the benefits in terms of improved incentives arguably outweigh them. Private equity firms routinely impose such restrictions on the managements of their portfolio companies. Furthermore, CEOs typically are wealthy enough that the benefits of diversification may not be so great.

Many corporate boards will decide to expense options and equity compensation even if they are not required to do so. We suspect that boards will discover that investors and the stock market have neutral or even positive reactions to such expensing (in contrast to the predictions of many executives). Sophisticated investors already know the extent of option issuance from its disclosure in footnotes. Expensing will provide the additional signal to these investors that the board and the company are serious about compensation and corporate governance.[37]

Boards of directors and compensation committees also will begin to change their behavior in issuing options and equity-based compensation. This will be particularly true of boards that decide to expense options. Expensing the options will make their costs more clear and will reduce the size of option grants, particularly large one-shot grants. Moreover, some companies that do expense equity compensation will choose to issue restricted stock rather than options. Restricted stock grants have the advantages of being easier to value, providing incentives that do not vary with stock price movements, and thus being less vulnerable to repricing.[38]

Concluding Remarks

Despite its alleged flaws, the U.S. corporate governance system has performed very well, both on an absolute basis and relative to other countries. It is important to recognize that there is no perfect system and that we should try to avoid the pendulum-like movement so typical of politically inspired system redesigns. The current problems arose in an exceptional period that is not likely to happen again soon. After all, it was almost seventy years ago that the corporate governance system last attracted such intervention.

The fact that the American public and political system became outraged and involved in corporate governance does not mean the system was broken. The U.S. public and the political system are part of the broader system of corporate governance. At the same time, an effort to regulate the system so that such outrage will never again occur would be overly costly and counterproductive. It would lead to inflexibility and fear of experimentation. In today's uncertain climate, we probably need more organizational experimentation than ever. The New Economy is moving forward, and in order to exploit the potential efficiencies inherent in the new information technologies, new business models and new organizational structures are likely to be desirable and valuable. Enron was an experiment that failed. We should take advantage of its lessons not by withdrawing into a shell, but rather by improving control structures and corporate governance so that other promising experiments can be undertaken.

Notes

Warren Batts, Don Chew, Art Kelly, Rick Melcher, Andrew Nussbaum, and Per Stromberg provided helpful comments. Part of this chapter draws on our earlier article, "Corporate Governance and Takeovers in the U.S.: Making Sense of the '80s and '90s," *Journal of Economic Perspectives* (Spring 2001), pp. 121–144.

1. For example, see Marco Becht, Patrick Bolton, and Ailsa Roell, "Corporate Governance and Control," in *Handbook of Economics and Finance*, ed. G. Constantinides, M. Harris, and R. Stulz (Amsterdam: North Holland, 2002); "CEOs Are Overpaid, Says Fed Banker," *Washington Post*, Sept. 11, 2002; and Claudia Deutsch, "After 10 Years, Corporate Oversight Is Still Dismal," *New York Times*, Jan. 26, 2003.
2. This is the most recent period for which data are available.
3. This section summarizes some of the arguments in Bengt Holmstrom and Steven Kaplan, "Corporate Governance and Takeovers in the U.S.: Making Sense of the '80s and '90s," *Journal of Economic Perspectives* (Spring 2001), pp. 121–144; and Steven

Kaplan, "The Evolution of U.S. Corporate Governance: We Are All Henry Kravis Now," *Journal of Private Equity* (1997), pp. 7–14.
4. See Gordon Donaldson and Jay Lorsch, *Decision Making at the Top* (New York: Basic Books, 1983); and Michael Jensen, "The Modern Industrial Revolution," *Journal of Finance* (1993), pp. 831–880.
5. See Brian Hall and Jeffrey Liebman, "Are CEOs Really Paid Like Bureaucrats?," *Quarterly Journal of Economics*, Vol. 112 (1998), pp. 653–691.
6. See Mark Mitchell and Harold Mulherin, "The Impact of Industry Shocks on Takeover and Restructuring Activity," *Journal of Financial Economics* (1996), pp. 193–229.
7. See Jensen (1993) and Andrei Shleifer and Robert Vishny, "The Takeover Wave of the 1980s," *Science*, Vol. 249 (1990), pp. 745–749.
8. See Raghu Rajan and Julie Wulf, "The Flattening Firm," Working paper, University of Chicago (2002); and Paul Gompers and Josh Lerner, "The Venture Capital Revolution," *Journal of Economic Perspectives* (2001), pp. 145–168.
9. Hall and Liebman (1998).
10. See Brian Hall and Kevin Murphy, "Stock Options for Undiversified Executives," *Journal of Accounting and Economics* (2002), pp. 3–42; and Brian Hall, "Six Challenges in Designing Equity-Based Pay," in this issue of the *Journal of Applied Corporate Finance* (2005), pp. 21–33.
11. The levels of executive compensation and managerial equity ownership appear to be high not only relative to 1980 but also relative to earlier periods. One study compares equity ownership by officers and directors in 1935 and 1995 and finds that equity ownership was substantially greater in 1995 than in 1935; see Cliff Holderness, Randall Kroszner, and Dennis Sheehan, "Were the Good Old Days That Good? Changes in Managerial Stock Ownership Since the Great Depression," *Journal of Finance* (1999), pp. 435–470.
12. See Becht, Bolton, and Roell (2002). See also Lucian Bebchuk, Jesse Fried, and David Walker, "Managerial Power and Rent Extraction in the Design of Executive Compensation," *University of Chicago Law Review* (2002), pp. 751–846.
13. For additional evidence consistent with this conclusion, see John Core and David Larcker, "Performance Consequences of Mandatory Increases in Executive Stock Ownership," *Journal of Financial Economics* (2002), who find that option grants or increases in equity ownership are related to improvements in stock and accounting performance.
14. See Steven Kaplan, "The Effects of Management Buyouts on Operations and Value," *Journal of Financial Economics* (1989), pp. 217–254.
15. P. Rogers, T. Holland, and D. Haas, "Value Acceleration: Lessons from Private-Equity Masters," *Harvard Business Review* (June 2002).
16. See Steven Kaplan and Antoinette Schoar, "Private Equity Returns: Persistence and Capital Flows," Working paper, University of Chicago (December 2002).
17. Other critiques are offered in Lucien Bebchuk, Jesse Fried, and David Walker, "Managerial Power and Rent Extraction in the Design of Executive Compensation," *University of Chicago Law Review*, Vol. 69 (2002), pp. 751–846; Becht, Bolton, and Roell (2002); Brian Hall, "Equity-Pay Design for Executives," Working paper, Harvard Business School (2002); and Tod Perry and Marc Zenner, "CEO Compensation in the 1990s: Shareholder Alignment or Shareholder Expropriation?," *Wake Forest Law Review* (2001).
18. See Jeremy Stein, "Efficient Capital Markets, Inefficient Firms: A Model of Myopic Corporate Behavior," *Quarterly Journal of Economics*, Vol. 104 (1989), pp. 655–669, for a model explaining this behavior. See also Joseph Fuller and Michael Jensen, "Just Say No to Wall Street," *Journal of Applied Corporate Finance*, Vol. 14, no. 4 (2002).

19. A part of the problem is that the press has traditionally reported the value of exercised options instead of the value of options at the time they have been granted. This is changing, too.
20. See Paul Gompers and Andrew Metrick, "Institutional Investors and Equity Prices," *Quarterly Journal of Economics* (2001); and James Poterba and Andrew Samwick, "Stock Ownership Patterns, Stock Market Fluctuations, and Consumption," Brookings Papers on Economic Activity (1995), pp. 295–357.
21. Jonathan Karpoff, "The Impact of Shareholder Activism on Target Companies: A Survey of Empirical Findings," Working paper, University of Washington (1998).
22. Paul Gompers and Andrew Metrick, "Institutional Investors and Equity Prices," *Quarterly Journal of Economics,* Vol. 116 (2001), pp. 229–260.
23. Jay Lorsch and Elizabeth MacIver, *Pawns or Potentates* (Boston: Harvard Business School Press, 1989).
24. See David Yermack, "Higher Market Valuation of Companies with a Small Board of Directors," *Journal of Financial Economics,* Vol. 40 (1996), pp. 185–202.
25. For a summary of these changes, see Ben Hermalin and Michael Weisbach, "Boards of Directors as an Endogenously Determined Institution: A Survey of the Economic Literature," *Economic Policy Review* (2003).
26. See M. Huson, Robert Parrino, and Laura Starks, "Internal Monitoring Mechanisms and CEO Turnover: A Long-Term Perspective," *Journal of Finance* (2001), pp. 2265–2297.
27. On the other hand, research shows that CEO turnover was less sensitive to industry-adjusted stock performance from 1990 to 1995 than in earlier years; see Kevin J. Murphy, "Executive Compensation," in *Handbook of Labor Economics,* ed. O. Ashenfelter and D. Card (Amsterdam: North Holland, 1999), pp. 2485–2525. Rakesh Khurana, in *Searching for a Corporate Savior: The Irrational Quest for Charismatic CEOs* (Princeton, NJ: Princeton University Press, 2002), has argued that the CEO labor market is flawed because it is overly focused on outsider, charismatic CEOs. The operating performance evidence in Rakesh Khurana and Nitin Nohria, "The Effects of CEO Turnover in Large Industrial Corporations: A Study of the *Fortune* 200 from 1978–1993," Working paper, Harvard Business School (2000), however, is not consistent with such a conclusion.
28. Paul Gompers, Joy Ishi, and Andrew Metrick, "Corporate Governance and Equity Prices," Working Paper 8449, National Bureau of Economic Research (2001).
29. Rick Escherich and Paul Gibbs, *Global Mergers and Acquisitions Review,* J. P. Morgan (April 2002).
30. Brian Hall, "Incentive Strategy II: Executive Compensation and Ownership Structure," Harvard Business School, Teaching Note N9-902-134 (2002).
31. See, for example, Michael Porter, "Capital Disadvantage: America's Failing Capital Investment System," *Harvard Business Review* (Sept.–Oct. 1992), pp. 65–83.
32. This provision could lead to a modest substitution of cash compensation for equity-based compensation. However, this would have to be accomplished entirely through salary increases because cash bonuses are also subject to the same disgorgement provisions.
33. We thank Andrew Nussbaum for suggesting this possibility.
34. J. Dahya, J. McConnell, and Nickolaos Travlos, "The Cadbury Committee, Corporate Performance, and Top Management Turnover," *Journal of Finance,* Vol. 57 (2002), pp. 461–483.
35. Andy Grove, chairman of Intel, disagreed with the majority in not recommending expensing of stock options, while Paul Volcker, former chairman of the Board of

Governors of the Federal Reserve System, argued that fixed-price stock options should not be used at all. Both filed dissenting opinions.

36. See Brian Hall and Thomas Knox, "Managing Option Fragility," Harvard NOM Research Paper 02-19, Harvard Business School (2002). It is interesting that fairness arguments often lead people to advocate options with exercise prices set well above current market price (for instance, Michael Jensen argues that the exercise price should rise with the cost of capital). Given the problems of fragility, this takes us in exactly the wrong direction. Restricted stock (an option with a zero exercise price) is more appealing, because its incentive effect is robust to variations in the stock price.

37. The argument that options cannot be expensed because no one knows their true value is wrong. On that basis, one could argue that we should not depreciate assets because it is impossible to measure the assets' true rate of depreciation. Nevertheless, it remains to be seen how fluctuations in the value of stock options will influence the information content of reported earnings. The never-ending debate over the best way to handle depreciation suggests that expensing options is going to be discussed for years to come.

38. See Hall (2002) for a detailed discussion.

CHAPTER 3

U.S. Corporate Governance: Accomplishments and Failings

A Discussion with Michael Jensen and Robert Monks

FINANCIAL MANAGEMENT ASSOCIATION,
ORLANDO, FLORIDA, OCTOBER 19, 2007

Ralph Walkling: Good morning, I'm Ralph Walkling, current president of the Financial Management Association. Both in this role, and as Director of the Center for Corporate Governance at Drexel University's LeBow School of Business, I'm excited—and indeed honored—to be moderating this panel on U.S. corporate governance with Robert Monks and Michael Jensen, two of the most prominent authorities on the subject. The original title for this event, as proposed by Mike Jensen, was just "Failings of the U.S. Corporate Governance System." But we later decided that, given Mike's and Bob's reputations for plain speaking, we could change the title a bit without dampening people's expectations for a provocative discussion.

And let me say a bit here about our two main speakers:

Robert Monks has been a passionate advocate of corporate governance reform for nearly 30 years, and a leader in putting such reform into practice. In 1985, Bob and Nell Minow founded Institutional Shareholder Services, a private firm that advises investors on proxy voting and how to respond to issues of corporate governance generally. In 1992, Bob and Nell sold ISS and started the shareholder activist investment firm called LENS. Much like today's activist hedge funds, LENS bought large stakes in underperforming companies with what Bob and Nell felt were unacceptable governance systems—Sears, Westinghouse, and Eastman Kodak, among others—and then engaged management in a dialogue to bring about change. Bob has served on the boards of directors of at least ten publicly held companies. He is also the co-author, with Nell Minow, of six books on corporate governance, books that many of us now use in our classrooms.

Michael Jensen is the Jesse Isidor Straus Professor of Business Administration Emeritus at Harvard Business School. But Mike's academic career did not start at Harvard. While at the University of Rochester in the 1970s, he wrote a paper with Bill Meckling on "Agency Costs and the Theory of the Firm" that revolutionized the study of corporate finance. It did so by focusing the attention of finance academics on the conflict of interest and incentives between management and shareholders that ends up reducing the value of most if not all public companies. In writing this paper, moreover, Mike and Bill anticipated what was going to become the central corporate governance challenge of the 1980s: getting managers to pursue the interests of their shareholders by maximizing the *value*, and not the size or diversity, of their organizations.

After moving to Harvard in the '80s, Mike became the most prominent academic spokesman for leveraged buyouts, or what is now known as "private equity," as a way of overcoming this agency problem in public companies. In fact, Mike was so impressed by the private equity model of corporate governance that, in 1989, he published an article in the *Harvard Business Review* called "The Eclipse of the Public Corporation." There he argued that, at least in the mature sector of the U.S. economy—those companies that no longer had major growth opportunities requiring outside capital—the greater efficiencies of the LBO or private equity model would cause it to replace the public corporation as the dominant organizational form.

Now, if Mike Jensen and Bob Monks can be thought of as perhaps the preeminent spokesmen for the U.S. shareholder activist movement, the other, pro-management end of the U.S. corporate governance spectrum can be represented by Martin Lipton, the inventor of the poison pill and probably the best-known critic of shareholder activism within our borders. And I think it says a lot about our panel that in a speech Marty gave here in Orlando this past February, the title was "Shareholder Activism and the 'Eclipse of the Public Corporation'," and the speech began by pointing to Mike's 1989 article: "It was an article," Marty starts by saying, "that, at the time it was published, I publicly disagreed with. But I now find it has new vitality. I'll return to Professor Jensen in my conclusion."

Then, in his very next sentence, Marty cites our other panelist as follows: "One can date shareholder activism from the watershed year of 1985 . . . [the year] Bob Monks and Nell Minow started ISS and the City of New York and State of California Pension funds started the Council of Institutional Investors."

And here are a few representative statements from the rest of the speech:

"The shareholder activism movement is destroying the role, focus, and collegiality of the board of directors . . . Activist investors create pressure on boards to manage for short-term share performance rather than long-term value. . . . The key issue for American business is whether the institution of the corporate board of directors as we know it today can cope with shareholder activism and survive as the governing organization."

 What Marty Lipton neglected to mention is that in the almost three decades since Mike Jensen and Bob Monks began working toward the reform of U.S. corporate governance, the productivity and value of U.S. companies have increased dramatically. And most economists would argue that the kind of shareholder activism advocated and practiced by Monks and Jensen has played an important role in these gains.

—Ralph Walkling

At the end of the speech, Marty says, "Now I come back to Michael Jensen. In 1989, Professor Jensen wrote, 'the publicly held corporation, the main engine of economic progress in the United States, has outlived its usefulness.' I now find myself embracing Professor Jensen's 1989 article, less for the reasons he espoused, and more as a solution to the problems created by rampant, unrestrained, and unregulated shareholder activism."

What Marty Lipton neglected to mention, of course, is that in the almost three decades since Mike Jensen and Bob Monks began working toward the reform of U.S. corporate governance, the productivity and value of U.S. companies have increased dramatically. And most economists would argue that the kind of shareholder activism advocated by Monks and Jensen has played an important role in these gains. So, again, let me point out once more that we are privileged to have with us this morning two of the country's leading authorities on corporate governance.

I have organized today's session around three topical aspects of corporate governance and we'll address each in turn. The first of the three concerns the wisdom of expanding investor access to the proxy. Does giving shareholders greater ability to nominate directors amount to shareholder democracy, or will it lead to disruption and corporate anarchy? The second question has to do with private equity as a model for public companies. What, if anything, can the successes of LBOs and private equity tell us about how public companies should be managed? And third and last is the perennial controversy over executive pay in public companies: Have we reached a level of pay that is clearly excessive? Or do the even higher rewards now held out to the top managers of private equity–controlled companies suggest that CEO pay could possibly, in some cases, be too low?

Expanding the Shareholder Vote

And before turning to Mike and Bob, let me say a word about recent proposals to expand shareholder democracy. Since passing Sarbanes-Oxley, Congress has continued to consider other measures that would give shareholders greater influence in the boardroom. Initiatives relating to shareholder access to the proxy and the procedures by which directors are elected have been debated, and in some cases are pending, in Congress. These measures are designed to transfer power from boards of directors to the investors whose interests the boards are supposed to be pursuing.

So, let me start by mentioning some new evidence on the influence of shareholders in electing boards of directors. In a working paper, my Drexel colleagues Jie Cai, Jacqueline Garner, and I looked at about 2,400 director elections with the aim of answering three questions about shareholder voting: Do shareholders vote as if firm performance matters? Do they vote as if the performance of the directors matters? And, third, do they vote as if the quality of governance matters? Our findings suggest that the answer to each of these questions is yes. Directors received a smaller percentage of the vote under the following circumstances: (1) when firm performance was substandard; (2) when the performance of the individual director was deemed to be substandard; and (3) when the firm's governance system, as reflected in several indexes of shareholder rights, was viewed as inadequate.

But then we asked a fourth question: Do the votes themselves matter, in the sense of affecting the reputation and labor market value of directors and influencing the performance of the firm itself? Here's what we found: Even if you are a poorly performing director in a poorly performing firm with bad governance, you're still likely to win almost 90% of the votes cast. What's more, the votes do not appear to affect election outcomes and director turnover. In other words, the voting appears to have no effect on directors' reputations in the sense that they don't lose their seats after getting lower votes. The voting also has almost no discernible effect on future firm performance.

At the same time, however, shareholder voting does appear to have two notable positive effects—one on CEO pay and one on antitakeover provisions. In cases where directors—especially members of the compensation committee—get significantly lower votes, the CEOs tend to get lower pay raises the following year, and companies are far more likely to get rid of poison pills and staggered boards.

So, let's come back to the key question and turn it over to our panelists. How much power should shareholders have in the boardroom, and for what types of decisions? And do you worry about single-issue advocates? Most of the proposals for majority voting, for example, are sponsored by unions. Bob, let's start with you.

Robert Monks: Let me start by telling you that I'm one of the few people in the world who has run as an uninvited candidate for the board of directors of a major U.S. company. And, as we talk about this issue, I think people really ought to understand how important—and restricted—access to the proxy is.

About ten years ago, I analyzed a whole bunch of companies to find one that clearly needed a change in its board. And when I did that, I found Sears. It was 497th out of 500 on *Fortune Magazine*'s list of most admired companies. So I ran for the board of Sears. I did everything you're supposed to do. I submitted my papers to their nominating committee—and they duly turned me down. Next I printed up a proxy, at my own expense. Then I had to get access to the shareholder list, which the law says that you're entitled to—but just try and get it.

Then I was sued by Marty Lipton, who was hired by Sears's board to protect themselves against me. Marty sued me on the grounds that I had "an improper reason" for wanting the shareholder list. He said I was trying to get a list to sell my book. The problem here is that even if you're faced with a lawsuit as absurd as this one, you still have to answer it—which costs a good deal of money. Finally, in the case of Sears, as in many companies, the employee benefit plans owned a lot of the stock. I had to try to prevent the trustee, who is hired by the company, from voting that stock automatically against me and allow the beneficiaries to make some kind of independent judgment.

I could go on, but each one of these steps costs an enormous amount of money. On top of that, if you have five or six hundred thousand shareholders, you're talking $5 million for a mailing. In the meantime, the management of the company is using shareholder funds to do mailings against you. And they mail not just once, but two or three times, and you have to answer those. So, it can run into very serious money. And that's why very few people have done what I did.

To sum up, then, I had long been interested in the field of corporate governance. And I viewed my experience with Sears as an investment in learning something about how shareholder democracy actually works in practice in the U.S. What I can tell you is that, under then prevailing practices—and this is still pretty much true today—it is economic folly to do what I did. What I found was not likely to encourage imitators. And while I don't profess to know the answer to Ralph's question about how much power shareholders ought to have, I think that this proxy question is a really important issue that needs to be addressed.

Walkling: Bob, do you worry about single-issue activists? You're very much an advocate of value and value creation. But do you worry, for example, about a union with some other agenda acquiring a major influence on corporate decision-making?

Monks: I worry about it, but it's way down on my list of worries. The question people really should be asking today is what does the board of an American corporation actually do—and what is it supposed to be doing? Without wanting to appear cynical, I have to say that there really isn't a consensus in America about what a board is supposed to do. In the United Kingdom, it's pretty clear what a board does. In America, a board does pretty much what the CEO wants it to do.

Now, in principle, American boards are supposed to do a lot. Just take a look at the statutory provisions for board responsibility. The reality, however, is that no one since the book of Genesis has ever been able to do all the things that boards are supposed to do. Therefore, everybody knows it's going to be something less than the complete requirement. And so, the question of which aspects of a company's governance system are in greatest need of reform is very much up for grabs in each company.

But, to come back to your question about single-issue advocacy, it's difficult for me to imagine a union member—or any single member—on a board causing much of a problem. The chairman of the board sets the agenda. When I campaigned for the Sears board, I kept telling myself, "We really ought to have two people running—because I can't even second my own motions." So, although I can imagine a single union representative being a minor nuisance, I can't see it threatening the foundation of corporate governance.

More on Corporate Boards

Walkling: Mike, can you tell us about your experiences as a director?

Michael Jensen: As Bob can tell you, I actually got elected to a board of directors in a hostile setting.

Monks: That's right, in the case of Armstrong World Industries.

Jensen: Right. The Belzberg family had purchased a large minority stake in the company and they invited me to run on a slate of directors. And I was the only one the Belzbergs put up who got elected. So, I was like the fox in the chicken house, I guess. But it was a very interesting experience.

Now, let me say that there were very good people on that board. But what was true at Armstrong—and I would guess that it's still true in almost every major public corporation today—is that even the outside directors basically see themselves as employees of the CEO. That's just the way it is. And the outside directors in this case seemed even more deferential and beholden to the CEO than the managers who actually reported to him.

I was put on the compensation committee. And at the first meeting of that committee, there was a proposal to give the management a substantial bonus for the excellent performance they'd had that year. The problem, however, was that the equity value of the company had fallen by roughly 50% over that period. So I was listening to this discussion—and, by the way, the CEO was there running the meeting whose main focus was his own compensation. And when I pointed out that it was really hard to argue that management had done a great job when the value of the company had fallen by 50%, my fellow members of the compensation committee acted as if they were shocked. The response I got was, "How did you calculate that?"

But again let me assure you that these fellow board members were not bad people. In fact, they were fine people. But they were just not accustomed to thinking about things like compensation and performance as being connected in any way to the share price.

Now eventually we did fire the CEO. And I kept asking hard questions. And then the next CEO fired me from the board because, as he put it, I had a tendency to ask "trick questions." And that, apparently, was inappropriate behavior. A trick question, as I gathered from this experience, is one that the CEO either can't answer or finds it uncomfortable to do so.

But contrary to what Bob just told you, my own experience suggests that one person on a board can make a difference. It took a couple of years, but we did fire the CEO for poor performance. I would show up at every board meeting and say, "We've destroyed $50 million since the last meeting." And finally things moved.

Now although things have improved in some ways since then, I would still argue that, under our current system, shareholders are one of the few interests that are really not effectively—or maybe "proactively" is a better word—represented in the boardroom. Even when a company is underperforming, until the market for corporate control—and today that means hedge funds and private equity firms—shows interest in the firm, shareholders really don't have much influence on management and boards. And for that reason, I think there is clearly room for giving shareholders more say in the nomination process.

But when we contemplate such changes, we also need to think hard about special interest groups and unintended consequences. I'm a bit more concerned than Bob about what might happen if we try to regulate or legislate changes in the boardroom nomination process. I say that because I believe that attempting to transfer the voting process that goes on in our political sector to board elections in the corporate sector would be a disaster. When Larry Summers came back from Washington a couple of years ago, I heard him describe the political process in Washington as one in which "nobody wants anybody else to succeed at *anything*." And if you just look at what comes out of Washington, that's pretty close to being correct.

So, again, I think we want to be very careful about legislating changes in the board nomination process. I find it easy to envision special interests, in a more open nomination system, getting board representation and taking actions to transfer wealth among different parties to the corporate contract. To cite just one example, giving shareholders a voice on executive pay could end up politicizing the corporate decision-making process. Look at what's happened to the Harvard Management Corporation since the pay of its chief investment officer became the focus of a public debate. The guy quit, went to work for a hedge fund, and got a huge increase in pay. We don't want that happening to our public corporations.

Walkling: Well, there is now a proposal in the House and Senate called "Say on Pay" that would allow shareholders to vote directly on executive pay packages, a practice that has been used in the U.K. for some time—and I want to come back to that later in this discussion. But it seems to me that we're going to need a lot more discussion and evidence to address this issue of the optimal level or form of shareholder democracy. And I do think that a lot of different forces are coming together on this issue, producing unusual coalitions.

Bob, do you see signs of things changing?

The U.K. Model of Shareholder Democracy

Monks: I think it's important to make very clear that the problem of shareholder involvement in the process of nominating directors is part of a larger question. And that question is the accountability of U.S. corporate management to anybody. That's really the issue.

Now, in every developed country in the world but the United States, that problem is solved in a very simple way: a relatively small percentage of shareholders have the right to call what in England is known as an "extraordinary general meeting," or an EGM. At an EGM, a majority of the shareholders who attend the meeting can remove any or all of the directors with or without cause.

Now that's a far more efficient and effective solution than the idea of having shareholders nominate people for the simple reason that shareholders are not particularly qualified to pick directors. Even very involved, financially sophisticated fiduciaries are not the best people to nominate directors. They really don't know the company business that well; that's not their comparative advantage and it's not their responsibility. You really want the company to do it—but at the same time, you want accountability.

So, I think we're going about this problem the wrong way. And this isn't black magic. As everybody knows, the state of corporation law in America reflects a power struggle and it's been an unequal power struggle. "Them that has the power," as the saying goes, "makes the law." And the result in this country is that, as a practical matter, shareholders don't have the power to remove directors. If they did, this problem would go away.

In every developed country in the world but the United States, the problem of management accountability is solved in a very simple way: a relatively small percentage of shareholders have the right to call what in England is known as an "extraordinary general meeting," or an EGM. At an EGM, a majority of the shareholders who attend the meeting can remove any or all of the directors with or without cause. That's a far more efficient and effective solution than the idea of having shareholders nominate people for the simple reason that even very involved, financially sophisticated fiduciaries are not the best people to nominate directors.

There is also greater respect for the monitoring function of boards in the U.K. The kind of people who serve as chairmen of U.K. companies also tend to be different from their U.S. counterparts. In the U.K. there is a recognized tradition of hiring very experienced executives who are in their second or third careers. And because these people are not afraid of risking their jobs or careers, they have a culture of independent-minded chairmen capable of providing a high level of oversight.

—Robert Monks

Walkling: Bob, does your endorsement of these extraordinary general meetings suggest that you think that U.K. companies are better directed and better managed than U.S. companies?

Monks: Better directed, but probably not better managed—because the U.K. doesn't have the same work culture that we have here. In America, for better or worse, there's a tendency to identify oneself very much with one's job. The level of commitment to that is huge, and that commitment contributes to effective management. In the U.K., by contrast, there's no confusion about whether a good life is a competitor with your job; a good life wins every time. So although I think the English have won the governance battle, we manage our businesses better.

But their governance really is a great deal better. For example, in the *Financial Times* this week, you might have read about a company called BAE, the principal British defense contractor. The independent board chairman of

BAE, who'd been there about three years, essentially forced the retirement of the CEO. And the same thing happened at British Petroleum with Lord Browne. But, in America, where the CEO is often the chairman, this just can't happen.

Jensen: Well, it can't happen unless there's a crisis, unless the troubles are so great they just can't be ignored.

Monks: Right, and Armstrong is a good example of that. But, to go back to my earlier point, there is greater respect for the monitoring function of boards in the U.K. There the directors' sources of information about the company are not limited to just the CEO and the people he chooses to give them access to. The kind of people who serve as chairmen of U.K. companies also tend to be different from their U.S. counterparts. In the U.K. there is a recognized tradition of hiring very experienced executives who are in their second or third careers. And because these people are not afraid of risking their jobs or careers, they have a culture of independent-minded chairmen capable of providing a high level of oversight.

So, in that sense, U.K. companies are better governed. But, as I suggested earlier, if you had to buy stock in two competitive companies, one British and one American, I'd probably take the American.

Jensen: My own experience with a handful of U.K. companies suggests that boards there take their monitoring and control function very seriously. They clearly see themselves as separate from the management. And it's very interesting to see American CEOs serving on those boards because the dominant model here is a supportive board. The function of a board member in the U.S. is basically to counsel and support the CEO. In the U.K., by contrast, there's a deep sense of obligation to exercise a control function, to hold management accountable. And that leads to much better governance. But at the same time, I also agree with Bob's suggestion that English companies tend not to be as efficient or well-run as U.S. firms.

Let me give you an example to illustrate Bob's point about U.K. governance. I was working with a fairly large English company where the outside members—one of whom hired me, by the way—outnumbered the insiders by a large number. And among these outsiders there was not a full-time, but essentially a half-time outside chairman who really ran the agenda independently of the CEO. Now, this is something I had been advocating for years. But until I worked for this U.K. company, I had no idea that any companies were actually doing it. What's more, any outside member of this board had the power to hire any expert or consultant he or she wanted. The only rule the outside board member had to observe was to notify the chairman or the CEO of their intent to hire, and to limit costs to reasonable levels. But there was literally no restriction on the kind of resources they were allowed to hire. And that's unheard of in American companies, at least to my knowledge. Bob, do you know of any U.S. companies that allow that?

Monks: No. In fact, I have ended up paying a bunch of pretty hefty legal fees myself because of this practice. In the case of Sears, for example, I submitted them the bill for my legal fees when trying to get on the proxy—and they submitted the bills right back to me.

Jensen: Right. And you can imagine the huge difference this makes in the attitude of the outside board members when they know the company is willing to spend money to give the board an independent view. So, again, this kind of independence is very different from the American system, where, as I said, even the outside board members see the CEO as their boss. They see themselves as employees of the CEO.

And this means that, in American companies, the CEO effectively has no boss. He or she is the boss unless and until there is an outside crisis that threatens the reputations of people on the board. Then the power shifts, the board members become the bosses, and you see people getting fired. But by that time, there's a whole lot of value destroyed that may not be recoverable.

Walkling: Bob, I want to follow up on your argument that companies in the U.K., although better governed, are not better managed. Can't that be construed as a failure of the U.K. governance system?

Monks: Not the way that I look at it. I see governance as concerned primarily with internal processes and accountability rather than performance. On the issue of accountability, if you want to take long lunches at the Grand National, that's a matter of choice. And whereas governance is a matter of process, performance is really a management question. And when people ask me management questions, my response is, "Hire McKinsey, not me." My expertise is in governing a company, not managing it.

Walkling: But, Mike, before we get off this topic, wouldn't you agree that the kind of discussion that took place at Armstrong is unimaginable today? I think today's boards of directors would be very aware that the stock price had underperformed by 50%. Hedge funds and private equity firms would be all over that board—and they would be forced to respond to that. And I wonder if that isn't an important part of the explanation for the performance of U.S. companies. Isn't it possible that the outside pressure, if not a perfect substitute, is a reasonably good substitute for effective governance?

Hedge funds and private equity play a critical role in maintaining the performance of U.S. companies. But let's not allow the effects of these forces to blind us to the problems that continue to exist in boardrooms, in the internal corporate governance system. So, yes, the control markets are a very important force—and a partial substitute—for more effective governance. And I have no doubt that U.S. companies today are far more efficient as a result of the LBOs and takeovers that took place in the 1980s and 1990s. But in the meantime, people like Marty Lipton continue to work to limit the effectiveness of those forces. And, as I said, most corporate board members continue to act as if they report to the CEOs instead of monitoring their performance and holding them accountable.

As a consequence, the CEOs of U.S. companies effectively have no boss. He or she is the boss unless and until there is an outside crisis that threatens the reputations of people on the board. Then the power shifts, the board members become the bosses, and you see people getting fired. But by that time, there's a whole lot of value destroyed that may not be recoverable.

—Michael Jensen

Jensen: Well, I think you're right to say that the outside pressures and corporate control markets are enormously important in bringing about change. And they were important a decade ago when I served on Armstrong's board. As I said, I was elected to the board as a result of the Belzbergs' acquiring a substantial minority interest. And after we fired the CEO and implemented a new management incentive plan, the value of the company doubled in a year. So, a big chunk of the lost value turned out to be recoverable—though things began to slide after that.

So, I agree with your point that those outside forces—the corporate control markets that today have increasingly taken the form of hedge funds and private equity—play a critical role in maintaining the performance of U.S. companies. But let's not allow the effects of those forces to blind us to the problems that continue to exist in boardrooms, in the *internal* corporate governance system. So, yes, the outside control markets are a very important force—and a partial substitute—for more effective governance. And I don't have any doubt that U.S.

companies today are far more efficient as a result of the LBOs and takeovers that took place in the 1980s and 1990s. But in the meantime, people like Marty Lipton continue to work to limit the effectiveness of those forces. And, as I said, most corporate board members continue to act as if they report to the CEOs instead of monitoring their performance and holding them accountable.

Walkling: One last question on this topic of shareholder voting: In a recent Harvard Law Review, the Delaware court's Leo Strine argued that shareholders may not deserve more shareholder democracy because "the majority of them are intermediaries, such as pension funds and mutual funds, which have governance problems of their own"—problems that could lead them to act against the interests of the people whose money they are investing.

Bob, let me put you on the spot by asking a pointed question. I know that you and Nell Minow sold Institutional Shareholder Services for a handsome price, and that ISS is now in the hands of a new owner. Our own estimates suggest that ISS effectively controls about 20% of votes in director elections, and thus can be a dominant factor in such elections. The question I have for you is, what are the potential conflicts inherent in a company that sells its services to the companies it rates?

Monks: Oh, there is a conflict; there's no question about it. I sold the venture before it started this practice. But I should also tell you that the Robert Monks who sold the venture is my son. And though he's a better businessman than I am, he is perhaps not as focused on internal governance issues as I would be.

This situation with ISS is a wonderful morality tale for early in the morning. When we started ISS back in 1985, you couldn't expect trustees, no matter how conscientious, to become well informed about all of the thousands of proxy issues that many of them have with regard to their portfolio companies. So we reasoned that if you wanted to have shareholders involved in corporate governance issues, you had to have some way for trustees to inform themselves about the issues. And ISS began to perform this very valuable function. Over time, it became such a dominant force that we ended up having, as you say, about 20% of the vote. And in addition to our influence on 20% of the vote, many of the clients have simply transferred their fiduciary responsibilities to ISS.

So, you want to be careful what you ask for—because you may get it. Now, as far as I know, ISS has never yet allowed, or been accused of allowing, payments from rated companies to influence its ratings. So far they have been clean. But one day I think that something will happen. It always does, but I hope I'm not around to see it. It isn't right to have a single intermediary becoming in effect the default fiduciary for everybody else.

The Private Equity Model

Walkling: Mike, since you just raised the subject of private equity, let's explore the main thesis of your 1989 *Harvard Business Review* article that the LBO represents a superior organizational form, a better model of corporate governance than that provided by the public corporation. What lessons can public companies learn from private equity? And why have they been so slow to learn them? And perhaps even more puzzling to economists, why are the private equity firms themselves becoming public companies? As a practitioner friend of mine, Joe Rizzi, likes to say, "When private equity firms go public, it's time to grab your wallet and run."

And let's start with Bob. What do you make of the recent wave of private equity deals, which now appears on its way down—and maybe even out?

Monks: I have long believed that you can increase a company's value by improving its governance system. That was the main premise underlying the kind of activism we practiced at LENS. And it seems equally clear to me that the truth of this proposition has been established by the successes of the private equity industry. Private equity exists mainly because there is a gap between public company governance and the governance structure the new owners plan to put in place once they've acquired the enterprise.

Rupert Murdoch did not pay $5 billion for the Dow Jones & Company because he wants to put *Wall Street Journal* editorials on his wall. The 60% or so premium he volunteered to pay over the stock's value under its former owners reflects his assessment of the extent of the underperformance—a failure that can be attributed in large part to the company's governance structure, to the dual-class stock ownership that long enabled the family to maintain control while destroying value. That premium can also be viewed as reflecting Murdoch's estimate of the value of the improvements he expects to make.

And private equity, to my way of thinking, plays essentially the same role. It's a form of arbitrage, if you will, between public and private equity markets in which active investors use leverage to acquire assets that, in their eyes, are not being managed to maximize value. Such investors are exploiting what I like to call a "governance value gap" between public and private companies.

Walkling: Mike, that sounds a lot like the thesis of your 1989 paper on "The Eclipse of the Public Corporation" that got Marty Lipton's attention. Can you tell us what you were thinking when you wrote that article?

Jensen: Well, let's start by thinking back to the beginning of the 1980s, when the shareholders of U.S. public companies were basically the only important stakeholder group that was not well represented in the corporate boardroom.

The inefficiencies that resulted from this lack of monitoring and accountability gave rise to corporate raiders and to the formation of these new organizations like KKR, Forstmann Little, and Berkshire Partners. When I started writing about them in the mid-'80s, I called them "LBO associations" or "LBO partnerships." But after LBOs got a bad name, the term "private equity" came into vogue. And let me just mention that what we call "private equity" today encompasses not just LBO firms like KKR but also classic venture capital firms like Kleiner Perkins. While there are important differences between these activities, there are also remarkable similarities between their ownership and governance systems, and that's why we lump them together.

But whatever you want to call them, these new organizations represented to me an important innovation in organizational form, a new model of governance and management, if you will—though I never could get my colleagues in strategy at the Harvard Business School to see it that way. What struck me was that the portfolios of assets put together by the LBO partnerships of the '80s were very similar to those of U.S. conglomerates, with lots of different businesses having no apparent synergies. But the LBO firms were set up very differently from the public conglomerates. Instead of raising capital from public equity markets, the LBO firms get most of their equity from private limited partnerships, for which the LBO firms serve as the general partners. Each unit or division of the LBO association is funded by debt and equity at the individual business unit or divisional level, not at the corporate level as in the conglomerates.

Now, if you think about how conglomerates operate, this difference in financial structure can make a huge difference. Every business effectively stands on its own, which means that financial problems that affect one operation cannot bring down another. And the level of the debt in these stand-alone operating businesses is also, of course, significantly higher. As I've argued in a number of papers, the high leverage in these transactions plays an important role, a very important control function. When a highly leveraged firm begins to underperform, the covenants get triggered, decision rights get changed, and, at the end, you could go into bankruptcy. The control benefit of debt can be seen by recognizing that if a company is leveraged to 90% of its value, management cannot destroy more than about 10% of firm value before these decision rights get substantially changed and outsiders begin to have influence or control. But if the same firm instead has only 10% debt, then management could have the opportunity to destroy as much as 90% of the value of the firm before any covenants get triggered. Reinforcing this control benefit, as I suggested earlier, is the inability of the LBO or private equity firm to use funds from one business or division to subsidize the activities of others.

Also very important, the operating heads of each business have significant equity stakes *in their own businesses*—as opposed to, say, stock options in a diversified collection of businesses over which they exercise almost no control. And the equity stakes of these operating heads were considerably larger than those of U.S. public company CEOs, especially back then. In a study of executive pay in U.S. public companies in the '70s and '80s, Kevin Murphy and I estimated that the average U.S. CEO in the '80s saw his personal wealth go up by about $3 for every $1,000 increase in the value of the firm. By comparison, Steve Kaplan's doctoral thesis found that the CEOs of businesses owned by LBO firms—the people who were previously running divisions inside conglomerates—earned about $64 for every $1,000 in shareholder wealth. So that's quite a change in incentives.

Finally, and in some ways most important, under the LBO or private equity governance system, the performance of the operating companies and their top managements is overseen by much smaller boards that consist mainly of the firm's largest investors. Other than the CEO, there are typically no insiders. And, as you can imagine, the kinds of discussions that take place in a room with just the firm's major owners and the CEO are just dramatically different from what goes on in most public company board meetings. In contrast to the public companies we have been talking about, the CEO in a private equity controlled firm does have a boss; he or she clearly reports to the board of directors, who are also the controlling investors. And if the board determines the company is not performing up to expectations, they will remove the CEO far more quickly than a public company board.

Now, there's also one other important aspect of private equity that I've neglected to mention—and that's the duration or term of the funds. The funds have clearly defined lives, ranging from seven to thirteen years. And that means that management has to give the funds back after a definite period of time. So, if you want to continue in operation, you have to ask the capital markets to give you back more money. It used to be a rule of thumb that, if two of your funds failed to beat the S&P 500 over the life of the fund, you were out of business. You wouldn't be able to raise money again.

That's a very important element of the private equity model, a critical source of discipline on the investment process. But that discipline goes away when a firm like KKR—as they did in Europe recently—raises "permanent" capital, public equity instead of the finite-term capital supplied by limited partnerships. And we all know from looking at closed-end mutual funds what happens when you have permanent capital. The market values the fund at a discount to its net asset value, a discount that I think clearly reflects what we now call "agency costs"—the loss of value from the potential divergence of interests between the fund's managers and its owners. So, when you buy public equity in a private equity firm, what you're essentially buying is a closed-end fund. And, as I said, it's well established that most closed-end funds trade at a discount to the value of the sum of their parts.

Now, when you take the next step, as the people at Blackstone and Fortress have done, and you turn the private equity firm itself into a public corporation, I think you've really put yourself in dangerous territory. I'm giving a talk here later today about the highly counterproductive game that most public companies are involved in. It's a game called "earnings management" that takes place between managements in corporations and the capital markets. There is a serious lack of integrity in this process and, as I have been arguing for the last few years, it ends up destroying enormous amounts of value.

So, when you take part of the private equity business public, you're putting yourself back into this other game. And I'll be very surprised if the private equity firms don't start to behave very much like other public corporations, with their reliance on earnings guidance and earnings management. So, Ralph, I'm in total agreement with your friend who said, "It's time to grab your wallet and run."

But, in terms of what public companies can learn from private equity, let me come back to their accomplishments, which have been pretty remarkable. After looking at all the evidence on LBOs—after considering the 30% or 40% premiums that are paid to the shareholders of the public companies that are being taken private, the returns to the limited partners, and the fees that are earned by the private equity firms themselves—there's absolutely no doubt in my mind that private equity has created huge amounts of value for the economy, huge amounts of social wealth.

However, because of the fees paid to buyout sponsors and the premiums paid to public shareholders in the buyout, average returns to private equity investors do not beat the market. Also remarkable is the consistency of the returns produced by the top quartile of firms—which are the best, and generally the oldest, firms in the business. We don't find that kind of consistency anywhere else in the capital markets; for, example, we don't find it in either our studies of mutual funds or in the work that I've seen to date on hedge funds.

But like all markets, private equity tends to overshoot. When things are going well, you get lots of new, inexperienced firms—Steve Kaplan calls them "tourists"—coming into the market. They will launch a couple of funds, perhaps have a couple of successes, and make a bunch of money. But when the tough times hit, they'll be gone. And thanks to the work of these inexperienced firms, private equity will get a bad rap during the next five or six years as the fallout from the most recent wave of deals begins to settle.

Public Companies and the Earnings Management Game

Walkling: Well, since you've brought it up, let's talk a bit more about the earnings management game that public companies either volunteer to play or, according to the managers of the companies themselves, are forced by the markets to play. A Duke University survey reported that almost 80% of some 400 responding U.S. CFOs said they would cut back investment in a project with a positive NPV in order to hit a short-term earnings target. And my question is: Who's really at fault here? Are investors being shortsighted, or are managers failing to understand the markets?

Monks: Well, again, I think this question is really one of accountability. A CFO works for a company, and the company is supposed to be run for its shareholders. And the shareholders are represented by the market. Now, does the market speak with a clear voice on corporate investments? Probably not. And even if there is clearly a market view of a particular project, should it be accepted without question by management? I don't think so. Although I might make an exception for large acquisitions, the precise evaluation of individual corporate projects is generally beyond the competency of the market.

On the other hand, the idea that corporate management should completely ignore the market's expectations in making large capital budgeting decisions is also clearly wrong. The market is the ultimate arbiter of the required return of the collection of corporate projects that make up the company. And that required return is the standard by which we judge what our managers are supposed to do.

But that raises the troublesome issue of net present values and their relevance to today's companies. NPV can take you a long way in valuing basic manufacturing companies, the kinds of companies that are good candidates for LBOs. But for companies whose values consist more of growth opportunities than cash-generating assets, we're going to need a somewhat broader finance vocabulary. We're going to have to understand more about the contributions of intangible assets and so-called real options to corporate values. And we're also going to have to begin to learn the language of sustainability—an area where Europe is well ahead of us, by the way.

If there's one subject on which most financial economists and practitioners agree, it's that the present system of accounting conveys very little information about underlying corporate values. Baruch Lev, one of the pioneering thinkers in this area, has concluded that, for today's companies, the percentage of value captured by corporate income statements and balance sheets has fallen to something like 20%. In other words, about 80% of corporate values today reflect things that aren't on the financial statements, that aren't picked up by NPV type of arithmetic. On the asset side, this is things like patents and other forms of intellectual property and corporate know-how. On the liability side are the costs of externalities like carbon emissions that are not borne by companies under present law—at least in the U.S.—but are likely to be imposed on them in the future. All of the attention to global warming would suggest that we're not very far away from having a broad social discussion about corporate sharing of the cost of the externalities now imposed on our communities.

So, again, I think that management needs to consider market signals and expectations when making major long-term strategic decisions. But I also think the current "linear" vocabulary of NPV is too limited for this discussion. And, as I said, there are major opportunities for leadership on the creation of a new language of accountability related to sustainability and long-term returns.

Walkling: I often hear corporate executives complain that they can't manage "for the long run." They have to hit that earnings target, and that means cutting back on projects that would create maximum value.

Monks: I have a good deal of skepticism about this argument. Long term and short term are in the eye of the beholder. While I know there can be a valuable discipline in being forced to meet short-term targets, I've rarely heard managers acknowledge this. But I've heard lots of managers try to justify abysmal performance by arguing that the profits are on the come. As used and abused by corporate managers in practice, "long term" and "short term" tend to be code words with little meaning behind them. The reality, of course, is that long-term performance is just a series of short-term results, and good management is about managing tradeoffs between a dollar of earnings today and a dollar plus tomorrow.

Peter Drucker once described effective management as "muddling through with a purpose." And I think that's a good description. The best managers have a pretty good idea of what they're doing and why. But even their companies are likely to end up somewhere different from where they expected to be—or they may end up in the same spot, but for reasons wholly different from what they anticipated. Marty Lipton ended up agreeing with Mike's article on the future of public companies, but for wholly different reasons. That's how our minds work. We begin with a set of priorities and expectations. And then experience causes us to adjust them.

So, to me the important question is whether management has a coherent and compelling explanation for why it is doing what it is doing at a given time. And whether someone characterizes that as short term or long term will depend on his or her expectations and requirements. But my own experience and intuition tell me that a manager with a compelling strategy is likely to find some group of investors who share that vision and are willing to ride out the bumps in performance. At the same time, it also seems clear that the firm that manages earnings to the penny will be abandoned by investors the moment it misses a target.

Jensen: I think this evidence of widespread earnings management produced by the Duke survey is very important. It confirms my own beliefs about the system, about this convoluted and distorted discussion of earnings that now tends to dominate at least the public dialogue between corporate management and the capital markets. And it is a corrupt system. It's a game that nobody can win, and it is reducing the long-run productivity and value of many of our public companies. And this in turn has a lot to do with why so many of our public companies have chosen to go private.

But what continues to puzzle me is the fact that the companies themselves don't seem to think they have any other options if they want to stay public. Most top managers say that they have to participate in this earnings guidance and earnings management game with analysts. But there are clearly other options. The best example, of course, is the disclosure policy of Warren Buffett, whose Berkshire Hathaway has long refused to provide earnings guidance. Buffett's success is proof that you can run a public company in pretty much the same way you would run a private firm, provided you do a good job of making clear your strategy and gain the confidence of investors. And the kind of disclosure and relationship with capital markets I'm talking about has nothing to do with earnings guidance. The practice of earnings guidance—and the pressure it puts on organizations to manage earnings to meet the targets—is more likely to undermine a company's relationship with its investors than to encourage the kind of sophisticated, longer-term holders that most managers claim to want.

Monks: That's right. Buffett doesn't give guidance and doesn't even talk to analysts—and his shares trade at a significant premium to the sum of the individual values of the companies that make up Berkshire Hathaway. Buffett's argument is that it's not his job to forecast earnings; that's the job for the analysts. Now if you hold up the example of Warren Buffett to corporate America, most CEOs tend to view Warren as too quirky to follow. But there are a number of successful and highly regarded companies—Goldman Sachs is one—that avoid guidance.

Jensen: Progressive Insurance is another good example. It's a fascinating story of a company that has never given guidance. The board thought about starting guidance when Reg. FD was passed in 2002. But they decided instead to provide monthly releases of their operating P&L—no earnings forecasts, just reports of actual premiums taken in and operating costs for the past month, including expected losses from claims. And since starting that policy, Progressive has seen the volatility of the stock—which many people thought would go up—fall by 50%.

But I will also predict that when Buffett and Charlie Munger are gone, Berkshire Hathaway is likely to revert to a more "normal" corporate behavior with all of the value destruction that will bring about.

So, we have this peculiar equilibrium that looks like collusion between the managers and the analysts and capital markets, but really isn't. In a market with that many different players, you can't really have an effective kind of collusion. And when I try to look at the whole picture, it absolutely doesn't make any sense. Most corporate managers think they have to engage in this game; if they don't, the capital markets will ignore them and their values will collapse. But I think the exact opposite is true. If they stopped guiding earnings and started a more substantive, forward-looking, strategic dialogue with investors, they would find themselves with a more sophisticated—and probably a more loyal—shareholder base.

The Issue of Executive Pay

Walkling: Now let's turn to another major controversy in U.S. corporate governance: the level of executive compensation and its correlation, or lack of it, with corporate performance. Mike has been studying this issue at least since the end of the 1980s; and if it was controversial then, it's even more controversial now.

But before I turn to Mike and Bob, let me mention some new evidence. A bill called "Say on Pay" was passed in the House this spring by a two-to-one vote, and supported by Democrats and Republicans alike. The same day Barack Obama introduced a companion bill in the Senate. Such bills would not limit CEO pay, but instead would allow nonbinding shareholder votes on all public company executive pay packages. So, shareholders would get to say yes or no—either they like the compensation for this firm or they don't. And companies can respond to the votes as they see fit. Let me also add that the Bush White House opposes the bill for essentially the same reason it claims to oppose expanding shareholder access to the proxy—that is, the possibility it creates for special interests to disrupt or distort corporate decision-making.

Now, in devising our study, we came up with three main hypotheses about how the stock market might respond to the announcements of these bills: The bill could either increase corporate values, reduce them, or have no effect. It might increase values by promising to give shareholders a voice, and perhaps greater influence, on executive pay. Alternatively, it could be viewed negatively by the market as promoting a destructive form of meddling by outsiders. It's not hard to envision a case—like the Harvard Management case Mike cited earlier—where populist voting discourages corporate boards from offering very large rewards for exceptional performance, and thereby causes companies to fail to retain a very effective CEO.

And then there's a third possibility—my own favorite—which is that a shareholder vote on pay could turn out to be what some economists call a "neutral mutation." First of all, even if the measure passes the senate, Bush's opposition is likely to prevent it from becoming law. And even if it passes, it's not binding and therefore doesn't have any teeth. If shareholders vote against a plan, who says the company will take action? And consistent with this third possibility, what evidence we now have on other nonbinding shareholder proposals supports this third hypothesis—not much of an effect.

So, my colleague Jie Cai and I performed the following experiment. We took 1,300 companies and examined the market reaction to the passing of this bill proposing "Say on Pay." And my initial expectation turned out to be right, at least on average: For the average company in our entire sample, there was no perceptible reaction to the bill.

But when we next divided companies into quartiles according to degree of CEO "overpayment"—we called it "positive unexplained CEO pay"—we found that the stock prices of the quartile of companies with the most overpaid CEOs had a positive reaction to the bill. This positive reaction was also more evident in companies deemed to have poor governance and those with greater ownership by activist investors. So, our findings were consistent with the idea that "Say on Pay" is expected to improve corporate performance and create value.

But now let me turn back to Bob Monks. Bob, in a recent article in the *Financial Times*, you were quoted as describing U.S. stock options as "history's greatest nonviolent transfer of wealth from one class to another." What have we learned about executive compensation and incentives, and where are we headed in this debate?

Monks: This has been a truly memorable week with regard to the subject of executive pay. The President of the United States, George W. Bush, publicly professed to be "astounded" by the level of U.S. executive pay. He went on to say that shareholders should get active and do something about it. Now, I don't know whether this is going to be any more of a self-executing decree than some of Bush's military pronouncements, but it is noteworthy that someone who is perhaps as responsible as anyone alive for the current hegemony of the CEO should profess astonishment at CEO pay—and then tell the shareholders to do something about it. So, this has been quite a week on that subject.

I want to say two things on the question of "Say on Pay." First, don't underestimate the idiosyncratic problems, the potential for mischief, stemming from the efforts of state and local governments in the U.S. to block any Federal initiative. As you know, substantive corporate law is passed by the individual states, which have long been in a race to the bottom to see who can pass the most permissive laws so as to encourage companies to charter there and produce tax revenues.

As a consequence, with one major exception, I don't believe there has been a single piece of substantive corporate law passed by the Congress since 1933. Every time a substantive corporation law comes up, the lobbying of 50 bar associations sees that it gets killed. Corporations are, of course, great clients for lawyers—and every state has lawyers and they're all active in politics. And they do not want to see their corporate law practices moved to Washington D.C. So literally every time some issue would come up, the corporate bar would lobby successfully not to have it passed.

Now, the one clear exception to this is Sarbanes–Oxley. It was an extraordinary event, one that could have been produced only by an extreme crisis. Large companies like Enron and WorldCom went bankrupt. And suddenly these bills that Paul Sarbanes had been sitting on for five or six years—which hadn't even gotten out of the Finance Committee—went through with a rush—and grabbed Michael Oxley along the way.

So, I'm not optimistic that this Say on Pay bill will become law in this country any time soon. But I think we should give it serious consideration. Giving investors a say on executive pay has been the practice in England now for about ten years and is widely regarded there as a successful measure. There's a weekly trade publication for governance junkies called "Global Proxy Watch" that comes out on Fridays. And in this morning's edition, it reports that a new academic study has concluded that, in the U.K., the shareholder votes on pay have had a measurable success in controlling executive compensation.

Walkling: There are at least two people in this room who are very interested in knowing the results of that study. To my knowledge, Jie and I were the only people who had looked at this.

Monks: That's right. According to this article, there had been anecdotal reports of the effectiveness of this measure, but no broad-based statistical evidence until now. But this morning I read that Professors Sudhakar Balachandran of Columbia University and Fabrizio Ferri and David Maber of the Harvard Business School examined 700 U.K. companies while using 1,800 U.S. firms as a control group. The study claims to have found evidence of an increase in the sensitivity of CEO total compensation to negative operating and stock performance following the passage of the new rule. What this means is that the U.K. votes on pay have resulted, as the article's caption puts it, in "markedly fewer rewards for failure." And such findings, as the article goes on to suggest, are expected to put "momentum behind the pending say on pay rise in the U.S. and elsewhere."

This article may well be onto something important. I say that because I think even the most ardent defenders of the U.S. pay system would agree that some of the packages given to our clearly failing CEOs have been unconscionable, outrageous, a disgrace to our system.

Walkling: Mike, what are your thoughts on this?

Jensen: First of all, compensation matters bring out the worst in human beings, whether you're talking about it across different levels in organizations or at the highest levels. And for that reason, I believe that publicizing and perhaps politicizing that process—and that includes putting executive compensation to a shareholder vote—could turn out to have unintended consequences. In fact, it could be a disaster.

In my paper with Kevin Murphy in the early '90s, we said in a fairly forceful way that, based on the evidence we had found, there was no way you could conclude that CEOs were overpaid. At the same time, it was clear to us that top executives were being paid in the wrong ways. The main determinant of pay was the size of the organization as measured by sales. And we argued that the relationship between size and pay contributed directly to value-destroying corporate behavior—to the pursuit of growth at all cost and, perhaps even worse, the building of conglomerates. Based on estimates of the value created when raiders began pulling conglomerates apart in the '80s, I would guess that U.S. conglomerates were routinely destroying anywhere from 25% to 50% of the total value of their operating companies by trying to run them from a single corporate headquarters.

Now, in the book that Kevin and I are writing today, our message is going to be a little different. We are still not especially troubled by the level of today's pay packages, at least on average. In fact, on that dimension, the rest of the world's companies now appear to be moving rapidly in our direction. But what we find disturbing is the way today's CEOs are getting paid enormous amounts of money for failure. Bob Nardelli earned something like $200 million at Home Depot for increasing earnings per share, even though the stock price fell over his four-year tenure. And making things worse, in fulfillment of the contract he negotiated when coming from GE, he got paid another $220 million after he got fired. So, as things worked out, he made more by being fired than he would have made had he stayed on board.

Now, to me that is a clear sign that there's something dramatically wrong in the way compensation decisions are being made in these organizations. And Nardelli's deal is not an aberration, by the way. In the process of researching our book, Kevin and Eric Wruck came across this tome produced by compensation consultants that collects, among many other documents, the "for cause" termination provisions in executive compensation contracts. (And, by the way, when we wrote our first article, executive CEO employment contracts were virtually unheard of—they were just coming into use.)

After looking at these contracts, we've come to at least one important conclusion: The near universality today of employment contracts for CEOs can be traced back to federal laws limiting golden parachutes, payments under changes of control. In other words, CEO employment contracts became a standard part of the executive labor market only after the federal government got in the way of the other corporate methods for getting rid of CEOs. And to me it seems very clear that golden parachutes are a far better solution to the problem of removing entrenched CEOs than today's employment contracts.

One of the major features of those contracts that Kevin and I have focused on are the terms and provisions that surround "for cause" dismissals. What we have found here represents to me an unbelievable failure of corporate compensation committees to fulfill their obligations to the company's shareholders. To cite one statistic, only 4% of the contracts we have examined allow a CEO to be dismissed "for cause" if he or she violates their fiduciary responsibilities. What that means is that 96% of U.S. corporate CEOs are entitled to the full value of their contracts even if they violate their fiduciary responsibilities to the firm and its financial stakeholders. Even more amazing, in the case of around 40% of CEOs, their companies would have to pay them the full values of their contracts *even if they are convicted of a felony.*

So, when I look at the provisions in these contracts, it just makes no sense whatsoever. And if U.S. boards are doing a bad job on obvious stuff like this, then it's not surprising that they're making mistakes elsewhere.

But having made these criticisms, let me also repeat what I've said many times before. There's no doubt in my mind that the shift in U.S. executive compensation during the '90s toward greater pay-for-performance, and away from pay based just on size of the organization, has had a huge impact on the productivity and value of U.S. corporations. And, as I already suggested, the fact that European companies are moving in this direction only lends support to this proposition. So I don't have any doubt that U.S. pay practices have brought about a big—and for the most part positive—change in the way corporations are run and operated.

But are those practices the best we can do? Clearly not. If Kevin and I were rewriting the paper we published in the early '90s, we would have paid much more attention to ensuring that executive stock options were indexed to the cost of equity capital so that the exercise price grows at the cost of equity capital. To give you an example of what I mean, suppose your company's stock is selling at $100, and you're going to give the CEO options with an exercise price of $100. And let's also assume the cost of equity capital is 10%. Given that information, we know that if the price of the stock isn't equal to at least $110 a year from now, value has been destroyed; the company has failed to provide its investors with the opportunity cost of their capital.

To give management a deal that is consistent with shareholders' interests, then, the exercise price of those options should rise at the end of the year to $110—or perhaps a bit lower, to reflect the managers' lack of liquidity and inability to diversity. And the exercise price should keep rising in each year thereafter. The problem, however, is that under the current regulations and tax law, there are big penalties for issuing such cost-of-capital-adjusted options; and as a result they have basically not been used.

Walkling: Mike, shouldn't options also be indexed for overall movements in markets, and perhaps for the performance of their competitors?

Jensen: I would argue against that. I know a lot of my colleagues in the business are very fond of these index-adjusted options. But that raises a whole set of complicated issues, especially if you're talking about industry-specific indexes instead of indexing to the general market. I'm convinced that indexing a firm's performance to its competitors is a bad idea. For example, if you go to competitor-adjusted performance measures, you absolutely have to change the decision rights. You can't let the CEO be deciding what industry he's in; those decision rights have to be taken into the hands of the board.

But, to come back to my earlier point, I think we can do a lot better in designing executive pay packages. We have a system that pays CEOs enormous bonuses for creating value, which I think is a good thing on the whole. But, at the same time, our system pays many executives large bonuses even when they destroy value, and that is something that clearly needs to change. And let me also say that I'm not in favor of the recent substitution by many companies of large restricted stock grants for options. I think that's a very expensive way to provide incentives for managers. And it doesn't provide nearly the incentives that options do. If I simply give you a million dollars' worth of restricted stock (instead of making you pay for it) and the stock price goes down by 20% over the next two years, you've still got $800,000 worth of stock. So you don't have much downside risk; you end up with a lot of money even if the stock goes down.

Now, options indexed to the cost of capital would take care of this problem. But, as I said, they are not being issued for a variety of legal and tax reasons. So, there's a lot to be untangled here. I don't know how to write rules and regulations that will fix this problem. And I don't think we understand the system well enough to say exactly what ought to be changed, especially when it comes to the laws. We need to have some people who know a lot more than I do about the long-run effects of legal and regulatory changes thinking about what actual rules one could put in place that would make a difference—changes that stand a better than 50% chance of making things better rather than worse.

More generally, I think we've got a long way to go to really understand the forces that operate in our compensations committees and to understand the incentives that actually get created. I would hate to revert back to the compensation practices we had in the '70s and '80s. In those days, executives had very little incentive to increase shareholder value. But I also believe that there are a lot of compensation rules and practices that have grown up since then that might need some rethinking.

For example, when Kevin and I get our book written, I think boards of directors and compensation committees will think harder about routinely including these for-cause provisions in executive pay contracts. The process by which certain practices become accepted as "best practice" in that industry is a very subtle one—and lawyers tend to do the same thing, by the way. People gather huge amounts of data, which allows them to identify trends or dominant practices. And then—presumably with the assumption that whatever prevails in a market process must be efficient—they go on to interpret them as *best* practices. But in many cases—particularly those involving clear conflicts of interest and unresolved agency problems—they are not best practices at all, nor are they the outcome of a true market process. They are simply summaries of what people do when left more or less to their own devices, when they're effectively insulated from market forces. But, as I said, these practices get labeled and sold as best practices—and this is very misleading.

So there are very complicated issues going on here with executive pay. Boards are given a very thick book showing what other executives get paid—and they're given another book on antitakeover devices and other corporate control practices and procedures. And, under the pretext of providing information about the best practices produced by a competitive market system, these books are viewed as providing protection to both companies and their shareholders.

Now, I haven't finished reading both of those volumes—and before our book gets done, Kevin and I will between us have read every page. But what I will say is that there is not a single example in what I've read so far where the consultants recommend executive compensation, golden parachutes, or antitakeover or corporate control provisions that make shareholders better off by making executives worse off. In other words, in what constitutes today's best practices, executives always win.

So, these findings and practices are sold in a very subtle and yet very powerful way that I believe has a big impact on the outcome of the discussions by compensation and governance committees. And I think that just exposing the methods and assumptions underlying this search for best practices will be very instructive.

Before Sarbanes-Oxley, there was a conflict in which the public accountants that audited companies were making more money from their consulting practices with their clients than from their audits. And that has been addressed by SOX. But, as Kevin and I have been complaining for years, we've also long had a conflict of interest in the compensation consulting business that is very much like what existed in the accounting business. A compensation consultant might get $250,000 for designing a CEO compensation contract for a top-level executive while at the same time earning as much as $10–25 million for actuarial work on rank-and-file compensation. And, as in the case of auditors, it's very hard to imagine this consultant taking a hard line against CEOs while asking their heads of human resources for $25 million of additional work. The consulting firms have a clear conflict of interest here.

How do we solve this problem? There are now Congressional hearings on this issue, but I wouldn't jump to passing a law. At the very least, it seems clear to me that the comp consulting industry needs to be reorganized so you don't have people facing that conflict. Towers Perrin and the other major compensation consultants have supposedly split up their practices. And Fred Cook does only top-level management compensation contracts, and no lower-level consulting. But even if this problem gets resolved as has been done in the public accounting sphere, you still have enormous conflicts of interest with outside consultants.

Walkling: Bob, do you want to respond to Mike on this, or give us any last words?

Monks: I have to confess that I feel privileged just to hear Mike talk about executive pay, since he probably has thought and written more about the subject than anybody in the world. And when he tells us that he doesn't have a legal or regulatory solution to obstacles to the design of better stock options, I find that a wonderful example of concern for getting things exactly right, for avoiding the problem of unintended consequences.

As Mike was just suggesting, it is amazing how little we know about the important factors and forces in setting the compensation of top executives. It's also disturbing to me to see consultants devoting so much ingenuity and effort to comply with the letter of disclosure requirements while flouting the spirit or intent of the regulations. I see it as an abandonment of basic standards of ethics and decency. And I don't see things changing any time soon. I recently asked the head of the SEC why he was so optimistic about the new disclosure requirements on CEO compensation. When I said to him, "I've been a director for 40 years, and the SEC has always had rules about disclosing compensation," he leaned back and said, "Bob, this time we really mean it."

So, let me end by inviting you to draw your own conclusions. What's important to keep in mind about disclosure and the governance of corporations is that they are not matters of law. And they are not matters of economics. They are matters of power. And the fixing of the pay of the top executives is the smoking gun, the indicator, of this power. The mechanisms that will correct this problem, whether they be legal or regulatory or governance, are going to result from investors meeting that power with their own. The difficulty at the moment is that the balance of power is with managements and boards. As we've been discussing at some length, the board views themselves as working for the CEO, so they're not going to be very effective in limiting the power of top management.

And recognizing their limited ability to influence boards or management, many shareholders who ought to participate in corporate governance have chosen not to. A good example of this is Harvard University, Mike's long-time employer and my alma mater. Harvard's endowment fund has long simply declined to involve itself in matters of governance. And why an institution where people take so much pride in teaching ethics refuses to practice effective governance is a question I leave to you.

Walkling: Well, let's leave it at that. Please join me in thanking our two panelists, Bob Monks and Mike Jensen, for a lively and provocative discussion.

Note

This chapter was previously published as an article in *Journal of Applied Corporate Finance*, Vol. 20, No. 1 (2008): 27–46. Photograph of Michael Jensen by Yvonne Gunner.

PART II

Internal Governance: Boards and Executive Compensation

CHAPTER 4

The Director's New Clothes

(or, The Myth of Corporate Accountability)

ROBERT MONKS AND NELL MINOW

A SCENE IN *BARBARIANS AT THE GATE* frames the question of accountability of corporate management perfectly. Ross Johnson, the man who somewhat impetuously initiated the leveraged buyout of RJR-Nabisco, meets with Henry Kravis and George Roberts of Kohlberg, Kravis, Roberts to discuss it. There is a brief discussion of the business before Johnson's central questions come up. "Now Henry, if you guys get this, you're not going to get into chickenshit stuff about planes and golf courses, are you?" (Johnson's perquisites included corporate jets and membership fees at twenty-four country clubs.)[1] Kravis is eager to gloss over this question, but Roberts is more candid: "Well, we don't want you to live a spartan life. But we like to have things justified. We don't mind people using private airplanes to get places, if there's no ordinary way. It is important that a CEO set the tone in any deal we do."

Johnson states his concern more directly: "I guess the deal we're looking for is a bit unusual." Johnson, as it turns out, wants to keep significant control of the company. Roberts responds even more directly: "We're not going to do any deal where management controls it. We'll work with you. But we have no interest in losing control." Johnson asks why. "We've got the money," Roberts says. "We've got the investors, that's why we have to control the deal." From the look in Johnson's eyes, Roberts can tell it wasn't the message he wanted to hear. "Well, that's interesting," Johnson says. "But frankly, I've got more freedom doing what I do right now."[2]

There's something wrong with this picture, because it took debt to make management accountable. It should have been accountable to shareholders, to the people who have "got the money."

What's wrong with this picture is the discrepancy between the expectations of the law and reality. The law generally assumes that "All corporation power shall be exercised by or under the authority of, and the business and affairs of the corporation managed under the direction of, its board of directors, subject to any limitation set forth in the articles of incorporation."[3] According to Melvin Eisenberg, "All serious students of corporate affairs recognize that notwithstanding the statutory injunction, in the typical large publicly held corporation the board does not 'manage' the corporation's business in the ordinary meaning of that term. Rather, that function is vested in the executives."[4] This reality is reflected in the erosion of the standard of performance for directors. *Barbarians at the Gate* documents in devastating fashion the way that Ross Johnson handled his boards, with a combination of lavish perquisites and meager information. So long as he was dazzling his hand-picked directors, who could expect them to complain about his jets and country clubs?

The corporate structure was designed to maximize profits through competition in the marketplace, but it has proven to be more successful at making profits, whether maximum or not, by imposing costs on others. Every single mechanism that has been set up as some kind of check to prevent this externalizing of costs has been neutralized, short-circuited, or co-opted. Shareholders, directors, state and federal legislatures—even the marketplace itself—all are part of the myth of corporate accountability, and all are part of the reality of corpocracy. In this chapter, we look at the convenient myth behind the mechanisms established to make sure that corporate activity was consistent with the public interest and the more convenient reality of the failure of these mechanisms to do so.

The Myth of the Director's Duty

In a corporation, management acts as agent for the owner, but it does not always have the same interests and incentives. What can we do to require—or at least encourage—people to treat other people's property with as much care as if it were their own?

The law has tried to answer this question of agency costs by developing its highest standard of behavior, the fiduciary standard, and applying it to those who hold and manage property for others. This standard applies to several different players in the process for establishing corporate behavior, including directors. At least in theory, they are fiduciaries for the shareholders. And the law books are filled with attempts, some almost poetic, to define that duty. Their actions must be "held to something stricter than the morals of the marketplace," with a "punctilio of an honor the most sensitive."[5]

That there is a fiduciary standard is perhaps the most powerful myth underlying the corporate system. Why is it so important to make clear that directors must take extraordinary measures to make sure that they are protecting the rights of shareholders? The reason is our belief that those who exercise power should be accountable to those who are affected by it. We delegate authority to the directors of private companies because they are accountable to the shareholders, just as we delegate authority to government officials because they are accountable to the electorate. Accountability is what makes delegated authority legitimate; without accountability, there is nothing to prevent abuse.

This was the conundrum that almost stopped corporations before they began. Karl Marx and Adam Smith did not agree on much, but they both thought that the corporate form of organization was unworkable, and for remarkably similar reasons. They questioned whether it is possible to create a structure that will operate efficiently and fairly, despite the fact that there is a separation between ownership and control. Put another way, is there any system to make a manager care as much about the company's performance as a shareholder does? Harvard Law School's Dean Robert Clark describes this issue when he says that the major problem addressed by corporate law is how to keep managers accountable to their fiduciary duties of care and loyalty while allowing them great discretionary power over the conduct of the business.[6]

This is a key question, for both economic and public policy reasons. The separation of ownership and control leads to externalities, imposition of costs on others—including shareholders, taxpayers, and the community. For example, a company that discharges untreated effluent into a river is making the community pay some of the costs of production, through government services for clean-up or increased health care costs. A company that uses political pull at the state level to thwart a worthwhile takeover attempt is making the shareholders foot the bill, not just for the lobbying efforts, but for the lost premium, and possibly for a less competitive company. And, of course, it was the shareholders who were paying for Ross Johnson's twenty-four country club memberships and (at least by one account) for his dog's trip on a jet from the corporate fleet, to say nothing of the devastatingly expensive mistake of the "smokeless cigarette."

The answer to this problem was supposed to be the board of directors, elected by shareholders and acting as fiduciaries on their behalf. The board is responsible for setting overall goals and making sure they are met, for hiring the CEO and monitoring his or her performance, and for watching corporate management on behalf of the shareholders, to make sure that the corporation is run in their interest. That's the theory—and the myth. The reality is that directors are "merely the parsley on the fish"[7] or the "ornaments on a corporate Christmas Tree."[8] As Peter Drucker put it many years ago, "Whenever an institution malfunctions as consistently as boards of directors have in nearly every major fiasco of the last forty or fifty years, it is futile to blame men. It is the institution that malfunctions."[9]

The Convenient Myth—and the More Convenient Reality

How can we justify a system in which investors purchase shares in a company that is far too big and complex to permit any meaningful shareholder involvement in governance? In theory, the accountability in our system is the enforceable allegiance that corporate directors and managers owe to shareholders. And that allegiance is enforceable in two ways. Dissatisfied shareholders can sue for violation of fiduciary duty, or, through the electoral process (proxy voting), they can throw the bums out and vote in directors who will do better.

Although difficult to believe in today's world, it is from the premise that shareholders can respond effectively to inadequate boards that much of corporate decision-making gets its legitimacy. It is directors, after all, who appoint the officers and determine their level of compensation, and who set the long-term goals and make sure that management takes appropriate steps to carry them out. The fiduciary standard is supposed to ensure that they take all of these actions on behalf of the shareholders. But this is little more than a vestigial notion in modern times. As the creation of instruments to finance takeovers of any company, of virtually any size, has presented directors with unprecedented challenges, they have found, as have the shareholders, that the traditional notion of a director's duty—and authority—is more myth than reality.

Dance with the One Who Brought You—or Else

Barbarians at the Gate detailed Ross Johnson's techniques for the care and feeding of his directors—everything from arranging for them to rub shoulders with celebrities to endowing chairs at their alma maters. Perquisites such as the use of corporate planes and apartments made it hard for directors to push him on tough questions. The same is true at most corporations. Directors are picked because the CEO knows them and knows that they are likely to be on his or her side. Many of them—even those termed "outside" directors by the New York Stock Exchange's definition—have some business or personal relationship with the CEO.[10] We were once informed by an investor of a prominent electronics company that the head of the board of directors' compensation committee was the chancellor of a college. The president of the company, in turn, was the chairman of the college's board of trustees, and the company has been a big contributor to the school—a nice, cozy arrangement.

Directors are not picked for their ability to challenge management. On the contrary, they are more often chosen for their business or personal ties, or for their ability to add symbolic luster. Compensation expert Graef Crystal describes boards as "ten friends of management, a woman and a black."

A vice president of one of the nation's largest conglomerates told us that during one period his company's board included a much-loved TV personality. "He always made a hit at annual meetings, where shareholders greeted him with long applause," said the vice president. "After the meeting, the directors would have cocktails and lunch, and the star would regale them with anecdotes and jokes. Then, when the Chairman banged the gavel, the star would put his head down on the table and sleep until the meeting was over. Someone sitting next to him would cast his vote, when required, claiming he or she had checked the star's position." On another board, a Nobel Prize–winning scientist was selected by management. An observer told us that "he always made a point to ask questions during board meetings, the kind of questions that an intelligent but uninformed layman might ask, but his material contributions were nil."

Since they are selected by management, paid by management, and—perhaps most important—informed by management, it is easy for directors to become captive to management's perspective. Information is the key, and it is often frustrating to directors to have such limited access. Former Supreme Court Justice Arthur Goldberg, a member of the board of TWA, suggested that the board form a committee to make periodic reports on the company's operations and that it have its own staff of experts, including a scientist, an economist, a public relations expert, an auditor, and, perhaps, a financial expert. The proposal was turned down, and Goldberg resigned from the board.[11]

Other directors who have tried to question management have fared even worse. Those directors who cannot be schmoozed, ignored, or avoided can be silenced. Ross Perot was brought to the General Motors board just for the skills and experience that had made his company, EDS, so successful. When he tried to give the board the benefit of that skill and experience, CEO Roger Smith paid Perot $742.8 million—$33 a share for stock that closed at $26 7/8 on the day of the trade, plus another $346.8 million for contingent notes and tax compensation—in order to get him off the board.[12] GM even established a $7.5 million penalty to be levied if either Perot or GM criticized each other, and they set up a three-man arbitration panel to evaluate possible violations.[13] So there was no opportunity for the shareholders to find out Perot's concerns about the company. There was also no opportunity for them to get that price; GM refused to buy back other shareholders' stock for the price they paid Perot.

An outside director of a company that went private in an MBO told us that his every attempt to question management was thwarted. The special committee convened to oversee that the deal was made up of directors selected for their history of going along with whatever management proposed. The projections for segments of the company previously expected to do well suddenly became dismal, as all of the assumptions changed to justify a low price. Even if a company is operating as a public company, it has every incentive to present its most optimistic forecasts to directors and shareholders. But a buyer and a seller have two different ways of valuing assets, and in an MBO, management switches sides. The "independent" investment banking firms hired to provide "fair" evaluations of the value of the assets owe their allegiance to management. Who owes allegiance to shareholders? In theory, it is the board of directors, who, as fiduciaries, are supposed to be better to shareholders than they would be to themselves. But the theory of fiduciary duty has given way to the reality of a duty so threadbare that it covers as little as the fabled emperor's new clothes.

The Empire Strikes Back: The Business Roundtable

With the birth of the Roundtable, big business in the United States may at last be said to have come of political age.[14]

The Business Roundtable is an association of approximately two hundred of the country's largest publicly held corporations, who have joined together to examine public issues that affect the economy and to develop positions that reflect "sound economic and social principles. The objectives of the Roundtable include fostering economic policies conducive to the wellbeing of the nation and its people."[15]

The Roundtable came about, indirectly, because its predecessor, the Business Council, was part of the Department of Commerce—a fact Kennedy's first commerce secretary, Luther Hodges, did not appreciate. Hodges felt that the council, a group that advised him as commerce secretary yet would not allow him to select its members or determine their meeting agendas, should not have a "special channel to government thinking."[16] Hodges and the council remained at loggerheads until the council went to Kennedy and told him that they would operate as a private group. Business was then represented by different umbrella organizations over the next decade, including a revived private Business Council, the U.S. Chamber of Commerce, the National Association of Manufacturers, and the National Federation of Independent Business. From the point of view of the business community, the inadequacy of its governmental relations was never more painful than during the Nixon and Ford administrations, when wage and price controls were installed, with almost no input from the business sector. According to one scholar, it was John Connally, long an ally of big business, who made it clear to prominent business leaders that "businessmen had to improve in political sophistication and techniques in Washington or else face political impotence."[17]

In March 1972, Frederick Borch of General Electric and John D. Harper of Alcoa convened about a dozen corporate CEOs as "the March Group" to involve themselves directly in lobbying and influencing. The result was the Business Roundtable, a disciplined, sophisticated, and effective political fighting machine. Its success is attributable to the prestige and effort of the leaders: Harper, Irving Shapiro of Dupont, Reg Jones of GE, GM's Thomas Murphy, Exxon's Clifton Garvin, and, more recently, GM's Roger Smith and Union Pacific's Drew Lewis.

The Roundtable's direction comes from its executive and policy committees. The organization has three unique characteristics. First, the CEOs are personally involved. Second, membership is limited to CEOs of large companies; there are no small or medium-sized businesses whose interests and priorities might be different—or inconvenient. Third, the organization carefully avoids involving itself with a single company or a single-interest pressure group. The Roundtable speaks for "big business," and it does so through its task forces. Typically, a subject for special attention will be selected and then a "lead company" designated. Usually, its CEO directs the task force, supplying the critical personnel from his or her own corporation or using people made available by other corporations. The Roundtable itself stays relatively small and discrete.

"Unable to persuade Congress to pass legislation curbing hostile takeovers,"[18] the Roundtable has devised an ambitious strategy to protect its members, including the devotion of substantial attention and energy to questions of internal corporate governance as a way of allowing what is, in essence, a hostile takeover from the inside. Although a great deal of the Roundtable's energy has been devoted to opposition to federal authority over corporate governance and support for state antitakeover legislation, one of its initiatives is noteworthy here: the recent drastic revisions of the Roundtable's own well-researched and thoughtful 1978 Statement on Corporate Governance.

The Roundtable on Governance, 1978 and 1990

There is no clearer indication of the Roundtable's views on corporate governance than in its own reports on the subject. In its brief existence, the Roundtable has profoundly changed its views, as revealed by a comparison of its papers issued in 1978 and 1990.

In January 1978, the Business Roundtable issued a statement entitled *The Role and Composition of the Board of Directors of the Large Publicly Owned Corporation*. The paper was the culmination of a project responding to a pattern of corporate criminal behavior involving illegal campaign contributions, bribery, and illicit involvement in the elections of other countries. The CEO members of the Roundtable evaluated how corporate boards of directors are selected, constituted, and function, in order to understand and to avoid further criminal behavior.

A distinguished scholars group was chaired by Dean David S. Ruder of the Northwestern University School of Law (who later became chairman of the SEC during the last part of the Reagan administration). He reported to the Roundtable's Committee on Corporate Organization Policy, chaired by J. Paul Austin (CEO of the Coca-Cola Company).

Their report was the state-of-the-art explanation in 1978 for the legitimacy of private power. It relies heavily on accountability as the safeguard from criminal and other activity that is contrary to the interests of society. The report describes the constraints on corporate action that are traditionally used to support its legitimacy. All of the limits listed in the report, however, were more myth than reality, and more often breached by corporate management than observed. The most noteworthy constraint cited by the Roundtable was its accountability to boards and shareholders—noteworthy precisely because, as that myth began to become reality with the takeovers of the 1980s, the Roundtable reversed its position. The 1990 version had the pomp of the earlier version, without the circumstance—no blue-ribbon panel of academics was brought in this time.

The 1978 report specified the accountability imposed by economic constraints—inadequate response to competition, both domestic and foreign—and raised the prospect of lower share prices, higher cost of capital, vulnerability to takeover, and diminished personal job security. It also cited accountability imposed by the formidable array of legal and regulatory requirements to which corporate management is subject: "Moreover, we have witnessed in recent years an increasing rigor on the part of state courts in applying fiduciary standards to evaluate behavior of corporate management. Contrary to some misconceptions, actions for management misconduct are in fact imposed and constitute an impressive system of deterrence."[19] The Roundtable in 1978 was acutely conscious of the necessity of an independent board of directors. In order to have meaningful independence, the report recognized that it might be necessary to give shareholders an explicit right to nominate directors. The following statement from the 1978 report may be the best definition of the ideal role of a board of directors: "The board of directors, then, is located at two critical corporate interfaces—the interface between the owners of the enterprise and its management, and the interface between the corporation and the larger society. The directors are stewards—stewards of the owners' interest in the enterprise and stewards also of the owners' legal and ethical obligations to other groups affected by corporate activity."[20] If only the Roundtable had stuck with it.

The Roundtable Retreats: Corporate Governance in 1990

The transformation of the issues of corporate governance in the 1980s is reflected in the revisionist approach taken twelve years later in the Roundtable's 1990 report, *Corporate Governance and American Competitiveness*. Its basic conclusion is that American business is doing just fine and does not need interference from anyone, especially shareholders. The Roundtable responded to the threat of government involvement in 1978 by emphasizing private accountability; it responded in 1990 to the threat of private accountability by stressing CEO supremacy.

Whereas the 1978 report contemplated a board of directors directly accountable to shareholders and constructively capable of independent evaluation and monitoring of management, the 1990 statement's version is closer to a structure of vertical authority, with the CEO on top and the board of directors one among several operating departments. The report contemplates the selection of directors who are acceptable to the CEO,[21] who attend meetings presided over by the CEO, and who discuss agenda items selected by the CEO.[22]

As a practical matter, the board contemplated by the report is self-perpetuating; there is no more suggestion of shareholder involvement in nominations, even informally. And the essence of the report is that owners cannot be trusted and therefore should not be permitted to make the fundamental decisions concerning the corporation's operations. "Shareholder voting on such things as acquisitions and divestitures can put immediate shareholder financial return ahead of sound longer-term growth which may have the potential of being even more rewarding to the corporation, its shareholders and its other stakeholders."[23]

This begs the question. No one is in favor of an overly short-term outlook, but *long-term* may be a euphemism for something that never happens. The real question is whose perspective is riskier. Why aren't shareholders—as those whose interest is at risk—just as knowledgeable and even more entitled than directors to set the overall direction of the company? Whose perspective is likely to be longer term—the index fund[24] pledged to hold the stock indefinitely or the CEO, who could lose his job in a change of control?

The critical question is on what basis directors and managers will make their choices. To the extent that directors have authority to allocate corporate resources on any basis other than long-term value enhancement, they are undermining the basis for the grant of power to private entities in a free society.

The 1990 Roundtable report, in all its essentials, is a wiring diagram for CEO monarchy. First, it cautions against direct shareholder involvement: "Excessive corporate governance by referendum in the proxy statement can also chill innovation and risk-taking."[25] Second, it diminishes the authority and independence of the board by depicting it as a necessarily self-perpetuating body ("Because effective corporate boards function as a cohesive whole, the directors are in the best position to recommend the slate of nominees for board membership which is presented to the shareholders for election at the annual meeting")[26] and by implying that the chairman and presiding officer of the board must be the CEO ("To ensure continuing effective board operations, the CEO can periodically ask the directors for their evaluation of the general agenda items for board meetings and any suggestions they may have for improvement").[27]

In the fall of 1990, the Business Roundtable further demonstrated its view of the role of shareholders by telling all of its members to refuse to respond to a survey of directors submitted by the California Public Employees' Retirement

System. The Roundtable responded as if merely asking questions of directors to determine their personal views was not appropriate:

> Some of the questions do not lend themselves to broad generalizations because the answers depend on particular facts and circumstances, others require a more complex response than the questionnaire's format allows, and still others suggest that directors' responses will be used to create "good" and "bad" rankings for director nominees in spite of the disavowal of any such intent.[28]

The letter itself provides the most telling evidence of the Roundtable's vision of the role of shareholders, directors, and management: It assumes that when shareholders seek information about the directors they are asked to elect, managers have not only the right but the obligation to interfere.[29]

This is quite a departure from the earlier commitment to acting as stewards for owners. Indeed, other than a vague acknowledgment of the obligation to maximize value, shareholders are mentioned only in the context of either being incapable of providing direction or having their rights considered along with those of other "stakeholders." This diminished role for shareholders is a startling retreat for the Roundtable. It also parallels the diminished role for the shareholders' representatives, the board.

Notes

This chapter is an excerpt from chapter 3 of *Power and Accountability* (New York: Harper-Business, 1990). Reprinted here with permission of the publisher.

1. Bryan Burrough and John Helyar, *Barbarians at the Gate* (New York: Harper & Row, 1990), p. 93. The book also notes that "Johnson's two maids were on the company payroll."
2. Ibid., p. 255.
3. See Committee on Corporate Laws of the Section of Corporation, Banking and Business Law, American Bar Association, *Model Business Corporation Act* (Prentice-Hall Law and Business, 1990), p. 781. "Thirty-two jurisdictions follow the language of the Model Act ... the remaining 20 jurisdictions provide the corporation's affairs should be managed by a board of directors," p. 788.
4. Melvin Aron Eisenberg, *The Structure of the Corporation: A Legal Analysis* (Boston: Little, Brown, 1976), p. 140.
5. Benjamin N. Cardozo, *Meinhard v. Salmon*, 249 N.Y. 458, 464 (1928).
6. Robert Clark, *Corporate Law* (Boston: Little, Brown, 1986), pp. 33–34.
7. Arthur Fleischer, Jr., Geoffrey C. Hazard, Jr., and Miriam Z. Klipper, *Board Games* (Boston: Little, Brown, 1988), p. 3.
8. Jay W. Lorsch with Elizabeth MacIver, *Pawns or Potentates: The Reality of America's Corporate Boards* (Boston: Harvard Business School Press, 1989), p. 4.
9. Peter Drucker, "The Bored Board," in *Toward the Next Economics and Other Essays* (New York: Harper & Row, 1981), p. 10.

10. According to preliminary figures in the ISS Database, 843 out of 5,848 director positions in the ISS Director Database were "affiliated" outsiders, with some business connection to the company.
11. Lorsch (1989), pp. 57–58.
12. Maryann Keller, *Rude Awakening: The Rise, Fall, and Struggle for Recovery of General Motors* (New York: William Morrow, 1989), p. 188.
13. Doron P. Levin, *Irreconcilable Differences: Ross Perot Versus General Motors* (Boston: Little, Brown, 1989), p. 324.
14. Kim McQuaid, *Big Business and Presidential Power: From FDR to Reagan* (New York: William Morrow, 1982), p. 308.
15. Brief of petitioner The Business Roundtable, Case #99–1651, Court of Appeals, D.C. Circuit (August 22, 1989), p. ii.
16. McQuaid (1982). Ibid., p. 308
17. Ibid., p. 284.
18. Tim Smart, "Knights of the Roundtable: Tracking Big Business' Agenda in Washington," *Business Week,* October 21, 1988, p. 39.
19. The Business Roundtable, *The Role and Composition of the Board of Directors of the Large Publicly Owned Corporation* (available from the Business Roundtable, 200 Park Ave., New York, NY 10166), 1978, p. 3.
20. Ibid., p. 8.
21. The Business Roundtable, *Corporate Governance and American Competitiveness* (available from the Business Roundtable, 200 Park Ave., New York, NY 10166), 1990, p. 13 ("... while the CEO must be involved...").
22. Ibid., p. 14 ("To ensure continuing effective board operations, the CEO can periodically ask the directors for their evaluation of the general agenda for board meetings and any suggestions they may have for improvement.").
23. Ibid., p. 16.
24. An index fund is a type of "passive portfolio" that tracks an index. An example is the Standard & Poor's Index. Investment managers do not make buy/sell decisions based on analysis of individual companies but hold the stock as long as it is in the index.
25. The Business Roundtable, *Corporate Governance and American Competitiveness,* p. 16.
26. Ibid., p. 9.
27. Ibid., p. 14.
28. Letter from Bruce Atwater, chairman, Corporate Governance Task Force of the Business Roundtable, November 7, 1990.
29. "We suggest you advise your directors not to respond..." (ibid.).

CHAPTER 5

Best Practices in Corporate Governance:

What Two Decades of Research Reveals

ANIL SHIVDASANI AND MARC ZENNER

INVESTOR, REGULATORY, AND PUBLIC CONCERN about corporate governance has prompted most companies to reassess the quality and structure of their governance systems. In this chapter, we survey a broad range of research (including our own) conducted over the past two decades on a variety of corporate governance topics. Our summary of the key findings is based on the most important and influential studies in this area. The sheer volume of the literature dictates that we focus on a few critical areas and emphasize the principal findings in each:

- What is the appropriate mix of inside, independent, and nonindependent outside directors on the board?
- Who qualifies as an independent director?
- What is the appropriate composition of board committees?
- What kinds of directors should companies seek to attract and how should they be compensated?
- What kinds of compensation policies for executives and directors create the most value for shareholders?
- What is the impact of various antitakeover provisions?

The existing research examines many, but not all, of the proposals under consideration or recently implemented by the NYSE, NASDAQ, and other organizations, such as the Institutional Shareholder Services. Most of the studies that we summarize are based on analyses of large numbers of public companies over several years. Therefore, the results of any specific study will not be directly applicable to all types of companies in all situations. Nonetheless, we believe that these studies highlight common themes, which should serve as a useful resource as boards evaluate and consider ideas for designing governance structures that enhance long-term shareholder value.

Should the Board Be Composed of a Majority of Independent Directors?

Few questions in academic work generate as much consensus as this one. The literature is filled with studies showing that in situations requiring a specific board decision, the outcome is more likely to be beneficial to shareholders when the board consists of a majority of independent outside directors—that is, when the board is "outside dominated." Studies have focused on the responsiveness of boards in the supervision of management, which is a primary board responsibility, and found the following:

- Outside-dominated boards are more likely to replace poorly performing CEOs (Weisbach, 1988).

- Outside boards are more likely to opt for a clean slate and hire the replacement CEO from outside the firm than promote an internal candidate (Borokhovich et al., 1996; Huson et al., 2000).

- Companies with outside-dominated boards tend to make better acquisitions, as reflected in the announcement-day reaction to acquisition bids (Byrd and Hickman, 1992); see figure 5.1.

- Outside-dominated boards tend to bargain more intensively when their companies become targets of takeover bids, resulting in larger stock price gains for the target shareholders (Cotter et al., 1997); see figure 5.2.

Although outside-dominated boards help companies make better specific decisions, existing research has not found any direct link between board composition and measures of financial performance or shareholder value. For companies with outside boards, valuation multiples[1] and metrics such as return on assets (ROA) or operating performance margins are typically comparable to those of companies with insider-dominated boards (Bhagat and Black, 1999; Hermalin and Weisbach, 1991; Mehran, 1995). But board composition is itself affected by financial performance in that companies typically react to deteriorating performance by adding outside directors to the board. Research shows that independent director appointments tend to be associated with share price appreciation (Rosenstein and Wyatt, 1990). In general, the advantages of an active outside board are most visible when a specific issue such as an acquisition proposal or the replacement of the CEO needs to be voted on. Operating performance, which is tied most closely to the quality of day-to-day management of the company, tends to be less directly affected by board composition.

FIGURE 5.1

Announcement-Day Returns for Acquiring Companies

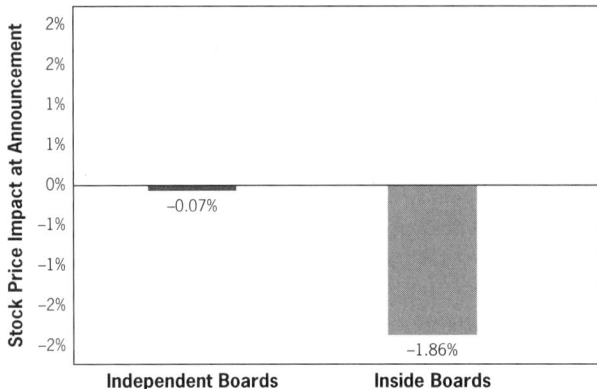

Source: Byrd and Hickman (1992).

FIGURE 5.2

Takeover-Period Returns for Target Companies

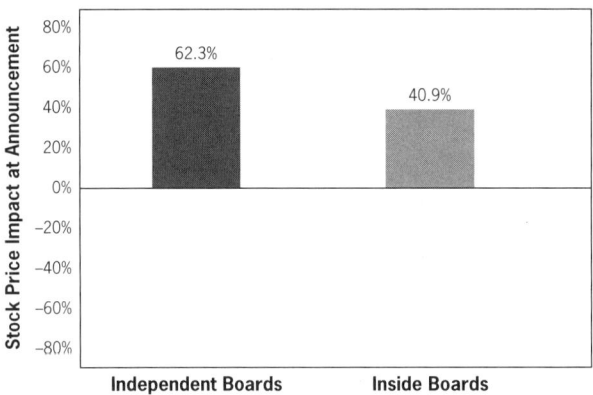

Source: Cotter et al. (1997).
Note: Returns are calculated as the market-adjusted stock return from inception to completion of bid.

Who Qualifies as an Independent Director?

Studies have shown that the impact of outside directors on corporate governance depends critically on whether they are independent or share some affiliation with management. Several types of affiliations have been identified as creating the potential for conflicts of interest:

- Past employment with the company as an executive. However, studies have not yet examined whether the five-year cooling-off period for an executive under the adopted NYSE guidelines overcomes potential conflicts when former executives serve on the board.
- Any consulting or contractual arrangement with the company from which a director may derive a pecuniary benefit. Directors who are executives of suppliers or customers, for example, would not be considered independent.
- Relatives of the top management team.
- Commercial bankers, investment bankers, and lawyers—even if no business ties currently exist—because of the potential for conflict of interest and the possibility that business ties may be sought.
- Outside directors with interlocked directorships with the top management team (such as CEOs that reciprocally serve on each other's boards).

Studies do find, however, that representatives of large shareholders on the board can have a positive impact on corporate governance (Fich and Shivdasani, 2002).

Should the CEO Be the Only Insider?

Although the evidence in support of an outside-dominated board is overwhelming, studies have not typically found much evidence that increasing the proportion of independent directors beyond 50 percent adds incremental value. This is perhaps not surprising, because most board decisions are determined by majority rule. In fact, it can be highly beneficial to have nonindependent directors on the board:

- Surveys of independent directors reveal that one of the biggest challenges is when the CEO is the primary conduit of information presented to the board (Lorsch and MacIver, 1989). With one or two non-CEO executives on the board, it is more likely that a comprehensive view of the company is presented to the outside board members. Particularly in today's environment, the CFO might be a logical candidate for the board.

When the board includes the top one or two internal candidates for CEO succession, outside directors are better able to assess their capabilities and to evaluate whether the next CEO should be internal or external (Hermalin and Weisbach, 1988).

- The presence of outside directors with financial expertise, such as investment and commercial bankers, can add value in certain situations. For small and medium-sized companies with limited access to in-house financial expertise, appointments of investment bankers and commercial bankers lead to a positive stock price reaction, suggesting that affiliated directors can add value in some circumstances (Lee et al., 1999).

Should the Chairman and CEO Positions Be Separate?

The question of whether the chairman and CEO positions should be separated is controversial and has been studied extensively. Some of the findings are as follows:

- In many companies, CEOs gain the title of chairman after having outperformed their peers. Brickley et al. (1997) argued that the title of chairman serves as a reward to a new CEO who has demonstrated superior performance and represents an implicit vote of confidence by outside directors. In their view, requiring companies to separate the positions of CEO and chairman would deprive boards of an important tool to motivate and reward new CEOs, even though it confers greater power on the CEO.
- Combining the CEO and chairman duties makes it harder for a board to replace a poorly performing CEO, which can reduce the flexibility of a board to address significant declines in performance (Goyal and Park, 2002).
- Among large industrial companies, those with non-CEO chairmen traded at higher price-to-book multiples (Yermack, 1996).
- Banks with non-CEO chairmen had higher ROAs and cost-efficiency ratios (Pi and Timme, 1993).

How Should Committees Be Structured?

The composition of the audit, nominating, and compensation committees has been studied in the literature, with the following findings:

- Earnings releases tend to be more informative to equity investors (that is, they have a more significant stock price impact) when the audit committee is independent (Klein, 2002). This result suggests that, on average, equity investors place greater reliance on earnings releases when the audit committee has a majority of independent directors.
- CEO involvement in the director nomination process has been shown to have a significant impact on the types of directors that are appointed to

boards. When CEOs either participate directly in the selection of new board appointees or serve on the nominating committee, or when no nominating committee exists, companies tend to appoint fewer independent outside directors and more affiliated outside directors with potential conflicts of interests (Shivdasani and Yermack, 1999).

- The stock market reaction to appointments of independent outside directors is more positive when the director selection process is viewed to have relatively little CEO involvement (Shivdasani and Yermack, 1999).
- When the CEO sits on the nominating committee, the audit committee is less likely to have a majority of independent directors (Klein, 2002).
- CEOs are more likely to receive excessive cash compensation when they sit on the nominating committee (Klein, 2002).
- Research for the period prior to 1992–1993 has shown that a greater proportion of a CEO's compensation was equity-based if retired or current executives dominated the compensation committee (Anderson and Bizjak, 2002). When CEOs served on their own compensation committee, there was no evidence of excessive compensation (Anderson and Bizjak, 2002). Thus, research has not found that CEO presence on the compensation committee leads to weaker governance, although this may simply reflect the fact that very few CEOs actually serve on the compensation committee.

How Often Should the Board Meet?

Board meetings serve as key forums in which executives and directors share information on company performance, plans, and policies. Frequent meetings allow for better communication between management and directors. However, frequent meetings might also distract the firm's managers from their day-to-day operational responsibilities and may deter the board participation of directors with other time-consuming responsibilities. Research suggests that boards should balance the costs and benefits of board meeting frequency and should be willing to increase meeting frequency whenever the situation requires significant board input and supervision.

- Boards increase meeting frequency after poor performance. On average, higher meeting frequency does not lead to poor performance but is a reaction to deteriorating performance (Vafeas, 1999).
- The recovery from poor performance is faster if board meeting frequency is increased (Vafeas, 1999).

How Large Should the Board Be?

The size of the board has a material impact on the quality of corporate governance. Several anecdotal accounts support the idea that large boards can be dysfunctional; for example, an outside director of American Express who organized the removal of the CEO in 1993 cited the unwieldy nineteen-person board as an obstacle to change (Monks and Minow, 1995). This view has been confirmed in two broad statistical studies (Eisenberg et al., 1998; Yermack, 1996):

- Among the largest five hundred companies ranked by Forbes, those companies with the highest valuation multiples had boards that included eight or fewer people, while companies with a board membership of more than fourteen displayed the lowest multiples.
- In addition to lower multiples, companies with large boards experienced lower ROAs and operating efficiency metrics.
- Companies with large boards are slower to replace CEOs in the face of declines in performance.
- Significant changes in the size of the board have a material valuation impact.[2] Companies that announced decreases in board size had an average market-adjusted stock return of 2.9 percent at the announcement, while those that increased board size saw the stock price decrease by 2.8 percent adjusted for market movements.

This evidence suggests that some boards may be larger than optimal and that it may be worthwhile for companies to reevaluate their optimal board size. However, the rationale for a board reduction should be carefully communicated to investors because news of the departure of a well-respected director may be received negatively.

How Many Boards Should Directors Sit On?

Despite the popular view in the media that serving on multiple boards lowers the ability of independent directors to perform their duties, most academic studies suggest that directors with multiple board seats are generally likely to be individuals with strong reputations whose services are in demand by many boards. Among the findings:

- Companies at which a large percentage of directors had multiple appointments were less likely to have been targets of unsolicited, hostile, or disciplinary takeover bids (Shivdasani, 1993). Being a target of an unsolicited, hostile bid is often viewed in the finance and economics literature as an indication that a company's internal governance is weak.

- Companies that were targets of takeover negotiations extracted higher premiums for their shareholders when more directors held multiple board appointments (Cotter et al., 1997).
- Companies announcing appointments of outside directors with at least three other board seats experienced a positive stock price effect at the announcement of the directors' appointment (Pritchard et al., 2003).
- Directors with three or more other board seats were more likely to serve on board committees and had higher board attendance (Pritchard et al., 2003).
- Securities litigation is no more likely for companies with independent directors serving on more than three boards (Pritchard et al., 2003).

Of course, time constraints dictate that there is a limit to how many boards on which any individual can effectively serve:

- Core et al. (1999) define directors to be "busy" if they serve on more than three boards while holding full-time employment or if they sit on more than six boards while retired. They find that the presence of such directors on the board correlates with excessive CEO compensation and imply that busy directors do not contribute significantly to effective corporate governance.
- Companies were more likely to be sued for financial statement fraud when directors served on multiple boards (Beasley, 1996).
- When companies announce the appointment of an outside director who is a full-time executive at another firm and who holds three or more other board seats, the market's reaction tends to be negative (Perry and Peyer, 2002).

Should Top Executives Hold More Stock?

Stock and option holdings link a CEO's wealth to company performance,[3] and a large body of literature suggests that, for most companies, executive equity ownership increases shareholder value and promotes better decision-making.[4]

- Firm valuation multiples are higher when executives and insiders own more stock and stock options (McConnell and Servaes, 1990; Morck et al., 1988).

- Acquisition decisions are received more positively by the market when executives have larger ownership stakes (Lewellen et al., 1985).
- CEOs are less likely to resist tender offers for their companies when executives own more stock (Cotter and Zenner, 1994; Walkling and Long, 1984).

The evidence suggests that there is a positive relationship between managerial ownership and firm value, and therefore that compensation committees and boards should make CEO stock ownership a key component of their compensation structure. However, the literature also illustrates that large CEO stock holdings have potential drawbacks:

- Once CEO stock ownership (or control of voting rights) increases beyond the level at which the CEO has effective control of the firm (say 25 percent), CEO ownership has a declining effect on value (McConnell and Servaes, 1990; Morck et al., 1988); see figure 5.3.
- When stock ownership confers effective control on the CEO, the company is less likely to consider changes in control (Stutz, 1988), and takeover bids for the company are less likely to succeed (Cotter and Zenner, 1994). Furthermore, CEO compensation may be "abnormally high" (Core, 1997; Holderness and Sheehan, 1988), and CEO turnover occurs less promptly after poor performance (Denis et al., 1997).
- The evidence supports granting stock to executives but also highlights the need for a strong and independent board, particularly when the CEO controls a large fraction of the voting rights. In addition, nonvoting stock may represent an effective tool for compensating CEOs when they already control a substantial fraction of the voting stock of the company.

Does Option Compensation Create Value for Shareholders?

Companies tend to make greater use of stock option awards when there is a need for strong managerial incentives to make appropriate investment decisions, as when the company has significant growth opportunities or is research and development intensive (Core and Guay, 2001; Yermack, 1995). Firms with a cash flow shortfall or poor access to capital markets also use options more frequently (Core and Guay, 2001). But the use of stock options can also lead to abuses or to suboptimal decision-making by executives:

- Large option awards tend to be granted prior to favorable news releases and stock price appreciation, raising the possibility that option awards are "timed" in advance of favorable events (Yermack, 1997).

FIGURE 5.3

Relationship between Insider Stock Ownership and Firm Value

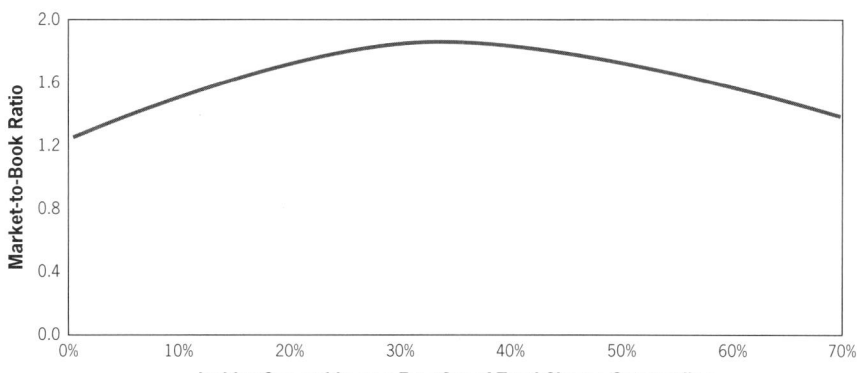

Source: McConnell and Servaes (1990).

- Gold-mining companies hedged price risk to a greater extent if executive stock ownership was large, but less so if executive *option* ownership was large (Tufano, 1996). Stockholders may prefer lower risk, while option holders may prefer more volatility because of their disproportionate payoff.
- After the initiation of stock option grants, companies have reduced their dividend payouts, making the options more valuable (Lambert et al., 1989).

Option repricings appear to provide executives with a downside safety net that shareholders do not have. But if poor performance is not caused by poor executive decisions, repricing may be needed to maintain incentives:

- Companies that reprice options have largely been poor performers with low equity ownership prior to the repricing (Chance et al., 2000). After the repricing, their performance stabilizes. The evidence does not, however, conclusively suggest that repricings either hurt or help shareholders.

Should Directors Also Be Compensated with Options?

Increasingly, companies are compensating their directors with stock options. Who adopts such director incentive plans, and are they beneficial for shareholders?

- Companies that use director incentive plans have low CEO stock ownership, independent boards, and greater institutional ownership (Perry, 2002), suggesting that boards adopt incentive plans to better align the directors' interests with those of shareholders.
- Boards replace the CEO more quickly following poor performance when directors are compensated in stock and the board is independent (Perry, 2002), suggesting that directors who receive incentive pay oversee management more actively.

What Are the Implications of Increased Compensation Disclosure?

In 1992–1993, the SEC adopted regulations that significantly increased disclosure of CEO compensation. In particular, disclosure on stock options had to be reported in tables, and companies were asked to value their annual options grants. (Previously, the number of options granted over a three-year period was reported only in the body of the proxy statement, and no valuation was required.) There was a general expectation that this increased disclosure would reduce the use of executive stock options and possibly reduce the overall level of CEO pay. Research showed the following:

- After increased CEO compensation disclosure, total compensation and the use of options actually rose dramatically (Perry and Zenner, 2001). However, this finding does not suggest that increased disclosure *caused* the increase in option compensation. The enactment of IRC 162(m) limiting deductibility of executive compensation in excess of $1 million when it is not tied to company performance may have enhanced the case for stock options (Perry and Zenner, 2001) and led to salary reductions for some firms whose CEO earned a salary of more than $1 million.

What Types of Governance Issues Do Institutional Shareholders Care About?

Institutional shareholders have been active in promoting corporate governance by endorsing independent boards and other board composition issues, stronger ties between compensation and performance, the repeal of antitakeover defenses, and voting rights provisions (Abuaf, 1998; Strickland et al., 1996). Various studies have examined the effectiveness of these actions:

- The most common proposals have included the removal of poison pills, the implementation of confidential voting, shareholder voting on golden parachutes, and the establishment of an independent board with independent committees. Proposals targeting the removal of poison pills have received the most shareholder support. A study of one shareholder activist, the United Shareholder Association, found that shareholders reacted positively to the announcement of negotiated settlements with the company (Strickland et al., 1996).

- Institutional shareholder targeting by the California Public Employees' Retirement System (CalPERS) has had a positive effect on shareholder value in the short term (Smith, 1996), but institutional targeting has had a mixed effect on long-term returns. Del Guercio and Hawkins (1999) did not find positive long-term returns. On the other hand, Nesbitt (1994) examined the performance of forty-two companies targeted by CalPERS between 1987 and 1992 and found more positive results: The stock price of the forty-two targeted companies trailed the S&P 500 Index by 66 percent in the five-year period before CalPERS acted—but outperformed that index by 41 percent in the following five years.

- Institutional targeting has not had a beneficial impact on operating performance (Wahal, 1996).

Do Antitakeover Measures Destroy Shareholder Value?

Institutional shareholders have often been vocal in their opposition to poison pills and other antitakeover mechanisms. Early studies showed that, on average, the adoption of a poison pill led to a decline in the company's stock price (Ryngaert, 1988). Research conducted on SB 1310, Pennsylvania's antitakeover law, suggested that companies with antitakeover provisions such as poison pills were also more likely to seek additional protection from state antitakeover laws to shore up their takeover defenses (Wahal et al., 1995).

However, research also shows that antitakeover measures can actually be beneficial in certain situations:

- Recent studies suggest that when the board of directors is independent, the adoption of a poison pill is not, on average, viewed negatively by equity investors (Brickley et al., 1994). The shareholder returns during takeovers are higher for takeover targets that have an independent board and a poison pill, suggesting that independent boards use poison pills to bargain for higher takeover premiums (Cotter et al., 1997).

- Poison pills have not reduced the likelihood of being the target of a successful takeover, and the negative stock market response to poison pill adoptions is limited primarily to those companies that adopted pills in the early 1980s (Comment and Jarrell, 1995).

- If poison pills harm shareholders, then rescission of an existing poison pill should be good news for investors. However, the evidence shows that poison pill removals do not lead to stock price appreciation (Bizjak and Marquette, 1998).

- When companies announce that they have reincorporated in part to have better takeover defenses, their stock price drops, on average. When companies reincorporate to establish limits on director liability, their stock price tends to react positively (Heron and Lewellen, 1998).

In sum, the evidence suggests that while antitakeover provisions may help entrench management, they can also benefit shareholders by giving independent boards increased bargaining power.

Concluding Observations

Our corporate governance recommendations and conclusions are based on independent research into various aspects of corporate governance. There is empirical support for many of the policies recently adopted by the NYSE and other corporate governance organizations, as summarized in table 5.1. The evidence strongly supports board independence, independent nominating committees, and incentive compensation for directors. But there is limited support of other activist recommendations, such as the separation of the CEO and board chairman function or the repeal of poison pills (currently not on the NYSE's list). Of course, these results are primarily driven by U.S. corporations. In the Anglo-Saxon model that underlies U.S. corporate law, the board's objective is shareholder wealth maximization. This may not be the board's primary official duty in other jurisdictions. Important governance differences exist across the world, driven by local regulations, laws, and cultural forces, and must be examined on a case-by-case and country-by-country basis.

When designing a corporate governance structure, boards and shareholders alike should take into account the industry, its growth opportunities, its size, and its need for different skills and expertise. No single set of governance rules fits all firms and situations. We recommend that companies proactively engage their major shareholders in a governance dialogue and implement value-adding governance proposals in a firm-appropriate way and in accordance with applicable laws and regulations.

TABLE 5.1

Comparison of Corporate Governance Principles

Principle	Empirical Support	CalPERS Governance Principle	ISS Corporate Governance Quotient Item	NYSE Rules
Board should be independent	Strong support	Yes	Yes	Yes
Board meets at least once a year without the CEO and nonindependent directors	No evidence	Yes	Yes[a]	Yes
Need for a lead director (if CEO acts as chairman)	Mixed support	Yes	Yes	No
Some committees consist entirely of independent directors	Moderate support	Yes	Yes	Yes
No director may serve as consultant	No support	Yes	Yes/No[b]	No
Director compensation is mix of cash and options	Moderate support	Yes	Yes	No

Sources: CalPERS, Institutional Shareholder Services, and the New York Stock Exchange.

a. ISS examines the published board guidelines and grants a company higher points if the guidelines mention that independent directors will also meet without the CEO.

b. In developing its Corporate Governance Quotient (CGQ), ISS grants a higher point value if the board is independent (i.e., independent directors constitute more than 50 percent) and grants the company a second set of points if independent directors constitute more than 75 percent of the board. The presence of director-consultants, while not prohibited, will reduce the likelihood of reaching the 75 percent mark.

APPENDIX A
INSTITUTIONAL SHAREHOLDER SERVICES (ISS) CORPORATE GOVERNANCE QUOTIENT SCORECARD (AS OF AUGUST 2002)

Board

1 Board composition
2 Nominating committee
3 Compensation committee
4 Audit committee interlocks
5 Governance committee
6 Board structure
7 Board size
8 Cumulative voting

9 Boards served on
10 Former CEOs
11 Chairman/CEO separation

12 Board guidelines
13 Response to shareholder proposals

Charter Bylaws

14–20 Features of poison pills
20–21 Vote requirements
22 Written consent

23 Special meetings
24 Board amendments
25 Capital structure

State of Incorporation

26–32 Takeover provisions applicable under state law—has company opted out?

Executive Director Compensation

33 Cost of option plans
34–35 Option repricing
36 Shareholder approval of option

37 Compensation committee plans
38 Director compensation
39 Pension plans for nonemployee directors

Qualitative Factors

40 Company performance and record of corporate governance
41 Retirement age for directors
42 Board performance reviews

43 Meetings of outside directors
44 CEO succession plan
45 Outside advisors available to board
46 Directors resign upon job change

Ownership

47 Director ownership
48 Executive stock ownership guidelines

49 Director stock ownership guidelines
50 Officer and director stock ownership

Director Education

51 Director education

Source: ISS Corporate Governance Quotient Homepage (http://www.isscgq.corn).
Note: ISS examines fifty-one factors to develop its CGQ. However, these factors do not necessarily carry the same number of points. For example, the fact that poison pill features relate to questions 14–19 does not necessarily mean that poison pills carry more weight than, for example, the first question on board composition.

APPENDIX B
NYSE NEW AND FORMER CORPORATE GOVERNANCE RULES (AS OF AUGUST 2002)

NYSE Committee Recommendation— Recently Adopted	Prior Rules
Independent directors must constitute a majority of the board.	Listed company must have an audit committee composed of at least three independent directors.
Nonmanagement directors must meet without management in regular executive sessions.	No such requirement.
Listed companies must have an audit committee, a nominating committee, and a compensation committee, each composed solely of independent directors.	Listed companies must have an audit committee composed solely of independent directors. No requirement for establishment or composition of nominating or compensation committees.
The chair of the audit committee must have accounting or financial management experience.	All committee members must be financially literate, and at least one must have accounting or financial management expertise.
Audit committee must have sole responsibility for hiring and firing the company's auditors, and for filing any significant non-audit work by the auditors.	Audit committee charter must provide that selection, and firing of the independent auditor is subject to the "ultimate" authority of the audit committee and the board of directors.
For a director to be deemed "independent," the board must affirmatively determine that the director has no material relationship with the listed company (either directly or as a partner, shareholder, or officer of an organization that has a relationship with the company).	Existing definition precludes any relationship with the company that may interfere with the exercise of director's independence from management and the company.
Independence also requires a five-year "cooling-off" period for former employees of the listed company, or of its independent auditor; for former employees of any company whose compensation committee includes an officer of the listed company; and for immediate family members of the above.	Cooling-off period is three years; does not specifically apply to former employees of the auditor or any company whose compensation committee includes an officer of the listed company. Board of directors can make an exception for one former officer, provided the reason is explained in the next proxy statement.

continued

NYSE Committee Recommendation—Recently Adopted	Prior Rules
Director's fees must be the sole compensation an audit committee member receives from the listed company; further, an audit committee member associated with a major shareholder (one owning 20% or more of the listed company's equity) may not vote in audit committee proceedings.	No such requirements.
Listed companies must adopt a code of business conduct and ethics and must promptly disclose any waivers of the code for directors or executive officers.	No such requirements.
Shareholders must be given the opportunity to vote on all equity-based compensation plans. Brokers may only vote customer shares on proposals for such plans pursuant to customer instructions.	Shareholder approval required of equity-compensation plans in which officers or directors may participate, but broad-based plans and one-time employment inducements are exempt. Broker can vote customer shares except when given instructions from the customer, or when the action is contested.
Listed companies must publish codes of business conduct and ethics and key committee charters. Waivers of such codes for directors or executive officers must be promptly disclosed.	No such requirements.
Listed foreign private issuers must disclose any significant ways in which their corporate governance practices differ from NYSE rules.	No such requirements.
Each listed company's CEO must certify annually that the company has established and complied with procedures for verifying the accuracy and completeness of information provided to investors and that he or she has no reasonable cause to believe that the information is not accurate and complete. The CEO must further certify that he or she has reviewed with the board those procedures and the company's compliance with them.	No such requirements.
CEOs must also certify annually that they are not aware of any company violations of NYSE rules.	No such requirements.

NYSE Committee Recommendation—Recently Adopted	Prior Rules
Upon finding a violation of an Exchange rule, the NYSE may issue a public reprimand letter to any listed company and ultimately suspend or de-list an offending company.	No provision for a public reprimand.
The NYSE urges every listed company to establish an orientation program for new board members.	No such recommendation has been made previously.
In conjunction with leading authorities in corporate governance, the NYSE will develop a Directors Institute.	NYSE has generally supported educational initiatives, but this will be the first formalized program designed for directors.

Source: The New York Stock Exchange.

APPENDIX C
CALPERS CORPORATE GOVERNANCE GUIDELINES (AS OF AUGUST 2002)

Core Principles of Board Independence and Leadership

1. A substantial majority of the board consists of directors who are independent.

2. Independent directors meet periodically (at least once a year) alone, without the CEO or other nonindependent directors.

3. When the chair of the board also serves as the company's chief executive officer, the board designates—formally or informally—an independent director who acts in a lead capacity to coordinate the other independent directors.

4. Certain board committees consist entirely of independent directors. These include the committees who perform the following functions:

    - Audit
    - Director nomination
    - CEO evaluation and management compensation
    - Compliance and ethics

5. No director may also serve as a consultant or service provider to the company.

6. Director compensation is a combination of cash and stock in the company. The stock component is a significant portion of the total compensation.

Source: CalPERS Corporate Governance Web Site (http://www.calpers-governance.org).

Notes

We thank Doina Hares, Andrew Farris, Dean Pimenta, and Shakira Sanchez for assistance in compiling the research described in this study; Celia Gong for her assistance with the publication process; Todd Perry from Arizona State University for his helpful comments and suggestions; and David Head, Robert Hoglund, Eric Lindenberg, Hans Morris, and Dan Pakenharn for their support and insightful comments. A substantially similar version of this chapter was originally published by Salomon Smith Barney, a member of Citigroup (Shivdasani and Zenner, 2002).

1. Most of the studies reviewed here have examined the price-to-book multiple or the Q ratio, which represents the ratio of firm market value to replacement cost of assets, as valuation multiples. When studying large samples of companies across numerous industries, studies have found that these metrics produce more reliable inferences than the price/earnings ratio because of the cyclical nature of earnings in many industries and the numerous nonoperating charges that can affect an individual company's earnings in any given year.
2. In Yermack (1996), the set of companies with "significant changes" included six companies that decreased board size by four to seven directors and four companies that increased board size by four to six directors.
3. See, for example, Jensen and Murphy (1990); Hall and Liebman (1998); and Perry and Zenner (2001).
4. Most of the research on employee ownership has focused on the impact of top executive ownership and not on the impact of board employee ownership on firm value.

References

Abuaf, N., *An Executive's Guide to Shareholder Activism.* Salomon Smith Barney, 1998.

Anderson, R., and J. Bizjak, "An Empirical Examination of the Role of the CEO and the Compensation Committee in Structuring Executive Pay," Working Paper, American University (2002).

Beasley, M., "An Empirical Analysis of the Relation Between the Board of Director Composition and Financial Statement Fraud," *Accounting Review*, Vol. 71 (1996), pp. 443–465.

Bhagat, S., and B. Black, "The Uncertain Relationship Between Board Composition and Firm Performance," *Business Lawyer,* Vol. 54 (1999), pp. 921–963.

Bizjak, J., and C. Marquette, "Are Shareholder Proposals All Bark and No Bite? Evidence from Shareholder Resolutions to Rescind Poison Pills," *Journal of Financial and Quantitative Analysis,* Vol. 33 (1998), pp. 499–521.

Borokhovich, K., R. Parrino, and T. Trapani, "Outside Directors and CEO Selection," *Journal of Financial and Quantitative Analysis,* Vol. 31 (1996), pp. 337–355.

Brickley, J., J. Coles, and G. Jarrell, "Leadership Structure: Separating the CEO and Chairman of the Board," *Journal of Corporate Finance,* Vol. 3 (1997), pp. 89–220.

Brickley, J., J. Coles, and R. Terry, "Outside Directors and Adoption of Poison Pills," *Journal of Financial Economics,* Vol. 35 (1994), pp. 371–390.

Byrd, J., and K. Hickman, "Do Outside Directors Monitor Managers? Evidence from Tender Offer Bids," *Journal of Financial Economics,* Vol. 32 (1992), pp. 195–207.

Chance, D., R. Kumar, and R. Todd, "The 'Repricing' of Executive Stock Options," *Journal of Financial Economics,* Vol. 57 (2000), pp. 129–154.

Comment, R., and G. Jarrell, "Corporate Focus and Stock Returns," *Journal of Financial Economics,* Vol. 37 (1995), pp. 67–87.

Core, J., "On the Corporate Demand for Directors' and Officers' Insurance," *Journal of Risk and Insurance,* Vol. 64 (1997), pp. 63–87.

Core, J., and W. Guay, "Stock Option Plans for Non-Executive Employees," *Journal of Financial Economics,* Vol. 61 (2001), pp. 253–287.

Core, J., R. Holthausen, and D. Larcker, "Corporate Governance, Chief Executive Officer Compensation, and Firm Performance," *Journal of Financial Economics,* Vol. 51 (1999), pp. 371–406.

Cotter, J., A. Shivdasani, and M. Zenner, "Do Independent Directors Enhance Target Shareholder Wealth During Tender Offers?," *Journal of Financial Economics,* Vol. 43 (1997), pp. 195–218.

Cotter, J., and M. Zenner, "How Managerial Wealth Affects the Tender Offer Process," *Journal of Financial Economics,* Vol. 35 (1994), pp. 63–97.

Del Guercio, D., and J. Hawkins, "The Motivation and Impact of Pension Fund Activism," *Journal of Financial Economics,* Vol. 52 (1999), pp. 293–340.

Denis, D., D. Denis, and A. Sarin, "Ownership Structure and Top Executive Turnover," *Journal of Financial Economics,* Vol. 45 (1997), pp. 193–221.

Eisenberg, T., S. Sundgren, and M. Wells, "Larger Board Size and Decreasing Firm Value in Small Firms," *Journal of Financial Economics,* Vol. 48 (1998), pp. 35–54.

Fich, E., and A. Shivdasani, "Impact of Stock Option Compensation for Outside Directors and Firm Value," Working Paper, University of North Carolina (2002).

Goyal, V., and C. Park, "Board Leadership Structure and CEO Turnover," *Journal of Corporate Finance,* Vol. 8 (2002), pp. 49–66.

Hall, B., and J. Liebman, "Are CEOs Really Paid Like Bureaucrats?," *Quarterly Journal of Economics,* Vol. 113 (1998), pp. 653–691.

Hermalin, B., and M. Weisbach, "The Determinants of Board Composition," *Rand Journal of Economics,* Vol. 19 (1988), pp. 589–606.

Hermalin, B., and M. Weisbach, "The Effects of Board Composition and Direct Incentives on Firm Performance," *Financial Management,* Vol. 20 (1991), pp. 101–112.

Heron, R., and W. Lewellen, "An Empirical Analysis of the Reincorporation Decision," *Journal of Financial and Quantitative Analysis,* Vol. 33 (1998), pp. 549–568.

Holderness, C., and D. Sheehan, "The Role of Majority Shareholders in Publicly Held Corporations: An Exploratory Analysis," *Journal of Financial Economics,* Vol. 20 (1988), pp. 317–346.

Huson, M., R. Parrino, and L. Starks, "Internal Monitoring and CEO Turnover: A Long-Term Perspective," Working Paper, University of Texas (2000).

Jensen, M., and K. Murphy, "Performance Pay and Top-Management Incentives," *Journal of Political Economy,* Vol. 98 (1990), pp. 225–264.

Klein, A., "Economic Determinants of Audit Committee Independence," *Accounting Review,* Vol. 77 (2002), pp. 435–452.

Lambert, R., W. Lanen, and D. Larcker, "Executive Stock Option Plans and Corporate Dividend Policy," *Journal of Financial and Quantitative Analysis,* Vol. 24 (1989), pp. 409–425.

Lee, Y., S. Rosenstein, and J. Wyatt, "The Value of Financial Outside Directors on Corporate Boards," *International Review of Economics and Finance,* Vol. 8 (1999), pp. 421–431.

Lewellen, W., C. Loderer, and A. Rosenfeld, "Merger Decisions and Executive Stock Ownership in Acquiring Firms," *Journal of Accounting and Economics,* Vol. 7 (1985), pp. 209–231.

Lorsch, J., and E. MacIver, *Pawns or Potentates: The Reality of America's Corporate Boards.* Boston: Harvard Business School Press, 1989.

McConnell, J., and H. Servaes, "Additional Evidence on Equity Ownership and Corporate Value," *Journal of Financial Economics,* Vol. 27 (1990), pp. 595–612.

Mehran, H., "Executive Compensation Structure, Ownership, and Firm Performance," *Journal of Financial Economics,* Vol. 38 (1995), pp. 163–184.

Monks, R., and N. Minow, *Corporate Governance.* Cambridge, MA: Blackwell Publishers, 1995.

Morck, R., A. Shleifer, and R. Vishny, "Management Ownership and Market Valuation: An Empirical Analysis," *Journal of Financial Economics,* Vol. 20 (1988), pp. 293–316.

Nesbitt, S., "Long-Term Rewards from Shareholder Activism: A Study of the 'CalPERS Effect,'" *Journal of Applied Corporate Finance,* Vol. 6 (Winter 1994), pp. 75–80.

Perry, T., "Incentive Compensation for Outside Directors and CEO Turnover," Working Paper, Arizona State University (2002).

Perry, T., and U. Peyer, "Shareholder Value and the Number of Outside Board Seats Held by Executive Officers," Working Paper, Arizona State University (2002).

Perry, T., and M. Zenner, "Pay for Performance? Government Regulation and the Structure of Compensation Contracts," *Journal of Financial Economics,* Vol. 62 (2001), pp. 453–488.

Pi, L., and S. Timme, "Corporate Control and Bank Efficiency," *Journal of Banking and Finance,* Vol. 17 (1993), pp. 515–530.

Pritchard, A., S. Ferris, and M. Jagannathan, "Too Busy to Mind the Business? Monitoring by Directors with Multiple Board Appointments," *Journal of Finance,* Vol. 58 (2003).

Rosenstein, S., and J. Wyatt, "Outside Directors, Board Independence, and Shareholder Wealth," *Journal of Financial Economics,* Vol. 26 (1990), pp. 175–184.

Ryngaert, M., "The Effect of Poison Pill Securities on Shareholder Wealth," *Journal of Financial Economics,* Vol. 20 (1988), pp. 377–417.

Shivdasani, A., "Board Composition, Ownership Structure, and Hostile Takeovers," *Journal of Accounting and Economics,* Vol. 16 (1993), pp. 167–198.

Shivdasani, A., and D. Yermack, "CEO Involvement in the Selection of New Board Members: An Empirical Analysis," *Journal of Finance,* Vol. 54 (1999), pp. 1829–1854.

Shivdasani, A., and M. Zenner, "Best Practices in Corporate Governance: What Two Decades of Research Reveals." Salomon Smith Barney, 2002.

Smith, M., "Shareholder Activism by Institutional Investors: Evidence for CalPERS," *Journal of Finance,* Vol. 51 (1996), pp. 227–252.

Strickland, D., K. Wiles, and M. Zenner, "A Requiem for the USA: Is Small Shareholder Monitoring Effective?," *Journal of Financial Economics,* Vol. 40 (1996), pp. 319–338.

Stulz, R., "Managerial Control of Voting Rights: Financing Policies and the Market for Corporate Control," *Journal of Financial Economics,* Vol. 20 (1988), pp. 25–54.

Tufano, P., "Who Manages Risk? An Empirical Examination of Risk Management Practices in the Gold Mining Industry," *Journal of Finance,* Vol. 51 (1996), pp. 1097–1137.

Vafeas, N., "Board Meeting Frequency and Firm Performance," *Journal of Financial Economics,* Vol. 53 (1999), pp. 113–142.

Wahal, S., "Pension Fund Activism and Firm Performance," *Journal of Financial and Quantitative Analysis,* Vol. 31 (1996), pp. 1–23.

Wahal, S., K. Wiles, and M. Zenner, "Who Opts out of State Antitakeover Protection?: The Case of Pennsylvania's SB 1310," *Financial Management,* Vol. 24 (1995), pp. 22–39.

Walkling, R., and M. Long, "Agency Theory, Managerial Welfare, and Takeover Bid Resistance," *Rand Journal of Economics,* Vol. 15 (1984), pp. 54–68.

Weisbach, M., "Outside Directors and CEO Turnover," *Journal of Financial Economics,* Vol. 20 (1988), pp. 431–460.

Yermack, D., "Do Corporations Award CEO Stock Options Effectively?," *Journal of Financial Economics,* Vol. 39 (1995), pp. 237–269.

Yermack, D., "Higher Valuation of Companies with a Small Board of Directors," *Journal of Financial Economics,* Vol. 40 (1996), pp. 185–212.

Yermack, D., "Good Timing: CEO Stock Option Awards and Company News Announcements," *Journal of Finance,* Vol. 52 (1997), pp. 449–476.

CHAPTER 6

Pay without Performance

Overview of the Issues

LUCIAN A. BEBCHUK AND JESSE M. FRIED

> *In judging whether Corporate America is serious about reforming itself, CEO pay remains the acid test. To date, the results aren't encouraging.*
> —Warren Buffett, letter to shareholders
> of Berkshire Hathaway Inc. (February 2004)

IN OUR RECENT BOOK, *Pay without Performance*,[1] and in several accompanying and subsequent papers,[2] we seek to provide a full account of how managerial power and influence have shaped executive compensation in publicly traded U.S. companies. Financial economists studying executive compensation have typically assumed that pay arrangements are produced by *arm's-length contracting*—contracting between executives attempting to get the best possible deal for themselves and boards trying to get the best deal for shareholders. This assumption has also been the basis for the corporate law rules governing the subject. We aim to show, however, that the pay-setting process in U.S. public companies has strayed far from the arm's-length model.

Our analysis indicates that managerial power has played a key role in shaping executive pay. The pervasive role of managerial power can explain much of the contemporary landscape of executive compensation, including practices and patterns that have long puzzled financial economists. We also show that managerial influence over the design of pay arrangements has produced considerable distortions in these arrangements, resulting in costs to investors and the economy. This influence has led to compensation schemes that weaken managers' incentives to increase firm value and even create incentives to take actions that *reduce* long-term firm value.

The dramatic rise in CEO pay during the last two decades has been the subject of much public criticism, which intensified following the corporate governance scandals that began erupting in late 2001. The wave of corporate scandals shook confidence in the performance of public company boards and drew attention to possible flaws in their executive compensation practices. As a result, there is now widespread recognition that many boards have employed compensation arrangements that do not serve shareholders' interests. But there is still substantial disagreement about the scope and source of such problems and, not surprisingly, about how to address them.

Many take the view that concerns about executive compensation have been exaggerated. Some maintain that flawed compensation arrangements have been limited to a relatively small number of firms, and that most boards have effectively carried out their role of setting executive pay. Others concede that flaws in compensation arrangements have been widespread, but maintain that these flaws have resulted from honest mistakes and misperceptions on the part of boards seeking to serve shareholders. According to this view, now that the problems have been recognized, corporate boards can be expected to fix them on their own. Still others argue that, even though regulatory intervention was necessary, recent reforms that strengthen director independence will fully address past problems; once these reforms are implemented, boards can be expected to adopt shareholder-serving pay policies.

Our work seeks to persuade readers that such complacency is unwarranted. To begin with, flawed compensation arrangements have not been limited to a small number of "bad apples"; they have been widespread, persistent, and systemic. Furthermore, the problems have not resulted from temporary mistakes or lapses of judgment that boards can be expected to correct on their own; rather, they have stemmed from structural defects in the underlying governance structure that enable executives to exert considerable influence over their boards. The absence of effective arm's length dealing under today's system of corporate governance has been the primary source of problematic compensation arrangements. Finally, while recent reforms that seek to increase board independence will likely improve matters, they will not be sufficient to make boards adequately accountable; much more needs to be done.

Another, broader aim of our work has been to contribute to a better understanding of some basic problems with the U.S. corporate governance system. The study of executive compensation opens a window through which we can examine our current reliance on boards to act as guardians of shareholders' interests. Our corporate governance system gives boards substantial power and counts on them to monitor and supervise company managers. As long as corporate directors are believed to carry out their tasks for the benefit of shareholders, current governance arrangements—which insulate boards from intervention by shareholders—appear acceptable. Our analysis of the executive pay landscape casts doubt on the validity of this belief and on the wisdom of insulating boards from shareholders.

A full understanding of the flaws in current compensation arrangements, and in the governance processes that have produced them, is necessary to address these problems. After providing a full account of the existing problems, our work also puts forward a set of proposals for improving both executive pay and corporate governance. We provide detailed suggestions for making both the amount of pay and its performance sensitivity more transparent. Such transparency will provide a better check on managers' power to influence their own pay. It will also eliminate existing incentives to choose compensation arrangements that are less efficient but more effective in camouflaging either the amount of pay or its insensitivity to managers' own performance.

Furthermore, our analysis of the many ways in which pay schemes weaken or distort managerial incentives provides a basis for recommending how corporate boards could strengthen the link between pay and performance and thereby improve incentives. Finally, we propose a number of reforms that would make directors not only more independent of insiders but also more dependent on shareholders, thus improving board accountability to shareholders. Such reforms may well offer the most promising route for improving executive compensation and corporate governance more generally.

In this chapter, we outline some of the main elements of our critique of contemporary executive compensation and corporate governance arrangements, as well as our proposals and suggested reforms. We start by describing the limitations of the official arm's-length model of executive compensation. We then turn to the managerial power perspective. We show that managerial influence can explain many features of the compensation landscape and explain how this influence has led to opaque and distorted pay arrangements. We conclude with a discussion of our proposals for making pay more transparent, improving the design of pay arrangements, and increasing board accountability.

Before proceeding, we want to emphasize that our critique of existing pay arrangements and pay-setting processes does not imply that most directors and executives have acted less ethically than others would have in their place. Our problem is not with the moral caliber of directors and executives, but rather with *the system* of arrangements and incentives within which directors and executives operate. As currently structured, our corporate governance system unavoidably creates incentives and psychological and social forces that distort pay choices. Such incentives and forces can be expected to lead most people to go along with arrangements that favor their colleagues or individuals who can in turn favor them, as long as these arrangements are consistent with prevailing practices and conventions and thus not difficult to justify to themselves and to others. If we were to maintain the basic structure of the system and merely replace current directors and executives with a different set of individuals, the new directors and executives would be exposed to the same incentives and forces as their predecessors, and by and large, we would not expect them to act any differently. To address the flaws in the pay-setting process, we need to change the governance arrangements that produce these distortions.

The Stakes

What is at stake in the debate over executive pay? Some might question whether executive compensation has a significant economic impact on shareholders and the economy. The problems with executive compensation, it might be argued, do not much affect shareholders' bottom line, but instead are mainly symbolic. However, the question of whether and to what extent pay arrangements are flawed is important for shareholders and policymakers because defects in these arrangements can impose substantial costs on shareholders.

Let's start with the excess pay that managers receive as a result of their power—that is, the difference between what managers' influence enables them to obtain and what they would get under arm's-length contracting. As a recent study by Bebchuck and Grinstein documents in detail,[3] the amounts involved are hardly pocket change for shareholders. Among other things, this study provides figures for the aggregate compensation of the top five executives of publicly traded U.S. firms. According to the study's estimates, which are shown in table 6.1, these companies paid their top five executives a total of $351 billion during the eleven-year period 1993–2003, with about $192 billion paid during the five-year period 1999–2003. Note that the aggregate compensation figures reported by the study reflect only those amounts reported in each firm's annual summary compensation table. As will be discussed later, standard executive compensation data sets (like the ExecuComp data set used in the study) omit many significant forms of compensation, such as the substantial amounts of retirement benefits received by executives. Thus, the aggregate compensation figures may significantly understate the actual compensation received by top executives during this period.

Table 6.2 displays the ratio of aggregate top-five compensation to aggregate corporate earnings for publicly traded U.S. firms. Such aggregate compensation accounted for 6.6 percent of the aggregate earnings (net income) of publicly traded U.S. firms during the period 1993–2003. Moreover, during the most recent three-year period examined by the study (2001–2003), aggregate top-five compensation jumped to 9.8 percent of aggregate earnings, up from 5 percent during the period 1993–1995.

These figures indicate that if compensation levels could be cut without weakening managerial incentives, the gain to investors would not be merely symbolic; it would have a discernible effect on corporate earnings. But excess pay is unlikely to be the only or even the main cost of current compensation practices. Managers' influence over their compensation arrangements can result

TABLE 6.1

Aggregate Top-Five Compensation, 1993–2003 (in Billions of 2002 Dollars)

	Period	All ExecuComp Firms	Non-ExecuComp Firms	All Firms
Full period	1993–2003	212	139	351
First five years	1993–1997	68	55	123
Last five years	1999–2003	122	70	192

Source: Bebchuk and Grinstein, "The Growth of Executive Pay."
Note: The table shows aggregate compensation paid by a large set of public firms to their top five executives. The sample includes all ExecuComp firms and Compustat firms with market cap larger than $50 million except for REITs, mutual funds, other investment funds (SIC codes 67xx), and firms with missing Compustat data. The compensation paid to executives of non-ExecuComp firms is estimated using the coefficients from annual regressions of compensation on firm characteristics in ExecuComp firms.

TABLE 6.2

Compensation and Corporate Earnings

	Period	Aggregate Top-Five Compensation to Aggregate Earnings
Three year periods	1993–1995	5.0%
	1994–1996	4.9%
	1995–1997	5.2%
	1996–1998	5.5%
	1997–1999	6.0%
	1998–2000	6.5%
	1999–2001	8.6%
	2000–2002	12.8%
	2001–2003	9.8%
Five year periods	1993–1997	5.2%
	1999–2003	8.1%
Full period	1993–2003	6.6%

Source: Bebchuk and Grinstein, "The Growth of Executive Pay."
Note: The table shows, for a large set of public firms, the ratio of the aggregate compensation of these firms' top-five executives to the aggregate earnings (net income) of these firms. The set of firms includes all ExecuComp firms and Compustat firms with market cap larger than $50 million except for REITs, mutual funds, other investment funds, and firms with missing Compustat data. Income information is from Compustat, and the estimates of aggregate top-five compensation are calculated in the same way as in Table 6.1.

in the weakening and distortion of managerial incentives. In our view, the dilution and distortion of incentives could well impose a larger cost on shareholders than excessive compensation per se.

Existing pay arrangements have been producing two types of incentive problems. First, compensation arrangements have provided weaker incentives to increase shareholder value than would have been provided under arm's-length contracting. Both the non-equity and equity components of managerial compensation have been more sharply decoupled from managers' contribution to company performance than appearances might suggest. Making pay more sensitive to performance could therefore have substantial benefits for shareholders.

Second, prevailing practices not only fail to provide cost-effective incentives to increase value but also create perverse incentives. For example, managers' broad freedom to unload company options and stock can lead them to act in ways that reduce shareholder value. Executives who expect to unload shares have incentives to report misleading results, suppress bad news, and choose projects and strategies that are less transparent to the market. The efficiency costs of such distortions may well exceed—possibly by a large margin—whatever liquidity or risk-bearing benefits executives obtain from being able to unload their options and shares at will. Similarly, because existing pay practices often reward managers for increasing firm size, they provide executives with incentives to pursue expansion through acquisitions or other means, even when that strategy is value-reducing.

The Arm's-Length Contracting View

According to the "official" view of executive compensation, corporate boards setting pay arrangements are guided solely by shareholder interests and operate at arm's length from the executives whose pay they set. The premise that boards contract at arm's length with executives has long been and remains a central tenet in the corporate world and in most research on executive compensation by financial economists. In the corporate world, the official view serves as the practical basis for legal rules and public policy. It is used to justify directors' compensation decisions to shareholders, policymakers, and courts. These decisions are portrayed as being made largely with shareholders' interests at heart and therefore deserving of deference.

The premise of arm's-length contracting has also been shared by most of the research on executive compensation. Managers' influence over directors has been recognized by those writing on the subject from legal, organizational, and sociological perspectives, as well as by media commentary on executive pay. But the vast majority of research on executive pay has been done by financial economists, and most of their work assumes that corporate boards adopt pay arrangements that serve shareholders by providing managers with cost-effective incentives to maximize value. Because boards and executives operating at arm's length have incentives to avoid inefficient provisions, the arm's-length contracting view has led researchers to assume that executive compensation arrangements will tend to increase value.[4] Some financial economists, whose studies we discuss at length in our book, have reported findings they viewed as inconsistent with the arm's-length model.[5] However, most work in the field has started from the premise of arm's-length contracting between boards and executives.

Financial economists, both theorists and empiricists, have largely worked within the arm's-length model in attempting to explain common compensation arrangements as well as differences in compensation practices among companies.[6] In fact, upon discovering practices that appear inconsistent with the cost-effective provision of incentives, financial economists have labored to come up with clever explanations for how such practices might be consistent with arm's-length contracting after all. Practices for which no explanation has been found have been described as "anomalies" or "puzzles" that will ultimately either be explained within the paradigm or disappear.

In our book, we identified many compensation practices that are difficult to understand under the arm's-length contracting view but can readily be explained by managerial influence over the pay-setting process. In response, critics suggested reasons why some of these practices could still have an explanation within an arm's-length contracting framework and argued that we have therefore not succeeded in ruling out completely the possibility of arm's-length dealing. For example, in response to our account of the significant extent to which pay is decoupled from performance, John Core, Wayne Guay, and Randall Thomas argue that there are circumstances in which large amounts of non–performance pay might be desirable.[7] Similarly, in response to our criticism of the widespread failure of firms to adopt option plans that filter out windfalls, both Jeff Gordon and Bengt Holmstrom argue that our analysis has not completely ruled out the possibility of explaining such failure within the arm's-length contracting model.[8]

These arguments reflect an implicit presumption in favor of arm's-length contracting: pay arrangements are assumed to be the product of arm's-length contracting unless one can prove otherwise. The presumption of arm's-length contracting, however, does not seem warranted. As we discuss below, an examination of the pay-setting process suggests that managerial influence seems likely to play a key role. Thus, given the a priori likelihood of managerial influence, the burden of proof should be on those arguing that executive pay arrangements are not significantly shaped by such influence. In any event, the fact that financial economists continue implicitly or explicitly to use arm's-length contracting as their baseline presumption indicates the dominance and power of this long-held view.

Limits of the Arm's-Length View

The official arm's-length story is neat, tractable, and reassuring. But it fails to account for the realities of executive compensation.

The arm's-length contracting view recognizes that managers are subject to an agency problem and do not automatically seek to maximize shareholder value. The potential divergence between managers' and shareholders' interests makes it important to provide managers with adequate incentives. Under the arm's-length view, the board attempts to provide such incentives cost-effectively through managers' compensation packages. But just as there is no reason to assume that managers automatically seek to maximize shareholder value, there is no reason to expect that directors will either. Indeed, an analysis of directors' incentives and circumstances suggests that director behavior is also subject to an agency problem.

Directors have had and continue to have various economic incentives to support, or at least go along with, arrangements that favor the company's top executives. A variety of social and psychological factors—collegiality, team spirit, a natural desire to avoid conflict within the board, friendship and loyalty, and cognitive dissonance—exert additional pull in that direction. Although many directors own some stock in their companies, their ownership positions are too small to give them a financial incentive to take the personally costly, or at the very least unpleasant, route of resisting compensation arrangements sought by executives. In addition, limitations on time and resources have made it difficult for even well-intentioned directors to do their pay-setting job properly. Finally, the market constraints within which directors operate are far from tight and do not prevent deviations from arm's-length contracting outcomes in favor of executives. Below we briefly discuss each of these factors.

Incentives to Be Reelected

Besides an attractive salary, a directorship is also likely to provide prestige and valuable business and social connections. The financial and nonfinancial benefits of holding a board seat naturally give directors an interest in keeping their positions.

In a world where shareholders select individual directors, board members might have an incentive to develop reputations as shareholder serving. Typically, however, the director slate proposed by management is the only one offered. The key to retaining a board position is thus being placed on the company's slate. And because the CEO has significant influence over the nomination process, displacing the CEO is likely to hurt one's chances of being put on the company slate. Directors have thus had an incentive to go along with the CEO's pay arrangement as long as the compensation package remains within the range of what can plausibly be defended and justified. In addition, developing a reputation as a director who blocks compensation arrangements sought by executives can only hurt a director's chances of being invited to join other boards.

The new stock exchange listing requirements, which attempt to give independent directors a greater role in director nominations, weaken but do not eliminate executives' influence over director nominations. The CEO's wishes can be expected to continue to influence the decisions of the nominating committee; after all, the directors appointed to the board are expected to work closely with the CEO. As a practical matter, director candidates who are opposed by the CEO are not expected to be offered board nomination and would likely decline the nomination if it were offered.[9] Even if the CEO had no influence over nominations, members of the nominating committee would be unlikely to look favorably on an individual who has taken a tough position on the CEO's pay. They might wish to avoid the friction and unpleasantness accompanying disputes over the CEO's pay, or might simply side with the CEO for other reasons discussed below.

CEOs' Power to Benefit Directors

There are a variety of ways in which CEOs can benefit individual directors or board members as a group. For one thing, CEOs have influence over director compensation. As the company leader, usually as a board member, and often as board chairman, the CEO can choose either to discourage or encourage increases in director pay. Independent directors who are generous toward the CEO might reasonably expect the CEO to use his or her bully pulpit to support higher director compensation. At a minimum, generous treatment of the CEO contributes to an atmosphere that is conducive to generous treatment of directors. And in fact, a study finds that companies with higher CEO compensation have higher director compensation as well—and that such high pay levels appear to reflect insider "cooperation" rather than superior corporate performance.[10]

CEOs also have often used their power over corporate resources to reward individual directors who were particularly cooperative. The new stock exchange listing standards place some limits on CEOs' ability to reward independent directors, but they do leave CEOs with substantial power in this area. For example, these requirements allow the company to pay $100,000 in additional compensation to an independent director. And there is no limit to how much the firm can pay an independent director's immediate family members, as long as they are nonexecutive employees.

Similarly, the requirements limit but do not prohibit business dealings between a company and an independent director's firm, and they place no limit on the company's dealings with the director's firm before or after the director qualifies for independent director status. The standards also permit unlimited contributions to charitable organizations that independent directors run, are affiliated with, or simply favor. In sum, executives' control over corporate resources continues to enable them to provide many directors with rewards—rewards that generally outweigh the small direct personal cost to most directors of approving pay arrangements that fail to serve shareholder interests.

Friendship and Loyalty

Many independent directors have some prior social connection to the company's CEO or other senior executives. Even directors who did not know the CEO before their appointment may well have begun their service with a sense of obligation and loyalty to the CEO. The CEO often will have been involved in recruiting the director to the board. As a result, directors often start serving with a reservoir of good will toward the CEO, which will contribute to a tendency to favor the CEO on compensation matters. This kind of reciprocity is expected and observed in many social and professional contexts. Not surprisingly, studies find that compensation committees whose chairs have been appointed after the CEO takes office have tended to award higher CEO compensation.[11]

Collegiality and Authority

In addition to friendship and loyalty considerations, there are other social and psychological forces that make it difficult for directors to resist executive-serving compensation arrangements. The CEO is the directors' colleague, and directors are generally expected to treat their fellow directors collegially. The CEO is also the company's leader, the person whose decisions and visions have the most influence on the firm's future direction. In most circumstances, directors treat the CEO with respect and substantial deference. Switching hats to contract at arm's length with one's colleague and leader is naturally difficult.

Cognitive Dissonance and Solidarity

Many members of compensation committees are current and former executives of other companies. Because individuals have a tendency to develop views that are consistent with their self-interest, executives and former executives are likely to have formed beliefs that support the type of pay arrangements from which they themselves have benefited. An executive who has benefited from a conventional option plan, for example, is more likely to resist the view that such plans provide executives with excessive windfalls.

Further reinforcing such cognitive dissonance, an executive who serves as a director in another firm might identify and feel some solidarity or sympathy with that firm's executives and naturally would be inclined to treat these executives the same way he or she would like to be treated. Not surprisingly, there is evidence that CEO pay is correlated with the pay levels of the outside directors serving on the compensation committee.[12]

The Small Cost of Favoring Executives

Directors typically own only a small fraction of the firm's shares. As a result, the direct personal cost to board members of approving compensation arrangements that are too favorable to executives—the reduction in the value of their shareholdings—is small. This cost is therefore unlikely to outweigh the economic incentives and social and psychological factors that induce directors to go along with pay schemes that favor executives.

Ratcheting

It is now widely recognized that the rise in executive compensation has in part been driven by many boards seeking to pay their CEO more than the industry average; this widespread practice has led to an ever-increasing average and a continuous escalation of executive pay.[13] A review of reports of compensation committees in large companies indicates that a large majority of them used peer groups in determining pay and set compensation at or above the fiftieth percentile of the peer group.[14] Such ratcheting is consistent with a picture of boards that do not seek to get the best deal for their shareholders, but are happy to go along with whatever can be justified as consistent with prevailing practices.

Limits of Market Forces

Some writers have argued that even if directors are under the considerable influence of corporate executives, market forces will force boards and executives to adopt the compensation arrangements that arm's-length contracting would produce. Our analysis, however, finds that market forces are neither sufficiently fine-tuned nor sufficiently powerful to compel such outcomes. The markets for capital, corporate control, and managerial labor do impose some constraints on executive compensation. But these constraints are by no means stringent and they permit substantial deviations from arm's-length contracting.

Consider, for example, the market for corporate control—the threat of a takeover. Most companies have substantial defenses against takeovers. For example, a majority of companies have a staggered board, which prevents a hostile acquirer from gaining control before two annual elections are held, and often enables incumbent managers to block hostile bids that are attractive to shareholders. To overcome incumbent opposition, a hostile bidder must be prepared to pay a substantial premium.[15] The disciplinary force of the market for corporate control is further weakened by the prevalence of golden parachute provisions, as well as by payoffs made by acquirers to target managers to facilitate the acquisition. The market for corporate control thus exerts little disciplining force on managers and boards, leaving them with considerable slack and the ability to negotiate manager-favoring pay arrangements.

New CEOs

Some critics of our work have assumed that our analysis of managerial influence does not apply when boards negotiate pay with a CEO candidate from outside the firm.[16] However, while such negotiations might be closer to the arm's-length model than negotiations with an incumbent CEO, they still fall quite short of this benchmark.

Among other things, directors negotiating with an outside CEO candidate know that, after the candidate becomes CEO, he or she will have influence over their renomination to the board and over their compensation and perks. The directors will also wish to have good personal and working relationships with the individual who is expected to become the firm's leader and a fellow board member. And while agreeing to a pay package that favors the outside CEO imposes little financial cost on directors, a breakdown in the negotiations, which might embarrass the directors and force them to reopen the CEO selection process, would be personally costly to them. Finally, directors' limited time forces them to rely on information shaped and presented by the company's human resources staff and compensation consultants, all of whom have incentives to please the incoming CEO.

Firing of Executives

Some have suggested that the increased willingness of directors to force out CEOs over the past decade, especially in recent years, provides evidence that boards do in fact deal with CEOs at arm's length.[17] However, firings or resignations under fire are still limited to unusual situations in which the CEO is accused of legal or ethical violations (such as in Fannie Mae, AIG, Boeing, and Marsh) or is viewed by revolting shareholders as having a record of terrible performance (such as in Morgan Stanley and HP). Without strong outside pressure to fire the CEO, mere mediocrity is far from enough to get a CEO pushed out. Furthermore, in the rare cases in which boards fire executives, boards often provide the departing executives with benefits beyond those required by the contract to sweeten the CEO's departure and alleviate the directors' guilt and discomfort. All in all, boards' record of dealing with failed executives does not support the view that boards treat CEOs at arm's length.

In sum, a realistic picture of the incentives and circumstances of board members reveals many incentives and tendencies that lead directors to behave very differently than boards contracting at arm's length with their executives over pay. Recent reforms, such as the new stock exchange listing requirements, may weaken some of these factors but will not eliminate them. Without additional reforms, the pay-setting process will continue to deviate substantially from arm's-length contracting.

Power and Pay

The same factors that limit the usefulness of the arm's-length model in explaining executive compensation suggest that executives have had substantial influence over their own pay. Compensation arrangements have often deviated from arm's-length contracting because directors have been influenced by management, insufficiently motivated to insist on shareholder-serving compensation, or simply ineffectual. Executives' influence over directors has enabled them to obtain "rents"—benefits greater than those obtainable under true arm's-length contracting.

In our work, we find that the role of managerial power can explain many aspects of the executive compensation landscape. It is worth emphasizing that our conclusion is not based on the amount of compensation received by executives. In our view, high absolute levels of pay do not by themselves imply that compensation arrangements deviate from arm's-length contracting. Our finding that such deviations have been common is based primarily on an analysis of the process by which pay is set and an examination of the inefficient, distorted, and nontransparent structure of pay arrangements that emerge from this process. For us, the "smoking gun" of managerial influence over pay is not high levels of pay, but rather such things as the correlation between power and pay, the systematic use of compensation practices that obscure the amount and performance insensitivity of pay, and the showering of gratuitous benefits on departing executives.

Power-Pay Relationships

Although top executives generally have some degree of influence over their boards, the extent of their influence depends on various features of the company's governance structure. The managerial power approach predicts that executives who have more power should receive higher pay—or pay that is less sensitive to performance—than their less powerful counterparts. A substantial body of evidence does indeed indicate that pay is higher, and less sensitive to performance, when executives have more power.

First, there is evidence that executive compensation is higher *when the board is relatively weak or ineffectual* vis-à-vis the CEO. In particular, CEO compensation is higher when the board is large, which makes it more difficult for directors to organize in opposition to the CEO; when more of the outside directors have been appointed by the CEO, which could cause them to feel gratitude or obligation to the CEO; and when outside directors serve on three or more boards, and thus are more likely to be distracted.[18] Also, CEO pay is 20–40 percent higher if the CEO is the chairman of the board, and it is negatively correlated with the stock ownership of compensation committee members.[19]

Second, studies find a negative correlation between the *presence of a large outside shareholder* and pay arrangements that favor executives. A large outside shareholder might engage in closer monitoring and thereby reduce managers' influence over their compensation. One study finds a negative correlation between the equity ownership of the largest shareholder and the amount of CEO compensation; more specifically, doubling the percentage ownership of a large outside shareholder is associated with a 12–14 percent reduction in a CEO's non-salary compensation.[20] Another study finds that CEOs in companies without a 5 percent (or larger) outside shareholder tend to receive more "luck-based" pay—that is, pay associated with profit increases that are generated entirely by external factors (such as changes in oil prices and exchange rates) rather than by managers' own efforts.[21] This study also finds that, in companies lacking large outside shareholders, boards make smaller reductions in cash compensation when they increase CEOs' option-based compensation.

Third, there is evidence linking executive pay to the *concentration of institutional shareholders,* which are more likely to monitor the CEO and the board. One study finds that more concentrated institutional ownership leads to lower and more performance-sensitive compensation.[22] Another study finds that the effect of institutional shareholders on CEO pay depends on the nature of their relationships with the firm.[23] This study reports that CEO pay is negatively correlated with the presence of "pressure-resistant" institutions—institutions that have no other business relationship with the firm and thus presumably are concerned only with the firm's share value. But CEO pay is positively correlated with the presence of "pressure-sensitive" institutions—those having business relationships with the firm (such as managing its pension funds) and thus more vulnerable to management pressure.

Finally, studies find a connection between pay and *antitakeover provisions,* arrangements that make CEOs and their boards less vulnerable to a hostile takeover. One study finds that CEOs of companies adopting antitakeover provisions enjoy above-market compensation before adoption of the provisions and that adoption is followed by further significant increases in pay.[24] This pattern is not readily explainable by arm's-length contracting; indeed, if risk-averse managers' jobs are more secure, shareholders should be able to pay the managers less. Another study finds that CEOs of companies that became protected by state antitakeover legislation enacted during the period of 1984–1991 reduced their holdings of shares (which became less important for the purpose of maintaining control) by an average of 15 percent.[25] Arm's-length contracting, by contrast, might predict that CEOs protected by antitakeover legislation would be *required by their boards* to increase their shareholdings to restore their incentive to generate shareholder value.

Limits of Managerial Influence

There are, of course, limits to the arrangements that directors will approve and executives will seek. Although market forces are not sufficiently powerful to prevent significant deviations from arm's-length outcomes, they do impose *some* constraints on executive compensation. If a board were to approve a pay arrangement viewed as egregious, for example, shareholders would be less willing to support incumbents in a hostile takeover or a proxy fight.

In addition, directors and executives adopting such an arrangement might bear social costs. Directors approving a clearly inflated and distorted pay package might be subject to ridicule or scorn in the media or in their social and business circles. Most directors would wish to avoid such treatment, even if their board positions were not at risk, and these potential social costs reinforce the constraints imposed by market forces. Like market forces, these potential costs cannot preclude significant deviations from shareholder-serving arrangements, but they may discourage the adoption of arrangements that are patently abusive and indefensible.

One important building block of the managerial power approach is therefore "outrage" costs. When a board approves a compensation arrangement favorable to managers, the extent to which directors and executives bear economic costs (such as heightened risk of takeover) and social costs (such as embarrassment) will depend on how the arrangement is perceived by outsiders whose views matter to the directors and executives. The more outrage a compensation arrangement is expected to generate, the larger will be the potential economic and social costs, and thus the more reluctant directors will be to approve it and the more hesitant managers will be to propose it in the first place.

There is evidence that the design of compensation arrangements is indeed influenced by how outsiders perceive them. One study finds that, during the 1990s, CEOs who were the target of shareholder resolutions criticizing executive pay had their annual (industry-adjusted) compensation reduced over the following two years.[26]

Camouflage and Stealth Compensation

The critical role of outsiders' perception of executives' compensation and the significance of outrage costs explain the importance of yet another component of the managerial power approach: "camouflage." The desire to minimize outrage gives designers of compensation arrangements a strong incentive to try to legitimize, justify, or obscure—or, more generally, to camouflage—the amount and performance insensitivity of executive compensation.

The desire to camouflage has an important effect on pay structures. We show that compensation designers' attempts to obscure the amount and performance insensitivity of compensation have led to arrangements that undermine and distort managerial incentives, thereby weakening firm performance. Overall, the camouflage motive turns out to be quite useful in explaining many otherwise puzzling features of the executive compensation landscape.

Among the arrangements that disguise or downplay the amount and performance insensitivity of compensation are executive pension plans, deferred compensation arrangements, and post-retirement perks. Most executive pensions and deferred compensation arrangements do not enjoy the large tax subsidy granted to the standard retirement arrangements provided to other employees. In the case of executives, such arrangements merely shift tax liability from the executive to the firm. The efficiency grounds for providing compensation through in-kind retirement perks are also far from clear.

All of these arrangements, however, make executives' compensation less visible to investors, regulators, and the general public. Among other things, existing disclosure rules do not require companies to place a dollar value on— or include in their publicly filed summary compensation tables—the amounts provided to executives after they retire. Although the existence and terms of executives' retirement arrangements must be disclosed in various places throughout the firm's public filings, this disclosure is less visible because outsiders, including compensation researchers and the media, focus on the dollar amounts reported in the compensation tables.

In a recent empirical study, Bebchuk and Jackson used information provided in proxy statements to estimate the value of the executive pension plans of S&P 500 CEOs.[27] About two-thirds of CEOs have such plans, and the study estimated the value of these plans for all the CEOs who had recently left their firms or were close to retirement age. For the median CEO in the study's sample, the actuarial value of the CEO's pension was $15 million, which made up about one-third of the total compensation (both equity-based and non-equity) they had received during their service as CEOs.

Furthermore, the study indicates that, when pension value is included in calculating executive pay, compensation is much less linked to performance than commonly perceived. After pension value is included, the percentage of a CEO's total compensation that is "salary-like" (i.e., the portion that consists of fixed annual payments, such as basic salary during the CEO's service and pension payments afterward) increases from 16 percent to 39 percent. The study documents that the current omission of retirement benefits from standard compensation data sets has distorted investors' picture of pay arrangements. In particular, this omission has led to (1) significant underestimations of the total amount of pay, (2) considerable distortions in comparisons among executive pay packages, and (3) substantial overestimations of the extent to which executive pay is linked to performance.

Although companies do not make the value of executive pensions transparent, they are required to disclose enough information to enable diligent researchers to estimate the value of these pensions. In contrast, the information provided about deferred compensation arrangements does not allow even the most careful analyst to estimate with any precision the value conferred on executives through these arrangements. Thus, this form of compensation is especially effective in camouflaging potentially large amounts of non–performance pay.

Gratuitous Goodbye Payments

In many cases, boards give departing CEOs payments and benefits that are not required under the terms of a CEO's compensation contract. Such gratuitous "goodbye payments" are common even when CEOs perform so poorly that their boards feel compelled to replace them. For example, when Mattel CEO Jill Barad resigned under fire, the board forgave a $4.2 million loan, gave her an additional $3.3 million in cash to cover the taxes for forgiveness of another loan, and allowed her unvested options to vest prematurely. These gratuitous benefits were offered in addition to the considerable benefits that she received under her employment agreement, which included a termination payment of $26.4 million and a stream of retirement benefits exceeding $700,000 per year.

It is not easy to reconcile such gratuitous payments with the arm's-length contracting model. The board has the authority to fire the CEO and pay no more than the CEO's contractual severance benefits. There should be no need to "bribe" a poorly performing CEO to step down. In addition, the signal sent by the gratuitous goodbye payment will, if anything, only weaken the incentive of the next CEO to perform.

The making of such gratuitous payments, however, is quite consistent with the existence of managerial influence over the board. Because of their relationship with the CEO, some directors might be unwilling to replace the existing CEO unless he or she is very generously treated. Other directors might be willing to replace the CEO even without a gratuitous goodbye payment but prefer to give it either to reduce their personal discomfort in forcing out the CEO or to make the separation process less personally unpleasant. In all of these cases, directors' willingness to make such payments stems from their relationships with the CEO.

Of course, taking managerial power *as given,* providing gratuitous payments to fired CEOs could be beneficial to shareholders in some instances. If many directors are loyal to the CEO, such payments might be necessary to assemble a board majority in favor of replacing the executive. In this case, the practice helps shareholders when the CEO's departure yields a benefit larger than the cost of the goodbye payment. For our purposes, however, what is important is that these gratuitous payments, whether or not they are beneficial to shareholders (given managers' power), reflect the existence and significance of managerial influence.

The Decoupling of Pay from Performance

In the early 1990s, prominent financial economists such as Michael Jensen and Kevin Murphy urged shareholders to be more accepting of large pay packages that would provide high-powered incentives.[28] Shareholders, it was argued, should care much more about providing managers with sufficiently strong incentives than about the amounts spent on executive pay. Defenders of current pay arrangements view the rise in pay over the past fifteen years as the necessary price—and one well worth paying—for improving executives' incentives.

The problem, however, is that executives' large compensation packages have been much less sensitive to their own performance than has been commonly recognized. Shareholders have not received the most bang for their buck. Companies could have generated the same increase in incentives at a much lower cost to their shareholders, or they could have used the amount spent to obtain more powerful incentives.

Non-Equity Compensation

Although the equity-based fraction of managers' compensation has increased considerably during the past decade and has therefore received more attention, non-equity compensation continues to be substantial. In 2003, non-equity compensation represented on average about half the total compensation of both the CEO and the top five executives of S&P 1500 companies not classified as new economy firms.[29]

Although significant non-equity compensation comes in the form of base salary and sign-up "golden hello" payments that do not purport to be performance related, much non-equity compensation comes in the form of bonus compensation that does purport to be performance based. Nonetheless, empirical studies have failed to find any significant correlation between non-equity compensation and managers' own performance during the 1990s.[30]

A close examination of compensation practices suggests why non-equity compensation is not tightly connected to managers' own performance. First of all, many companies use subjective criteria for at least some of their bonus payments. Such criteria could play a useful role in the hands of boards guided solely by shareholder interests. However, boards favoring their top executives can use the discretion provided by these plans to ensure that executives are well paid even when their performance is substandard.

Furthermore, when companies do use objective criteria, these criteria and their implementation are usually not designed to reward managers for *their own contribution* to the firm's performance. Bonuses are typically based not on how the firm's operating performance or earnings increased relative to its peers but rather on other metrics. And when companies fail to meet the established targets, the board can reset the target (as happened at Coca-Cola in 2001 and at AT&T Wireless in 2002) or compensate the executives by setting even lower figures going forward.

Finally, many boards award bonuses to managers simply for buying other companies. In about 40 percent of large acquisitions during the period 1993–1999, the acquiring-firm CEO received a multimillion dollar bonus for completing the deal.[31] But making acquisitions hardly appears to be something for which managers should receive a special reward—that is, a payment above and beyond whatever benefit they get from the effect of the acquisition on the value of the managers' options, shares, and earnings-based bonuses. Executives do not lack incentives to make value-increasing acquisitions. If anything, investors' concern is that executives may engage in empire building and make too many acquisitions. Thus, although the making of a large acquisition might provide a convenient excuse for a large bonus, acquisition bonuses are not called for by incentive considerations.

Windfalls in Equity-Based Compensation

In light of the historically weak link between non-equity compensation and managerial performance, shareholders and regulators wishing to make pay more sensitive to performance have increasingly encouraged the use of equity-based compensation, often in the form of stock options. We strongly support equity-based compensation, which in principle can provide managers with desirable incentives. In practice, however, the design of executives' stock options has enabled executives to reap substantial rewards even when their own performance was merely passable or even poor.

Rewards for Market-Wide and Industry-Wide Movements. Conventional stock options enable executives to gain from any increase in the nominal stock price above the grant-date market value. This in turn means that executives can profit even when their companies' performance significantly lags that of their peers, as long as market-wide and industry-wide movements provide sufficient lift for the stock price. A substantial fraction of stock price increases is due to such movements, rather than to firm-specific factors that might reflect the manager's own performance.

Although there is a variety of ways in which market- and industry-driven windfalls could be filtered out, very few companies have adopted equity-based plans that even attempt to filter out such windfalls. Unfortunately, most of the boards now changing their equity-based compensation plans in response to outside pressure are still choosing to avoid plans that would effectively eliminate such windfalls. Instead, they are moving to plans based on restricted stock that fail to eliminate, and sometimes even increase, these windfalls.

Rewards for Short-Term Spikes. Option plans have been designed, and largely continue to be designed, in ways that enable executives to make considerable gains from temporary spikes in the company's stock price, even when long-term stock performance is poor. Companies have given executives broad freedom to unwind equity incentives, a practice that has been beneficial to executives but costly to shareholders. In addition to being granted the freedom to exercise their options as soon as they vest and sell the underlying stock, executives often have considerable control over the timing of sales, enabling them to benefit from their inside information. Compounding the problem, many firms have adopted reload plans that make it easier for executives to lock in profits from short-term spikes. The features of option plans that reward managers for short-term spikes not only decouple pay from managers' own performance, but also provide incentives to manipulate earnings. There is in fact significant evidence linking executives' freedom to unload options with earnings manipulation and financial misreporting.[32]

Compensation at and after Departure

As already noted, the dollar value of a substantial portion of executive compensation is not reported in firms' publicly filed summary compensation tables and is therefore not included in standard compensation data sets. This "stealth compensation" includes executive pensions, deferred compensation arrangements, and post-retirement consulting contracts and perks. These less visible forms of compensation have tended to be insensitive to managerial performance, thus further contributing to a decoupling of pay from performance.

Take, for example, Franklin Raines, who was forced to retire as Fannie Mae's CEO in late 2004. Upon departure, Fannie owed him (and his surviving spouse after his death) an annual pension of approximately $1.4 million, an amount specified without any connection to the firm's stock performance under Raines. In a case study of his compensation, we estimated the value of this non-performance element of pay at about $25 million.[33]

Further decoupling pay from performance are severance payments given to departing executives. Executives pushed out by their boards are typically paid a severance amounting to two or three years' worth of annual compensation. These payments are not reduced even when the executive's performance has been clearly and objectively dismal. Furthermore, standard severance provisions do not reduce the severance payment even if the executive quickly finds other employment.

It is doubtful that these severance arrangements reflect efficient arm's-length contracting. Non-executive employees are both more likely to be terminated than executives and less financially capable of bearing this risk. But they are not protected from having to bear a substantial monetary loss in the event of termination. If executive severance provisions were driven by risk-bearing considerations, one would expect non-executive employees to have such provisions as well.

More important, if executives' high pay is justified by the importance of providing them with incentives, one would expect their compensation arrangements to be *more* sensitive to performance than non-executive pay and to provide *less* protection in the event of dismal failure. Current corporate severance practices not only fail to strengthen the link between pay and performance, but undermine it by diminishing the difference between payoffs for good and bad performance.

Improving Transparency

We now turn to our proposals for improving pay arrangements and the governance processes that produce those arrangements. We start with a reform that we view as a "no-brainer," one for which we see no reasonable basis for opposition. In particular, the SEC should require public companies to make the amount and structure of their executive pay packages more transparent.

Financial economists have paid little attention to transparency. They tend to focus on stock price behavior and assume that any publicly available information, even if understood by only a small number of professionals, becomes incorporated into stock prices. Thus, economists are typically interested in *whether* certain information is publicly available, not *how* it is disclosed. As we have discussed, SEC regulations already require detailed disclosure of the compensation of a company's CEO and its four other most highly paid executives. Thus, from economists' stock-pricing perspective, there is already a significant amount of information available about executive compensation.

In our view, however, is it critical to recognize the importance of making such disclosures transparent. The purpose of executive compensation disclosure is not merely to enable accurate pricing of corporate securities, but to provide some check on arrangements that are too favorable to executives. This goal is not well served by disseminating information in a way that makes the information understandable to a small number of market professionals but opaque to others.

Public officials, governance reformers, and investors should work to ensure that compensation arrangements are and remain transparent. Transparency would provide shareholders with a more accurate picture of total pay and its relationship to performance and thereby provide some check on departures from arrangements that serve shareholder interests. Furthermore, transparency would eliminate the distortions that currently arise when pay designers choose particular forms of compensation for their camouflage value rather than for their efficiency. Finally, transparency would impose little cost on companies because it would simply require them to clearly disclose information they have or can obtain at negligible cost.

Although we support improved mandatory disclosure requirements, nothing prevents companies in the meantime from voluntarily making pay more transparent. Investors should demand more openness, and companies should not continue to follow a "lawyerly" approach of not disclosing more than is legally required. The measures described below could substantially increase the transparency of pay arrangements.

Recommendation 1: Place a Dollar Value on All Forms of Compensation

Companies should be required to place a dollar value on all forms of compensation and to include these amounts in the summary compensation tables contained in company SEC filings. Executives routinely receive substantial "stealth compensation" in the form of pensions, deferred compensation, and post-retirement perks and consulting contracts. Although certain details of these benefits appear in various SEC filings, companies have not been required to place a dollar value on any of these forms of benefits and to include this value in the summary tables that receive the most attention from investors and the media. These benefits have not even been included in the standard database used by financial economists to study executive compensation.

In our view, companies should be required to place a monetary value on each benefit provided or promised to an executive, and to include this value in the summary compensation table in the year the executive becomes entitled to it. Thus, for example, the compensation tables should include the amount by which the expected value of an executive's promised pension payments increases during the year. In addition, it might be desirable to require companies to place a dollar value on and report any tax benefit that accrues to the executive at the company's expense (for example, under deferred compensation).

Recommendation 2: Disclose All Non-Deductible Compensation

The tax code permits companies to deduct certain payments to executives but not others. Companies routinely include in their disclosure boilerplate language notifying shareholders that some of the arrangements may result in the firm being unable to deduct a portion of an executive's compensation. But they do not provide details about what particular amounts end up not being deductible. Companies should provide full details about the components of pay that are not deductible, place a monetary value on the costs of this non-deductibility to the firm, and disclose this dollar cost to investors.

Recommendation 3: Expense Options

Options should be expensed. From an accountant's perspective, expensing is desirable because it leads to a more accurate reflection of the company's financial situation. In our view, expensing is beneficial because it makes the costs imposed by option-based compensation more visible to investors on an ongoing basis.

Rationalizing the accounting treatment of option plans would also level the playing field among different types of options. It would eliminate a major excuse used to avoid indexed and other reduced-windfall options. The fact that such options must be expensed while conventional options need not be has long been a convenient excuse for using conventional options that reward managers for general market or sector rises.

Recommendation 4: Report the Relationship between Pay and Performance

Companies should report to their shareholders how much of their executives' profits from equity and non-equity compensation is attributable to general market and industry movements. This could be done by requiring firms to calculate and report the gains made by managers from the exercise of options (or the vesting of restricted shares, in the case of restricted share grants) and to report what fraction, if any, reflects the company's success in outperforming its industry peers. Such disclosure would help clarify the extent to which the company's equity-based plans reward the managers for good relative performance.

Recommendation 5: Disclose Option and Share Unloading

Companies should be required to make transparent to shareholders on a regular basis the extent to which their top five executives have unloaded any equity instruments received as part of their compensation. Although a diligent and dedicated researcher can obtain this information by sifting through stacks of executive trading reports filed with the SEC, requiring the firm to compile and report such information would highlight for all investors the extent to which managers have used their freedom to unwind incentives.

Improving Pay Arrangements

Well-designed executive compensation can provide executives with cost-effective incentives to generate shareholder value. We have argued, however, that the promise of such arrangements has not yet been realized. Below we note various changes that companies should consider, and investors should urge companies to adopt, in order to strengthen the link between pay and performance and thereby improve executives' incentives.

Recommendation 1: Reduce Windfalls in Equity-Based Compensation

Investors should encourage firms to adopt equity compensation plans that filter out at least some of the gains in the stock price that are due to general market or industry movements. With such filtering, the same amount of incentives can be provided at a lower cost, or stronger incentives can be provided at the same cost. This can be done not only by indexing the exercise price of stock options, but in other ways as well. For example, by linking the exercise price of options to changes in the stock price of the worst-performing firms in the industry, market-wide movement can be filtered out without imposing excessive risk on executives. It is also important to note that moving to restricted stock is not a good way to address the windfalls problem. In fact, grants of restricted stock provide even larger windfalls than conventional options.

Recommendation 2: Reduce Windfalls in Bonus Plans

For similar reasons, companies should design bonus plans that filter out improvements in financial performance due to economy- or industry-wide movements. Even assuming that it is desirable to focus on accounting rather than stock price performance, as most bonus plans seek to do, rewarding executives for improvements in accounting measures enjoyed by all companies in the industry is not a cost-effective way to provide incentives. Thus, bonus plans should not be based on absolute increases in earnings, sales, revenues, and so forth, but rather on such increases relative to peer companies.

Recommendation 3: Limit the Unwinding of Equity Incentives

Investors should also seek to curtail executives' broad freedom to unwind the equity-based incentives provided by their compensation plans. It may be desirable to separate the vesting of options and managers' ability to unwind them. By requiring that executives hold vested options (or the shares resulting from the exercise of such options) for a given period after vesting, boards would ensure that options already belonging to executives will remain in their hands for some time, continuing to provide incentives to increase shareholder value. Furthermore, such restrictions would eliminate the significant distortions that can result from rewarding executives for short-term spikes in the stock price that do not subsequently hold. To prevent circumvention, such restrictions should be backed by contractual prohibitions on executives' hedging or using any other scheme that effectively eliminates some of their exposure to declines in the firm's stock price.

In addition, it might be desirable, as Fried proposed some time ago, to require executives to disclose *in advance* their intention to sell shares, providing detailed information about the intended trade, including the number of shares to be sold.[34] Providing executives with opportunities to sell their shares when their inside information indicates the stock price is about to decline can dilute and distort their incentives.

Recommendation 4: Tie Bonuses to Long-Term Performance

Even assuming it were desirable to reward managers for improvements in accounting results, such rewards should not be given for short-term results but only for improvements that are sustained over a considerable period of time. Rewarding executives for short-term improvements is not an effective way to provide beneficial incentives and indeed might create incentives to manipulate short-term accounting results.

Compensation contracts should also generally include "clawback" provisions that require managers to return payments based on accounting numbers that are subsequently restated. Such return of payments is warranted, regardless of whether the executive was in any way responsible for the misreporting. When the board believes it is desirable to tie executive payoffs to a formula involving a metric whose value turns out to have been inflated, correctly applying the formula requires reversing payments that were based on erroneous values. The governing principle should be: "What wasn't earned must be returned."

Recommendation 5: Be Wary of Paying for Expansion

Because running a larger company increases managers' power, prestige, and perquisites, executives might have an incentive to expand the company at the expense of shareholder value. Executive compensation arrangements should seek to counter rather than reinforce this incentive.

A recent study by Bebchuk and Grinstein finds that executives' decisions to expand company size—by issuing new equity to finance acquisitions or investments or by avoiding distributions—are associated with increases in subsequent executive pay.[35] Controlling for past performance, the compensation of continuing CEOs is positively and substantially correlated with firm expansion during their service. While a larger firm size might lead the board to raise executive pay, boards should keep in mind that an expectation that expansion will result in higher pay can provide executives with incentives to expand even when doing so would not be value maximizing.

Recommendation 6: Restore Dividend Neutrality

Under current option plans, terms are not updated to reflect the payment of dividends, and as a result, executives' payoffs are reduced when they decide to pay a dividend. There is evidence that companies run by executives whose pay has a large option component tend to pay lower dividends and instead distribute cash through share repurchases,[36] which have a less adverse effect on the value of managers' options but may not be the most efficient form of payout.[37] To reduce distortions in managers' payout decisions, all equity-based compensation should be designed in such a way that it neither encourages nor discourages the payment of dividends. In particular, in the case of option plans, the exercise price of options should be adjusted downward to reflect a dividend payment.

Recommendation 7: Rethink Executive Pensions

There are reasons to doubt the efficiency of the widespread practice of using Supplemental Executive Retirement Plans (SERPs) to provide executives with a major component of their career compensation. Unlike pension plans used for non-executive employees, SERPs do not enjoy a tax subsidy. And given that companies have been moving away from defined benefit plans to defined contribution plans for non-executive employees, it is far from clear that providing executives with defined benefit plans is required by risk-bearing considerations. Unlike defined contribution plans, which force the employee to bear the risk of poor investment performance, defined benefit plans shift the risk of investment performance to the firm. However, executives do not seem less able to bear such risk than other employees. While the efficiency benefits of SERPs are far from clear, SERPs impose incentive costs. They provide executives with pay that is largely independent of performance, thereby weakening the overall link between total pay and performance. Boards would thus do well to reconsider their heavy use of SERPs.

Recommendation 8: Avoid Soft-Landing Arrangements

Soft-landing arrangements, which provide managers with a generous exit package when they are pushed out due to failure, dilute executives' incentives. While companies spend large amounts on producing a payoff gap between good and poor performance, the money spent on soft-landing arrangements works in the opposite direction, narrowing the payoff gap between good and poor performance.

At present, executives are commonly promised generous severance arrangements in the event of termination, unless the termination is triggered by an extremely narrow set of circumstances (such as criminal indictment or "malfeasance"). Boards should consider provisions that make the termination payoff depend on the reasons for the executive's termination and the terminated executive's record. Even if companies stick to the existing broad definition of termination without cause, the payoff in such a termination should depend in part on the firm's performance relative to its peers during the executive's service. An executive who is terminated against a background of extremely poor stock performance should get less than an executive who is terminated when the company's performance is reasonable.

Improving Board Accountability

Past and current flaws in executive pay arrangements have resulted from underlying problems within the corporate governance system: specifically, directors' lack of sufficient incentives to focus solely on shareholder interests when setting pay. If directors could be relied on to focus on shareholder interests, the pay-setting process, and board oversight of executives more generally, would be greatly improved. The most promising route to improving pay arrangements is thus to make boards more accountable to shareholders and more focused on shareholder interests. Such increased accountability would transform the arm's-length contracting model into a reality. It would improve both pay arrangements and board performance more generally.

Recent reforms require most companies listed on the major stock exchanges (the New York Stock Exchange, NASDAQ, and the American Stock Exchange) to have a majority of independent directors—directors who are not otherwise employed by the firm or in a business relationship with it. These companies must also staff compensation and nominating committees entirely with independent directors. Although such reforms are likely to reduce managers' power over the board and improve directors' incentives somewhat, they fall far short of what is necessary.

Our analysis shows that the new listing requirements weaken executives' influence over directors but do not eliminate it. More important, there are limits to what independence can do by itself. Independence does not ensure that directors have incentives to focus on shareholder interests or that the best directors will be chosen. In addition to becoming more independent of insiders, directors also must become more *dependent on shareholders.* To this end, we should eliminate the arrangements that currently entrench directors and insulate them from shareholders.

To begin with, shareholders' power to replace directors should be turned from myth into reality. Even in the wake of poor performance and shareholder dissatisfaction, directors now face very little risk of being ousted. Shareholders' ability to replace directors is extremely limited. A recent study by Bebchuk provides evidence that, outside the hostile takeover context, the incidence of electoral challenges to directors has been practically negligible in the past decade.[38] This state of affairs should not continue.

To improve the performance of corporate boards, impediments to director removal should be reduced.[39] As a first step, shareholders should be given the power to place director candidates on the corporate ballot. In addition, proxy contest challengers that attract sufficient support should receive reimbursement of their expenses from the company. Furthermore, it would be desirable to limit the use of staggered boards, a feature of most public companies, to impede director removal. Staggered boards provide powerful protection from removal in either a proxy fight or a hostile takeover. And a recent study by Bebchuk and Cohen finds that staggered boards are associated with economically significant reductions in firm value. Shareholders should be able to replace all the directors each year or at least every other year.[40]

In addition to making shareholder power to remove directors viable, boards should not have veto power—which current corporate law grants them—over proposed changes to governance arrangements in the company's charter. Shareholders should have the power, which they now lack, to initiate and adopt changes in the corporate charter. Under current rules, shareholders can pass only nonbinding resolutions. And, as documented in a recent empirical study, boards often choose not to follow resolutions that receive majority support from shareholders, even if these resolutions have passed two or three times.[41] This state of affairs should change.

Allowing shareholders to amend the corporate charter would over time improve the entire range of corporate governance arrangements without outside regulatory intervention. If there is concern that shareholders are influenced by short-term considerations, shareholder-initiated changes could require approval by majority vote in two successive annual shareholder meetings. But we should not continue denying shareholders the power to change the corporate charter, no matter how widespread and long-lasting the shareholder support for such a change. Allowing shareholders to set governance arrangements would help make boards more accountable to shareholders.

To fully address the existing problems in executive compensation and corporate governance, structural reforms in the allocation of power between boards and shareholders are necessary. Given political realities, such reforms will not be easy to pass. But the corporate governance flaws that we have discussed—and have shown to be pervasive, systemic, and costly—call for such reforms.

Notes

This chapter is a revision of an article prepared for the summer 2005 issue of the *Journal of Corporation Law*. For financial support, we would like to thank the John M. Olin Center for Law, Economics, and Business and the Guggenheim, Lens, and Nathan Cummins Foundations (Bebchuk); and the Boalt Hall Fund and the U.C. Berkeley Committee on Research (Fried).

1. Lucian A. Bebchuk and Jesse M. Fried, *Pay without Performance: The Unfulfilled Promise of Executive Compensation* (Cambridge, MA: Harvard University Press, 2004). Earlier articles on which the book draws include Lucian A. Bebchuk, Jesse M. Fried, and David I. Walker, "Managerial Power and Rent Extraction in the Design of Executive Compensation," *University of Chicago Law Review,* Vol. 69 (2002), pp. 751–846; and Lucian A. Bebchuk and Jesse M. Fried, "Executive Compensation as an Agency Problem," *Journal of Economic Perspectives,* Vol. 17 (2003), pp. 71–92.

2. These studies include Lucian A. Bebchuk and Jesse M. Fried, "Stealth Compensation via Retirement Benefits," *Berkeley Business Law Journal,* Vol. 2 (2004), pp. 291–325; Lucian A Bebchuk and Jesse M. Fried, "Executive Compensation at Fannie Mae: A Case Study of Perverse Incentives, Nonperformance Pay, and Camouflage," *Journal of Corporation Law,* 30, 4 (2005) pp. 807–822; Lucian A. Bebchuk and Yaniv Grinstein, "The Growth of Executive Pay," *Oxford Review of Economic Policy,* Vol. 21 (2005),

pp. 282–303; Lucian A. Bebchuk and Robert Jackson, Jr., "Executive Pensions ," *Journal of Corporation Law,* 30, 4 (2005), pp. 823–855; and Lucian A. Bebchuk and Yaniv Grinstein, "Firm Expansion and CEO Pay," Working Paper, Harvard Law School and NBER (2005).
3. Bebchuk and Grinstein, "The Growth of Executive Pay."
4. The link between arm's-length contracting and efficient arrangements has led us to label arm's-length contracting as "efficient contracting" or "optimal contracting" in some of our earlier work. See Bebchuk, Fried, and Walker (2002); Bebchuk and Fried (2003).
5. See, e.g., Olivier Jean Blanchard, Florencio Lopez-de-Silanes, and Andrei Shleifer, "What Do Firms Do with Cash Windfalls?," *Journal of Financial Economics,* Vol. 36 (1994), pp. 337–360; David Yermack, "Good Timing: CEO Stock Option Awards and Company News Announcements," *Journal of Finance,* Vol. 52 (1997), pp. 449–476; and Marianne Bertrand and S. Mullainathan, "Are CEOs Rewarded for Luck? The Ones without Principals Are," *Quarterly Journal of Economics,* Vol. 116 (2001), pp. 901–932.
6. For surveys from this perspective in the finance and economics literature, see, e.g., John M. Abowd and David S. Kaplan, "Executive Compensation: Six Questions That Need Answering," *Journal of Economic Perspectives,* Vol. 13 (1999), pp. 145–168; and John E. Core, Wayne Guay, and David F. Larcker, "Executive Equity Compensation and Incentives: A Survey," *Economic Policy Review,* Vol. 9 (2003), pp. 27–50.
7. See, e.g., John E. Core, Wayne R. Guay, and Randall S. Thomas, "Is U.S. CEO Compensation Inefficient?," *Michigan Law Review,* Vol. 103 (2005), pp. 1142–1185.
8. See Bengt Holmstrom, "Pay without Performance and the Managerial Power Hypothesis: A Comment," *Journal of Corporation Law,* 30, 4 (2005), pp. 703–715.; Jeffrey Gordon, "Executive Compensation: If There's a Problem, What's the Remedy? The Case for 'Compensation Disclosure and Analysis,'" *Journal of Applied Corporate Finance* 17, 4 (2005), pp. 24–45.
9. Daniel Nasaw, "Opening the Board: The Fight Is on to Determine Who Will Guide the Selection of Directors in the Future," *Wall Street Journal* (October 27, 2003), p. R8.
10. Ivan E. Brick, Oded Palmon, and John K. Wald, "CEO Compensation, Director Compensation, and Firm Performance: Evidence of Cronyism," *Journal of Corporate Finance,* 12, 3 (2006), pp. 403–423.
11. Brian G. M. Main, Charles A. O'Reilly III, and James Wade, "The CEO, the Board of Directors, and Executive Compensation: Economic and Psychological Perspectives," *Industrial and Corporate Change,* Vol. 11 (1995), pp. 292–332.
12. Ibid.
13. Kevin J. Murphy, "Executive Compensation," in *Handbook of Labor Economics,* edited by Orley Ashenfelter and David Card (New York: Elsevier, 1999).
14. John M. Bizjak, Michael L. Lemmon, and Lalitha Naveen, "Has the Use of Peer Groups Contributed to Higher Levels of Executive Compensation?," Working paper (2003).
15. Lucian Bebchuk, John Coates IV, and Guhan Subramanian, "The Powerful Antitakeover Force of Staggered Boards: Theory, Evidence, and Policy," *Stanford Law Review,* Vol. 54 (2002).
16. Kevin J. Murphy, "Explaining Executive Compensation: Managerial Power vs. the Perceived Cost of Stock Options," *University of Chicago Law Review,* Vol. 69 (2002), pp. 847–869.
17. See, e.g., Holman W. Jenkins, "Outrageous CEO Pay Revisited," *Wall Street Journal* (October 2, 2002), p. A17.

18. John Core, Robert Holthausen, and David Larcker, "Corporate Governance, Chief Executive Compensation, and Firm Performance," *Journal of Financial Economics*, Vol. 51 (1999), pp. 371–406.
19. Ibid.; Richard Cyert, Sok-Hyon Kang, and Praveen Kumar, "Corporate Governance, Takeovers, and Top-Management Compensation: Theory and Evidence," *Management Science*, Vol. 48 (2002), pp. 453–469.
20. Cyert, Kang, and Kumar (2002).
21. Marianne Bertrand and Sendhil Mullainathan, "Agents with and without Principals," *American Economic Review*, Vol. 90 (2000), pp. 203–208.
22. Jay C. Hartzell and Laura T. Starks, "Institutional Investors and Executive Compensation," *Journal of Finance*, Vol. 58 (2003), pp. 2351–2374.
23. David Parthiban, Rahul Kochar, and Edward Levitas, "The Effect of Institutional Investors on the Level and Mix of CEO Compensation," *Academy of Management Journal*, Vol. 41 (1998), pp. 200–208.
24. Kenneth A. Borokhovich, Kelly R. Brunarski, and Robert Parrino, "CEO Contracting and Anti-Takeover Amendments," *Journal of Finance*, Vol. 52 (1997), pp. 1503–1513.
25. Shijun Cheng, Venky Nagar, and Madhar V. Rajan, "Identifying Control Motives in Managerial Ownership: Evidence from Antitakeover Legislation," *Review of Financial Studies*, Vol. 8 (2005), pp. 637–672.
26. Randall S. Thomas and Kenneth J. Martin, "The Effect of Shareholder Proposals on Executive Compensation," *University of Cincinnati Law Review*, Vol. 67 (1999), pp. 1021–1065.
27. See Bebchuk and Jackson (2005).
28. Michael C. Jensen and Kevin J. Murphy, "Performance Pay and Top-Management Incentives," *Journal of Political Economy*, Vol. 98 (1990), pp. 225–264; and Michael C. Jensen and Kevin J. Murphy, "CEO Incentives: It's Not How Much You Pay, but How," *Harvard Business Review*, Vol. 68 (1990), pp. 138–153.
29. Bebchuk and Grinstein, "The Growth of Executive Pay."
30. See Murphy (1999).
31. Yaniv Grinstein and Paul Hribar, "CEO Compensation and Incentives: Evidence from M&A Bonuses," *Journal of Financial Economics*, Vol. 71 (2004), pp. 119–143.
32. Daniel Bergstresser and Thomas Philippon, "CEO Incentives and Earnings Management: Evidence from the 1990s," *Journal of Financial Economics*, 80, 3 (2006), pp. 511–529; Scott L. Summers and John T. Sweeney, "Fraudulently Misstated Financial Statements and Insider Trading: An Empirical Analysis," *Accounting Review*, Vol. 73 (1998), pp. 131–146.
33. Bebchuk and Fried (2005).
34. See Jesse M. Fried, "Reducing the Profitability of Corporate Insider Trading Through Pretrading Disclosure," *Southern California Law Review*, Vol. 71 (1998), pp. 303–392.
35. Bebchuk and Grinstein, "Firm Expansion and CEO Pay."
36. Christine Jolls, "Stock Repurchases and Incentive Compensation," NBER Working Paper No. 6467 (1998). Jolls's findings were subsequently confirmed by George Fenn and Nellie Liang, "Corporate Payout Policy and Managerial Stock Incentives," *Journal of Financial Economics*, Vol. 60 (2001), pp. 45–72.
37. See Jesse M. Fried, "Informed Trading and False Signaling with Open Market Repurchases," *California Law Review* 93 (2005), pp. 1323–1386.
38. Lucian Bebchuk, "The Case for Shareholder Access to the Ballot," *The Business Lawyer*, Vol. 59 (2003), pp. 43–66.

39. For a fuller analysis of the ways in which shareholder power to remove directors could be made viable, see Lucian Bebchuk, "The Myth of the Shareholder Franchise," Working paper, Harvard Law School (2005).
40. Lucian Bebchuk and Alma Cohen, "The Costs of Entrenched Boards," *Journal of Financial Economics,* Vol. 78 (2005), pp. 409–433.
41. Lucian Bebchuk, "The Case for Increasing Shareholder Power," *Harvard Law Review,* Vol. 18 (2005), pp. 833–914.

CHAPTER 7

Is U.S. CEO Compensation Broken?

JOHN E. CORE, WAYNE R. GUAY,
AND RANDALL S. THOMAS

CRITICS OF U.S. EXECUTIVE PAY practices have raised four major concerns: (1) executive pay is too high; (2) CEO contracts do not provide strong enough incentives to increase value (that is, there is too little pay for performance); (3) options and other equity-based pay provide "windfalls," or large payoffs that reflect good luck more than good performance; and (4) CEOs have too much freedom to unwind their incentives.[1] This negative, and increasingly mainstream, assessment of the state of U.S. executive compensation has led many observers to conclude that executive pay practices are fundamentally flawed and that systemic reform is needed. The purpose of this chapter is to shed light on some common misconceptions about executive pay and, in so doing, to provide some balance to what we find to be an increasingly one-sided debate.

Before getting into the details, we think it is important to keep in mind a number of facts about the performance of U.S. companies relative to their international competitors. In a 2003 article in the *Journal of Applied Corporate Finance* called "The State of U.S. Corporate Governance," MIT's Bengt Holmstrom and the University of Chicago's Steve Kaplan offered the following assessment:

> [T]he U.S. stock market has generated returns at least as high as those of the European and Pacific markets during each of the five time periods [we] considered—since 2001, since 1997, since 1992, since 1987, and since 1982.... Stock returns ... reflect publicly available information about executive compensation ... [and,] therefore, are measured net of executive compensation payments. The fact that the shareholders of U.S. companies earned higher returns even after payments to management does not support the claim that the U.S. executive pay system is designed inefficiently; if anything, shareholders appear better off

with the U.S. system of executive pay than with the systems that prevail in other countries.[2]

Our objective in this chapter is not to convince the reader that U.S. CEO compensation is completely free of problems. Instead, we offer arguments for why observed practices should not be taken as clear evidence of inefficiency, and how these practices may well be part of a cost-effective contracting environment between companies and their CEOs.

U.S. CEOs Have Substantial Performance Incentives

In this section, we show that U.S. CEOs do in fact have substantial incentives to increase corporate efficiency and value. We define a CEO as having greater incentives when his or her wealth is more sensitive to changes in a given performance measure, such as the company's stock returns.

Clearly there are both benefits and costs associated with requiring executives to bear incentive risk. The benefits of incentives come from their ability to encourage CEOs to make decisions that increase firm value. The costs of these incentives stem from the additional risk they impose on CEOs. The additional risk means that CEOs will demand higher levels of total compensation as the risk of their pay packages goes up. If a CEO's contract imposes too much risk for the total compensation offered, the CEO will either quit and work elsewhere or will act conservatively to reduce firm risk and may avoid valuable, but risky, new projects. But if the contract offers too much total compensation for the level of risk imposed, then the CEO's pay could be cut without adversely affecting the probability of retention, or the CEO's interests will not be sufficiently aligned with those of the shareholders. Thus, incentives can be too low or *too high,* and the appropriate level of pay depends upon the appropriate level of incentives.

There are two common ways of providing executives with incentives to increase value. One is to make their annual pay (salary and bonus plus any stock or option grants) vary with some measure of operating or stock price performance. The other is to require executives to hold company stock and options, the value of which varies directly with stock price performance.[3]

We will show that these two methods can provide identical incentives. This illustration is instructive because many critics focus exclusively on the performance component of *annual* pay, which, as stated, consists mainly of salary, bonus, and *new grants* of stock and options. Such critics often argue that CEO annual pay does not appear particularly sensitive to firm performance. For example, a given CEO's pay might consist of $1 million in salary, a $2 million bonus, and $2 million in option grants in a good year (say, a 20 percent increase in stock price), and fall to $1 million in salary, a $1.5 million bonus, and $1.5 million in option grants in a bad year (say, a 10 percent decrease in stock price). If salary, bonus, and option grants were the only components of the CEO's compensation contract, one might conclude from the $1 million difference in pay between good and bad years that this pay package is relatively insensitive to performance.

But, as we point out below, if this CEO also holds $25 million in stock and previously granted options, he or she has very strong incentives to increase value, far greater than what could reasonably be provided through variation in annual pay. If the return to shareholders was −10 percent instead of 20 percent, the CEO's portfolio would experience a $2.5 million loss instead of a $5 million gain—a difference of $7.5 million.

To see this point more clearly, suppose that a board of directors wants to provide incentives for its CEO to outperform the market. To do this, it focuses on market-adjusted stock returns, measured as the difference between the return on the firm's stock and the return on a broad market index. For simplicity, assume that the expected return on the firm's stock is the same as the expected return on the market (that is, the firm has an equity beta of one). Suppose further that the CEO is worth $20 million and prefers to hold this wealth in a well-diversified portfolio that mimics the market index. Assume also that the board has decided that the right package of incentives for this CEO is one in which the CEO's wealth increases by $100,000 for every percentage point by which the company's stock return outperforms the market return, and drops by $100,000 for every percentage point the stock underperforms. For example, if the company's stock return is 5 percent and the market return is 10 percent, the board wants the CEO's wealth to decrease by $500,000. Finally, assume that this CEO requires $2 million in annual compensation to work for the firm under these conditions. We emphasize here that the contract we use in our example rewards the CEO only when the company's performance exceeds market performance (that is, the contract has no "windfalls").

There are two different kinds of contracts that can be used to achieve these incentives—and let's call them "Pay Incentives" and "Portfolio Incentives." To illustrate these contracts, assume that the Pay Incentives contract consists of a salary of $2 million and a bonus equal to the product of $10 million and the company's market-adjusted return. This bonus would cause the CEO's wealth to change by $100,000 for each 1 percent deviation between the stock return and the market return ($10 million × 1% = $100,000). Note, moreover, that the expected bonus is zero since the expected return on the firm's stock is the same as the expected return on the market. Let's assume further that if the firm's stock return is less than the market return (that is, the market-adjusted return is negative), the bonus would actually be *negative*. For example, as shown in table 7.1, if the market-adjusted return is −50 percent, the CEO would have to pay the firm $5 million.[4] The CEO's expected pay from this contract is $2 million ($2 million salary + an expected bonus of zero).

To illustrate the Portfolio Incentives contract, we assume that the firm requires the CEO to maintain $10 million in company stock (that is, half of his $20 million wealth) and pays the CEO a salary of $2 million, but does not have a bonus plan.[5] By holding the $10 million position in company stock, the CEO is effectively forgoing the return on the market portfolio (which is where the CEO would like to hold all of his or her wealth). Thus, this contract also has a payoff of $100,000 for each 1 percent deviation between the firm return and the market return ($10 million times the market-adjusted return). Again, under the assumption that the expected returns are the same for the firm and the market, the CEO's expected pay from this plan is $2 million ($2 million in salary).

Table 7.1 shows that these two contracts provide identical incentives, as measured by the change in CEO wealth for each 1 percent difference between the return on the firm's stock return and the market return. The table displays payments and CEO wealth changes associated with these contracts for a firm stock return of −40 percent, 10 percent, and 60 percent. To make the example more straightforward, we assume that the market return for the year is 10 percent in all scenarios, and so the market-adjusted returns are −50 percent, 0 percent, and 50 percent. The Pay Incentives contract shown in the upper panel delivers these wealth changes through a bonus, and the Portfolio Incentives contract shown in the lower panel delivers these wealth changes through changes in stock value. The Pay Incentives contract and the Portfolio Incentives contract result in identical risk exposures and therefore provide identical incentives.

Despite identical compensation and incentives, however, the *observed* payment stream from the two plans is quite different. With the Pay Incentives contract, the structure of the CEO's bonus will cause pay to vary directly with firm performance, and the CEO's incentives are clearly visible to the casual observer. With the Portfolio Incentives contract, the CEO's annual pay will be $2 million no matter how good or bad firm performance turns out to be. A shareholder who did not look at the CEO's stock ownership in the proxy statement might conclude that the CEO had no performance incentives (even though a market-adjusted return of −50 percent would result in a $5 million reduction in the CEO's wealth).

Our main point, then, is that companies do not need to construct complex bonus plans to provide executives with powerful incentives. Executives' stock and option holdings can also provide powerful incentives. And, as we discuss below, the incentives provided to most U.S. CEOs look much more like those in the Portfolio Incentives contract than in the Pay Incentives contract.[6]

As a case in point, consider the compensation of Steven Ballmer, CEO of Microsoft. Mr. Ballmer's total reported compensation for the fiscal years 2000–2004 consisted of salary, annual cash bonus, and a small amount of other pay. These amounts are shown in Column 1 of table 7.2. His total compensation

TABLE 7.1

Comparison of "Pay Incentives" and "Portfolio Incentives" Contracts

	Scenario 1	Scenario 2	Scenario 3
Firm and market stock returns			
Firm return	−40%	10%	60%
Market return	10%	10%	10%
Market-adjusted return	−50%	0%	50%
CEO compensation and incentives			
Salary	$2	$2	$2
Bonus	$(5)	$0	$5
Change in firm stock value	$0	$0	$0
Change in market holdings	$2	$2	$2
Total wealth change	$(1)	$4	$9

Note: "Pay Incentives"—CEO receives salary of $2 million plus a bonus that is equal to the product of $10 million and the firm's market-adjusted return, and has $20 million of wealth invested in the market portfolio.

	Scenario 1	Scenario 2	Scenario 3
Firm and market stock returns			
Firm return	−40%	10%	60%
Market return	10%	10%	10%
Market-adjusted return	−50%	0%	50%
CEO compensation and incentives			
Salary	$2	$2	$2
Bonus	$0	$0	$0
Change in firm stock value	$(4)	$1	$6
Change in market holdings	$1	$1	$1
Total wealth change	$(1)	$4	$9

Note: "Portfolio Incentives"—CEO receives salary of $2 million, invests $10 million of wealth in firm stock, and has $10 million of wealth invested in the market portfolio.

varied very little from year to year, from a low of $633,514 in 2000 to a high of $909,532 in 2004. Further, these swings in pay were uncorrelated with either Microsoft's stock return (shown in Column 2) or its market-adjusted return (shown in Column 3).

Does Mr. Ballmer have incentives to increase the value of Microsoft? The answer, as indicated by his more than $10 billion worth of stock holdings as

TABLE 7.2

Compensation Package of Steven A. Ballmer, CEO of Microsoft (2000–2004)

Year	(1) Ballmer's Total Compensation	(2) Microsoft Stock Return	(3) Microsoft Market-Adjusted Stock Return	(4) Ballmer's Stock Holdings
2000	$633,514	−11%	−18%	$19.2 billion
2001	$670,620	−9%	6%	$17.5 billion
2002	$758,810	−25%	−7%	$12.8 billion
2003	$871,114	−7%	−7%	$10.5 billion
2004	$909,532	12%	−7%	$11.7 billion

shown in Column 4, is an emphatic yes. Although the magnitude of incentives in Mr. Ballmer's case may not be representative, it helps us make a simple point: an examination of a CEO's performance incentives should focus not on whether *annual pay* varies with firm performance, but on the extent to which the CEO's *wealth* varies with firm performance.

Although few executives have incentives as high-powered as Ballmer's, most U.S. executive incentives are designed much more like Portfolio Incentives than Pay Incentives. In a 1998 study of U.S. CEO compensation and incentives over the period 1980–1994, Brian Hall and Jeff Liebman summarized their results as follows: "Using a new fifteen-year panel data set of CEOs in the largest, publicly traded U.S. companies, we document a strong relationship between firm performance and CEO compensation. This relationship is generated almost entirely by the changes in the value of CEO holdings of stock and options."[7]

In table 7.3, we extend Hall and Liebman's analysis to cover the period 1993–2003. We report the size of U.S. CEOs' equity incentives in relation to their total pay by presenting data on annual compensation and beginning-of-year stock and option portfolio values for S&P 500 CEOs. The first column shows annual pay, including stock and options grants in that year as well as salary and bonus. The second column reports the market value of stock and option holdings at the beginning of that year.[8] The third column shows a measure of the median CEO's beginning-of-year equity-based incentives—namely, the change in the value of his or her stock and option portfolio when the stock price changes by 1 percent.[9]

To illustrate how this incentive measure works, consider the median CEO with $430,000 in incentives in 2003. If this CEO's firm experienced a return of −20 percent during the year, his or her portfolio would fall in value by $8.6 million

(20 × $430,000). Note that this $8.6 million loss by the median CEO would have represented a considerable penalty, one that exceeds the median CEO's total annual pay for 2003 of $6.6 million.

Table 7.3 illustrates the point that regardless of whether changes in annual CEO pay are correlated with shareholder returns (and the empirical correlation between annual pay and returns is fairly weak), when one takes account of CEOs' portfolios of stock and options (shown in Column 2), the potential gains to most CEOs from increasing share values are clearly considerable.

TABLE 7.3

Median CEO Pay, Portfolio Value, and Incentives for S&P 500 Firms (1993–2003)

Year	(1) Total Annual Pay ($)	(2) Beginning-of-Year Portfolio Value ($)	(3) Beginning-of-Year Incentives (S)	(4) % of Value Vested
1993	1,983,000	9,275,000	125,000	76.7
1994	2,444,000	10,306,000	152,000	75.6
1995	2,765,000	10,623,000	157,000	70.8
1996	3,257,000	13,220,000	191,000	72.8
1997	3,989,000	19,574,000	286,000	71.3
1998	4,578,000	27,563,000	403,000	69.2
1999	5,470,000	37,041,000	492,000	65.9
2000	6,947,000	43,484,000	567,000	63.8
2001	7,351,000	50,215,000	647,000	60.1
2002	6,585,000	38,105,000	552,000	58.8
2003	6,578,000	30,137,000	430,000	52.8
Ten-Year Growth Rate	12.7%	12.5%	13.2%	−3.7%

Note: Data are from S&P's ExecuComp and Compustat databases for S&P 500 CEOs from 1993 to 2003. Values are not inflation-adjusted. *Total Annual Pay* is median CEO salary, bonus, stock and option grants, and other pay for the year shown. *Beginning-of-Year Portfolio Value* is the median total value of stock plus the value of exercisable and unexercisable options held by the CEO at the beginning of the year shown. To compute the value and incentives of the CEOs' option portfolio, we used a method that we developed previously (see John Core and Wayne Guay, "Estimating the Value of Employee Stock Option Portfolios and Their Sensitivities to Price and Volatility," *Journal of Accounting Research*, Vol. 40, 2002) with a modification that assumes time-to-exercise equal to 70 percent of the stated time-to-maturity. *Beginning-of-Year Incentives* is an estimate of the change in the beginning-of-year value of CEO stock and option holdings for a 1 percent change in stock price. *Fraction of Value Vested* is the fraction of *Beginning-of-Year Portfolio Value* that the CEO could obtain if all vested stock were sold and all vested in-the-money options were exercised (for options, the value vested is the intrinsic value, which is equal to the beginning-of-year stock price less the exercise price times the number of options).

Are U.S. CEOs Overpaid?

The popular focal point of the criticism about executive pay is the contention that U.S. CEOs are overpaid. The obvious question here is: "Overpaid compared to what?"

The appropriate level of CEO pay can be thought of as consisting of two components: (1) the market wage of the CEO based on skill, reputation, expected productivity, and outside employment opportunities; and (2) a premium for bearing incentive risk. As discussed above, a risk-averse executive will demand greater compensation as the firm requires the executive to bear greater incentive risk, other things being equal. For example, a CEO who is required to bear incentives that cause his or her wealth to fluctuate by $500,000 per 1 percent change in stock price will require more total pay than if the CEO's wealth fluctuated by only $100,000 per 1 percent change in stock price.

Misconceptions about the appropriateness of U.S. CEO pay levels arise from the failure to consider the extent of equity-based incentives and the resulting demand for higher total pay. To illustrate this point, consider the fact that U.S. CEOs have higher annual pay than their European and Japanese counterparts and that these differences are frequently cited by critics as evidence that U.S. CEOs are overpaid. What most critics fail to consider is that U.S. CEOs' higher annual pay could conceivably be justified by the larger equity-based incentives and the associated risk borne by U.S. CEOs.[10] For example, Conyon, Core, and Guay (2006) report that U.S. CEOs in 2003 were paid about 1.6 times more than their British counterparts, but that U.S. CEOs also held 5.2 times more stock and options.[11] Given the larger incentives held by U.S. CEOs, it is not clear that U.S. CEOs receive excessive annual pay relative to their British counterparts.

The predicted economic relationship between incentives and pay can also be applied to the growth in CEO pay over the last decade that some critics point to as prima facie evidence of excessive pay. In the early 1990s, academics such as Michael Jensen and Kevin Murphy and various industry observers called for an increase in executive pay for performance. Consistent with this call, table 7.3 shows that during the period from 1993 to 2003, the market value of the median CEO's beginning-of-year stock and option portfolio grew from $9.3 million at the beginning of 1993 to $30.1 million at the beginning of 2003, for an annual increase of 12.5 percent (see Column 2). At the same time, the median incentives provided by the CEOs' beginning-of-year stock and option portfolios increased from $125,000 for each 1 percent increase in the stock price in 1993 to $430,000 in 2003, representing annual growth of 13.2 percent (see Column 3).

If the efficiency of CEO compensation contracts calls for an increase in the incentive risk borne by CEOs over time, an increase in annual pay will be required to achieve this end. Thus, one cannot identify the growth in pay as a problem without considering the accompanying growth in incentives. A significant growth in pay without a corresponding increase in incentive risk borne by executives would lead economists to suspect a problem with either the level of pay or the level of incentives. However, a simultaneous increase in the level of pay and incentives is at least consistent with efficient contracting.

Table 7.3 shows that, during the period 1993–2003, high pay growth went hand in hand with high growth in incentives. As shown in Column 1, the median CEO's total pay increased from $2 million in 1993 to $6.6 million in 2003, an annual increase of 12.7 percent over the ten-year period and nearly identical to the 12.5 percent growth rate in stock and option holdings shown in Column 2.

We also note that, during this time period, the market value of the median S&P 500 company increased from $3.6 billion in 1993 to $9.1 billion in 2003. Empirical evidence suggests that both CEO pay and target incentives increase with the size and complexity of the firm (pay because these variables capture variation in the required market wage, and incentives because these variables capture variation in the difficulty the boards have in monitoring CEOs).

In summary, while we cannot prove that U.S. CEO pay levels or growth in pay are optimal or value maximizing, our finding that pay, incentives, and firm size have grown at the same rate during the last decade or so is at least consistent with this proposition. That is, the growth in U.S. executive pay during the 1990s may represent a cost-effective response to two major changes: (1) investor demand for U.S. CEOs to bear greater equity risk; and (2) an increase in the size and complexity of U.S. companies, with a resulting increase in the demand for exceptionally capable CEOs. And as we mentioned at the outset of this chapter, the productivity of the U.S. economy and the stock market performance of U.S. companies over this period provide no grounds for believing that U.S. pay practices are less cost-effective than those of their international competitors.

Should Equity Incentives Be Indexed to Eliminate "Windfalls"?

We turn next to the critics' argument that the design of stock and option plans should be changed to ensure that executives are not rewarded mainly for favorable market- and sector-wide movements in stock prices. As we argue below, we feel that this criticism reflects a failure to appreciate what we view as a fundamental strength of equity-based incentives.

Critics of non-market-adjusted stock and options argue that they reward good luck rather than good performance, and that the indexing of stock and options to adjust for market performance is necessary to remove the possibility of excess pay due to this market exposure. To explain why this criticism is likely to be misguided, let us go back to the Portfolio Incentives plan described above. It is true, as critics claim, that much of the change in the value of stock and option portfolios will be caused by market- and industry-wide events beyond management's control. What most people fail to recognize, however, is the extent to which the Portfolio Incentives contract increases the manager's exposure to firm-specific performance. Moreover, as we will show below, this increase in exposure is effectively accomplished without changing the manager's market exposure.

To see this, remember that the CEO in table 7.1, with the Portfolio Incentives plan, has $20 million in total wealth that he or she would prefer to invest in the market portfolio. The CEO's Portfolio Incentives contract instead requires maintaining $10 million of that wealth in firm stock. That is, the contract requires holding $10 million less of the market portfolio and $10 million more of firm stock than the CEO would prefer. Next consider that the company's stock return, R_{firm}, can be thought of as having two components: the market return and the firm-specific (or net-of-market) return. In equation form, $R_{firm} = R_{market} + (R_{firm} - R_{market})$.

Although the executive would prefer to hold a portfolio that earns the market return ($20 million $\times R_{market}$), the contract requires holding a portfolio weighted toward the firm's stock return [($10 million $\times R_{firm}$) + ($10 million $\times R_{market}$)], which is the same as holding $20 million in the market portfolio and $10 million in a security whose return is $R_{firm} - R_{market}$.[12] The key insight here is that this latter security has the same payoffs as the *indexed* security that compensation critics have been calling for.

Thus, when one starts by recognizing a CEO's preference for holding a diversified portfolio rather than company stock or options, it is easier to see why firms might avoid market-adjusting executive stock and options. This practice is consistent with an optimal contracting perspective that attempts to balance two conflicting demands: shareholders' interest in giving CEOs incentives to increase value, and CEOs' preference to hold a significant part of their wealth in well-diversified portfolios. And thus the advantage of equity-based incentives that are not indexed may be their ability to expose CEOs to what proves to be an optimal mix of market risk—their preferred risk exposure—and firm-specific risk, which supplies most of the incentive to increase efficiency and value.

Do U.S. CEOs "Unwind" Their Incentives?

The exercise of executive stock options and the sale of stock by CEOs are frequently cited as evidence that CEOs have too much freedom to exploit their informational advantage over investors by "timing" their sales and unwinding their incentives. But given the natural preference to diversify one's portfolio, executives' decisions to sell their stock are not at all surprising. And if CEOs were allowed complete freedom to diversify their portfolios, many if not most would likely avoid accumulating substantial quantities of firm-specific equity. Indeed, from a pure wealth management perspective, one would expect CEOs to sell restricted stock shortly after vesting, and to exercise options (and sell the stock) as options become exercisable and sufficiently in the money to reap a reasonable fraction of the options' value.[13] But the evidence provides little support for the claim that executives behave this way. First of all, the level of CEO equity holdings, which continues to be larger in the United States than in any other country, has risen substantially in the last twenty years and shows no sign of declining. In 2003, the median CEO held more than $30 million in stock and options, a dollar amount roughly five times the median annual pay. In fact, roughly 20 percent of all CEOs with three or more years of tenure held stock and options with value in excess of fifteen times annual pay. Moreover, as can be seen in the last column of table 7.3, in 2003 the median CEO could have realized 53 percent of his or her company-specific wealth (but presumably chose not to) by exercising and selling vested stock and options.[14] These large equity holdings and their increase in value over time suggest that a powerful force, likely an implicit or explicit contractual agreement, is restraining CEOs from selling their vested stock and options.[15]

A further point on unwinding incentives is that, in some cases, it is optimal for the firm to allow and even encourage the CEO to sell equity. For example, consider the case in which the stock price has risen substantially faster than the market over a number of years. As the portfolio of stock and options becomes a greater proportion of the CEO's overall wealth, incentive risk could increase beyond the optimal level. In addition to the higher risk premiums the CEO will demand, unnecessarily high incentives can also cause the CEO to behave in an overly risk-averse manner, shunning valuable but risky projects. In such cases, it may be optimal to allow the CEO to exercise options and sell stock for portfolio rebalancing purposes.

Further, restricted stock and options are sometimes granted for reasons other than to increase incentives, such as for tax and financial accounting benefits, or to ease cash constraints.[16] For example, Michael Dell, founder and former CEO of Dell, Inc., routinely received large stock option grants even though he owned several billion dollars of Dell stock and clearly had sufficient equity incentives. When equity pay is used for reasons other than to increase incentives, CEOs should be allowed to rebalance their portfolios. Consistent with this argument, a recent study suggests that executives with higher levels of stock ownership sell stock to "undo" the new risk imposed by equity grants.[17]

Conclusion

In this chapter, we address four major concerns about the pay of U.S. CEOs: (1) failure to pay for performance; (2) excessive levels of pay; (3) failure to index options and other equity-based pay, resulting in "windfalls"; and (4) too much unwinding of incentives. Most if not all of these concerns are exaggerated by the popular tendency to focus on the annual income of CEOs (consisting of salary, bonus, and new stock and option grants) while ignoring their existing holdings of company equity.

Taking into account the effect of stock price changes on CEO wealth leads us to a number of interesting findings:

- First, the strength of the pay-for-performance relationship is large and has grown significantly in recent years.

- Second, what may appear to be above-normal growth in levels of annual CEO pay may well be necessary to compensate for the increased risk associated with the CEOs' growing level of equity-based incentives.

- Third, viewed as a combination of market risk and firm-specific risk, conventional (that is, unindexed) stock and options may provide an optimal solution to two conflicting demands: (1) shareholders' demand for executive rewards tied to company performance and (2) executives' preference to diversify their wealth.

- Fourth, U.S. CEOs show little evidence of widespread "unwinding" of incentives. Furthermore, CEOs can sometimes have too much company-specific wealth and income, in which case it is appropriate to allow and encourage the CEO to exercise options and sell stock for portfolio rebalancing purposes.

Notes

This chapter draws on our paper "Is U.S. CEO Compensation Inefficient Pay without Performance?," *Michigan Law Review* (May 2005).

1. For example, see J. M. Abowd and D. S. Kaplan, "Executive Compensation: Six Questions That Need Answering," *Journal of Economic Perspectives,* Vol. 13 (1999), pp. 145–168; L. A. Bebchuk and J. Fried, *Pay without Performance: The Unfulfilled Promise of Executive Compensation* (Cambridge, MA: Harvard University Press, 2004); and M. C. Jensen, K. J. Murphy, and E. G. Wruck, "Remuneration: Where We've Been, How We Got to Here, What Are the Problems, and How to Fix Them," Harvard NOM Working Paper No. 04–28; ECGI—Finance Working Paper No. 44/2004 (2004).
2. Bengt Holmstrom and Steven N. Kaplan, "The State of U.S. Corporate Governance: What's Right and What's Wrong?," *Journal of Applied Corporate Finance,* Vol. 15, No. 3 (Spring 2003), p. 9.
3. In a discussion of executive compensation, it is important to distinguish between the executive's "pay" and the executive's "incentives." We define incentives as the *sensitivity* of executive wealth to changes in performance, and we define pay (cash, stock, options, etc.) as the remuneration that the executive receives for the labor he or she provides the firm and the risk premium he or she demands given the imposed incentive

risk. A major source of incentives is stock and options owned by the executive, which change in value when the stock price changes. Pay in the form of stock or options does not necessarily imply an increase in incentives, just as cash pay does not necessarily imply the absence of incentives. As we illustrate further on in this chapter, cash pay can be structured to provide powerful incentives. Pay in the form of stock or options provides additional incentives only when either (1) the value of the stock or options granted from year to year varies with the executive's performance or (2) a new grant of stock or options increases the sensitivity of the executive's wealth to the firm's stock price. Empirically, the former is only weakly descriptive of the data, and the latter applies only to executives who hold smaller portfolios of stock and options than their peers.

4. We recognize that although there is nothing to prevent companies from using negative bonuses, they generally do not do so. Our illustration requires a negative bonus in order to generate the same negative wealth changes for poor performance that can be achieved with equity ownership incentives. For our purposes, the key point is simply that a bonus plan can be structured with high-powered incentives that mimic the incentives in equity holdings.

5. For purposes of our illustration, it does not matter precisely *how* the CEO satisfies the contractual requirement to hold $10 million in firm stock, whether by liquidating outside wealth and investing it directly in firm stock, or after a "ramp up" period by allowing the firm to weight compensation in the early years of the contract toward equity pay. What is important for our illustration is simply that our CEO has settled into a portfolio position that satisfies the contractual obligation to maintain half of the CEO's wealth in firm stock.

6. One last point before moving on: although the incentives provided by the Portfolio Incentives and Pay Incentives contracts are the same, the Pay Incentives contract requires an after-the-fact settling up that is more difficult to enforce. In particular, it requires that both the company and the executive can credibly commit to make cash transfers in the future when the firm's stock price changes. Executives would be tempted to renege (or file for bankruptcy) after large price declines (when they would owe a large bonus to the firm), and a company might be inclined to renege after a large price run-up (when it would owe a large bonus to the manager). Because the Portfolio Incentives contract is effectively fulfilled once the manager purchases the stock, it is simple to enforce: the executive benefits directly from any stock price increases and is punished by decreases. This more straightforward structure may account for why most CEO contracts (at least in the United States) look more like the Portfolio Incentives contract than like the Pay Incentives contract—a subject to which we next turn.

7. Brian Hall and Jeff Liebman, "Are CEOs Really Paid Like Bureaucrats?," *Quarterly Journal of Economics*, Vol. 113 (1998), p. 653.

8. We measure incentives at the beginning of the year and pay over the course of the year to keep a clear distinction between the executive's "pay" and the executive's "incentives." As discussed above, we define incentives as the sensitivity of executive wealth to changes in performance. In table 7.2, following the evidence in Hall and Liebman's analysis, we focus on the executive's stock and option holdings as the major source of incentives, and we ignore the contribution to incentives that comes from variation in annual pay. We note that pay in the form of stock or options does not imply an increase in incentives. Stock or option grants increase incentives only if the values of the grants vary over time with performance, or if the grant increases the executive's equity holdings (i.e., the executive does not sell stock in response to the grant).

9. Our method follows the one developed by Michael Jensen and Kevin Murphy in their paper, "Performance Pay and Top-Management Incentives," *Journal of Political Economy,* Vol. 98 (1990).
10. This higher level of incentives reflects the more diffuse shareholder ownership patterns in the United States. See Randall S. Thomas, "Explaining the International CEO Pay Gap: Board Capture or Market Driven?," *Vanderbilt Law Review,* Vol. 57 (2004).
11. See Martin Conyon, John E. Core, and Wayne R. Guay, "How High Is US CEO Pay? A Comparison with UK CEO Pay," working paper, Wharton, 2006.
12. The idea that non-indexed grants of stock and options do not impose excess market risk on executives is becoming well recognized. See John E. Core, Wayne R. Guay, and David F. Larcker, "Executive Equity Compensation and Incentives: A Survey," Federal Reserve Bank of New York *Economic Policy Review,* Vol. 9 (2003); Gerald Garvey and Todd Milbourn, "Executive Compensation When Executives Can Hedge the Market: Evidence of Relative Performance Evaluation in the Cross Section," *Journal of Finance,* Vol. 58 (2003); and Li Jin, "CEO Compensation, Diversification, and Incentives," *Journal of Financial Economics,* Vol. 66 (2002).
13. It is true that a CEO may be reluctant to sell large quantities of stock or exercise large quantities of options due to concerns about sending a negative signal to the market about the company's financial condition. To substantially mitigate this problem, executives can carry out a personal trading program that meets the requirements of SEC Rule 10b5-1. This rule requires the executive to enter into a binding contract that specifies in advance the amount and timing of equity sales. By announcing equity sales well in advance, the executive can reduce or eliminate the signaling effects of these sales.
14. Although there is a declining trend in the percentage of value vested during this time period, executives are holding much more equity now than in 1993. Thus, the dollar value of their vested holdings is far greater today than it was ten years ago, even though the fraction of value vested is lower.
15. Some of these CEOs could be hedging the firm-specific risk in their equity portfolios through derivative securities such as caps and collars that are negatively correlated with firm-specific price changes. These instruments can reduce the CEO's exposure to the firm's stock price and the price-based incentives provided by their portfolios. Recent research indicates that some CEOs use these techniques, but the small sample size suggests that this behavior is limited; see J. Bettis, J. Bizjak, and M. Lemmon, "Managerial Ownership, Incentive Contracting, and the Use of Zero-Cost Collars and Equity Swaps by Corporate Insiders," *Journal of Financial and Quantitative Analysis,* Vol. 36 (2001). Although it is possible that some CEOs engage in this behavior and do not file required SEC disclosures, the fact that secret hedging activities violate SEC disclosure and insider trading rules reduces the likelihood that this behavior is widespread.
16. These points are made in recent research; see B. Hall and K. Murphy, "The Trouble with Stock Options," *Journal of Economic Perspectives,* Vol. 49 (2003), and Core, Guay, and Larcker (2003).
17. E. Ofek and D. Yermack, "Taking Stock: Equity-Based Compensation and the Evolution of Managerial Ownership," *Journal of Finance,* Vol. 55 (2000).

PART III

External Governance: Ownership Structure

CHAPTER 8

Just Say No to Wall Street

Putting a Stop to the Earnings Game

JOSEPH FULLER AND MICHAEL C. JENSEN

> *We do not want to maximize the price at which Berkshire shares trade. We wish instead for them to trade in a narrow range centered at intrinsic business value. . . . [We] are bothered as much by significant overvaluation as significant undervaluation.*
> —Warren Buffett, "Berkshire Hathaway
> Annual Report," 1988

First there were whispers and informal advisories to favored analysts of what to expect in coming earnings announcements. Then the conversations became more elaborate, engendering a twisted kind of logic. No longer were analysts trying to understand and analyze a company so as to predict what it might earn; instead the discussion revolved around the analysts' forecasts themselves. Will expectations be met? What will management do to ensure that? Rather than the forecasts representing a financial by-product of the firm's strategy, the forecasts came to drive those strategies. While the process was euphemistically referred to as "earnings guidance," it was, in fact, a high-stakes game with management seeking to hit the targets set by analysts—and being punished severely if they missed.

Last year, the Securities and Exchange Commission recognized that private conversations between executives and analysts had become extensive, with analysts gaining access to critical data not otherwise broadly available to shareholders. The new regulations on fair disclosure addressed the mechanics of the conversation, but did little to change its underlying logic. The result has been blizzards of filings and dozens of press releases and many more company-run conference calls. But such changes in the outward forms of corporate disclosure have done little if anything to deflect the underlying momentum of the earnings guidance game.

Nevertheless, there are some encouraging signs. In the past few months, a few courageous CEOs—notably, USA Networks' Barry Diller and Gillette's Jim Kilts—have attempted to put a halt to the earnings game by simply saying no. In a recent SEC filing, Diller balked at the sophisticated art form known as managing expectations, saying publicly what many have said privately for a long time: "The process has little to do with running a business and the numbers can become distractingly and dangerously detached from fundamentals."[1]

An Overvalued Stock Damages a Company

Witness the part that Wall Street's rising expectations played in the demise of once high flyers like Enron, Cisco, and Nortel. With analysts pushing these companies to reach for higher and higher growth targets, the managements of the companies responded with actions that have generated long-term damage. To resolve these problems, managers must abandon the notion that a higher stock price is *always* better and recognize that an overvalued stock can be as dangerous to a company as an undervalued stock. The proper management of investor expectations means being willing to take the necessary actions to eliminate such overvaluation when it occurs.

In his first meeting with analysts after taking over Gillette, James Kilts stood firm against the tide, refusing to be forced into making predictions for his company. The *New York Times* reports that, in a June 2001 meeting with analysts, Kilts remained silent when Wall Street analysts repeatedly asked him for a more specific estimate of the company's performance: "Mr. Kilts stood on the stage, crossed his arms and refused to give it."[2] By taking positions that we believe will benefit all the players in this game, Kilts and Diller have seized an important opportunity—even an obligation—to reshape and reframe the conversation for a new era.

Over the last decade, companies have struggled more and more desperately to meet analysts' expectations. Caught up by a buoyant economy and the pace of value creation set by the market's best performers, analysts challenged the companies they covered to reach for unprecedented earnings growth. Executives often acquiesced to increasingly unrealistic projections and adopted them as a basis for setting goals for their organizations.

There were several reasons executives chose to play this game. Perhaps the most important was favorable market conditions in many industries, which enabled companies to exceed historical performance levels and, in the process, allowed executives and analysts alike to view unsustainable levels of growth as the norm. Adding to favorable conditions and exceptional corporate performance was a massive, broad-based shift in the philosophy of executive compensation. As stock options became an increasing part of executive compensation, and managers who made great fortunes on options became the stuff of legends, the preservation or enhancement of short-term stock prices became a personal (and damaging) priority for many a CEO and CFO. High share prices and earnings multiples stoked already amply endowed managerial egos, and management teams proved reluctant to undermine their own stature by surrendering hard-won records of quarter-over-quarter earnings growth. Moreover, overvalued equity "currency" encouraged managers to make acquisitions and other investments in the desperate hope of sustaining growth, continuing to meet expectations, and buying real assets at a discount with their overvalued stock.

Parallel developments in the world of the analysts completed a vicious circle. Once analysts were known to a handful of serious investors and coveted a spot on Institutional Investor's annual All-American team. In recent times, analysts became media darlings. An endless parade appeared on an increasing array of business programming. The views of celebrity analysts were accorded the same weight as the opinions of leading executives. Analysts Mary Meeker and Jack Grubman were quoted in the same breath and, more important, credited with the same insight as Cisco's CEO John Chambers and Qwest's Joe Nacchio. With the explosion in the markets came an explosion in analyst compensation, as leading analysts shared in the bonus pools of their investment banking divisions and thus had incentives to issue reports favorable to their banks' deals. Analysts with big followings, a reputation built on a handful of good "calls," and an ability to influence large investment banking deals sold by their firms commanded multimillion dollar salaries. In sum, analysts had strong incentives to demand high growth and steady and predictable earnings performance, both to justify sky-high valuations for the companies they followed and to avoid damage to their own reputations from missed predictions. In too many instances, too many executive teams and too many analysts engaged in the equivalent of liar's poker.[3]

Many will say, "So what? If overly aggressive analysts drove executives to create more shareholder value faster, what's the harm?" What they fail to recognize is that this vicious cycle can impose real, lasting costs on companies when analyst expectations become unhinged from what is possible for firms to accomplish. As the historic bankruptcy case of Enron suggests, when companies encourage excessive expectations or scramble too hard to meet unrealistic forecasts by analysts, they often take highly risky value-destroying bets. In addition, smoothing financial results to satisfy analysts' demands for quarter-to-quarter predictability frequently requires sacrificing the long-term future of the company. Because the inherent uncertainty in any business cannot be made to disappear, striving to achieve dependable period-to-period growth is a game that CEOs cannot win. Trying to mask the uncertainty inherent in every industry is like pushing on a balloon—smoothing out today's bumps means they will only pop up somewhere else tomorrow, often with catastrophic results.

More important, we have witnessed the consequences of executives' futile attempts to record growth rates that consistently and materially exceed growth in primary demand in their markets. Stated simply, companies participating in markets with 4 percent underlying growth in demand cannot register 15 percent growth in earnings quarter over quarter, year over year, indefinitely.

The technology and telecommunications sectors provide good examples of the effects of sustained pressure from analysts. In the last decade, analysts' expectations consistently and vastly exceeded what high-tech and telecom companies were capable of achieving. Managers collaborated in this fiction, either because they themselves had unrealistic expectations for their companies or, worse yet, because they used analysts' expectations to set internal corporate goals. The resulting destructive effects of overvaluation of corporate equity manifested itself in ill-advised actions aimed at fulfilling these unrealistic expectations--notably, value-destroying acquisitions and greenfield investments. When the fiction finally became obvious, the result was massive adjustments in earnings and growth projections and, consequently, in equity valuations.

In many cases, the very survival of the affected companies came into question. Enron is perhaps the most dramatic example.

The Case of Enron

Enron was in many ways an extraordinary company. It boasted significant global assets, genuine achievements, dramatic innovations, and a promising long-run future. Taking advantage of a rapidly deregulating market and capitalizing on its deep knowledge of the industry, Enron had seized what was probably a once-in-a-corporate-lifetime opportunity to reinvent itself as a market maker in natural gas and energy.

Wall Street responded to this and other innovations by Enron with a series of positive reports and ever-higher valuations, eventually labeling Enron one of the best companies in the economy, even comparing it to Microsoft and GE.[4] However, the aggressive targets that Wall Street set for Enron's shares made the company a captive of its own success. To be sure, it was a game that Enron willingly played—but it's one the company clearly lost, with considerable consequences for not only the company's stockholders, but for its creditors, customers, employees, and other major stakeholders.

To begin to see what went wrong, consider that Enron's peak valuation of $68 billion (in August 2001) effectively required the company to grow its free cash flow at 91 percent annually for the next six years (and then to grow at the average rate for the economy)—a pace that required it to continuously come up with what were, in effect, one-time-only innovations. As if to confirm these expectations, one analyst blithely predicted that Enron would come to "dominate the wholesale energy market for electricity, natural gas, coal, energy derivatives, bandwidth, and energy services on three continents."[5] And Enron, to its own detriment, took up the challenge. In seeking to meet such expectations, it expanded into areas, including water, broadband, and even weather insurance, in which it had no specific assets, expertise, or experience.

Yet it didn't have to be this way. Had management not met Wall Street's predictions with its own hubris, the result could have been very different. As Gillette's Kilts is demonstrating, managers can refuse to collude with analysts' expectations when they don't fit with their strategies and the underlying realities of their markets. They can decline to bow to analysts' demand for highly predictable earnings.

If Enron's management had confronted the analysts with courage and conviction and resisted their relentless focus on outsized earnings growth, the company could have avoided questionable actions taken to please the analysts and markets. The result may well have been a lower-valued company, but a stable and profitable one with a promising future. And, as in other companies, these questionable actions went beyond the decisions to launch unwise investments and acquisitions, and included apparent manipulation of the information it provided to Wall Street. Some of these practices are currently being investigated by the SEC, including aggressive revenue recognition practices, off-balance-sheet financing that reduced Enron's apparent debt, and partnerships that allowed the company to show higher earnings.

When discovered, such practices—coupled with missed earnings expectations—first stirred Wall Street's concern and eventually caused the crisis of confidence that destroyed the company's most valuable asset—its ability to make markets in energy. As a result, by January of 2002, Enron's stock price had fallen by more than 99 percent from its peak just four months earlier. While the partnerships brought to the forefront issues of credibility for Enron and the integrity of their financial reporting, they also served to highlight the importance of Wall Street analysts and the nature of their relationship with the companies they cover.

The Case of Nortel Networks

The story of Nortel is similar. Nortel's CEO, John Roth, launched a strategy in 1997 to transform the company from one dependent on its traditional strength in voice transmission into one focused on data networking. Nortel acquired nineteen companies between 1997 and early 2001. And as its stock price soared (to reach a total capital value of $277 billion in July 2000), it came under pressure to do deals to satisfy the analysts' growth expectations. Ultimately, it paid over $32 billion—mostly in stock—for these companies. Most of those acquisitions have now been sold off for modest amounts or shut down and written off entirely.

The quest to transform Nortel clearly damaged this former mainstay of the telecommunications sector. With a year-end 2001 valuation of just $24 billion, the company's stock has fallen by more than 90 percent from its peak in September of 2000. In July 2001 it reported a record $19.4 billion second-quarter loss followed by a $3.6 billion loss in the third quarter. Its CEO resigned effective November 1, 2001, but remains as vice-chairman until the end of 2002. Employment has shrunk from 72,900 people when Roth took over (and from a high of 94,500) to a projected 45,000 by the end of 2002. As of the end of 2001, Nortel's (adjusted) stock price was 44 percent lower than its level of $13.16 on Oct. 1, 1997, when Roth took over as CEO.[6] As these numbers make clear, the decline suffered by Nortel involved far more than the elimination of its overvaluation; it involved a significant destruction of value, mainly, again, through acquisitions and massive overinvestment. It is this kind of damage that can be stopped if managers can just say no to the pressure to fulfill unrealistic market expectations.

A number of factors encouraged Nortel's managers to collaborate in the fiction of a $270 billion valuation. One was the incentive to maintain the value of managerial and employee stock options. Another was the understandable reluctance of top management to admit they were not as good as analysts were projecting. And a third was management's unwillingness to give up the overvalued equity currency that gave them the leeway (and purchasing power) to make unwise, value-destroying investments. In sum, management's reluctance to bear the unpleasantness associated with correcting the market sooner led to far greater pain down the road.

This cycle is not without its costs for the financial community. Of course, many stockholders have incurred huge losses. Analysts, too, have taken their lumps. Their integrity has been called into question in congressional hearings. The press has pilloried many of the most prominent analysts, contrasting their earnings projections with actual results. Many unhappy clients have terminated long-standing relationships. One even went so far as to sue a prominent analyst in federal court.[7] And though that action proved unsuccessful, extensive coverage of the suit in the popular press reflects the depth of disillusionment. Where there is smoke from the public having been burned, political fire soon follows. If the SEC were willing to spend years and significant political capital pursuing restrictions on accounting firms providing consulting services to their statutory audit clients, it cannot be long before regulators become interested in the potential conflict of interest between the investment banking and the security analysis sides of investment banks.

Restarting the Conversation

Putting an end to this destructive cycle will require a new approach to disclosure based on a few simple rules of engagement.

Managers must confront the capital markets with courage and conviction. They must not collude with analysts' expectations that don't fit with their strategies and the underlying characteristics of their markets. They must not bow to analysts' demands for highly predictable earnings. The art of analysis includes the capacity to understand phenomena like seasonality, cyclicality, and random events. Companies do not grow in a constant fashion with each quarter's results better than the last. In the long run, conforming to pressures to satisfy the market's desire for impossible predictability and unwise growth leads to the destruction of corporate value, shortened careers, humiliation, and damaged companies. Managers must be forthright and promise only those results they have a legitimate prospect of delivering, and they must be clear about the risks and uncertainties involved. They must dispel any air of unreality that settles over their stock and highlight what they cannot do, and they should do so as readily as they trumpet their prospects. While this can cause the stock price to fall, the associated pain is slight compared with colluding in myth-telling. This reflects more than the good conscience of a boy scout. It is, in fact, an act of self-preservation.

Managers must recognize that an overvalued stock can be damaging to the long-run health of the company, particularly when it serves as a pretext for overpriced acquisitions. As the experience of companies like Nortel and WorldCom demonstrates, buying overpriced companies with overvalued stock not only fails to add value, but can end up demoralizing once successful organizations. While leveling with the markets can cause the stock price to fall to a sustainable level, the associated personal and organizational pain is slight compared with that arising from colluding in myth-telling.

Managers must work to make their organizations far more transparent to investors and to the markets. USA Networks' Diller, for example, has chosen to provide analysts with actual business budgets broken down by business segments. At the very least, companies should state their strategies clearly, identify associated value drivers, and report auditable metrics on both. They should also address the "unexplained" part of their firm's share price—that part not directly linked to observable cash flows—through a coherent description of the growth opportunities they foresee and be willing to tell the markets when they see their stock price as overvalued.

Similarly, to limit wishful thinking, managers must reconcile their own company's projections to those of the industry and their rivals' projections. Analysts develop models of an industry's growth. If the company's expectations lie outside what is widely viewed as the industry's growth rate, its managers must be able to explain how and why they will be able to outperform their market. Some executives will be concerned or complain that making this all clear to the analysts will reveal valuable information to their competitors. To this we have a simple response: if your strategy is based on your competitor not knowing what you are doing, as opposed to not being able to do what you can do, you cannot be successful in the long run no matter who knows what.

Finally, managers would be wise to remember that analysts are not always wrong. In fact, analysts have a vital monitoring role to play in a market economy. While recent history may have obscured that role, managers should not simply presume that analysts are wrong when disagreement occurs. It is worth noting that during the 1970s and 1980s managers regularly complained that analysts were undervaluing their companies. Yet, analysts were generally correct that managers of that era were not making effective use of corporate resources. They continued to invest in industries and activities with substantial excess capacity and consequent low returns, refused to downsize and distribute free cash flow to shareholders, and pursued inefficient, value-destroying conglomerate mergers. In response to such value destruction, there emerged an active market for corporate control, as reflected in the wave of hostile acquisitions and LBOs, in which competing management teams took over and replaced the managers and directors of underperforming companies and created vast new value.

Contrasting the decades of the 1970s and 1980s with the recent era thus yields an important lesson: managers and analysts must pay close attention to each other's views. Both analysts and managers bring important information and important perspectives to the conversation, and both sides benefit when each does their task well. Managers for their part must stop encouraging analysts to reach for ever-higher valuations and return to managing their companies. Analysts must stop making Nostradamus-like predictions and instead return to their true roots—the creation of original research and analysis.

The Securities Industry Association issued an excellent statement entitled "Best Practices for Research" in 2001 that lays the foundations for resolving many of the conflicts of interest on the part of analysts. We look forward to its early and widespread implementation.[8]

Stock prices are not simply abstract numbers that exist apart from the reality of corporate enterprises. Gyrations initiated by Wall Street or managers have real effects on companies and society. The price that Wall Street puts on a company's securities and the trajectory of those prices affect the nature of the strategies firms adopt and, hence, their prospects for success. Stock prices also drive a company's cost of capital, its borrowing capacity, and its ability to make acquisitions. Ultimately, the viability of the companies themselves is at stake.

A dysfunctional conversation between Wall Street and Main Street is not the esoteric stuff of business school classroom discussions. It can rob investors of savings, cost employees their jobs, erode the nest eggs of retirees, and undermine the viability of suppliers and communities. Clearly, it is time to restart the conversation on a new, stable, and enduring footing.

Notes

© Copyright The Monitor Company and M. C. Jensen. Excerpts of this chapter were published in the *Wall Street Journal* "Manager's Journal" column under the title "Dare To Keep Your Stock Price Low," December 31, 2001, and in the *Financial Times,* January 22, 2002 under the title "End the Myth-Making and Return to True Analysis." We thank Nancy Nichols, Pat Meredith, Jennifer Lacks Kaplan, Hardy Tey, Stephanie Mayer, and Shibanee Verma, who contributed to this effort. This paper can be downloaded without charge from the Social Science Research Network Electronic Library at: http://papers.ssrn.com/abstract=297156.

1. USA Networks, 2001. "USA Provides Internal Budget to Investment Community," *SEC Form 425.1,* October 24, 2001.
2. Julian E. Barnes, "Gillette's Chief Is Critical of the Company's Misstep," *New York Times,* June 7, 2001, http://college2.nytimes.com/guests/articles/2001/06/07/852365.xml.
3. Evidence of the distortion of information provided to investors by companies, and of the collaboration of some financial intermediaries and analysts in this distortion, has grown considerably. For an excellent compilation and analysis of this evidence, see the paper by Gene D'Avolio, Efi Gildor, and Andrei Shleifer, "Technology, Information Production, and Market Efficiency," Harvard Institute of Economic Research Discussion Paper Number 1929, September 2001. This paper can be downloaded without charge from the Social Science Research Network eLibrary at: http://papers.ssrn.com/abstract=286597 and at http://post.economics.harvard.edu/hier/2001papers/2001list.html.
4. David N. Fleischer, "Enron Corp. Gas and Power Convergence," Conference Call Transcript, Goldman Sachs, July 12, 2001, New York.
5. Edward J. Tirello, Jr., "Enron Corporation: The Industry Standard for Excellence," Analyst Report, Deutsche Banc Alex. Brown., September 15, 2000, New York.
6. The breakeven share price for Nortel investors as of December 31, 2001, was $21.33, assuming a 12 percent cost of equity capital net of dividends. This implies that the breakeven total value of Nortel at the end of 2001 was $68.5 billion. Thus, investors lost a total of $44.5 billion as a result of the failed strategy.
7. Keith Regan, "Lawsuit against Noted Internet Analyst Tossed," www.EcommerceTimes.com, August 22, 2001, http://www.newsfactor.com/perl/story/13001.html.
8. Securities Industry Association, "Best Practices for Research," 2001, http://www.sia.com/publications/pdf/best.pdf.

CHAPTER 9

Identifying and Attracting the "Right" Investors

Evidence on the Behavior of Institutional Investors

BRIAN BUSHEE

In our opinion, outside pressures too often tempt companies to sacrifice long-term opportunities to meet quarterly market expectations . . . If opportunities arise that might cause us to sacrifice short-term results but are in the best long-term interests of our shareholders, we will take these opportunities. . . . We would request that our shareholders take the long-term view.
—Larry Page and Sergey Brin,
Google's founders[1]

After the IPO, they [Google's management] are going to have to think in terms of predictable quarterly results and momentum.
—Gordon Eubanks, who took
Symantec Corp. public in 1989[2]

THE ENTRY OF GOOGLE INC. into the public equity market has rekindled the debate over the extent to which U.S. capital markets encourage short-sighted decisions by corporate managers. In the above statement from their "'Owner's Manual' for Google's Shareholders," the company's founders declared their intent to avoid the "numbers game" in which companies guide and then try to meet Wall Street's quarterly earnings projections, in many cases by "managing" earnings.[3] The second statement reflects the widespread skepticism that Google can simply opt out of the numbers game. But there are several recent examples of companies trying to do just that. Coca-Cola has stopped issuing quarterly earnings forecasts because management felt that the practice was drawing attention away from its emphasis on long-term strategy.[4] Gillette, AT&T, and PepsiCo have done much the same.[5] In such cases, managers say they are trying to attract investors whose primary concern is long-run value creation and not the next quarter's earnings.

But how do companies find the "right" investors? And having identified them, how do they persuade them to buy the firm's shares without attracting the "wrong" investors?

In an ideal world, managers would have farsighted investors that insulate the firm's operations from undue pressure for short-term performance and from excess stock price volatility. With such investors, corporate managers might be better able to avoid market overreactions to earnings surprises, especially the negative price responses that often lead to lawsuits and can limit companies' ability to raise capital for promising investment opportunities.[6]

While many observers believe that at least some U.S. companies would benefit from less pressure for short-term performance, there is no clear consensus about which kinds of investors provide more "patient" capital. Some investor relations consultants recommend the targeting of individual investors. Others urge the recruiting of foreign institutional investors, and still others advise corporate Investor Relations (IR) departments to focus their efforts on investors holding the shares of comparable firms.[7] Thus, it is not obvious which set of investors would provide managers more leeway in avoiding pressure for short-term performance.

Researchers have produced persuasive evidence that institutional investors as a group are more sophisticated than retail investors in the sense that they are more likely to see through obvious earnings management.[8] They are also easier to target. But if institutions as a group are better able to understand value drivers beyond reported earnings, there is also evidence that institutions react more aggressively to short-term events, thereby creating excess price volatility.[9] Moreover, institutional investors are not a homogeneous group—they differ greatly in terms of investment styles (such as preferences for value or growth stocks), trading frequency, competitive pressures, and legal restrictions, all of which affect their sensitivity to the short-term performance of their portfolio companies.

For the past seven years, I have been conducting research that aims to answer a number of questions about institutional investors. First, what are the significant differences among institutional investors in time horizon and other trading practices, and can such investors be classified into types on the basis of their behavior? Second, do corporate managers respond differently to the pressures created by different types of investors—and, by implication, are certain kinds of investors more desirable from corporate management's point of view? Third, what kinds of companies tend to attract each type of investor, and how does a company's disclosure policy affect that process?

In this chapter, I summarize my main findings and discuss their implications for managing a company's investor base through strategic disclosure. I begin by presenting my method of classifying institutional investors based on their trading behavior. My approach identifies three categories of institutional investors: (1) "transient" institutions, which exhibit high portfolio turnover and own small stakes in portfolio companies; (2) "dedicated" institutions, which provide stable ownership and take large positions in individual firms; and (3) "quasi-indexers," which also trade infrequently but own small stakes (similar to an index strategy).

Next, I discuss research findings on the influence of each category of institution on corporate management's decision-making. The disproportionate presence of transient institutions in a company's investor base appears to intensify pressure for short-term performance while also resulting in excess volatility in the stock price. My research also suggests that transient investors are attracted to companies with investor relations activities geared toward forward-looking information and "news events," like management forecasts, that constitute trading opportunities for such investors. By contrast, quasi-indexers and dedicated institutions are largely insensitive to short-term performance, and their presence is associated with lower stock price volatility. Quasi-indexers are attracted to companies with "high-quality" annual and quarterly report disclosure, whereas dedicated institutions appear to be insensitive to the quality of disclosure.

My research suggests that managers who focus their disclosure activities on historical information that helps investors to monitor corporate performance (as opposed to earnings forecasts, which seem to invite speculative trading) will attract quasi-indexers instead of transient investors, thereby reducing the sensitivity of their stock price to short-term developments. Such a change in investor base should encourage managers to make the best decisions for long-run value with less concern about short-term consequences.

Classifying Institutional Investors

A common approach to classifying institutions is by their legal type. For example, bank trusts may invest differently than insurance companies, and the investment practices of both may differ significantly from those of investment companies and advisers (including mutual funds) and pension funds. Each of these types is governed by different fiduciary responsibility laws. Bank trusts and pensions are subject to more stringent fiduciary standards than investment advisers and so tilt their portfolios toward safer stocks.[10] In addition, the competitive pressures faced by each type differ. Investment advisers encounter much more "churn" in their sources of funds than pensions and endowments, which results in trading that is more sensitive to the current performance of portfolio companies.[11] The advantage of this classification scheme is that legal type is readily available in most databases of institutional investor holdings. The key disadvantage is that there is tremendous variation within these groups in terms of investment horizons and sensitivity to short-term news.

My approach is to classify institutional investors based on their observed investment and trading behavior. This approach was inspired by Michael Porter's comparison of the behavior of U.S. investors with that of German and Japanese investors.[12] Porter observed that U.S. institutional investors tend to make small investments in a large number of companies, which they either turn over frequently or passively ignore (e.g., indexers). By contrast, German and Japanese markets are dominated by investors that own large, long-term equity stakes, which provide companies with patient capital as well as effective governance. While this argument tends to overlook the presence of U.S. "value" investors like Berkshire Hathaway (as well as major shortcomings of the German and Japanese governance systems), it does provide the insight that important differences among investors can be represented by two key variables: (1) ownership stability and (2) the size of the ownership stake. I use these two factors to classify U.S. institutional investors.

Here is how the method works. First, I calculated various measures of both ownership stability and stake size using publicly available information on institutional investor portfolio holdings. To measure stability, I computed quarterly portfolio turnover (measured as the total market value of sales during the quarter divided by the total market value of the portfolio at the beginning of the quarter) and the percentage of the institution's portfolio stocks that have been held continuously for the past two years. To measure stake size, I calculated the average percentage ownership in portfolio companies, the percentage of the portfolio stocks in large block holdings (that is, greater than a 5 percent stake), and the average dollar investment in portfolio firms.[13] I then used factor analysis to combine these portfolio characteristics into the two "common factors," ownership stability and stake size.

Next I used a grouping technique called cluster analysis to form three groups of institutions based on where they rank on both factors. As mentioned earlier, I have labeled the groups "transient," "dedicated," and "quasi-indexer." Transient institutions, which accounted for 31 percent of all institutions during the period 1983–2002, are characterized by low ownership stability and small stakes. Table 9.1 provides a representative example of a transient investor, Numeric Investors L.P., which describes itself as "an active quantitative manager of U.S. and international equity portfolios offering investment strategies with aggressive investment objectives."[14] Using quarterly averages for the year 2001, the table shows that Numeric sold almost 75 percent of its total portfolio market value every quarter and that only 25 percent of its portfolio holdings were in stocks that had been held continuously for two years. Numeric's average percentage ownership in its portfolio companies was less than 1 percent, it held no blocks greater than 5 percent, and its average investment size was $6 million per portfolio firm. Given such high portfolio turnover and small stake sizes, transient investors like Numeric clearly have short investment

TABLE 9.1

Portfolio Characteristics for a Representative Institution in Each Category of Institutional Investors

(Using 2001 Averages)	Numeric Investors (Transient)	Berkshire Hathaway (Dedicated)	CalPERS (Quasi-Indexer)
Ownership stability			
Quarterly portfolio turnover (market value of sales/beginning total portfolio market value)	73.7%	0.6%	8.0%
Percent of portfolio stocks held continuously for past two years	25.1%	75.0%	98.1%
Ownership stake size			
Average percentage ownership in portfolio firms	0.4%	10.9%	0.8%
Percent of portfolio stocks that are large block holdings (greater than 5%)	0.0%	52.5%	0.1%
Average investment size in portfolio firms (millions)	$6.0	$1,065.5	$21.6
Number of stocks in portfolio	501.1	26.2	1,988.3

horizons and likely have little incentive to understand drivers of long-run value.

Dedicated institutions, which amounted to 8 percent of all institutions during the same twenty-year period, are characterized by stable ownership and large stakes. Table 9.1 provides a representative example of a dedicated investor, Berkshire Hathaway, the insurance/holding company managed by Warren Buffett. The table shows that, in 2001, Berkshire Hathaway sold less than 1 percent of its portfolio market value each quarter and had held 75 percent of its portfolio holdings continuously for at least two years. Its average ownership in its portfolio companies was over 10 percent, and it owned greater than a 5 percent block in over half (52.5 percent) of its portfolio firms. As these numbers suggest, dedicated investors like Berkshire Hathaway follow a "relationship investing" strategy of buying and holding large stakes in a small number of companies.

Quasi-indexer institutions, a category that encompassed 61 percent of all institutions for the period 1983–2002, are identified by their high ownership stability and small ownership stakes. The representative example in table 9.1 is the California Public Employees' Retirement System (CalPERS). In 2001, CalPERS sold about 8 percent of its portfolio market value each quarter while

FIGURE 9.1

Percent of Each Category of Institutional Investors by Legal Type (1983–2002)

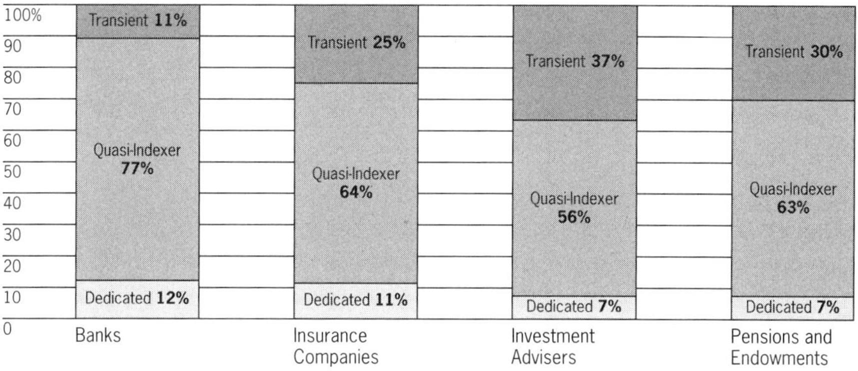

	Banks	Insurance Companies	Investment Advisers	Pensions and Endowments
Transient	11%	25%	37%	30%
Quasi-Indexer	77%	64%	56%	63%
Dedicated	12%	11%	7%	7%

having held 98 percent of its portfolio companies for at least two years. Its average ownership of portfolio firms and percentage of large block investments were both less than 1 percent. As these statistics suggest, quasi-indexers tend to make buy-and-hold investments in a broad set of companies and trade only when there is a major change in a given firm.

Figure 9.1 shows what happens when my classification scheme is imposed on each of the different legal types of institutions. Apart from the somewhat-lower-than-average representation of transient investors among banks, the three types of investment styles appear to be distributed fairly evenly across legal types. Thus, grouping institutions by whether they are banks or investment advisers would be only a weak proxy for whether the institutions create pressures for managers to focus on short-term results. In the next section, I provide evidence on how these different categories of institutions are associated with a key aspect of managerial decision-making—earnings management.

Does Investor Behavior Influence Managers?

My classification method allowed me to come up with a direct test of Michael Porter's assertion that transient ownership creates incentives for managers to sacrifice long-term investment to avoid a decline in current earnings. As described in a study published in the *Accounting Review* in 1998, I began by identifying all the companies that, during the period 1983–1994, were in a position to reverse an expected decline in earnings (relative to the prior year's) by cutting research and development (R&D) expenditures.[15] I found that managers with higher total institutional ownership were less likely to cut R&D to meet their earnings targets. My interpretation of this finding is that institutional investors, because of their greater sophistication, are more likely than individual investors to understand that an increase in earnings achieved by cutting productive R&D would be bad news, deterring managers from taking this step.

It was in the second part of this study that my classification scheme for institutional investors came into play. Here I found that, in cases where a company's investor base was dominated by transient institutions, managers were significantly more likely to cut R&D to avoid an earnings drop than if the investor base was dominated by quasi-indexers or dedicated institutions. Thus, managers faced with a high proportion of transient institutional ownership appear to cut investment in order to avoid an earnings decline that could trigger large-scale selling by such institutions.

In later work, researchers Bin Ke and Kathy Petroni used my classification method to examine what happens to companies whose earnings fall relative to their expected trend. Their own previous study (with Steve Huddart) had reported negative price reactions to breaks in strings of positive earnings growth, both at the announcement of the break and during the thirty days leading up to it.[16] When they then examined the patterns of institutional trading around the earnings breaks using my classification method, they found it was primarily the transient institutions that bought heavily during strings of earnings increases—and that when a break in the string became imminent, transient investors began dumping the stock, often up to a quarter before the break was announced.[17] In contrast, quasi-indexers and dedicated institutions tended to hold the stock during the quarters before, during, and after the break in the earnings sequence.

These studies have two implications. First, they provide additional evidence that my institutional investor classification approach can help companies identify the institutions that are more likely to create pressure on managers to manipulate earnings. More important, and contrary to the conventional wisdom, they imply that a corporate policy that aims to create continuous earnings growth is likely to be a double-edged sword. Such earnings "momentum" will attract transients who may drive up the stock price for a time; but their tendency to sell at the first sign of a downturn will make for a bumpy ride down, and management may be better off avoiding the artificial creation of such earnings strings in the first place.[18]

This brings us to the question of how managers can avoid attracting transient institutional investors to their stock, which I address in the next section.

What Attracts Institutional Investors?

In a study published in 2001, I attempted to determine what kinds of companies are more likely to attract each of the different categories of institutional investors.[19] More specifically, the study began by testing whether some groups of institutional investors focus more on expected near-term earnings than on long-run value in making their investment decisions. After putting together all companies followed by Value Line between 1980 and 1992, I used a valuation model that decomposed each firm's year-end market value into three components: (1) its accounting book value, (2) its expected earnings over the next one to four years, and (3) expected long-term earnings (beyond four years out). The second and third components were estimated using Value Line forecasts of future earnings, dividends, and book values.

I found that transient institutions invest more heavily in companies with larger proportions of their value in near-term earnings and a lower proportion in long-run value. Such companies typically have relatively high earnings and persistent earnings growth, in contrast to firms with low and volatile earnings whose market value stems primarily from expected long-run performance. Companies with more persistent earnings growth also tend to have larger price reactions to earnings surprises, providing greater potential trading profits for transient investors speculating on upcoming earnings news. In contrast, quasi-indexers and dedicated institutions are fairly insensitive to earnings volatility and the amount of firm value that will be realized in future earnings.

Transient institutions also prefer companies with greater liquidity (generally, larger firms with high share turnover), low dividend yields, and good past performance in terms of both stock returns and earnings. Liquidity is important to transient investors because it allows them to move in and out of stocks without having their trading profits eroded by round-trip transaction costs. Since dividends are theoretically a substitute for higher capital gains, high dividend yields tend to mean lower potential profit from short-term capital appreciation. The preference for good past performance reflects the momentum strategies employed by many transient investors. In contrast, quasi-indexers tend to prefer large, mature firms that are part of the S&P 500 index and have higher dividend yields and lower risk. Dedicated institutions show similar preferences for mature, low-risk, dividend-paying firms. But the fact that my regression model explained very little of the variation in dedicated investor ownership suggests that dedicated investors pay less attention to financial variables per se than to intangible factors such as the quality of management.

These results suggest that managers might be able to influence the composition of their company's investor base by changing some corporate characteristics. Perhaps the most important step that managers could take would be to discourage transient ownership by refusing to manage (that is, smooth) reported earnings. Such a step, when combined with changes in disclosure policy discussed below, could also conceivably affect the investor base by reducing the liquidity of its stock.

In the next section, I discuss some recent research that examines the link between disclosure policy and institutional ownership.

How Does Disclosure Policy Affect Institutional Investors?

Many studies have found important benefits from better disclosure, including a lower cost of capital, increased liquidity, a stronger analyst following, and greater institutional ownership.[20] In a study I co-authored with Christopher Noe, we investigated whether different categories of institutional investors are more or less sensitive to a company's disclosure practices.[21] We were particularly concerned about the possibility that certain kinds of disclosure—more specifically, what tends to be viewed in the business and analyst communities as "higher-quality" disclosure—could lead to greater liquidity and hence more transient ownership. If this were the case, there could be an important unintended consequence from more disclosure: greater stock price volatility.

We measured disclosure "quality" using security analysts' ratings from the Association for Investment Management and Research (AIMR). From 1979 to 1996, AIMR produced annual assessments of disclosure quality based on consideration of annual reports, interim reports, and investor relations activities (using criteria such as the accessibility and cooperativeness of company contacts, the timeliness of presentations to analysts, and the frequency of meetings with management). We found that higher disclosure quality was associated with higher ownership by both transient institutions and quasi-indexers. We attributed these results to transient institutions' preference for the liquidity that tends to accompany a high level of disclosure. For quasi-indexers, we suggested that greater disclosure reduces their costs of monitoring a large portfolio of stocks. Dedicated investors appeared to be largely insensitive to disclosure quality, at least as rated by the AIMR. The most likely explanation of this finding is that, because of the size of their ownership stakes, such investors will typically supplement required disclosure with their own research—and in many cases their ownership block may entitle them to an insider role, including a seat on the board of directors.

Our study also found that transient institutions focus specifically on investor relations activities and interim reports, which help companies maintain continuously high liquidity. In addition, IR activities such as conference calls and management forecasts provide transient investors with "information events" that present opportunities for speculative trading. In contrast, quasi-indexers tend to be most concerned with the quality of interim and annual reports, which reduce the cost of their ongoing monitoring activity. Since such investors are generally not looking to trade in the short term, management forecasts of quarterly earnings and other timely investor relations activities are relatively unimportant to them.

In sum, companies that provide more forthcoming and detailed disclosures of historical information in their annual reports are likely to attract more stable, quasi-indexer ownership. Companies with extensive investor relations activities, especially forward-looking information centered on near-term forecasts and news events, tend to attract transient investors. And as suggested earlier, the presence of transient investors could increase the volatility of the stock price, a possibility I take up in the next section.

Does Disclosure Affect Stock Price Volatility?

To provide evidence on the link between disclosure quality and stock price volatility, the study I co-authored with Christopher Noe examined the volatility consequences of attracting different categories of institutional investors. We began by arguing that differences in disclosure could have both direct and indirect effects on volatility. The expected direct effect of more disclosure is to lower volatility by reducing what academics refer to as information "asymmetries"—loosely speaking, gaps in information about a company's prospects between managers and outside investors, as well as among different groups of outside investors.[22] At the same time, however, more disclosure could also have the opposite ("indirect") effect of raising volatility by attracting transient investors.

We defined stock price volatility three ways: (1) the standard deviation of daily stock returns over a year; (2) the standard deviation of daily stock returns in the five days surrounding each earnings announcement; and (3) the number of days in a year with stock price drops larger than 1 percent. The first measure is relevant because it affects the market's perception of the firm's normal level of risk, which in turn should be incorporated into investors' required returns and the firm's cost of capital. The last two measures matter because large stock price drops in response to information events could trigger lawsuits or at least temporarily limit the firm's ability to raise capital (possibly foreclosing a time-sensitive investment opportunity).

As expected, we found that the direct effect of disclosure on volatility is negative; that is, more disclosure is generally associated with lower return volatility.[23] At the same time, we found that a higher percentage ownership by transient institutions was associated with incrementally higher stock price volatility using all three measures, and that higher percentage ownership by quasi-indexers and dedicated institutions was associated with lower volatility. As shown in figure 9.2, we found that the volatility-increasing effect of greater disclosure resulting from transient investors was largely offset by its volatility-

FIGURE 9.2

Summary of the Relationship among Disclosure Quality, Institutional Investors, and Stock Return Volatility

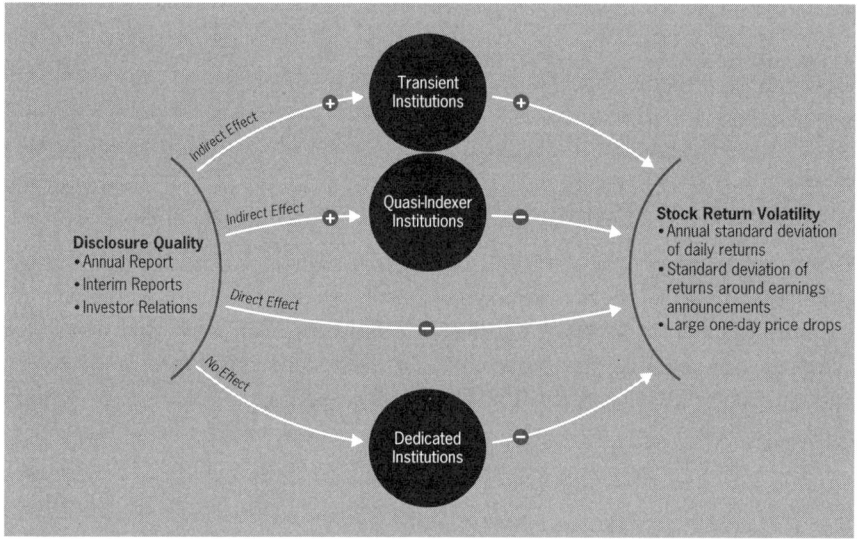

Direct effect of disclosure
Higher level of disclosure leads to lower stock return volatility

Indirect effects of disclosure
- Higher level of disclosure (especially investor relations) leads to greater ownership by transient institutions, which in turn increases stock return volatility
- Higher level of disclosure (especially annual reports) leads to greater ownership by quasi-indexer institutions, which in turn reduces stock return volatility

dampening effect of attracting quasi-indexers. But we also discovered that when a company made a major "improvement" in disclosure (as measured by the AIMR), transient investors reacted more quickly than quasi-indexers, leading to a temporary increase in volatility (lasting generally until quasi-indexers responded to the change, typically over the next year or two).

These results also differed in predictable fashion across the different aspects of disclosure rated by the AIMR. For example, we found that the increased volatility associated with the attraction of transient owners was most pronounced in the case of improvements in investor relations activities. In other words, more timely investor relations activities can actually increase volatility by attracting short-term-focused institutional investors with a preference for aggressive trading. At the same time, the reduction in volatility resulting from an increase in ownership by quasi-indexers was most evident in the case of improvements in the annual report.

Implications for Corporate Disclosure

One potentially troubling implication of these findings is that certain kinds of disclosure activities—while generally serving to reduce the cost of capital and increase the liquidity of the firm's stock—can create a series of short-term "news" events that facilitate the numbers game, attract transient investors, and destabilize the stock price. Without careful consideration of their company's potential to attract transient investors and the format and type of its investor relations activities, managers may be exposing the firm to significant costs stemming from excess price volatility.

The first step for managers is to examine their investor base and determine whether their company is likely to attract transient investors. Large companies with persistent earnings, high liquidity, low dividend yields, and strong past performance tend to fall into this category. Such companies may want to redesign their investor relations activities to downplay the significance of quarterly earnings reports and avoid creating additional news events. For example, managers might want to consider dropping quarterly forecasts and bundling conference calls or analyst presentations with earnings announcements.

As part of their effort to shift investor focus from quarterly earnings to questions of longer-run value, managers should be sensitive to the information demands of their longer-term investors, both quasi-indexers and dedicated institutional investors. Improving the quality of annual report disclosure will attract more quasi-indexers, whose low propensity to trade will dampen return volatility around news events. By orienting more of their disclosure activities toward historical information that helps investors in monitoring performance (as opposed to forecasts, which tend to invite speculation), managers may be able to attract quasi-indexers to take the place of transients. Also, because transient investors react more quickly than quasi-indexers to changes in disclosure practices, most companies should be cautious about making major changes in many disclosure practices all at once—since the likely effect is a spike in transient ownership. Finally, managers should consider the possibility of cultivating dedicated investors with the aim of turning them into blockholders. But to be confident enough to entrust investors with what amounts to an insider role, management must have a credible strategy, an effective means of communicating it, and a sufficiently sophisticated and well-capitalized investor group to take the long view.

In sum, my research suggests that changes in disclosure practices have the potential to shift the composition of a firm's investor base away from transient investors and toward more patient capital. This shift will remove some of the external pressures for short-term results and encourage managers to return their focus to establishing a culture based on long-run value maximization.

Notes

1. Quoted in Larry Page and Sergey Brin, "Letter from the Founders: 'An Owner's Manual' for Google's Shareholders," Google Inc. Form S-1 SEC filing, pp. i–vi, Apr. 29, 2004.
2. Quoted in Michael Liedtke, "Google Files Its Long-Awaited IPO Plans," Associated Press, Apr. 29, 2004.
3. See "The 'Numbers Game,'" speech by SEC Chairman Arthur Levitt to the NYU Center for Law and Business, Sept. 29, 1998, http://www.sec.gov/news/speech/speecharchive/1998/spch220.txt.
4. See "Coke, Quarterly Estimates and 'The Numbers Game,'" Knowledge@Wharton, Jan. 29, 2003, http://knowledge.wharton.upenn.edu/index.cfm?fa=viewArticle&id=706.
5. The Treasurer of Progressive Insurance discusses how its management refuses to give earnings guidance and values accuracy over smoothing, even at the expense of more volatile earnings in Tom King, "Making Financial Goals and Reporting Policies Serve Corporate Strategy: The Case of Progressive Insurance." *Journal of Applied Corporate Finance*, Vol. 16, 4 (2004), pp. 17–27.
6. For lawsuit evidence, see Jennifer Francis, Donna Philbrick, and Katherine Schipper, "Shareholder Litigation and Corporate Disclosures," *Journal of Accounting Research* (Autumn 1994), pp. 137–164.
7. See, respectively, Editorial Staff, "Targeting Retail Investment Can Help Buoy a Stock," *Investor Relations Bulletin* (July 2002), p. 1; John Byrne, "When Capital Gets Antsy: How Stock Churning Is Reshaping Corporate America," *BusinessWeek* (Sept. 13, 1999), p. 72; and Peggie Elgin, "Strategic Pairings Uncork Blessings for Investors, Issuers," *Corporate Cashflow* (Sept. 1992), p. 7.
8. For an example, see John Hand, "A Test of the Extended Functional Fixation Hypothesis," *The Accounting Review* (Oct. 1990), pp. 740–763.
9. See Gordon Potter, "Accounting Earnings Announcements, Institutional Investor Concentration, and Common Stock Returns," *Journal of Accounting Research* (Spring 1992), pp. 146–155; and Richard Sias, "Volatility and the Institutional Investor," *Financial Analysts Journal* (Mar./Apr. 1996), pp. 13–21.
10. See Diane Del Guercio, "The Distorting Effect of the Prudent-Man Laws on Institutional Equity Investments," *Journal of Financial Economics* (Jan. 1996), pp. 31–62.
11. See Mark Lang and Maureen McNichols, "Institutional Trading, Corporate Earnings, and Returns," Working paper, Stanford University (Oct. 1997).
12. Michael Porter, "Capital Choices: Changing the Way America Invests in Industry," *Journal of Applied Corporate Finance* (Summer 1992), pp. 4–16.
13. In practice, I used multiple measures of each of these variables to reduce the error in the methodology. For more details on the exact variables used, interested readers should consult my article, "Do Institutional Investors Prefer Near-Term Earnings over Long- Run Value?," *Contemporary Accounting Research*, Vol. 18 (2001), pp. 207–246.
14. Numeric Investors L.P. Web site (http://www.numeric.com).
15. See my article, "The Influence of Institutional Investors on Myopic R&D Investment Behavior," *Accounting Review* (July 1998).
16. See Bin Ke, Steve Huddart, and Kathy Petroni, "What Insiders Know about Future Earnings and How They Use It: Evidence from Insider Trades," *Journal of Accounting & Economics* (Aug. 2003), pp. 285–314.
17. See Bin Ke and Kathy Petroni, "How Informed Are Actively Trading Institutional Investors? Evidence from Their Trading Behavior Before a Break in a String of Con-

secutive Earnings Increases," *Journal of Accounting Research* 42, No. 5 (2004), pp. 895–927.
18. This sentiment is echoed in the philosophy of Progressive Insurance, King (2004), note 5.
19. See my 2001 article, cited earlier (note 13).
20. See Amy Hutton, "Beyond Financial Reporting—An Integrated Approach to Disclosure," *Journal of Applied Corporate Finance*, Vol. 16, No. 4, pp. 8–16.
21. See Brian Bushee and Christopher Noe, "Corporate Disclosure Practices, Institutional Investors, and Stock Return Volatility," *Journal of Accounting Research*, Vol. 38 (2000), pp. 171–202.
22. See Mark Lang and Russell Lundholm, "Cross-Sectional Determinants of Analysts Ratings of Corporate Disclosures," *Journal of Accounting Research* (Autumn 1993).
23. This result is consistent with Progressive's experience after introducing monthly disclosures (see King [2004], note 5).

CHAPTER 10

U.S. Family-Run Companies—They May Be Better Than You Think

HENRY MCVEY AND JASON DRAHO

THE CONVENTIONAL WISDOM is that effective control of large U.S. corporations has largely passed from the active owner-managers of old, like Henry Ford, to today's professional managers. What's more, many investors may have viewed the recent scandals at Adelphia and Parmalat as further confirmation of their suspicion that family firms are run primarily for the benefit of family members at the expense of the other shareholders. But recent research, some of it done at Morgan Stanley, suggests that the conventional wisdom about family-run firms may be wrong or in need of some important qualifications.

First of all, although studies have long reported that family ownership predominates among exchange-listed companies in continental Europe, Asia, and Latin America, recent work suggests that the influence of families on U.S. public companies is far more pervasive than commonly thought.[1] For example, in a study published in the *Journal of Finance* in 2003, academics Ronald Anderson and David Reeb reported evidence of family control in over 35 percent of S&P 500 industrial companies and family ownership of nearly 18 percent of the outstanding equity in those firms.[2]

The second major surprise is the performance of such family companies. A number of studies, including Anderson and Reeb's and a follow-on report by *Business Week* (also published in 2003), provided striking evidence that U.S. family-run companies have outperformed their non-family counterparts in recent years.[3] For example, over the period 1992–1999, Anderson and Reeb found that family companies earned an average return on assets (ROA; EBITDA/Total Assets) that was 6.6 percent higher than the ROA of non-family firms. And the *Business Week* study reported that, over the ten-year period 1993–2002, family companies produced an average annual return to shareholders of 15.6 percent, as compared with 11.2 percent for non-family firms.

Why do family companies perform better? The answer may have a lot to do with the unusual "governance model" of the typical family company. A family that both owns and controls a company avoids the classic agency problem—namely, the natural tendency of professional managers to pursue private interests at the expense of their shareholders.[4] On the cost side, however, family ownership, like the presence of any large blockholder, also creates another potential agency conflict—the temptation of the controlling shareholder to use corporate resources in ways that do not benefit the minority shareholders.[5] To the extent that the reduction in the first kind of agency costs resulting from significant family ownership exceeds the increase in the second kind, family companies can be expected to outperform their non-family counterparts.

Besides examining their governance model, we also point to some distinctive "psychological" or "behavioral" attributes of family companies that could also provide insight into their performance. Families that own and help run a company for generations have some potential advantages over professional managers—knowledge of the business, longer planning horizons, and well-established reputations and ties with corporate stakeholders (including employees and local communities)—that could translate into systematically higher returns. The downside of family control, as mentioned, is the greater possibility for expropriation of corporate resources—a possibility that includes the "entrenchment" of an unqualified family management. These benefits and drawbacks are likely to depend on the family's willingness to relinquish control when it is clearly no longer serving the interests of their co-owners, the other shareholders.

In this chapter, we describe our own recent efforts to identify and then analyze the performance of family-run companies in the S&P 500. One of the major difficulties in conducting such analysis is determining what constitutes a "family-run" company. In contrast to previous studies that classified over a third of the S&P 500 as family companies, our sample turned out to be much smaller (sixty-three). One reason for our smaller sample was our decision to exclude "founder companies" like Dell and Microsoft, which, as discussed later, fall outside our concept of a family company. But even when we exclude such relatively new and highly successful firms, our sample of family companies has also "outperformed" in recent years, producing stock returns well in excess of their non-family counterparts. Of course, not all family companies have prospered, and our study casts light on one factor that may help in distinguishing successful from unsuccessful firms. The roughly one-third of family companies with dual-class shares produced lower returns than firms with a single-share class. And among the family firms with dual-class structures, those with insider-dominated boards fared even worse. In short, corporate governance seems to matter.

The Benefits and Costs of Family Control

Families represent only one type of owner-manager. Management buyouts, reverse LBOs, and companies with active blockholders all have, at least on paper, similar ownership structures. But these alternative forms lack certain family traits that can lead to better performance. Primary among them is the extra motivation stemming from the family's long ownership of and association with the company. Family wealth is typically concentrated in the company for generations. Using *Forbes*'s Wealthiest Americans Survey data, Anderson and Reeb reported that, in their sample of family companies, the average family had over 69 percent of its wealth invested in its company and its average holding period was seventy-nine years. Whether as managers, board members, or active monitors, such families have strong incentives to make their companies succeed. And in addition to their financial and emotional investments, family owners also often acquire a knowledge of their companies' operations, history, and culture that outsiders would find impossible to gain on their own.

To the extent founding families view their companies as legacies to be bequeathed to their heirs—which is clearly consistent with a seventy-nine-year average holding period—they may think harder than many professional managers about the long-term consequences of their actions and decisions. A long-term focus has two immediate consequences that could give family companies a leg up over non-family rivals. First, they may be less likely to respond to external pressure for higher current earnings by making cutbacks in productive long-term investment. Second, the continuing presence of a highly regarded family can strengthen the company's relationships with customers, suppliers, and capital providers.

The Downside to Family Control

An estimated 30 percent of all family companies make it through the second generation, 12 percent survive through the third, and just 3 percent continue to operate through the fourth generation and beyond.[6] While a number of factors contribute to the downfall of a company, specific aspects of family control weigh on its performance and long-term survival. Family risk aversion can lead to an emphasis on value preservation rather than value maximization. Poor planning and weak economic incentives are obstacles to making a successful transition to the next generation. Failure to define early on the future roles of individual family members in the company—ideally in a "constitution" that outlines the procedures for generational transfer of control—can result in destructive squabbles and tension when the current generation steps down. But even with good planning, the gradual dispersion of ownership among a growing number of increasingly passive family members can create problems—and, if things are not going well, pressure for change.

The possibility for entrenchment, however, is likely to be the biggest potential drawback of family control. A dominant family can enjoy the so-called private benefits of control, which can range from the relatively benign—modest consumption of perks—to more serious value destruction that results from efforts to build a corporate empire through value-reducing acquisitions. Outright expropriation is also a possibility, but the strong legal protection in the United States of non-controlling shareholders and concerns about family reputation typically limit such behavior. On the other hand, entrenched family control effectively eliminates the possibility of all but a friendly takeover, which is likely to put a ceiling on the value of a poorly performing company.

Is There an Optimal Ownership Level?

The proposition that a large ownership block helps address the owner-manager agency conflict while simultaneously creating conflicts between controlling and minority shareholders suggests that there may be an optimal level of ownership—one that balances the two concerns. Some economists have hypothesized that the optimal controlling block is around 20–30%. Consistent with this conjecture, Anderson and Reeb found that ROA rises with increases in the family stake up to around 30% and then falls thereafter, reaching the ROA of non-family firms at around 60%.

But the conjectured relationship between ownership and performance is a matter of ongoing academic debate. In theory, ownership levels and performance are jointly determined, conditional on other factors, as the outcome of a value-maximizing strategy.* In other words, whereas a small controlling stake might be optimal for one company under one set of circumstances—say, a biotech company that requires a large infusion of equity to bring a new drug to market—a large block may be best in others—say, a mature company that clearly needs to shrink. To the extent this is true, there should be no observable correlation between the two values—and this is what some researchers have found.**

*See H. Dernsetz and K. Lehn. "The Structure of Corporate Ownership: Causes and Consequences," *Journal of Political Economy*, Vol. 93 (1985), pp. 155–177.
**See H. Dernsetz and B. Villalonga, "Ownership structure and Corporate Performance," *Journal of Corporate Finance*, Vol. 7 (2001), pp. 209–233. They tested for the joint determination of the ownership and performance variables, and concluded that there was no relationship.

One final drawback of family companies worth noting is their inclination to reserve senior executive positions, especially the CEO, for family members. In cases where there are clearly better candidates, nepotism of this kind can not only lead to substandard performance but also demoralize managers and other employees.

In sum, the greatest cost to family control is not the expropriation of company resources, but rather the possible persistence of inferior management and poor investment decisions that can result from an entrenched position.

How to Recognize a "Family Company" When You See One

A family can maintain control of a company through either explicit or informal methods. Official control is a direct function of the voting rights held by the family. A simple majority ensures the family's controlling position, but effective control can often be achieved with far fewer votes. Indeed, as long as the firm performs well, the family can continue to exert a controlling interest over the strategic direction of the company. For example, no one disputes that Anheuser-Busch is a family company, even though the Busch family owns only 1.3 percent of the stock.

Another means commonly used by U.S. family companies to maintain control is the issuance of two classes of shares. This dual-class ownership structure has the effect of creating a "wedge" between the family's voting rights, which are typically a majority, and its far fewer cash flow rights. The larger the wedge between a family's votes and its percentage claim on corporate cash flows, the greater is the potential conflict of incentives between the family and the minority shareholders over the best use of corporate assets. In cases where the family has voting control and a relatively small claim on dividends and earnings, family shareholders bear only a fraction of the cost of decisions to use corporate resources for other than value-increasing activities. And while family members often derive "private" benefits from such activities, minority shareholders bear most of the costs.

The absence of a clear threshold for stock ownership that confers control means that classifying public companies as "family-controlled" involves some degree of subjective judgment. Some cases are clear—Ford, W. M. Wrigley, and Wal-Mart immediately come to mind—but others are not. Most studies have identified family companies as those in which (1) the founder or the founder's family (including foundations and trusts) is the largest shareholder or (2) the founders' descendants serve on the board or in senior management. When using these criteria, Anderson and Reeb classified over one-third of the S&P 500 as "family companies," and *Business Week* identified 177 such firms.

In coming up with our own sample of family companies in the S&P 500, we decided to make two major changes. First, candidate firms—those that satisfied one of the two conditions above—were also subjected to a "market test," which consisted of asking Morgan Stanley equity analysts whether investors actually view the company as a family firm. The purpose of this test was to exclude companies where, although the family may still have a material ownership stake, it appears to have become a passive investor. Eli Lilly is a good example of a company that did not pass our test. Although the Lilly Foundation owns 14 percent of the stock, no family member is in senior management or on the board.[7]

The second condition is that the company is no longer a "founder" firm—that is, a company in which the founder is the only family member involved with the firm, most likely as the CEO or chairman. Our distinction between family and founder companies—a category that includes Dell, Oracle, and Microsoft—is important because such companies are likely to differ in significant ways. Founder CEOs typically possess unique skills and experience, as well as the managerial talent to run a large corporation—traits that are not necessarily passed on to their descendants. Founders also typically have more invested in the firm than their descendants, both in terms of their ownership stake and their commitment to building the business. Founder companies have also not had to deal with the complex issues associated with family succession, including the allocation of ownership and decision-making rights among the future heirs. In fact, many founders choose not to pass on significant ownership or control to family members, but sell to outsiders instead.

Sixty-three companies in the S&P 500 met our definition of a family company. Moreover, as shown in figure 10.1, twenty companies, or almost one-third of our sample, had multiple classes of stock (as compared with just 8 percent for the entire S&P 500). The founder was still active, either in management or on the board, in 43 percent of our sample companies, which was true of only 15 percent of the S&P 500. Family members other than the founders were active in management or the board in 97 percent of our sample firms.[8]

Not surprisingly, the media group contains the largest concentration of family-run companies, accounting for 14 percent of our sample. In fact, family companies constitute about half of that industry's companies (and market capitalization) in the S&P 500. Figure 10.2 shows the percentage of family companies in each of seventeen different industries, along with their percentage of the total industry market cap. In addition to media, as shown in the figure, the two industries with the next largest representations of family companies are consumer services and food, beverage, and tobacco. Also worth noting is the domination of the food and staples retailing group by Wal-Mart, which alone accounts for 80 percent of the group's market cap.

FIGURE 10.1

Family Company Defining Characteristics

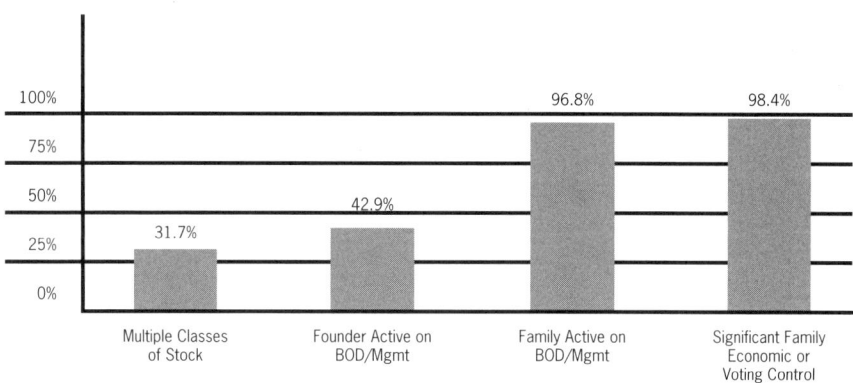

(% of 63 Company Family Universe)

Source: Company data, The Corporate Library, Morgan Stanley Research.
BOD = Board of directors.

FIGURE 10.2

Family Company Representation in the S&P 500

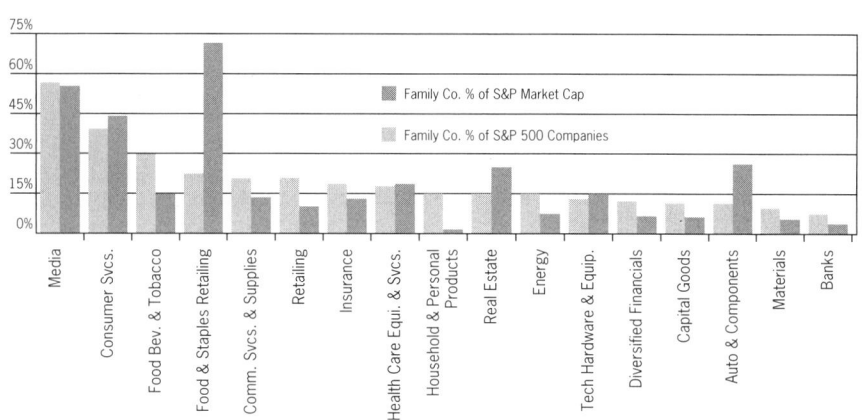

Source: FactSet, Morgan Stanley Research.

Performance

To determine whether our sample of family companies outperformed their non-family rivals, we calculated their stock returns over one-, three-, and five-year periods each ending on August 5, 2005, and benchmarked those returns

TABLE 10.1

Family Company Performance Relative to the S&P 500 (August 5, 2000–August 5, 2005)

	1 Year	3 Years	5 Years
All family companies (63)	4.4%	19.6%	109.7%
Companies without active founder or dual-class stock (24)	7.8%	21.2%	120.5%
Companies with active founders (27)	7.2%	34.0%	116.6%
Companies with dual-class stock (20)	−5.7%	−2.2%	72.2%

Source: Company data, Morgan Stanley Research.
Note: The returns assume an equal-weighted portfolio and represent total return including dividends.

against the S&P 500. As shown in table 10.1, the family firms outperformed the index by 4.4 percent, 19.6 percent, and 109.7 percent over the progressively longer periods. Our sample firms also outperformed their respective industry groups by 43 percent over the five-year period. Nevertheless, there was a lot of variation in the five-year returns, as evidenced by a standard deviation of 120 percent and a range of −85 percent to 490 percent. This snapshot shows that although family companies have recently done very well as a group, some are lagging far behind.

The higher stock returns of these family companies did not translate into larger dividends, which might come as a surprise since these companies had more cash as a percentage of assets (10.7 percent vs. 8.9 percent). The dividend yield for family firms averaged 1.1 percent, as compared with 1.7 percent for the S&P 500. The best explanation seems to be that companies with paltry or no dividends, such as Comcast and Danaher, retained the cash to make acquisitions or other strategic investments. At the same time, many other family companies, including Viacom and Marriott, chose to return their excess cash through share buybacks rather than dividends. Consistent with this idea, the average net buyback yield for family companies was 1.7 percent, as compared with 1.2 percent for the S&P 500 as a whole.

The Governance Effect

As discussed earlier, the performance and value of family companies can suffer from agency costs associated with family entrenchment and poor decision-making as company control passes through the generations. To explore whether such problems actually do affect performance, we divided our sample into three categories:

1. companies with an active founder in senior management or on the board;
2. companies without an active founder, but with descendant family members involved in either or both management and the board; and
3. companies with a dual-class share ownership structure.

As shown in table 10.1, which lists the returns for each of the three subgroups benchmarked against the S&P 500, both companies with active founders and those with active family members performed very well—and the returns of the two groups were nearly identical. The returns of the dual-class stock companies were lower than those of the other two groups over all three periods, and less than those of the S&P 500 over the one- and three-year horizons (though, to be fair, they did significantly outperform in the preceding two years, giving them higher five-year returns). These results, along with those from other studies, suggest that control-enhancing devices like dual-class shares that entrench the family and create a wedge between cash flow and control rights generally destroy value.

The board of directors, although a critical governance component in all companies, appears to take on additional significance in family companies. Families that are actively involved in running the company can suffer from insular decision-making, and an independent board with experienced external senior executives can provide an objective assessment of the company strategy. Even more important in some cases is the board's ability to mediate between competing family members, thereby preventing decisions from becoming "personal."

The average overall board effectiveness of our sample, based on metrics produced by The Corporate Library, is only moderately below that of the S&P 500. Figure 10.3 shows the distribution of grades, ranging from A to F, with a median of C. Not surprisingly, companies with dual-class stock receive noticeably worse grades than the broader group of family firms. This is largely because they have low percentages of independent directors—another indication of the family's unwillingness to share control. These "low grade" dual-class companies also exhibited worse performance, trailing the returns of other dual-class firms.

A more recent (2005) study by Anderson and Reeb demonstrates the importance of a well-constructed, independent board for family companies.[9] They showed that, over the period 1992–1999, the "Q" ratio (a variant of market to book) of S&P 500 industrial companies was 12 percent higher for family companies with an independent board (at least 51 percent independent) compared with insider-dominated boards (less than 25 percent independent). This result

FIGURE 10.3

Board of Director Effectiveness

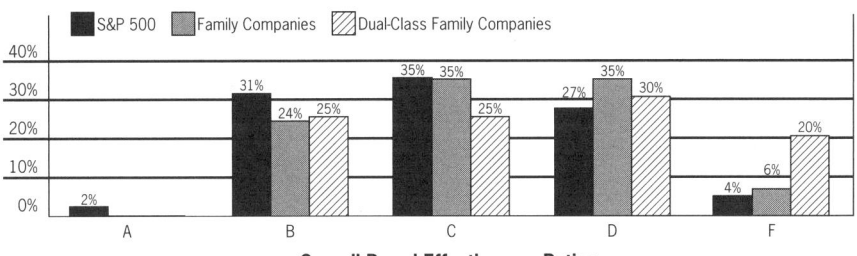

Overall Board Effectiveness Rating

Source: The Corporate Library.

contrasts with the consistent finding that board independence is generally unrelated to value for all S&P 500 companies. Anderson and Reeb also noted that only those independent directors who are also outside executives are associated with significantly higher value; other independent director classifications appear to have little effect. Again, this supports the conjecture that it is important to have directors with the ability to question and challenge the family's strategy.

Family Companies in Practice

Governance structure and succession planning are only one of many possible factors that affect the performance of family companies. The quality of the business plan, the effective implementation of the plan, the competitive environment, and even luck all unite to decide the company's fate. To understand the high mean and variance of the returns, we try to identify a number of other factors, including the relationship between business strategy and the family's attitude toward control, that seem to play important roles in the performance of family companies.

Whether the benefits of family ownership outweigh the costs depends in large part on the actions and strategy pursued by the family. Investment policies can be shortsighted if the family is risk averse or suffers from inertia. Similarly, the family does not have to be entrenched; instead, it could turn over considerable decision-making authority to professional managers as well as give investors some power to intervene should things go wrong. The decisions the family makes regarding strategy and control are an overall reflection of their philosophy toward the company. More precisely, they reflect the beliefs and ability of the CEO, especially one who is the founder.

> ### Family Companies and Disclosure
>
> One way for controlling families to reassure minority investors is to adopt an effective disclosure policy—one that provides more than the information mandated by the SEC. Investors reward companies that provide more and better disclosure with a lower cost of capital, creating an incentive for families to develop a good disclosure reputation.
>
> A 2005 study found that family companies reported higher-quality earnings than did non-family firms.* One possibility is that because families are well-informed, active monitors of management, they have less need for accounting-based pay-for-performance compensation, and so their managers have less incentive to manage reported earnings to their benefit.** Family companies were also quicker to issue management earnings forecasts in the face of bad news, measured as negative changes in quarterly earnings. Since the market penalizes companies with a reputation for withholding bad news and families are long-term investors, disclosing bad news quickly can head off greater damage in the future.
>
> Perhaps as a result of these two disclosure practices, the study also found that family companies have larger analyst followings, lower dispersion of forecasts, smaller forecast errors, less volatile earnings forecast revisions, and smaller bid-ask spreads. These findings show that families, far from being secretive about their business, understand the benefits of good disclosure.
>
> *See A. All, T. Chen, and S. Radhakrishnan, "Corporate Disclosures by Family Firms," Working paper, University of Texas at Dallas (2005). They measured reported earnings quality by the ability of its components to predict future cash flows and the earnings association with contemporaneous stock returns.
> **Other studies have found that CEO performance pay is significantly smaller in family firms, both in absolute terms and as a percentage of total compensation. See Anderson and Reeb (2003), cited elsewhere, and T. Chen, "Executive Compensation Contracts of Family Firms," Working paper, University of Texas at Dallas (2005).

The critical question here is the amount of control the family is prepared to give up. The family's willingness to cede either a little or a lot of control can greatly affect both corporate strategy and financial policy. For example, an aggressive growth strategy will require both significant risk-taking and, most likely, external capital that either increases the probability of financial distress, in the case of debt, or dilutes the family's controlling stake, as with an equity offering. A growth strategy through mergers and acquisitions fits this scenario. Depending on the family's control preferences, this may not be an attractive option. Relinquishing control also means bringing in professional management when merited and acquiescing to its decision-making authority, an action difficult for some families. But, as we will try to show using a number of cases from our sample, there are a number of ways of carrying out an ambitious and risky business strategy while still retaining effective control.

Maintaining Control

A preference for retaining control does not require a large ownership position or a dual-class structure. In many cases, families have effective control with very few votes. The Grainger family controls W. W. Grainger with a little over 10 percent of the stock; the Pigott family controls Paccar with 5.7 percent; and the Plank family runs Apache Corp. with only 0.08 percent. All of these companies have market-leading positions within their industry, highly regarded franchises, and a single-class share structure—and they have all generated high returns for investors. Outside investors tend to give such families considerable "slack" before challenging their right to control.

The beer industry offers a good case study of the different methods of maintaining control. The Busch family controls Anheuser-Busch with only 1.3 percent of the stock. Two competitors, Coors and Molson, were both family controlled using dual-class structures before their 2005 merger, and that remains the case with the new Molson-Coors. The Busch family's ability to maintain control with far fewer votes may reflect the companies' differing fortunes over the past two decades. Anheuser-Busch is the largest brewer in the United States, with a market share that has doubled over that period to approximately 50 percent. Investors have reaped the rewards, as the stock price increased from about $3 in October 1985 to $50 in July 2004—a 1,550 percent return. By comparison, Coors, with an 11 percent U.S. market share, saw its share price increase from about $12 to $70 over the same period—a 480 percent return—prior to its announced merger with Molson. (The return to the S&P 500 over the same period was also 480 percent.)

The experience of Anheuser-Busch and the preceding examples demonstrates that families can maintain control with a relatively small stake, provided the company has performed well. But if the performance of a company like Apache Corp. (with minimal family ownership) deteriorates sufficiently, investors will press for change, which could mean a drastically reduced role for the family. Chris Galvin, grandson of the founder of Motorola, resigned in 2003 as CEO over a disagreement with the board over the company's turnaround strategy; most investors no longer think of Motorola as a family company.

One implication of this dynamic is that the sixty-three companies in our sample of public family companies, especially those with small stakes, reflect a kind of "survivorship" bias. Given the tendency of families to relinquish control (voluntarily or otherwise) of poorly performing businesses, it is not completely surprising that the performance of family companies is well above average. But this reasoning does not apply with the same force to companies with entrenched families, such as those with dual-class stock. Their lower average performance is consistent with governance structures that are more tolerant of managerial failure to add value.

Long-Term Focus

All companies and managers are likely to claim that they focus on long-term value creation. In reality, concerns about meeting the short-term earnings expectations of analysts and investors can result in managers passing up value-increasing investment opportunities.[10] Family owners should be somewhat insulated from external pressure and therefore have longer investment horizons.

A number of our sample companies have attempted to discourage investor focus on quarterly earnings, presumably with the aim of focusing on longer-term value creation. Progressive Insurance, for example, has never provided earnings guidance. This philosophy originated with Peter Lewis, the current chairman and son of the founder. According to Lewis, the corporate pursuit of steady growth in earnings per share can cause operating managers to make short-sighted decisions that reduce value. Paccar Inc. is another company that pays little heed to analysts' forecasts and how actual earnings measure up to the consensus. Over the past few years of rising commodity prices, Apache Corp. has resisted the temptation to grow its oil and gas business by "paying up for assets." Instead, it prefers to wait for special, reasonably priced asset deals that complement its existing businesses.

A more clear-cut example of longer-term investment horizons is Simon Property Group, a real estate investment trust specializing in shopping malls. Controlled by the Simon family, the company acquired Corporate Property Investors and its portfolio of high-quality assets in 1998. While the transaction instantly transformed the value of Simon's holdings, analysts were concerned with the highly dilutive short-term effect on earnings per share. The stock price subsequently fell from $33 at the merger announcement in February 1998 to $23 in the fall of 1999. But the stock now trades around $75, thanks in part to the payoff from the acquisition of CPI. In the face of investor opposition, career concerns, and a belief at the time that Internet commerce would erode the value of shopping malls, professional managers may have been less likely to do what has turned out to be a great deal.

Managerial Talent

The performance of family firms, as with any company, is a function of managerial talent. Almost by definition, founder CEOs possess the right skills to be excellent managers; otherwise the company never would have grown and survived. Studies routinely show that founder-CEO firms trade at a premium relative to other companies.[11] The challenge arises once the founder steps down: is the family willing to hand over the reins to the best candidate, regardless of bloodline? People who grow up immersed in the family business could have an advantage over outsiders who lack the same level of operational knowledge. The desire to match or even surpass the performance of highly successful predecessors could also provide an extra bit of motivation over an outside manager. On the other hand, the family offers a very small pool of talent, especially in contrast with the market for professional managers.

The experiences of three companies demonstrate the consequences of the CEO choice. The current CEO of AFLAC, Dan Amos, is the son of one of the cofounding brothers. The decision to "keep it in the family" is justified by the fact that investors routinely vote Amos as the best CEO in the industry in an annual *Wall Street Journal* poll. Apollo Group Inc., a provider of higher education for working adults, has taken a different approach. Founder John Sperling and his son Peter both sit on the board of directors but take a hands-off approach to the business. While it is impossible to know how the company would have fared under their control, the five-year return of 310 percent the company has achieved with its professional managers would have been hard to surpass. Thus, the Sperlings' decision to step back appears to have been a good one, even though they still have voting control.

The drug store chain Rite Aid had a less successful experience with appointing a descendant as CEO. Martin Grass succeeded his father and the company's founder, Alex, as CEO in 1995. The younger Grass quickly embarked on a series of debt-financed acquisitions, and by 1999, the company was having difficulty matching past earnings and obtaining necessary financing. This led to questionable earnings reports, charges of falsifying board minutes, and ultimately the resignation of Grass as CEO. The Grass family is no longer involved in Rite Aid.[12]

Although Rite Aid is an extreme example, it is consistent with a general pattern. The performance record of descendant CEOs is typically poor relative to professional managers, and the market reacts negatively to their appointment.[13] But some descendants have clearly proved themselves capable. A 2001 study found that when the descendant CEO attended a selective university—a proxy for ability—the firm experienced no decline in operating performance relative to firms that appointed outside managers.[14] But descendant CEOs without the prestigious education were associated with a substantial performance decline.

> ## Family Companies and the Cost of Debt
>
> Although a family's controlling block raises concerns about conflicts with other shareholders, it could serve to reduce agency conflicts with bondholders. In their pioneering article on agency costs, Jensen and Meckling* showed that shareholders, as the residual claimant, have an incentive to increase firm risk as a way of transferring wealth from bondholders to themselves. In anticipation of such actions, bondholders demand higher premiums.
>
> Families are long-term investors with substantial wealth at risk. They also regularly access the debt markets. Any attempt at risk shifting in the short term could prove costly in the long run as the family's reputation with debt holders is damaged. In this way, a family's concern about protecting its reputation effectively reassures potential bondholders and other creditors, thus reducing its cost of debt. Consistent with this argument, one study found that family companies in the S&P 500 paid 32 basis points less than comparable non-family firms for bonds with comparable terms and risk.** This was not a size or leverage effect, as family companies and non-family companies have similar debt ratios. The savings were greatest when the families had smaller ownership stakes and if a non-family member or the founder was CEO.
>
> *M. Jensen and W. Meckling, "Theory of the Firm: Managerial Behavior, Agency Costs and Ownership Structure," *Journal of Financial Economics*, Vol. 3 (1976), pp. 305–360.
> **R. Anderson, S. Mansi, and D. Reeb, "Founding-Family Ownership and the Agency Cost of Debt," *Journal of Financial Economics*, Vol. 68 (2003), pp. 263–285.

Interestingly, the performance of the descendant CEOs in our sample of family companies runs counter to the results of the above study. Of the twenty-four companies in our sample with active family members, six had descendants as CEOs. The one-, three-, and five-year returns of these six companies were 41 percent, 141 percent, and 153 percent, respectively. The comparable returns for the eighteen remaining firms were roughly half those, at 19 percent, 70 percent, and 83 percent.[15]

Cost of Dual-Class Shares

Dual-class share structures entrench families, allowing them to enjoy the private benefits of control unavailable to minority shareholders. One indication of the value of the control benefits, and thus the cost to minority shareholders, is the price discount of the low-vote relative to the high-vote shares. In the United States, the best estimate of this discount is about 5–10 percent.[16] One company in our sample, Alberto-Culver, eliminated its dual-class structure in 2003, and the publicly traded low-vote shares experienced a 1.8 percent jump in price on the day of the announcement. At least part of this effect could be attributed to the announcement of quarterly earnings that took place on the same day. But the fact that the price rose by such a small amount suggests that minority investors did not feel particularly harmed by the greater possibility of family entrenchment stemming from the dual-class structure.

The market reaction in this case is actually quite insightful. Keep in mind that the chance of a takeover when the family owns the high-vote shares is negligible. In such a case, the value of both classes of stock then reflects the earnings potential and dividend payout policy of the company under family control. Since U.S. laws afford minority shareholders considerable protection, there should be at most a small discount in the value of low-vote shares, which is what we observe.

But the situation changes when the family's controlling block becomes either splintered or at risk. A change of control then becomes a real possibility, which makes the high-vote shares much more valuable. Consider the experience of Wang Laboratories, controlled by the Wang family. In 1989, An Wang, founder and majority holder of the family's shares, forced his son out as president and announced plans to bring in an outside manager. With the Wang family's control over the company in jeopardy, the premium for the high-vote shares jumped from 5 percent to 62 percent.[17] The increase in the discount suggests that the actual value of control might be a lot more than 5 or 10 percent because investors will pay a significant premium for it when it is available.

Summary

Although the common perception is that public family-run companies make for poor investments, the evidence shows that they actually perform quite well and that there are good reasons for this. The family's concentrated, long-term investment in the company and knowledge of the business make them highly effective and motivated monitors. Their relatively permanent presence also means they can focus on long-term investment and strategy, with less concern for short-term results. Such companies also benefit from the reputations they develop over time with their investors and other stakeholders.

At the same time, family ownership is clearly no guarantee of superior performance. Families can choose to entrench themselves with their controlling position, often through a dual-class share structure, which can lead to risk-averse decision-making and underinvestment. Families are also often inclined to choose one of their own to run the company instead of bringing in and empowering more qualified outside professional managers. Families enjoy the private benefits that come with control, but which can, and often do, occur at the expense of minority shareholders. However, none of these problems condemns an enterprise to failure; whether they do often depends on the family's willingness to surrender at least some control and decision-making authority to outsiders.

Notes

This chapter is based on a research report put out by Henry McVey and his team in August 2005 titled "A Family Portrait." The report benefited greatly from the contributions of Parul Saini, David McNellis, Frances Lim, and Nicole Davison. A number of Morgan Stanley analysts shared their insights on family companies: David Adelman, Douglas Arthur, Lloyd Byrne, Scott Coleman, Nigel Dally, Scott Davis, Chris Gutek, Matt Ostrower, Robert Ottenstein, Bill Pecoriello, Jamie Rollo, Jami Rubin, Stephen Volkmann, and Mark Wiltamuth. Damaris Skouras also provided invaluable insight into family-run companies. Any remaining errors are the responsibility of the authors alone.

1. The first study of public corporation ownership around the world was by R. La Porta, F. Lopez-de-Silanes, and A. Shleifer, "Corporate Ownership Around the World," *Journal of Finance,* Vol. 54 (1999), pp. 471–517.
2. R. Anderson and D. Reeb, "Founding-Family Ownership and Firm Performance: Evidence from the S&P 500," *Journal of Finance,* Vol. 57 (2003), pp. 1301–1328.
3. See J. Weber, L. Lavelle, T. Lowry, W. Zellner, and A. Barrett, "Family, Inc.," *Business Week* (Nov. 2003). B. Villalonga and R. Amit, in "How Do Family Ownership, Control, and Management Affect Firm Value?," Working paper, Wharton School, University of Pennsylvania (2004), concluded that value was created (higher market-to-book) if the founder was still involved, but value was destroyed if the second generation was active in management. B. Maury, in "Family Ownership and Firm Performance: Empirical Evidence from Western European Corporations," *Journal of Corporate Finance,* Vol. 12, No. 2 (2006), pp. 321–341, examined family companies in thirteen Western European countries. He found that for the closest fiscal year ending in 1998, family companies had a 16 percent higher ROA than non-family firms.
4. The agency conflict was first pointed out by A. Berle and G. Means in their classic *The Modern Corporation and Private Property* and was later formulated into a full-blown theory by M. Jensen and W. Meckling in "Theory of the Firm: Managerial Behavior, Agency Costs and Ownership Structure," *Journal of Financial Economics,* Vol. 3 (1976), pp. 305–360.
5. Jensen and Meckling also pointed out the potential for agency conflicts between controlling and minority shareholders.
6. Joseph Astrachan, editor of *Family Business Review,* produced these statistics.
7. One could, of course, argue that the size of the foundation's stake limits the company's potential as an acquisition candidate. One could also argue that, if performance deteriorated sufficiently, the trustees of the foundation could become active. But if this provides some degree of control, it is not the equivalent of either an active family monitor or an entrenched blockholder that destroys value.
8. In the two companies without family member involvement, Boston Scientific and International Flavors & Fragrances, the family owned a significant block of shares, either directly or through a trust.

9. R. Anderson and D. Reeb, "Board Composition: Balancing Family Influence in S&P 500 Firms," *Administrative Science Quarterly* (June 2004).
10. In a survey of CFOs conducted by John Graham and Campbell Harvey, over 40 percent of the 400 respondents said they would pass up a positive net present value (NPV) project just to meet the consensus analyst EPS estimate. See J. Campbell and C. Harvey, "How Do CFOs Make Capital Budgeting and Capital Structure Decisions?," *Journal of Applied Corporate Finance,* Vol. 15 (2002), pp. 8–23.
11. See D. Palia and A. Ravid, "The Role of Founders in Large Companies: Entrenchment or Valuable Human Capital," Working paper, Rutgers University (2002); and R. Fahlenbrach, "Founder-CEOs and Stock Market Performance," Working paper, Wharton School, University of Pennsylvania (2004).
12. For additional details, see R. Berner and M. Maremont, "As Rite Aid Grew, CEO Seemed Unable to Manage His Empire," *Wall Street Journal* (October 20, 1999), p. A1; Mike Bell, "What Happened to Rite Aid?," *Contemporary Topics in Finance,* mimeo, Villanova University.
13. See B. Smith and B. Amoako-Adu, "Management Succession and Financial Performance of Family Controlled Firms," *Journal of Corporate Finance,* Vol. 5 (1999), pp. 341–368; and F. Pérez-González, "Does Inherited Control Affect Performance?," Working paper, Columbia University (2001).
14. Pérez-González (2001), cited earlier, used Barron's (1980) definition of a selective college or university: an institution that considered applicants who ranked in the top 50 percent of their graduating class, a total of ninety colleges.
15. Given the small sample size and the many other factors that affect stock returns, we cannot infer too much from this result. Nonetheless, it is worth pointing out that our sample construction methodology differed considerably from the other studies. By focusing on a narrower definition of family firms, we might have a cleaner measure of descendant motivation and skill.
16. See L. Zingales, "What Determines the Value of Corporate Votes?," *Quarterly Journal of Economics,* Vol. 110 (1995), pp. 1047–1073; and R. Lease, J. McConnell, and W. Mikkelson, "The Market Value of Control in Publicly-Traded Corporations," *Journal of Financial Economics,* Vol. 11 (1983), pp. 439–471.
17. The example is taken from Zingales (1995), cited earlier, who found that, in general, a disruption in control led to a significant increase in the premium.

CHAPTER 11

The Evolution of Shareholder Activism in the United States

STUART L. GILLAN AND LAURA T. STARKS

SHAREHOLDER ACTIVISM IN THE U.S. is by no means a new phenomenon. In the early 1900s, American financial institutions such as insurance companies, mutual funds, and banks were active participants in U.S. corporate governance. In many cases, the representatives of such institutions—among them J. P. Morgan and his associates—served on corporate boards and played major roles in the strategic direction of the firm.

But over the next three or four decades, laws passed with the aim of limiting the power of financial intermediaries also prevented them from having an active role in corporate governance.[1] The Glass-Steagall Act prohibited U.S. banks from owning equity directly. And the regulatory reforms that followed the stock market crash of 1929 limited the liquidity of, and otherwise raised the costs to, investors of active participation in corporate affairs. The consequence of such laws and regulations was a progressive widening of the gap between ownership and control in large U.S. public companies—a process that continued until the emergence of corporate raiders and LBOs in the 1980s.[2]

The current wave of U.S. shareholder activism can be seen as dating from the SEC's introduction in 1942 of a rule (the predecessor of today's Rule 14a-8) that first allowed shareholders to submit proposals for inclusion on corporate ballots. Since that time, the identities of shareholder activists have changed along with the focus of their efforts to bring about change. From 1942 through the end of the 1970s, shareholder activism was dominated by individual investors. The 1980s, by contrast, saw an increase in the involvement of institutional investors, at first mainly public pension funds. These pension funds submitted shareholder proposals, pressured management "behind the scenes" for corporate reforms, and used the press to target the management and boards of poorly governed or performing companies. The 1980s also saw the rise of corporate raiders—perhaps the ultimate activists—who used the market for corporate control to try to impose discipline on boards and managements.

But with the decline of the takeover market during the 1990s and following regulatory changes that enhanced the ability of shareholders to communicate on voting issues, activist institutional investors again came to the fore. At the same time, labor union pension funds began to assume a major role in investor activism. Indeed, as discussed later, a number of innovations in the use of shareholder proposals can be attributed to union-based funds.

While these different varieties of activism can still be seen today, the evolutionary process continues. In particular, during the past few years, hedge funds and private equity funds have assumed prominence in the activist arena. These funds have become increasingly important players in financial markets, particularly in their capacity as monitors of corporate performance and agents of change. In many respects, the hedge funds that take large, relatively long-term positions in underperforming companies (and, contrary to popular perception, there are a significant number of such funds) can be viewed as the modern-day equivalent of the active investors who disciplined U.S. managers at the turn of the last century.

In the pages that follow, we review the evolution of shareholder activism since the establishment of the SEC in the 1930s, with emphasis on three main subjects: the kinds of companies that are targeted by activists; the motives of institutional investors for activism; and the effectiveness of activists in bringing about economically significant change at targeted companies. We finish with an analysis of the most recent changes that have occurred with the entry of hedge funds into shareholder activism.[3]

Varieties of Shareholder Activism

Shareholder activists are often viewed as investors who, dissatisfied with some aspect of a company's management or operations, try to bring about change within the company without a change in control. But one can also think of shareholder activism more broadly as encompassing a continuum of possible responses to corporate performance and activities. At one end, we could view shareholders who simply trade a company's shares as being "active." Through their initial purchases and subsequent decisions to hold or sell, shareholders are expressing their views of the corporation's performance. At the other end of the continuum is the market for corporate control, where investors initiate takeovers and LBOs aimed at accomplishing fundamental corporate changes. Between these extremes are intermediate points on the continuum that include, for example, blockholders who purchase minority stakes with the intent of influencing managerial decision-making.

Dissatisfied shareholders can simply vote with their feet—a practice known as "the Wall Street walk"—by selling their shares. And theoretical and empirical studies provide evidence that the act of selling shares can have disciplinary effects on companies that lead to changes in governance.[4] For example, the probabilities of CEOs being fired and replaced by executives from outside the firm are higher after large sell-offs by institutional investors. Dissatisfied shareholders who choose instead to hold their shares (perhaps because they are "indexed" and so unable to sell) have two choices: (1) do nothing (and thereby exhibit "loyalty") or (2) express their dissatisfaction using some means ranged on the continuum discussed above.[5] Our primary interest in this chapter is in the variety of ways that shareholders have "voiced" their dissatisfaction with managements and boards over the past six decades and how both the identity of the shareholders and the focus of their dissatisfaction have changed.[6]

A Short History of Shareholder Activism

In 1942, after a series of new laws and regulations forced active investors out of corporate governance, the SEC adopted a rule that was the predecessor of and paved the way for the current Rule 14a-8, which states that management must allow shareholder proposals that constitute a "proper subject for action by the security holders." In 1943, shareholders began to submit proposals aimed at improving corporate governance and performance. And the next three decades saw a flood of shareholder resolutions aimed at improving performance and raising share values.

But that was not the only intent of such proposals. In 1970, a federal court decision allowed a shareholder proposal to forbid the sale of napalm by Dow Chemical, and other proposals on social responsibility issues began to appear.[7] To get a sense of the proportion of shareholder proposals devoted to social issues at this time, consider that the member companies of the American Society of Corporate Secretaries reported that 611 of the 790 proposals they received during the 1978 proxy season dealt with governance issues and the other 179 with social issues. As for the disposition of these 790 proposals, 439 were voted on, 197 were excluded from the proxy statements, 125 were withdrawn, and the fate of the remaining 29 is unknown.[8]

Until the mid-1980s, the major proponents of shareholder proposals were individuals that came to be called "gadfly" investors.[9] For example, in 1982, almost 30 percent of the 972 resolutions submitted to 358 companies came from three individuals: Lewis and John Gilbert and Evelyn Davis.[10]

Starting in the mid-1980s, however, shareholder activists began to work in numbers, and a number of groups have arisen—and some have met their demise. For example, T. Boone Pickens established the United Shareholders Association (USA) in 1986 with the expressed intent of "upgrading shareholder awareness." After monitoring and targeting corporations and submitting corporate governance shareholder proposals for seven years, the group's board voted to disband in 1993.[11] Another coalition of individual shareholders, the

Investors' Rights Association of America (IRAA), began submitting proposals in 1995 and did so for a short time.

What is perhaps the newest group of prominent shareholder activists, known as the Investors for Director Accountability, was organized in March of 2006. Headed by luminaries that include John Bogle, T. Boone Pickens, and Robert Monks, the group has declared its goal to be the restoration of directors' accountability to shareholders.[12]

The Growing Role of Institutional Investors

With the suspension of hostile takeovers at the end of the 1980s, and the steady growth in their ownership of U.S. companies, U.S. institutional investors were forced to play a more active role in corporate governance. As can be seen in figure 11.1, institutional investors held only about 10 percent of U.S. equities in 1953, but their percentage ownership had jumped to over 70 percent by the end of 2006.

The beginnings of shareholder activism by institutional investors can be identified in the formation, in 1985, of the Council of Institutional Investors, which was led by Jesse Unruh, then treasurer of the state of California. As state treasurer, Unruh was responsible for the performance of two large institutional

FIGURE 11.1

Percentage Ownership of Institutional Investors in U.S. Stock Markets

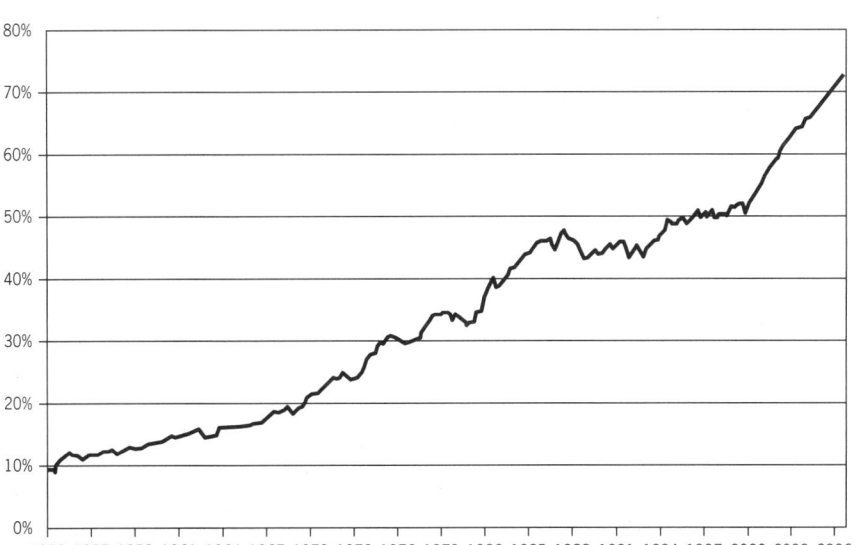

investment funds, the California Public Employees Retirement System (CalPERS) and the California State Teachers Retirement System (CalSTRS). Both of these funds were heavily invested in Texaco. Unruh formed the Council in response to learning that the Bass Brothers, after acquiring a 9.8 percent block in Texaco, sold the shares back to Texaco at a $137 million premium over the current market price—a repurchase offer that was not extended to other shareholders like CalPERS and CalSTRS. The purpose of the Council of Institutional Investors was to act as a lobbying group for shareholder rights.[13]

Still in existence today, the Council has evolved to the point of becoming a focal point for many institutional shareholder activists. Although started as an organization primarily for public pension funds, it now consists of more than 140 public, labor, and corporate pension funds that control in excess of $3 trillion in financial assets. Its stated objective is to enable institutional investors to pool their resources and "use their proxy votes, shareowner resolutions, pressure on regulators, discussions with companies, and, when necessary, litigation to protect plan assets."[14]

Such institutional activism expanded greatly in 1986 and 1987, as large public pension funds began to submit shareholder proxy proposals, both individually and in collaboration with one another. In our own study of proposals by institutional investors during the 1980s and 1990s,[15] we found that the three most common objectives of such proposals were the repeal of antitakeover amendments, the adoption of cumulative voting, and greater board independence. But, as we also discovered, public pension funds changed their approach to activism in the early 1990s. One important change was to submit fewer proxy proposals while trying harder to initiate a dialogue with targeted companies' managements and boards. Another was to make greater use of the media in targeting companies, while alerting other investors to the firm's problems and the activists' proposals.

Until the recent emergence of hedge funds, the most activist institutional investors have been public pension funds and union funds. In the mid-1990s, union funds began to account for a larger proportion of shareholder proposals while the public pension funds' share started to fall. But their labor affiliation notwithstanding, the goals of the union funds have been similar to those of other institutional investors. As Stuart Schwab and Randall Thomas commented in a 1998 *Michigan Law Review* article, "In most cases it is hard to find a socialist or proletarian plot in what unions are doing with their shares. Rather labor activism is a model for any large institutional investor." And since publication of this article, the union funds appear to have persisted in this behavior. Besides submitting shareholder proposals, the unions have pursued innovative forms of activism, not only in terms of developing new proposals, but also by using the media to pressure management (the Teamsters publicly target individual directors rather than just a particular company) and making proposals from the floor at annual meetings.[16]

Along with the rise of institutional investor activism in the mid-1980s, the Department of Labor, through its oversight of Employment Retirement Income Security Act (ERISA) portfolios, began to pressure corporate pension funds to assume a more active role in monitoring the companies in their portfolios. They advocated the voting of proxies by the pension funds rather than delegating that responsibility to their external managers, arguing that voting was part of their fiduciary duty.[17]

Although private pension funds and mutual funds did not generally participate in public shareholder activism, money managers purportedly played a major role in the ouster of some high-profile CEOs. For example, according to *Pensions and Investments,* the removal of James D. Robinson as chairman of American Express was the result of pressure by private money managers, not public pension funds. And Fidelity reportedly had a behind-the-scenes role in Kay Whitmore's departure as the CEO of Eastman Kodak.[18] Money managers have been involved in other types of activism as well. For example, in 2002, Fidelity announced that it would vote against directors if executive compensation was not sufficiently linked to corporate performance. And in that same year, Fidelity took private activism further by appointing one of its own executives, Steve Akin, as chief executive of Colt Telecom, the troubled U.S. telecommunications group.

While the efficacy of institutional activism continues to be the subject of debate, these activists achieved a considerable measure of influence. As one observer noted in 1996, "Fifteen years ago, the CEO and CFO did not know major holders and really didn't care. CEOs are now more accessible to money managers."[19]

Motives for Shareholder Activism

Shareholder activism is, at bottom, a response to the potential gains from addressing the agency conflict at the core of large publicly traded companies with absentee owners. In such companies, shareholders effectively delegate decision-making responsibility to managers whose interests can diverge from those of their shareholders.[20] The board of directors has a significant role in controlling such agency problems that comes with its fiduciary obligation to shareholders, which includes the responsibility to hire, fire, compensate, and monitor top management. The demand for activism arises when boards fail to perform these tasks.

There are a number of remedies for inadequate boards, starting with the fact that common stocks are bought and sold in a marketplace.[21] Precisely because investors can sell their shares to the highest bidder, there is a market for corporate takeovers—or, in academic parlance, a "market for corporate control"—that gives competing management teams, as well as unaffiliated active investors, the ability to gain control of companies, thereby circumventing ineffective managers and boards. But even in cases where there appear to be no bidders, the stock market performs an inherent monitoring function that exerts pressure on managers and boards to make decisions that serve the interests of shareholders. As Bengt Holmstrom and Jean Tirole have argued, the stock market may be the most reliable monitor of managerial performance because stock prices incorporate a variety of kinds of information about future performance and value that cannot be found in financial statements alone.[22]

We now have substantial theoretical and empirical evidence that documents the monitoring role played by institutional investors.[23] When interpreting such evidence, however, it's important to recognize that such investors differ in terms of their trading styles, incentives for managers, clienteles, legal and regulatory environments, and ability to gather and process information. These differences in turn imply differences among institutions' motives and capabilities for monitoring—and the evidence supports this contention. For example, empirical studies suggest that the presence of certain kinds of institutional shareholders in a company's ownership base influences (and is often influenced by) its executive compensation policy, its operating performance, and the market for corporate control that surrounds it. For example, companies with disproportionate holdings by independent investment advisers and mutual funds tend to place greater emphasis on pay for performance, produce consistently higher returns on capital, and avoid value-reducing mergers.[24]

On the other hand, institutional investors, such as corporate pension funds or insurance companies, may be reluctant to undertake activism against other corporations, particularly those with which the sponsoring company does business. Because of business relations with the corporation, some institutional investors may feel compelled to vote with management even though such behavior runs contrary to their fiduciary interests.[25]

Consistent with the idea that institutional investors may face potential conflicts of interest in monitoring companies, a study by Roberta Romano investigated a widely held hypothesis that public pension funds are more effective monitors of management because they vote their own shares, whereas private pension funds typically delegate their voting to external money managers. However, she found no evidence to support this hypothesis. Furthermore, according to a survey of institutional investors from the Investor Responsibility Research Center (IRRC), there has been no significant difference in voting policy between public and private pension funds: both groups tended to support management over the survey period.[26]

A 1993 survey of the forty largest U.S. pension funds, forty of the largest investment managers, and the twenty largest charitable foundations reported finding major differences among institutions—even institutions of the same type—in their attitudes and approaches to shareholder activism. For example, although we might expect to find indexed portfolios more engaged in activism, the survey indicated that while some index fund managers were highly active, most were completely passive. Based on follow-up interviews, the authors of the survey also reported that activist institutions preferred direct negotiation to proxy proposals, in large part because of the difficulty of persuading other institutions to agree on unified proxy strategies. Besides the need for arduous coalition-building among investors, another reason for avoiding proxy campaigns—at least prior to 1993—was regulatory constraints on communication among investors.[27]

Although some public pension funds have been praised for their advocacy of shareholder interests, a number of studies have shown that the incentives of the decision-makers at public pension funds may not be consistent with value-increasing shareholder activism.[28] A 2002 study comparing the relative value of companies held by public and private pension funds reported that corporate values were positively related to private pension fund ownership and negatively related to (activist) public pension ownership. In attempting to explain this finding, the author focused on political and social influences on public pension fund managers that divert their focus from maximizing value.[29]

Some legal scholars have even suggested that the costs of shareholder activism are likely to exceed the benefits, and that the SEC should accordingly consider raising the hurdles for submitting shareholder proposals.[30] In a similar spirit, others have argued that activist institutions often pursue narrow agendas that, rather than aimed at increasing value, have the potential to undermine the effectiveness of corporate boards.[31]

What Companies Get Targeted?

Until recently, the main criterion for the targeting of a corporation by shareholder activists has been poor performance. The targets have also often been characterized by large shareholdings by other institutional investors, low inside ownership, and what investors perceive to be a poor governance structure.[32] Although some of the early targeting by public pension funds and TIAA-CREF focused primarily on companies with questionable governance structures, that practice largely disappeared in the early 1990s. For example, CalPERS, after experimenting with a variety of indicators of substandard governance, settled on poor performance as its primary criterion for targeting in 1990.[33] While in some cases poor performance and poor governance still trigger activist campaigns, recent hedge fund activism has rekindled the focus on profitable companies.[34]

The Evolution of Shareholder Proposals: Issues and Sponsors

The findings of our own (previously cited) study of corporate governance shareholder proposals submitted during the period 1987–1994, when set against the findings of a later study by the proxy firm Georgeson for the period 2001–2005, allows us to see the main issues of interest to shareholder activists and how they have changed over time.[35] As can be seen in both table 11.1 and figure 11.2, both periods saw extensive efforts by activist shareholders to remove poison pills, classified boards, and supermajority antitakeover amendments from corporate charters. Concerns about board independence and executive pay, while certainly in evidence in the earlier period (accounting for 13.7 percent and 11.4 percent, respectively, of all proposals), became much more prevalent in the later period (at 20.4 percent and 33.1 percent). And while the general focus of some of the proposals remained unchanged, there were also notable changes. For example, in the earlier period, the two most common board-related proposals aimed at increasing director share ownership and limiting directors' terms. During the more recent period, the two most common board-related proposals were aimed at achieving director elections through majority vote and independent board chairmen.

Figure 11.3 shows that there were also large changes in the sponsors of the corporate governance proposals between the two periods. Union funds became a much larger force in shareholder activism, submitting over 40 percent of the proposals in 2004 and 2005, as compared with less than 10 percent during the 1987–1994 period. In contrast, public pension funds accounted for a much smaller share of proposals (4 percent, as compared with an earlier 14.2

TABLE 11.1

Number of Corporate Governance Proposals Submitted over Two Separate Periods

Major Issues	1987–1994	2001–2005
Repeal classified board	314	199
Eliminate poison pill	249	220
Cumulative voting	274	93
Supermajority	21	47
Audit-related	19	62
Board-related	279	353
Executive compensation	233	573
Other	653	183
Total	2,042	1,730

FIGURE 11.2

Corporate Governance Proposal Issues across Two Periods

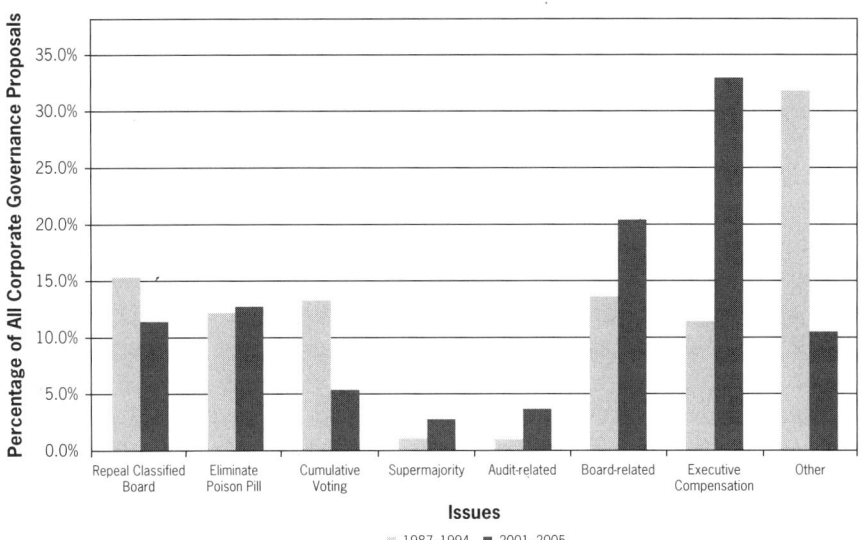

FIGURE 11.3

Sponsors of Corporate Governance Proposals

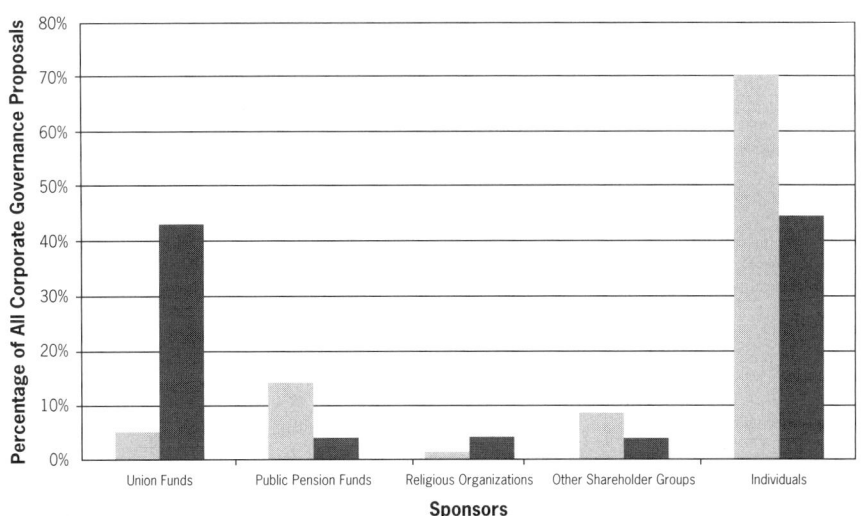

percent), as did unaffiliated individuals (44.5 percent, as compared with an earlier 70.4 percent).

Does Shareholder Activism Work?

Measuring the effectiveness of shareholder activism is a difficult task for several reasons. First, identifying cases of shareholder activism can be problematic. For example, when activists negotiate behind the scenes, there may be no external sign of the activity. Take the case of CalPERS and Texaco cited earlier. CalPERS submitted a shareholder proposal to the company calling for the creation of an advisory committee of major shareholders to work with management. After directly negotiating with Texaco and getting an agreement that management would nominate a pro-shareholder candidate to its board of directors, CalPERS withdrew its proposal.[36] Such activities are not detected by most studies of shareholder activism.

One exception is a study of direct negotiations with targeted companies by one notably activist shareholder, TIAA-CREF.[37] The study found that, of the forty-five companies contacted by TIAA-CREF, 71 percent reached a negotiated settlement prior to the vote on the proposal. The remaining 29 percent of the firms resisted TIAA-CREF's pressures, and the proposals went to a vote. These results suggest both the challenge for researchers posed by unreported events and the understatement of the extent of shareholder activism by studies that focus only on proposals that get put to a vote.

A second problem with such studies is the difficulty in establishing a causal link between shareholder activism and subsequent changes in governance, and between such governance changes and changes in corporate performance. In other words, are observed changes in governance the result of shareholder proposals, public pressure, behind-the-scenes negotiations with activists, or some other influence? And did the changes actually result in increases in the efficiency and value of the targeted firms?

For example, one major aim of shareholder activists has been to get more independent directors on the board. Although we can observe whether there are more independent directors, it is often difficult to attribute the increase to a particular shareholder action. And it is even harder to assess whether the change in the composition of the board led to higher profits and share values.

With these caveats in mind, we now present and discuss the empirical evidence on the effects of shareholder activism. Table 11.2 provides a summary of existing studies of shareholder activism, including the sample period, the type of activism, the identity of the shareholder activists, and the number of proposals and firms. As can be seen in the table, the sample periods all begin after 1985, the beginning of institutional investor activism.[38] Although many of the studies include all active institutions ("sponsors"), some focus on subsets of sponsors, such as public pension funds, labor unions, coordinated groups, or individual pension funds. Finally, the studies vary widely in the number of firms and activist "events" examined.

As might be expected with such a range of issues and sponsors, the studies produce some strikingly different assessments of the extent and effects of shareholder activism. In addition to analysis of the kinds of companies targeted by activists, researchers have devised and tested numerous measures of the influence of shareholder activism. Chief among them are short-term stock market reactions to announcement of shareholder initiatives, longer-term stock market and operating performance, outcomes of votes on shareholder proposals, and changes in corporate strategy and investment decisions in response to activism. In the following sections, we discuss the empirical evidence concerning each of these different ways of evaluating the effectiveness of shareholder activism.

Short-Term Stock Market Reactions

One potential measure of the effects of shareholder activism is whether the announcement of such activism is accompanied by an increase in the company's value. That is, do other investors change their expectations about the value of the firm because they believe that activism will lead to real economic changes? To measure such an increase, researchers commonly examine changes in stock prices around the date of the announcement of the activism. But this kind of analysis has a number of limitations.

One problem is the difficulty in ascertaining exactly when investors first receive the information that a company has been targeted by a shareholder activist. For example, in examining shareholder proposals, the researcher needs to decide whether the critical date is the date of any initial letter to the firm, the proxy mailing, the shareholders' annual meeting, or a separate press release. Given the private nature of communications between corporate management and public pension funds, most studies consider the date of the proxy mailing to be the earliest release of news of a shareholder proposal. If this news caused investors to reassess the firm's valuation, we would expect to be able to detect the change around this date.

On the other hand, some shareholder activists, including CalPERS and the Council of Institutional Investors, announce the list of companies they are targeting at the beginning of the proxy season. When this happens, some of the information has already reached other investors. In addition, many companies are repeat targets, in which case their inclusion may not convey news about the firm in that particular year.

Some studies have also examined stock returns around the date of the shareholders' annual meeting, with the idea that investors may change their

TABLE 11.2

Empirical Studies of Shareholder Activism

Study	Sample Period	Type of Activism	Sponsor of Activism	Number of Firms and Activism Events	Conclusions Regarding Outcomes
Gordon and Pound (1993)	1990	Governance proposals	All sponsors	266 proposals	Voting outcomes depend on governance and performance of target firm and ownership by insiders, institutions, ESOPS, and blockholders.
Nesbitt (1994)	1987–1992	All governance activism	CalPERS	42 firms	Targeted companies underperformed S&P 500 by 66% in five years before targeting and outperformed by 41% in five years after targeting.
Gillan (1995)	1986–1991	Governance proposals	All sponsors	1,019 proposals at 305 firms	While there is a positive stock market reaction to shareholder proposals in some subsamples, on average there is no improvement in long-term stock market performance or operating performance. Public pension fund sponsorship of shareholder proposals is positively associated with the percentage of votes received.
John and Klein (1995)	1991–1992	Social and governance proposals	All sponsors	344 proposals	The likelihood of a firm being the target of corporate governance proposals is significantly affected by firm size, presence of negative net income, percentage of outside directors with outside directorships in other S&P 500 firms, the percentage of institutional ownership and whether or not shareholders vote on the choice of auditor and last year's vote.

Karpoff, Malatesta, and Walkling (1996)	1986–1990	Governance proposals	All sponsors	522 proposals at 269 firms	There is no persuasive evidence that shareholder proposals increase firm values, improve operating performance, or influence firm policies.
D. G. Smith (1996)	1990–1995	Activism aimed at Kmart	All sponsors	1 firm	Concludes that problems were due to managerial incompetence and that shareholder activism is an ineffective mechanism for dealing with this type of problem.
M. Smith (1996)	1987–1993	All governance activism	CalPERS	51 firms	Shareholder wealth increased for firms that settled with CalPERS and decreased for firms that resisted. There were no statistically significant changes in operating performance.
Strickland, Wiles, and Zenner (1996)	1986–1993	Proposals and negotiated settlements	United Shareholders Association	216 proposals at 85 firms	Votes on proposals were higher when target had poor performance and more institutional investors. Out of proposals sponsored by USA found 53 negotiated agreements, which had a small average positive announcement return. Authors concluded USA's actions were successful.
Wahal (1996)	1987–1993	All proposals	Public pension funds	356 proposals at 146 firms	Finds no significant target firm wealth effects from shareholder activism.
Carleton, Nelson, and Weisbach (1998)	1992–1996	Negotiated agreements	TIAA-CREF	62 targetings of 45 firms	Negotiated agreements are generally successful in achieving goals, but whether there are short-term wealth effects depends on issue.

(continued)

TABLE 11.2 (*Continued*)

Study	Sample Period	Type of Activism	Sponsor of Activism	Number of Firms and Activism Events	Conclusions Regarding Outcomes
Johnson, Porter, and Shackell (1997)	1992–1995	Executive compensation proposals	All sponsors	184 firms	Find no effect of proposals on executive compensation.
Johnson and Shackell (1997)	1992–1995	Executive compensation proposals	All sponsors	169 proposals at 106 firms	Find no effect of proposals on executive compensation.
Bizjak and Marquette (1998)	1987–1993	Poison pill rescission proposals	All sponsors	191 proposals at 116 firms	Pill rescission proposals are submitted more frequently when firm performance has been poor, when the initial market reaction to the adoption of the pill is negative, and when insider and block ownership of stock is low. Firms that receive shareholder proposals regarding poison pills are more likely to restructure or rescind the pills.
Campbell, Gillan, and Niden (1998)	1997	All proposals	All sponsors	681 proposals at 394 firms	Governance-related proposals generally receive higher support than social-issue proposals. A high proportion of proposals sponsored by individual investors are omitted on technical grounds.
Crutchley, Hudson, and Jensen (1998)	1992–1997	Target list firms	CalPERS	47 firms	Success of CalPERS activism depends on time period studied. Unless management is pressured into making substantial changes, investors will not benefit from activism.

Del Guercio and Hawkins (1999)	1987–1993	Governance proposals	5 public pension funds	266 proposals at 125 firms	Shareholder proposals are not associated with accounting or stock market performance, but are associated with subsequent changes in corporate governance and corporate activities such as asset sales or restructurings.
Huson (1998)	1990–1992	All governance activism	CalPERS	18 firms	Found significant changes in the real activities of targeted firms. In addition, market reaction to such transactions was significantly more positive, on average, than to comparable transactions before the targeting.
Gillan, Kensinger, and Martin (2000)	1989–1992	Activism aimed at Sears Roebuck	All sponsors	1 firm	Suggestive of activism having a positive influence on Sears's value and that management was pressured to restructure faster than they would have done absent shareholder pressure.
Opler and Sokobin (1995)	1991–1994	Targeted firms on focus lists	Council of Institutional Investors (CII)	117 firms	In year after being listed, firms averaged an 11.6% increase in share price, suggesting that coordinated shareholder activism creates shareholder wealth.
Schwab and Thomas (1998)	1996–1997	Governance proposals	Labor unions	126 proposals at 91 firms	Argues that unions need to align with shareholders, and in so doing, they shift from an antagonistic player to a strategically cooperative player in corporate governance.
Thomas and Martin (1998)	1994	Governance proposals	All sponsors	309 proposals	Find that labor union proposals receive at least as much support as other shareholder group proposals.

(continued)

TABLE 11.2 (*Continued*)

Study	Sample Period	Type of Activism	Sponsor of Activism	Number of Firms and Activism Events	Conclusions Regarding Outcomes
Gillan and Starks (2000)	1987–1994	Governance proposals	All sponsors	2,042 proposals at 452 firms	Shareholder reaction and voting outcome on proposals depend on issue and identity of sponsor. Proposals sponsored by institutions receive much higher votes and more positive reactions.
Prevost and Rao (2000)	1988–1994	Governance proposals	Public pension funds	146 proposals	Find strong negative wealth effects on announcement of targeting.
Choi (2000)	1991–1995	Governance proposals	Institutions	362 proposals at 278 firms	Examines proposals before and after SEC changes in proxy reform rules and finds no difference in voting outcomes after the changes.
Caton, Goh, and Donaldson (2001)	1991–1995	Targeted firms on focus lists	Council of Institutional Investors(CII)	108 firms	Negative market reaction to list release, but increased earnings estimates by financial analysts for subsample companies with solid growth opportunities.
Hann (2002)	1989–1996	Targeted firms	5 public pension funds	150 targeted firms	Characteristics of target can explain whether activism results in successful changes. Can explain why so few studies find significant changes in target.
Song and Szewczyk (2003)	1991–1996	Targeted firms on focus lists	Council of Institutional Investors (CII)	156 firms	Find little evidence of the efficacy of shareholder activism by institutional investors.
English, Smythe, and McNeil (2004)	1992–1997	Target list firms	CalPERS	63 targetings of 47 firms	Announcement effects depend on index used. For some, significantly positive announcement effects, but no long-term abnormal performance after six months.

Study	Period	Focus	Sponsor	Sample	Findings
Wu (2004)	1988–1995	Target list firms in Forbes 500	CalPERS	37 firms	Public targeting is associated with a decrease in the number of inside directors, an increase in the likelihood of CEO dismissal, and an increase in the sensitivity of CEO turnover to performance.
Thomas and Cotter (2006)	2002–2004	Governance proposals	All sponsors	1,454 proposals	Examines shareholder proposals post-Enron and finds many similarities in voting outcomes and market reactions as compared with previous studies. Also reports that recent targeting is not restricted solely to poor performers, and that private investments groups and individuals are most effective in garnering voting support.
Barber (2006)	1992–2005	Target list firms	CalPERS	115 firms	Short-term market reaction to target announcements suggests positive returns.
Del Guercio, Wallis, and Woidtke (2006)	1996–2003	Just vote no campaigns	All sponsors	92 firms	Activism is associated with higher forced CEO and director turnovers, and forced CEO turnovers have positive valuation effects. Activism affects market for directors.
Nelson (2006)	1990–2003	Target list firms	CalPERS	91 firms	Studies on CalPERS activism have used biased parameters and too long a window, and do not exclude contaminating events. Once these are corrected, there are positive results pre-1994, but none post-1994.
Akyol and Carroll (2006)	1990–2004	Poison pill rescission	All sponsors (including company initiated removals)	126 firms	Companies remove pills due to shareholder pressure, including pressure by way of pill rescission proposals. Company-initiated pill removals are also associated with potential pressure from shareholders.

(continued)

TABLE 11.2 (*Continued*)

Study	Sample Period	Type of Activism	Sponsor of Activism	Number of Firms and Activism Events	Conclusions Regarding Outcomes
Prevost, Rao, and Williams (2006)	1998–2002	Governance proposals	Union funds	481 proposals at 232 firms	Results do not support the hypothesis that union fund proposals are indicative of conflicts of interest on the part of such funds seeking to extract gains for employees.
Zenner, Shivdasani, and Darius (2005)	2004–2005	All types of activism	Hedge funds	31 firms	Found significant returns on announcement of activism, primarily driven by returns to targets where the activism was related to merger and acquisition activity.
Bradley, Brav, Goldstein, and Jiang (2006)	1989–2003	Activism with regard to closed-end funds	All sponsors, most were hedge funds	Over 200 open-ending attempts	Activists target closed-end funds with high discounts but discounts shrink on activism.
Klein and Zur (2006)	2003–2005	All types of activism	Hedge funds	194 firms	Found significant returns for period surrounding 13D filing date; no improvement in accounting performance for year after filing, but hedge fund goals were at least partially met about 60% of time.
Brav, Jiang, Partnoy, and Thomas (2006)	2004–2005	All types of activism	Hedge funds	374 firms	Found significant returns for period surrounding 13D filing date; hedge fund achieved their goals in a third of cases and partially achieved their goals in another third of cases.

expectations based on the voting outcome of the shareholder proposals. The problem with this approach, however, is that other important information is often made public during annual meetings. And the same objection can be made to the use of the proxy mailing date, given the other information disclosed in corporate proxy statements.

The second problem with analysis of short-term market reactions is that it is not clear what the investors' responses should be on learning that a company has been targeted by an active shareholder. Shareholder proposals are advisory in nature, which means that even if the proposals pass with 100 percent of the vote, management is not required to implement their directives. In addition, there is a question as to whether the announcement is good news (because it means there is increased monitoring) or bad (because it implies institutional investors could not come to a negotiated agreement with management).

In general, for the overall samples of shareholder proposals, the studies have found no significant abnormal returns around the assumed date of information release.[39] This result tends to be true regardless of whether the study used the announcement date of the target list, the mailing dates of proxies, the annual meeting date, or the *Wall Street Journal* announcement date.

Nevertheless, some studies have reported significant responses to subsamples of the proposals or announcements. For example, some studies found a negative abnormal return for proposals to rescind poison pills, while others reported negative abnormal returns for board-related and antitakeover proposals (which could be driven by the poison pill rescission proposals in this category).[40] The study, discussed earlier, of proposals by TIAA-CREF found that for specific issues like board diversity and blank-check-preferred, there were significant market responses—negative in cases involving board diversity and positive for blank-check-preferred—around the dates of targeting letters from TIAA-CREF.[41] A more recent study by Andrew Prevost and Ramesh Rao focused on two subsamples—companies targeted by CalPERS's proposals and firms receiving proposals from public pension funds—and reported significantly negative stock returns in the three days surrounding the mailing date of the proxy statement containing the proposal.[42] One interpretation is that the failure of management to negotiate with activist shareholders is viewed as bad news in the marketplace. Another is that the event date is noisy, and the abnormal return being captured reflects information other than that related to the shareholder proposal or targeting event.

Some studies have examined the reaction to other aspects of shareholder activism. For example, Deon Strickland, Ken Wiles, and Marc Zenner found that the announcement of a negotiated settlement with a target firm is associated with significantly positive returns, on average.[43] One interpretation of this finding is that such settlements bring about a reduction of uncertainty about some potential liability while also conveying management's commitment to avoid the offending behavior in the future. Another recent study examines a particular activist practice in which institutional investors target the board rather than corporate governance practices by conducting "Just Vote No" campaigns during director elections.[44] The authors report that such campaigns are associated with higher forced CEO and director turnover and that the reputations of the targeted directors are affected by the campaigns.

Voting Outcomes on Shareholder Proposals

Another test of the efficacy of shareholder activism is to examine the voting outcomes of shareholder proposals. In so doing, several factors must be considered. First, shareholder proposals, as already noted, are only advisory; management is not required to adopt the proposal if it receives majority support. Moreover, shareholder activism conducted through the proxy process is subject to considerable managerial control in that managers have the ability to influence both the voting turnout and results. They can do so by excluding shareholder proposals from the proxy (subject to SEC oversight) and by hiring proxy solicitors to garner support for their position.[45]

Studies of voting outcomes on shareholder proposals for earlier periods (late 1980s to early 1990s) have reported that voting support for proposals has depended on a number of variables: the issue addressed by the proposal; the identity of the sponsor; insider ownership; institutional ownership; the number of times a proposal had been submitted; the governance structure and performance of the target firm; and whether the proposal was related to the removal of antitakeover mechanisms. Specifically, favorable votes have been higher in cases involving poison pill repeal proposals, proposals sponsored by public funds, companies with fewer insiders, smaller companies, and companies that had performed poorly in the stock market. Proposals sponsored by institutions, labor unions, or coordinated shareholder groups have also received substantially more support than proposals sponsored by individual investors.[46] Our own study (mentioned earlier) also found a general increase in votes supporting governance proposals over the period we studied (1987–1994).

In addition, research shows that governance proposals typically receive greater support than do social responsibility proposals. For example, a study of the 1997 proxy season reported that governance proposals received an average of 24 percent of votes cast during that year, while social proposals received an average of just 6.6 percent. Furthermore, less than one-third of all social proposals were voted on in contrast to almost 50 percent of governance proposals.[47]

According to the IRRC, 8,600 shareholder proposals were put on proxies during the period 1973–2004. Less than 10 percent of these won majority sup-

FIGURE 11.4

Voting Outcomes for Proposals

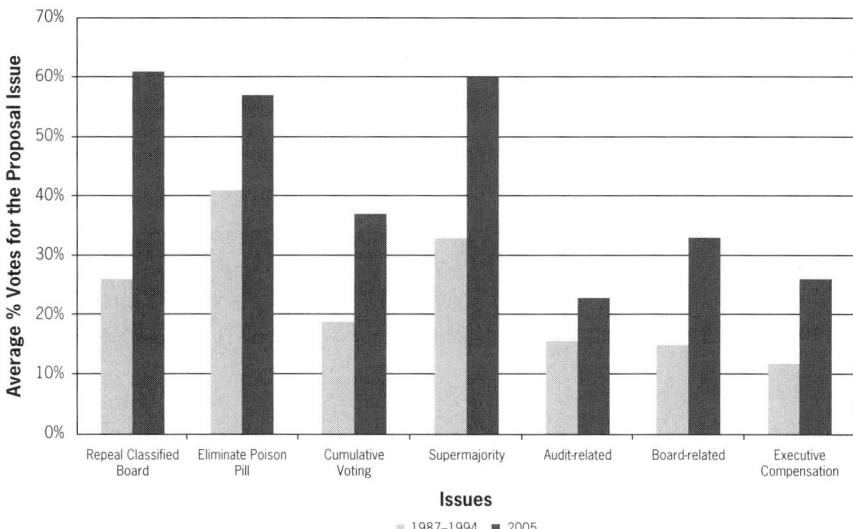

port, but, strikingly, more than half of the majority votes occurred in the 2000–2004 period. Figure 11.4 shows differences in voting outcomes for types of shareholder proposals submitted in 2005 as compared with the earlier 1987–1994 period. As the figure shows, votes in support of proposals have increased significantly, as have the number of proposals aiming to repeal classified boards, eliminate poison pills, and remove supermajority amendments that have commanded over 50 percent of the shareholder vote. Votes in favor of shareholder proposals on executive compensation have more than doubled, from 12 percent to 26 percent. The general increase in voting support for many shareholder proposals likely reflects a number of factors: more concerted action by institutional investors, the existence of proxy voting advisory firms, and the public disclosure of mutual fund proxy votes.[48] One example of more concerted action is the "Just Vote No" campaigns targeting boards of directors.[49]

Several studies have also examined the potential conflicts of interest faced by investment managers when voting on management and shareholder proposals. An early study by James Brickley, Ron Lease, and Cliff Smith suggested that institutional investors that have business dealings with portfolio companies may be pressured to vote with management.[50] However, the more recent evidence on this issue does not suggest that institutions, on average, are "captured" by their business ties.[51]

Studying potential conflicts of interest on the part of mutual funds has resurfaced with new SEC regulations requiring that funds disclose the way they vote their shares in portfolio firms. Two recent studies examining the voting practices of large mutual fund families suggest that the funds studied are no more likely to vote with management at client than nonclient firms. But if there is little direct evidence of conflicts of interest,[52] investment style does seem to influence voting decisions, with stock pickers tending to vote with management and passive indexers more likely to vote against management. Such studies have also reported that funds with longer investment horizons tend to vote in favor of shareholder proposals that are likely to increase shareholders' wealth and rights, and in cases involving companies with weaker governance or entrenched management.[53] Finally, other work suggests that, while shareholder support for management proposals has declined over time, there is no evidence to suggest that the requirement that funds disclose their votes has led to a change in mutual fund voting.[54]

Voting on Management Proposals

Here the studies suggest that management proposals generally pass (they are generally put to shareholder vote only when management is confident of a victory), and uncontested directors receive most of the votes. The evidence also suggests that the degree of shareholder support varies with corporate performance, ownership structure, and a number of characteristics of the proposal. For example, several studies conclude that the percentage of votes cast in favor of stock option plan proposals decreases with the perceived cost to shareholders, typically measured as the potential dilution from the plan.[55] Finally, while there is relatively little variation in voting for directors, recent evidence suggests that voting support for directors has been related to firm performance, director performance, and a firm's shareholder rights. More specifically, directors receive fewer votes when they attend less than 75% percent of board meetings and when Institutional Shareholder Services recommends that their clients vote against them.[56]

Long-Term Performance

The two previous measures of the effects of shareholder activism—stock market reactions to announcements of initiatives and voting outcomes on proposals—are both short-term in nature. But the effects of such activism are likely to show up only gradually over time. To investigate this possibility, studies have examined the long-term performance of the targeted companies, both their returns to shareholders and their operating performance.

The studies' definitions of what constitutes "long-term" have varied from one year to five years. The problem noted earlier of uncertainty about the linkage between cause and effect is exacerbated by long-term performance measures. Even in cases of activism that lead to significant improvements in operating performance or stock appreciation over the next several years, it is difficult to ascertain whether it was activism per se that caused the changes.

The general results of studies of the long-term stock performance of targeted companies have been mixed. An early study (by one of the present writers) focusing on companies targeted for the first time in 1990 or 1991 found no evidence of significant wealth effects.[57] Similarly, two other studies reported no evidence of significant wealth changes for companies targeted over the 1987–1993 period.[58] But studies of interventions by a single institutional investor come to a different conclusion. For example, Stephen Nesbitt's study of CalPERS's governance initiatives showed significant gains for shareholders.[59] And Michael Smith found that those of CalPERS's targets that cooperated with the fund's suggestions saw significant increases in shareholder wealth, while the shareholders of companies that resisted CalPERS's pressure experienced reductions in wealth.[60]

Virtually all studies of long-term operating performance have reported no statistically significant changes in the operating performance of targeted companies.[61] Another potential problem with studies of long-term performance is the choice of an appropriate control group when measuring "abnormal" performance. Since the control firms are usually selected on the basis of being in the same industry and having similar performance, two related questions arise: First, did other activists not included in the study target the control firms? Second, if the control firms were not targeted yet operate in the same industry and had the same performance, then why were the control firms not targeted as well (i.e., there must be important differences between them)?

With regard to the first question, there may be a time-period effect. That is, the activism may be attributed to one activist, or set of activists, when in fact the activism process had been initiated earlier by other investors. For example, a case study of Sears Roebuck (involving one of the present writers) showed that while Sears appeared on CalPERS's target list, the firm was also subject to a proxy fight for board representation by shareholder activist Bob Monks. Moreover, the activism at Sears, although leading to changes in the company's real activities and governance structure, took over three years to reach a "satisfactory" conclusion.

With regard to the second question, researchers need to be careful when assessing why the control firms were somehow insulated from targeting. Given the previous studies of the characteristics of targeted firms, one has to consider a number of possibilities: Were the control firms already in the process of change? Or were there other factors at work, such as lower institutional ownership or greater insider ownership? A related issue is whether any such differences in firm characteristics had an effect on the long-term performance, regardless of the targeting.

Changes in Other Aspects of the Target Firm

A number of studies have investigated how other aspects of the targeted companies have changed in response to shareholder activism. The primary focus of these studies has been on changes in governance structure, investment decisions, and management.

On changes in governance structure, Michael Smith reported that 72 percent of the companies targeted by CalPERS between 1988 and 1993 either adopted CalPERS's proposed changes or made changes resulting in a settlement with the investor. Similarly, poison pills were more likely to be restructured, removed, or put to a shareholder vote after being the subject of a shareholder proposal. Moreover, shareholder pressure has been particularly effective in pill removal post-Enron.[62] One study of pension fund activism showed that, during the three-year period after targeting, the targeted companies saw a greater frequency of governance events, including shareholder lawsuits, non-pension-fund sponsored shareholder proposals, or public "no" votes for directors.[63] On the other hand, another study conducted around the same time found no evidence that the submission of a shareholder proposal on executive compensation was followed by significant changes in compensation levels or pay-for-performance sensitivities.[64]

In an extensive study of the effect of CalPERS's activism on the real activities of targeted companies, Mark Huson found significant changes in the real activities of these firms. In particular, the targeted firms had significantly more divestitures, fewer acquisitions, and more joint ventures. The study also reported that the market reaction to such transactions was significantly more positive, on average, than to comparable transactions before the targeting.[65] Similarly, in their study of companies targeted by five major public pension funds, Diane Del Guercio and Jennifer Hawkins found a greater incidence of restructurings, including asset divestitures and employee layoffs than for a comparable control group of companies.[66]

In contrast, the results of studies focusing on management turnover have been mixed. Some studies reported finding no relation between CEO turnover and shareholder proposals, although there is evidence of higher turnover for other senior managers.[67] But other studies reported higher CEO turnover, as well as a decrease in board size, in companies targeted by CalPERS.[68]

One other way to test the effectiveness of investor activism is to examine the extent to which boards have implemented majority vote shareholder proposals, and how that has changed, if at all, over time. A recent study concluded that the frequency of implementations has more than doubled, from 16 percent in 1997 to over 40 percent in 2003–2004. Moreover, the probability that a proposal was implemented has increased with the percentage of votes cast in favor of the proposal and the percentage of stock owned by activist shareholders. At the same time, however, shareholder proposals related to board issues and executive pay have been less likely to be implemented than other kinds of proposals.[69]

New Kids on the Block: Hedge Funds and Shareholder Activism

During the past decade or so, hedge funds have not only entered the shareholder activism arena but have become a dominant force. Recent examples include Relational Investors and Home Depot, Pershing Square and Wendy's International, Icahn Partners and Time Warner, and Breeden Partners and Applebee's International.

The hedge funds have a variety of goals in their activism. The most common ones are as follows: changing management strategy or board decisions; seeking a board seat for either input, control, or information purposes; effecting corporate governance changes; forcing a buyout or sale of a division; and increasing cash distributions to shareholders through dividends or share repurchases. While the hedge funds use some of the same strategies as those employed by the traditional institutional activists—including shareholder proposals, direct negotiations, and use of the media—they also use other means such as proxy contests, litigation, or outright takeover.[70] Even their use of traditional institutional activist strategies is often different in its application. For example, one study concludes that the Hermitage Fund has been successful in lobbying the media to cover corporate governance violations of Russian public corporations, and thereby helping to bring about the Fund's desired changes in those companies.[71]

One form of shareholder activism that is sometimes practiced by hedge funds is relationship investing. By definition, this is an ongoing relationship between the institutional investors and the firm.[72] And for a number of reasons, the shareholder consequences of such activism are difficult to measure. As noted earlier (when discussing the case of Sears), when activism occurs over a number of years and often involves different investors, it is difficult to attribute the outcome to any single activist or strategy.

Although proxy contests were a traditional form of shareholder voice that was used extensively in the 1980s, the rising expense of waging a proxy battle caused use of this tactic to fall off sharply. But with the rise of hedge funds, the proxy contest has staged a comeback. For example, there were ninety-one proxy contests over board elections in 2006, up from forty in 2005 and thirty in 2004; most of the increase has been attributed to the growth and proliferation of hedge funds engaged in such contests.[73] Another likely contributor to the recent jump in proxy contests was the SEC's 1992 easing of rules limiting communication between shareholders.[74]

A number of questions have arisen about the effectiveness of hedge fund activism: For example, have hedge funds really succeeded in adding value to the companies they have targeted; or have most of the returns to hedge funds been short-term profits at the expense of other, longer-term shareholders? Do hedge funds have the appropriate organizational structure to bring about change in the underlying target firms? And do hedge funds' incentives for activism differ from those of other kinds of institutional activists?[75]

While there is no shortage of anecdotal reports of the failures (such as Icahn Partners' efforts with Blockbuster) and successes (Relational Investors' recent ouster of the CEO of Home Depot) of hedge fund activism, the general lack of information about hedge funds' activities and holdings has prevented researchers from assessing benefits and costs. Nevertheless, a handful of studies have attempted systematic investigations of the consequences of hedge fund activism using the information provided in the funds' filings of 13Ds. For example, in a recent study of 194 13D filings by 102 hedge funds during the period 2003–2005, the authors reported a sixty-one-day announcement period return of 10.3 percent.[76] Another study (by different authors) of 374 13D filings by 110 hedge funds during the period 2004–2005 reported a twenty-day announcement period return of 5–7 percent.[77]

These results indicate that there are short-term gains associated with hedge fund activism. But one problem with drawing firm conclusions from these results is our inability to ascertain when the hedge funds purchased and sold the shares, making it difficult to determine whether the hedge funds themselves earned abnormal returns on their investments. One study that may help resolve this issue examined the actual trades of a U.K. fund (the Hermes U.K. Focus Fund) and reported that the fund earned returns in excess of the benchmarks.[78] In the U.S., a study of Relational Investors' activities (by one of the present writers) provides evidence that the fund has succeeded in targeting underperformers and beating benchmark returns.[79]

It is also difficult to distinguish announcement effects that derive from the knowledge that a hedge fund is engaging in shareholder activism from the longer-term effects that actually result from the activism. The study of the Hermes fund cited above accomplished this by linking the (longer-term) excess returns derived from the fund's activism directly to the success of specific initiatives, such as replacing directors, blocking diversifying acquisitions, and increasing payouts. And consistent with these findings, two studies of U.S. hedge fund activism have reported that management often acquiesces to the hedge funds' demands (at least partially in over 60 percent of the cases examined).[80]

A study of the role of activism in "open-ending" closed-end funds provides further evidence of the success of shareholder activists, primarily hedge funds. Activists pressing for the open-ending of closed-end funds have used a variety of tactics, including negotiations, shareholder proposals, and proxy contests, with the latter accounting for a little over half of the attempts. No strategy has been completely reliable, as the authors report that the number of successful open-endings is much smaller than the number attempted. But even unsuccessful attempts at open-ending closed-end funds have tended to narrow the discounts at which the funds trade in relation to their net asset values (NAVs).[81]

On the other hand, legal scholars have expressed concern about potential problems related to some aspects of hedge fund activism. For example, Henry Hu and Bernie Black have noted potential problems associated with the separation of economic ownership from voting rights—a separation that, according to Hu and Black, has been exploited by hedge funds in their relatively new practice of voting on shares they no longer own. (Such a practice, known as "empty voting," could conceivably be used by short sellers to advocate measures that would reduce firm value.) Hedge funds can also achieve and maintain effective economic ownership without having to reveal it by forgoing voting rights (a condition the authors term "hidden ownership"). And if, as some have argued,[82] hedge funds have a shorter-term orientation than other investors, such ownership could cause problems.

Conclusion

Investor activism in the form of shareholder proposals has existed since the SEC's adoption in 1943 of Rule 14a-8. Between 1943 and the mid-1980s, the shareholder proposal process was almost exclusively the domain of individual shareholders and religious or political groups. But with the initiation of public pension fund activism in 1985, the involvement of large institutional shareholders increased dramatically.

The main motive for active participation by institutional investors in the monitoring of corporations has been the potential to enhance the value of their investments. But since the active investors incur *all* the costs associated with such activism (while the benefits accrue to all shareholders), only shareholders with large positions are likely to obtain a large enough return on their investment to justify the costs.

The evidence provided by empirical studies of the effects of shareholder activism is mixed. While some studies have found positive short-term market reactions to announcements of certain kinds of activism, there is little evidence of improvement in the long-term operating or stock-market performance of the targeted companies. Studies have reported significant changes in the business activities of companies targeted by shareholder initiatives, but it is difficult to establish a causal relationship between shareholder activism and these changes. The relatively recent entrance of hedge funds into shareholder activism has provided more evidence of gains from activism, but the long-term effects are still unknown and warrant more research.

Notes

1. See Roe (1990). Full citations of all articles appear in the References section.
2. See Bhide (1990, 1993).
3. For previous surveys of shareholder activism, see Black (1998), Gillan and Starks (1998), Karpoff (2001), and Romano (2000). Partnoy and Thomas (2006) contrast shareholder activism by hedge funds and institutional investors.
4. For analyses of the effects of selling shares on corporate governance, see Admati and Pfleiderer (2006); or Parrino, Sias, and Starks (2003).
5. Hirschman (1971).
6. Our focus in this review is on studies of corporate governance issues and attempts to link governance-based activism to shareholder value. This is notably different from the intent of, say, Tkac (2006), who provides an analysis of shareholder proposals with particular focus on social issues.
7. Manne (1972).
8. American Society of Corporate Secretaries, 1979, *Report on Shareholder Proposals July 1, 1978 to June 30, 1979*.
9. Some of the gadflies had been submitting proposals since they were first allowed in 1942. In fact, according to Talner (1983), the activism of the Gilbert Brothers can be traced to a 1932 annual shareholders meeting of Consolidated Gas in which the chairman never recognized any of the shareholders who had raised their hand to ask questions. Lewis Gilbert was reportedly appalled by the lack of communication between management and shareholders.
10. N. Ross, 1983, "Gadflies Set to Buzz Shareholders' Meetings," *Washington Post* (Apr. 17), G1.
11. See Strickland, Wiles, and Zenner (1996) and Speeches of T. Boone Pickens: http://digital.library.okstate.edu/Pickens/1988/062488A2.html.
12. Tiffany Kary, 2006, "Upstart Investors for Director Accountability Target Pfizer," Marketwatch.com.
13. See Monks and Minow (2003).
14. Council of Institutional Investors Website, 2006: http://www.cii.org.
15. Gillan and Starks (2000).
16. Prevost, Rao, and Williams (2006); and Schwab and Thomas (1998).
17. The 1994 release of the Department of Labor's Interpretative Bulletin 94-2 (IB 94-2) took an even stronger stance on the responsibility of corporate pension funds by stating that, "active monitoring and communication with corporate management is consistent with a fiduciary's obligations under ERISA where the responsible fiduciary concludes that there is a reasonable chance that such activities . . . are likely to enhance the value of the plan's involvement, after taking into account the costs involved."
18. See *Pensions and Investments*, 1993, "The Value of Activism" (Feb. 22), 12; and A. Myerson, 1993, "Wall Street, the New Activism at Fidelity," *New York Times* (Aug. 8), Section 3, 15.
19. Ettorre (1996).
20. Jensen and Meckling (1976).
21. Eugene Fama and Michael Jensen suggest that the unrestricted nature of common stock residual claims allows special market and organizational mechanisms for controlling these problems (Fama and Jensen, 1983).
22. Holmstrom and Tirole (1993).
23. Examples include Agrawal and Mandelker (1992), Almazan and Suarez (2003), Black (1992), Del Guercio and Hawkins (1999), Gillan and Starks (2000), Hartzell and Starks

(2003), Kahn and Winton (1998), Kaplan and Minton (1994), and Noe (2002). There is also a broad literature examining the role of shareholders in general: for example, Admati, Pfleiderer, and Zechner (1994); Black (1990); Bolton and von Thadden (1998); Chidambaran and John (1998); Coffee (1991); Huddart (1993); Maug (1998); Maug and Rydqvist (2006); Noe (2002); and Shleifer and Vishny (1986), among others.

24. Almazan, Hartzell, and Starks (2005); Borokhovich, Brunarski, Harman, and Parrino (2006); Brickley, Lease, and Smith (1988); Bushee (1998, 2001); Chen, Li, and Harford (2006); Cornett, Marcus, Tehranian (2004); Gaspar, Massa, Matos (2005); Pinkowitz (2003); and Qiu (2005).
25. Brickley, Lease, and Smith (1988); and Pound (1988).
26. Romano (1993).
27. Bradley, Brav, Goldstein, and Jiang (2006); and Useem, Bowman, Myatt, and Irvine (1993).
28. Murphy and Van Nuys (1994); and Woidtke, Bierman, and Tuggle (2003).
29. Woidtke (2002).
30. Romano (2000).
31. Bainbridge (2005).
32. Carleton, Nelson, and Weisbach (1998); Huson (1997); John and Klein (1995); Karpoff, Malatesta, and Walkling (1996); and Smith (1996).
33. Thomas and Cotter (2006).
34. Brav, Jiang, Partnoy, and Thomas (2006); and Klein and Zur (2006).
35. Data for the early period come from Gillan and Starks (2000). Data for the latter period come from Georgeson Shareholders' 2005 Annual Corporate Governance Review.
36. M. Parker, 1989, "It's Almost Spring, and That Means Proxy Fever," *New York Times* (March 5), Section 3, 8.
37. Carleton, Nelson, and Weisbach (1998).
38. The shortest analyses focus on proposals in a single year (e.g., Gordon and Pound, 1993; Campbell, Gillan, and Niden, 1998). The longest is our own study of the eight-year period 1987–1994 cited earlier (Gillan and Starks, 2000). Most of the studies examine the submission of shareholder proposals related to corporate governance, but some studies also include shareholder proposals aimed at social reforms (John and Klein, 1995; Campbell, Gillan, and Niden, 1998). In addition, some studies emphasize other types of activism: firms on focus lists (Anson, White, and Ho, 2004; Barber, 2006; Caton, Goh, and Donaldson, 2001; Crutchley, Hudson, and Jensen, 1998; English, Smythe, and McNeil, 2004; Nelson, 2006; Opler and Sokobin, 1995; Song and Szewczyk, 2003), negotiated agreements (Carleton, Nelson, and Weisbach, 1997; Strickland, Wiles, and Zenner, 1996), and all activism aimed at a single firm (Gillan, Kensinger, and Martin, 2000; D. Smith, 1996).
39. See, for example, Carleton, Nelson, and Weisbach (1998); Del Guercio and Hawkins (1999); Gillan and Starks (2000); Karpoff, Malatesta, and Walkling (1996); Prevost and Rao (2000); Smith (1996); Song and Szewczyk (2003); and Wahal (1996).
40. Bizjak and Marquette (1998) and Gillan and Starks (2000) find negative abnormal returns for pill rescission proposals; Del Guercio and Hawkins (1999) focus on board-related issues and the repeal of antitakeover measures (including pills).
41. See Carleton, Nelson, and Weisbach (1998).
42. Generalizations from some of these results should be viewed with caution, for the number of observations in the subsamples are small (twenty-two and sixteen in the Carleton, Nelson, and Weisbach [1998] paper and fifteen and twenty-three in the Prevost and Rao [2000] study).

43. Strickland, Wiles, and Zenner (1996).
44. Del Guercio, Wallis, and Woidtke (2006).
45. When seeking support for management proposals, management can bundle hard-to-pass decisions with other proposals and classify proposals as routine in order to increase the number of votes in their favor; Bethel and Gillan (2002).
46. See Bizjak and Marquette (1998), Gillan and Starks (2000), Gordon and Pound (1993), and Thomas and Martin (1998).
47. See Campbell, Gillan, and Niden (1998).
48. According to Alexander, Chen, Seppi, and Spatt (2006), proxy advisory services have significant effects on voting outcomes, and their recommendation announcements are associated with significant abnormal returns.
49. Del Guercio, Wallis, and Woidtke (2006).
50. Brickley, Lease, and Smith (1988).
51. To consider one example, Karen Van Nuys (1993), when examining the 1987 proxy fight at Honeywell, found that banks and insurance companies were more supportive of management-sponsored antitakeover proposals than public pension funds and independent investment managers. But, on closer inspection, Van Nuys found no evidence of business ties between Honeywell and its shareholders that would account for this pattern of voting.
52. Davis and Kim (2006) and Rothberg and Lilien (2005).
53. Ashraf and Nayaran (2006) and Rothberg and Lilien (2005).
54. Cremers and Romano (2006).
55. See Bethel and Gillan (2000); Martin and Thomas (2005); Morgan and Poulsen (2001); and Morgan, Poulsen, and Wolf (2006). In the context of mergers, Burch, Morgan, and Wolf (2004) report that voting support varies substantially with firm and deal characteristics.
56. Cai, Garner, and Walkling (2006); and Fischer, Gramlich, and Miller (2006).
57. Gillan (1995).
58. Del Guercio and Hawkins (1999) and Wahal (1996).
59. Nesbitt (1994).
60. Smith (1996). Another study, Opler and Sokobin (1995), reported that stock market performance improved after a company appeared on the Council of Institutional Investors' focus list. But more recent papers call this result into question. See, particularly, Song and Szewczyk (2003).
61. Del Guercio and Hawkins (1999); Karpoff, Malatesta, and Walkling (1996); Smith (1996); Strickland, Wiles, and Zenner (1996); and Wahal (1996).
62. Akyol and Carroll (2006) and Bizjak and Marquette (1998).
63. Del Guercio and Hawkins (1999).
64. Johnson and Shackell (1997); and Johnson, Porter, and Shackell (1997).
65. Huson (1997).
66. Del Guercio and Hawkins (1999).
67. Smith (1996); Karpoff, Malatesta, and Walkling (1996); and Del Guercio and Hawkins (1999) find that the target firms do not have a higher frequency of CEO turnover; however, Del Guercio and Hawkins (1999) do find a higher frequency of turnover for other executives.
68. Huson (1997) and Wu (2004) report increased turnover; Wu, in particular, reports that board size declines.
69. Ertimur, Ferri, and Stubben (2006).
70. Kahan and Rock (2006); Pearson and Altman (2006); and Zenner, Shivdasani, and Darius (2005).

71. Dyck, Volchkova, and Zingales (2006).
72. Any long-term relationship between large shareholders and companies can be termed relationship investing. For studies on block shareholders, see, for example, Bethel, Liebiskind, and Opler (1998); Denis and Kruse (2000); and Denis and Serrano (1996). For studies on relationship investing specifically, see Bethel and Gillan (2007); Bhagat, Black, and Blair (2004); Gillan, Kensinger, and Martin (2000); Martin and Kensinger (1996); Rock (1994); and Wruck and Wu (2005).
73. K. Whitehouse, 2007, "Proxy Fights Hit High in 2006, and More Seen for 2007," Dow Jones News Service.
74. See, for example, Collins and DeAngelo (1990), DeAngelo (1988), DeAngelo and DeAngelo (1989), Faleye (2004), Ikenberry and Lakonishok (1993), Mulherin and Poulsen (1998), and Pound (1988).
75. Kahan and Rock (2006).
76. Klein and Zur (2006).
77. Brav, Jiang, Portnoy, and Thomas (2006).
78. Becht, Franks, Mayer, and Rossi (2006).
79. Bethel and Gillan (2007).
80. Brav, Jiang, Portnoy, and Thomas (2006); and Klein and Zur (2006).
81. Bradley, Brav, Goldstein, and Jiang (2006).
82. Kahan and Rock (2006).

References

Admati, A., P. Pfleiderer, 2005, The Wall Street Walk as a Form of Shareholder Activism. Working paper, Stanford University.

Admati, A., P. Pfleiderer, and J. Zechner, 1994, "Large Shareholder Activism, Risk-Sharing, and Financial Market Equilibrium," *Journal of Political Economy* 102, 1097–1130.

Agrawal, Anup, and Gerald Mandelker, 1992, "Shark Repellants and the Role of Institutional Investors in Corporate Governance," *Managerial and Decision Economics* 13, 15–22.

Akyol, Ali C., and Carolyn Carroll, 2006, Removing Poison Pills: A Case of Shareholder Activism. Working paper, University of Alabama.

Alexander, C., M. Chen, D. Seppi, and C. Spatt, 2006, The Role of Advisory Services in Proxy Voting. Working paper, University of Maryland.

Almazan, Andres, Jay Hartzell, and Laura Starks, 2005, "Active Institutional Shareholders and Cost of Monitoring: Evidence from Executive Compensation," *Financial Management* 34, 5–34.

Almazan, Andres, and Javier Suarez, 2003, "Managerial Compensation and the Market Reaction to Bank Loans," *Review of Financial Studies* 16, 237–261.

American Society of Corporate Secretaries, 1953, *Analysis of Stockholder Proposed Resolutions Submitted under Rule X-14a-8 of the Securities and Exchange Commission.*

Anson, M., T. White, and H. Ho, 2004, "Good Corporate Governance Works: More Evidence from CalPERS," *Journal of Asset Management*, 5(3), 149–156.

Ashraf A., and N. Jayaraman, 2006, Determinants and Consequences of Proxy Voting by Mutual Funds on Shareholder Proposals. Working paper, Georgia Tech.

Bainbridge, S., 2005, Shareholder Activism and Institutional Investors. UCLA School of Law, Law-Economics Research Paper 05-20.

Barber, B., 2006, Monitoring the Monitor: Evaluating CalPERS Activism. Working paper, University of California at Davis.

Becht, M., J. Franks, C. Mayer, and S. Rossi, 2006, Returns to Shareholder Activism: Evidence from a Clinical Study of the Hermes U.K. Focus Fund. Working paper, ECGI-finance.

Bethel, J., and S. Gillan, 2002, "The Impact of the Institutional and Regulatory Environment on Shareholder Voting," *Financial Management* 31, 29–54.

Bethel, J., and S. Gillan, 2007, Relationship Investing, Corporate Change and Shareholder Value. Working paper, Babson College and Texas Tech University.

Bethel, J., J. Liebiskind, and T. Opler, 1998, "Block Share Purchases and Corporate Performance," *Journal of Finance* 53(2), 605–635.

Bhagat, S., B. Black, and M. Blair, 2004, "Relational Investing and Firm Performance," *Journal of Financial Research* 27, 1–30.

Bhide, A., 1990, "Efficient Markets, Deficient Governance: U.S. Securities Regulations Protect Investors and Enhance Market Liquidity. But Do They Alienate Managers and Shareholders?" *Harvard Business Review* 72(6), 128–140.

Bhide, A., 1993, "The Hidden Costs of Stock Market Liquidity," *Journal of Financial Economics* 34, 31–51.

Bizjak, J. M., and C. Marquette, 1998, "Shareholder Proposals to Rescind Poison Pills: All Bark and No Bite," *Journal of Financial and Quantitative Analysis* 33, 499–521.

Black, B. S., 1990, "Shareholder Passivity Reexamined," *Michigan Law Review* 89, 520–608.

Black, B. S., 1992, "Agents Watching Agents: The Promise of Institutional Investor Voice," *UCLA Law Review* 39, 811–893.

Black, B. S., 1998, "Shareholder Activism and Corporate Governance in the United States," in *The New Palgrave Dictionary of Economics and the Law,* ed. P. Newman. New York: Macmillan.

Bolton, P., and E. von Thadden, 1998, "Blocks, Liquidity, and Corporate Control," *Journal of Finance* 53, 1–25.

Borokhovich, K., K. Brunarski, Y. Harman, and Robert Parrino, 2006, "Variation in the Monitoring Incentives of Outside Blockholders," *Journal of Law and Economics* 49, 651–680.

Bradley, M., A. Brav, I. Goldstein, and W. Jiang, 2006, Costly Communication, Shareholder Activism, and Limits to Arbitrage. Working paper, Duke University, Wharton School, and Columbia University.

Brav, A., W. Jiang, F. Partnoy, and R. Thomas, 2006, Hedge Fund Activism, Corporate Governance and Firm Performance. Working paper, Duke University, Columbia University, University of San Diego, and Vanderbilt University.

Brickley, J., R. Lease, and C. Smith, 1988, "Ownership Structure and Voting on Antitakeover Amendments," *Journal of Financial Economics* 20, 267–292.

Burch, T. R., A. G. Morgan, and J. G. Wolf, 2004, "Is Acquiring Firm Shareholder Approval in Stock-for-Stock Mergers Perfunctory?," *Financial Management* 33(4), 45–69.

Burkart, Mike, Dennis Gromb, and Fausto Panunzi, 1997, "Large Shareholders, Monitoring and the Value of the Firm," *Quarterly Journal of Economics* 112(3), 693–798.

Bushee, Brian J., 1998, "The Influence of Institutional Investors on Myopic R&D Investment Behavior," *Accounting Review* 73, 305–333.

Bushee, Brian J., 2001, "Do Institutional Investors Prefer Near-Term Earnings over Long-Run Value?," *Contemporary Accounting Research* 18, 207–246.

Cai, J., J. L. Garner, and R. A. Walkling, 2006, Electing Directors. Working paper, Drexel University.

Campbell, C., S. Gillan, and C. Niden, 1999, "Current Perspectives on Shareholder Proposals: The 1997 Proxy Season," *Financial Management* 28, 89–98.

Carleton, W. T., J. M. Nelson, and M. S. Weisbach, 1998, "The Influence of Institutions on Corporate Governance Through Private Negotiations: Evidence from TIAA-CREF," *Journal of Finance*, 53(4), 1335–1362.

Caton, Gary, Jeremy Goh, and Jeffrey Donaldson, 2001, "The Effectiveness of Institutional Activism," *Financial Analysts Journal* 57(4), 21–26.

Chen, Xia, Jarrad Harford, and Kai Li, 2006, "Monitoring: Which Institutions Matter?," *Journal of Financial Economics*, 279–305.

Chidambaran, N., and K. John, 1998, Relationship Investing: Large Shareholder Monitoring with Managerial Cooperation. Working paper, New York University.

Choi, S., 2000, "Proxy Issue Contests: The Impact of the 1992 Proxy Reforms," *Journal of Law, Economics and Organizations* 16, 233–268.

Coffee, J., 1991, "Liquidity versus Control: The Institutional Investor as Corporate Monitor," *Columbia Law Review* 91, 1277–1368.

Collins, D. W., and L. DeAngelo, 1990, "Accounting Information and Corporate Governance: Market and Analyst Reactions to Earnings of Firms Engaged in Proxy Contests," *Journal of Accounting and Economics* 13(3), 213–248.

Cornett, M., A. Marcus, A. Saunders, and H. Tehranian, 2006, The Impact of Institutional Ownership on Corporate Operating Performance. Working paper, New York University.

Cremers, M., and R. Romano, 2006, Institutional Investors and Proxy Voting: The Impact of the 2003 Mutual Fund Voting Disclosure Regulation. Working paper, Yale University.

Crutchley, C., C. Hudson, and M. Jensen, 1998, "Shareholder Wealth Effects of CalPERS Activism," *Financial Services Review* 7, 1–10.

Davis, Gerald F., and E. Han Kim, 2006, "How Do Business Ties Influence Proxy Voting by Mutual Funds?," *Journal of Financial Economics*.

DeAngelo, Linda E., 1988, "Managerial Compensation, Information Costs, and Corporate Governance: The Use of Accounting Performance Measures in Proxy Contests," *Journal of Accounting and Economics* 10, 3–36.

DeAngelo, Linda E., and H. DeAngelo, 1989, "Proxy Contests and the Governance of Publicly Held Corporations," *Journal of Financial Economics* 23, 29–59.

Del Guercio, Diane, and Jennifer Hawkins, 1999, "The Motivation and Impact of Pension Fund Activism," *Journal of Financial Economics* 52, 293–340.

Del Guercio, Diane, Laura Wallis, and Tracie Woidtke, 2006, Do Boards Pay Attention when Institutional Investors 'Just Vote No'?: CEO and Director Turnover Associated with Shareholder Activism. Working paper, University of Tennessee.

Denis, D., and T. Kruse, 2000, "Managerial Discipline and Corporate Restructuring Following Performance Declines," *Journal of Financial Economics* 55, 391–424.

Denis, David, and Jan Serrano, 1996, "Active Investors and Management Turnover Following Unsuccessful Control Contests," *Journal of Financial Economics* 40, 239–266.

Dyck, A., N. Volchkova, and L. Zingales, 2006, The Corporate Governance Role of the Media: Evidence from Russia. Working paper, University of Toronto, New Economic School, and University of Chicago.

English, Philip C., Thomas I. Smythe, and Chris R. McNeil, 2004, "The CalPERS Effect Revisited," *Journal of Corporate Finance* 10, 157–174.

Ertimur, Yonca, Fabrizio Ferri, and Stephen R. Stubben, 2006, Board of Directors' Responsiveness to Shareholders: Evidence from Majority-Vote Shareholder Proposals. Working paper, Harvard Business School.

Ettorre, B., 1996, "When Patience Is a Corporate Virtue," *Management Review* 85(11), 28–32.

Faleye, O., 2004, "Cash and Corporate Control," *Journal of Finance,* 59(5), 2041–2060.

Fama, Eugene, and Michael Jensen, 1983, "Separation of Ownership and Control," *Journal of Law and Economics* Vol. 26, 301–325.

Fischer, Paul E., Jeffrey D. Gramlich, and Brian P. Miller, 2006, Are Uncontested Director Elections Meaningful? Working paper, Pennsylvania State University.

Gaspar, J. M., M. Massimo, and P. Matos, 2005, "Shareholder Investment Horizon and the Market for Corporate Control," *Journal of Financial Economics* 76(1), 135–165.

Gillan, S. L., 1995, "Shareholder Activism through the Proxy Mechanism: An Empirical Investigation," PhD diss., University of Texas at Austin.

Gillan, S. L., J. W. Kensinger, and J. D. Martin, 2000, "Value Creation and Corporate Diversification: The Case of Sears Roebuck & Co.," *Journal of Financial Economics* 55, 103–137.

Gillan, Stuart, and Laura Starks, 1998, "A Survey of Shareholder Activism: Motivation and Empirical Evidence," *Contemporary Finance Digest* 2, 10–34.

Gillan, Stuart, and Laura Starks, 2000, "Corporate Governance Proposals and Shareholder Activism: The Role of Institutional Investors," *Journal of Financial Economics* 57, 275–305.

Gordon, L., and J. Pound, 1993, "Information, Ownership Structure, and Shareholder Voting: Evidence from Shareholder-Sponsored Corporate Governance Proposals," *Journal of Finance* 47(2), 697–718.

Hann, Rebecca, 2002, On the Effectiveness of Pension Fund Activism. Working paper, University of Southern California.

Hartzell, Jay C., and Laura T. Starks, 2003, "Institutional Investors and Executive Compensation," *Journal of Finance* 58, 2351–2374.

Hirschman, A., 1971, *Exit, Voice and Loyalty: Responses to Decline in Firms, Organizations, and States*. Cambridge, MA: Harvard University Press.

Holmstrom, B., and J. Tirole, 1993, "Market Liquidity and Performance Monitoring," *Journal of Political Economy* 101(4), 678–709.

Hu, H., and B. Black, Hedge Funds, Insiders, and Decoupling of Economic and Voting Ownership in Public Companies: Empty Voting and Hidden (Morphable) Ownership. Working paper, University of Texas at Austin.

Huddart, S., 1993, "The Effect of a Large Shareholder on Corporate Value," *Management Science* 39, 1407–1421.

Huson, M., 1997, Does Governance Matter? Evidence from CalPERS Interventions. Working paper, University of Alberta.

Ikenberry, D., and J. Lakonishok, 1993, "Corporate Governance Through the Proxy Contest: Evidence and Implications," *The Journal of Business* 66(3), 405–436.

Jensen, M., and W. Meckling, 1976, "Theory of the Firm: Managerial Behavior, Agency Costs, and Capital Structure," *Journal of Financial Economics* 3, 305–360.

John, K., and A. Klein, 1995, Shareholder Proposals and Corporate Governance. Working paper, New York University.

Johnson, M., S. Porter, and M. Shackell, 1997, Stakeholder Pressure and the Structure of Executive Compensation. Working paper, University of Michigan.

Johnson, M., and M. Shackell, 1997, Shareholder Proposals on Executive Compensation. Working paper, University of Michigan.

Kahan, M., and E. Rock, 2006, Hedge Funds in Corporate Governance and Control. Working paper, New York University.

Kahn, C., and A. Winton, 1998, "Ownership Structure, Speculation, and Shareholder Intervention," *Journal of Finance* 53(1), 99–129.

Kaplan, Steven, and Bernadette Minton, 1994, "Appointments of Outsiders to Japanese Boards: Determinants and Implications for Managers," *Journal of Financial Economics* 36, 225–258.

Karpoff, J., 2001, The Impact of Shareholder Activism on Target Companies: A Survey of Empirical Findings. Working paper, University of Washington.

Karpoff, J., P. Malatesta, and R. Walkling, 1996, "Corporate Governance and Shareholder Initiatives: Empirical Evidence," *Journal of Financial Economics* 42, 365–395.

Kary, Tiffany, 2006, "Upstart Investors for Director Accountability Target Pfizer," http://www.marketwatch.com.

Klein, A., and E. Zur, 2006, Hedge Fund Activism. Working paper, New York University.

Martin, J., and J. Kensinger, 1996, *Relationship Investing: What Active Institutional Investors Want from Management,* Financial Executives Research Foundation, Morristown, NJ.

Maug, E., 1998, "Large Shareholders as Monitors: Is There a Trade-off between Liquidity and Control?," *Journal of Finance* 53(1), 65–98.

Maug, E., and K. Rydqvist, 2006, Do Shareholders Vote Strategically: Voting Behavior, Proposal Screening, and Majority Rules. Working paper, European Corporate Governance Institute.

Monks, R. A., and N. Minow, 2003, *Corporate Governance.* Cambridge, MA: Blackwell Publishers.

Morgan, A. G., and A. B. Poulsen, 2001, "Linking Pay to Performance: Compensation Proposals in the S&P 500," *Journal of Financial Economics* 62(3), 489–523.

Morgan, A. G., A. B. Poulsen, and J. Wolf, 2006, "The Evolution of Shareholder Voting for Executive Compensation Schemes," *Journal of Corporate Finance* 12(4), 714–737.

Mulherin, J. Harold, and Annette Poulsen, 1998, "Proxy Contests and Corporate Change: Implications for Shareholder Wealth," *Journal of Financial Economics* 47, 279–313.

Murphy, K., and K. Van Nuys, 1994, State Pension Funds and Shareholder Inactivism. Working paper, Harvard University.

Nelson, James, 2006, "The CalPERS Effect Revisited Again," *Journal of Corporate Finance* 12, 187–213.

Nesbitt, Stephen, 1994, "Long Term Rewards from Shareholder Activism: A Study of the CalPERS Effect," *Journal of Applied Corporate Finance* 6, 75–80.

Noe, Thomas, 2002, "Investor Activism and Financial Market Structure," *Review of Financial Studies* 15, 289–319.

Opler, T., and J. Sokobin, 1995, Does Coordinated Institutional Activism Work? An Analysis of the Activities of the Council of Institutional Investors. Working paper, Ohio State University and Southern Methodist University.

Parrino, R., R. Sias, and L. Starks, 2003, "Voting with Their Feet: Institutional Ownership Changes Around CEO Turnovers," *Journal of Financial Economics* 68, 3–46.

Partnoy, F., and R. Thomas, 2006, Gap-Filling, Hedge Funds, and Financial Innovation. Working paper, University of San Diego and Vanderbilt University.

Pearson, N., and K. Altman, 2006, "Hedge Funds and Shareholder Activism," *The Corporate Governance Adviser* (Aspen Publishers).
Pinkowitz, L., 2000, Monitoring by Transient Investors? Institutions and Corporate Control. Working paper, Georgetown University.
Pound, J., 1988, "Proxy Contests and the Efficiency of Shareholder Oversight," *Journal of Financial Economics* 20, 237–265.
Prevost, A., and R. Rao, 2000, "Of What Value Are Shareholder Proposals Sponsored by Public Pension Funds?," *Journal of Business* 73, 177–204.
Prevost, A., R. Rao, and Melissa Williams, 2006, Labor Unions as Shareholder Activists: Champions or Detractors? Working paper, Ohio State University.
Qiu, Lily, 2005, Which Institutional Investors Monitor? Evidence from Acquisition Activity. Working paper, Brown University.
Rock, E., 1994, "Controlling the Dark Side of Relational Investing," *Cardozo Law Review* 15, 987–1031.
Roe, M., 1990, "Political and Legal Restraints on Ownership and Control of Public Companies," *Journal of Financial Economics* 27, 7–41.
Romano, R., 1993, "Public Pension Fund Activism in Corporate Governance Reconsidered," *Columbia Law Review* 93, 795–853.
Romano, R., 2001, "Less Is More: Making Shareholder Activism a Valued Mechanism of Corporate Governance," *Yale Journal on Regulation* 18(2), 174–252.
Rothberg, B., and S. Lilien, 2005, Mutual Fund Proxy Votes. Working paper, City University of New York.
Schwab, S., and R. Thomas, 1998, "Realigning Corporate Governance: Shareholder Activism by Labor Unions," *Michigan Law Review* 96(4), 1018–1094.
Shleifer, A., and R. Vishny, 1986, "Large Shareholders and Corporate Control," *Journal of Political Economy* 94, 461–488.
Smith, D. G., 1996, "Corporate Governance and Managerial Incompetence: Lessons from Kmart," *North Carolina Law Review* 74(4), 1038–1139.
Smith, M., 1996, "Shareholder Activism by Institutional Investors: Evidence from CalPERS," *Journal of Finance* 51, 227–252.
Song, W., and S. Szewczyk, 2003, "Does Coordinated Institutional Investor Activism Reverse the Fortunes of Underperforming Firms?," *Journal of Financial and Quantitative Analysis* 38, 317–336.
Strickland, D., K. Wiles, and M. Zenner, 1996, "A Requiem for the USA: Is Small Shareholder Monitoring Effective?," *Journal of Financial Economics* 40, 319–338.
Talner, L., 1983, *The Origins of Shareholder Activism*. Washington, DC: Investor Responsibility Research Center.
Thomas, R., and J. Cotter, 2006, Shareholder proposals Post-Enron: What's Changed, What's the Same? Working paper, Vanderbilt Law School.
Thomas, R., and K. Martin, 1998, "Should Labor Be Allowed to Make Shareholder Proposals?," *Washington Law Review* 73(1), 41–80.

Tkac, P., 2006, "One Proxy at a Time: Pursuing Social Change Through Shareholder Proposals," *Federal Reserve Bank of Atlanta Economic Review* 91, 3, 1–20.

Useem, M., E. Bowman, J. Myatt, and C. Irvine, 1993, "U.S. Institutional Investors Look at Corporate Governance in the 1990s," *European Management Journal* 11(2), 175–189.

Van Nuys, K., 1993, "Corporate Governance Through the Proxy Mechanism: Evidence from the 1989 Honeywell Proxy Solicitation," *Journal of Financial Economics* 34(1), 101–132.

Wahal, S., 1996, "Pension Fund Activism and Firm Performance," *Journal of Financial and Quantitative Analysis* 31, 1–23.

Woidtke, T., 2002, "Agents Watching Agents? Evidence from Pension Fund Ownership and Firm Value," *Journal of Financial Economics* 63, 99–131.

Woidtke, T., L. Bierman, and C. Tuggle, 2003, "Reigning in Activist Funds," *Harvard Business Review* 8(3), 22–23.

Wruck, K., and Y. Wu, 2005, The Value of Relationship Investing: Evidence from Private Placements of Equity by U.S. Public Firms. Working paper, Ohio State University and Washington University.

Wu, Y., 2004, "The Impact of Public Opinion on Board Structure Changes, Director Career Progression, and CEO Turnover: Evidence from CalPERS' Corporate Governance Program," *Journal of Corporate Finance* 10, 199–227.

Zingales, L., 1998, "Corporate Governance," in *The New Palgrave Dictionary of Economics and the Law,* ed. P. Newman. New York: Macmillan.

PART IV

External Governance: The Market for Corporate Control

CHAPTER 12

Corporate Control and the Politics of Finance

MICHAEL C. JENSEN

THE U.S. MARKET FOR CORPORATE CONTROL reached the height of its activity and influence in the last years of the 1980s. Among its many accomplishments, mergers and acquisitions, LBOs, and other leveraged restructurings of the past decade sharply reduced the effectiveness of size as a deterrent to takeover. The steady increase in the size of the deals throughout the 1980s culminated in the $25 billion buyout of RJR-Nabisco in 1989 by KKR, a partnership with fewer than thirty professionals.

The effect of such transactions was to transfer control over vast corporate resources—often trapped in mature industries or uneconomic conglomerates—to those prepared to pay large premiums to use those resources more efficiently. In some cases, the acquirers functioned as agents rather than principals, selling part or all of the assets they acquired to others. In many cases, the acquirers were unaffiliated individual investors (labeled "raiders" by those opposed to the transfer of control) rather than other large public corporations. The increased asset sales, enlarged payouts, and heavy use of debt to finance such takeovers led to a large-scale return of equity capital to shareholders.

The consequence of this control activity has been a pronounced trend toward smaller, more focused, more efficient—and in many cases private—corporations.[1] And while capital and resources were being forced out of our largest companies throughout the 1980s, the small- to medium-sized U.S. corporate sector was experiencing vigorous growth in employment and capital spending. At the same time our capital markets were bringing about this massive transfer of corporate resources, the U.S. economy was experiencing a ninety-two-month expansion and record-high percentages of people employed.

The resulting transfer of control from corporate managers to increasingly active investors has aroused enormous controversy. The strongest opposition has come from groups whose power and influence have been challenged by corporate restructuring: notably, the Business Roundtable (the voice of managers of large corporations), organized labor, and politicians whose ties to wealth and power were being weakened. The media, always responsive to popular opinion even as they help shape it, have succeeded in reinvigorating the American populist tradition of hostility to Wall Street "financiers." The current controversy pitting Main Street against Wall Street has been wrought to a pitch that recalls the intensity of the 1930s. Newspapers, books, and magazines have obliged the public's desire for villains by furnishing unflattering detailed accounts of the private doings of those branded "corporate raiders."

Barbarians at the Gate, for example, the best-selling account of the RJR-Nabisco transaction, is perhaps best described as an attempt to expose the greed and chicanery that goes into the making of some Wall Street deals. And, on that score, the book is effective (though it's worth noting that, amidst the general destruction of reputations, the principals of KKR and most of the Drexel team come across as professional and principled). But what also emerges from the 500-plus pages—though the authors seem to fail to grasp its import—is clear evidence of corporate-wide inefficiencies at RJR-Nabisco, including massive waste of corporate "free cash flow," that would allow KKR to pay existing stockholders $12 billion over the previous market value for the right to bring about change.

Since that control change, KKR has defied skeptics not only by managing the company's huge debt load, but by creating another $5 billion in value (providing the original LBO warrant and equity holders with a compound annual rate of return of 59 percent), extracting almost $6 billion in capital through asset sales, and bringing the company public again.[2] In the process, it has also paid off almost $13 billion of the original $29 billion in debt (without, according to KKR, any losses to note- or bondholders). Thus, the consequences to date of the RJR buyout for all investors, buying as well as selling, appear to be a remarkable $17 billion in added value.[3]

For economists and management scientists concerned about corporate efficiency, the RJR story is deeply disturbing. What troubles us is not so much the millions of dollars spent on sports celebrities and airplanes—or the greed and unprofessional behavior of several leading investment bankers—but rather the waste of billions in unproductive capital expenditures and organizational inefficiencies.[4] Viewed in this light—although, here again, the authors don't seem aware of what they have discovered—*Barbarians* is testimony to the massive failure of the internal control system led by RJR's board of directors. As former SEC Commissioner Joseph Grundfest has put it, the real "barbarians" in this book were *inside* the gates.[5]

Moreover, the fact that Ross Johnson, RJR's CEO, could be held up by *Fortune* as a model corporate leader only months before the buyout[6] attests to the difficulty of detecting even such gross inefficiencies and thus suggests that organizational inefficiencies of this magnitude may extend well beyond RJR.

Although parts of corporate America may be guilty of underinvesting—as the media continually assert—there is little doubt that many of our largest U.S. companies have grossly *over*invested, whether in desperate attempts to maintain sales and earnings in mature or declining businesses or by diversifying outside of their core businesses. Many of our best-known companies—GM, IBM, Xerox, and Kodak come to mind most readily—have wasted vast amounts of resources over the last decade or so. The chronic overinvestment and overstaffing of such companies reflects the widespread failure of our corporate internal control systems. And it is this fundamental control problem that gave rise to the corporate restructuring movement of the 1980s.

The Media and the Academy

But the role of takeovers and LBOs in curbing corporate inefficiency is not the story told by our mass media. When media accounts manage to raise their focus above the "morality play" craved by the public to consider broader issues of economic efficiency and competitiveness, the message is invariably the same: leveraged restructurings are eroding the competitive strength of U.S. corporations by forcing cutbacks in employment, R&D, and capital investment. The journalistic method of inquiry is the investigation of selected cases, a process potentially subject to "selection bias." And the typical journalistic product is a series of anecdotes—stories that almost invariably carry with them a strong emotive appeal for the "victims" of control changes, with little or no attention paid to long-run efficiency effects.[7]

Using very different methods and language, academic economists have subjected corporate control activity to intensive study. And the research contradicts the popular rhetoric. Indeed, I know of no area in economics today where the divergence between popular belief and the evidence from scholarly research is so great.

The most careful academic research strongly suggests that takeovers—along with leveraged restructurings prompted by the threat of takeover—have generated large gains for shareholders and for the economy as a whole. My estimates indicate that over the fourteen-year period from 1976 to 1990, the $1.8 trillion of corporate control transactions—that is, mergers, tender offers, divestitures, and LBOs—created over $650 billion in value for selling-firm shareholders.[8] And this estimate includes neither the gains to the buyers in such transactions nor the value of efficiency improvements by companies pressured by control market activity into reforming without a visible control transaction.

Some of the shareholder gains in highly leveraged transactions (HLTs) have come at the expense of bondholders, banks, and other creditors who financed the deals. But the amount of such losses is not likely to exceed $50 billion; a current best estimate would probably run around $25 billion.[9] (To put this number into perspective, IBM alone has seen its equity value fall by $25 billion in the past six months.)[10] And thus far, there is no reliable evidence that any appreciable part of the remaining $600 billion or so of net gains to stockholders has come at the expense of other corporate "stakeholders" such as employees, suppliers, and the IRS.[11]

The well-documented increases in shareholder value have been largely dismissed by journalists and other critics of restructuring as "paper gains" having little bearing on the long-term vitality and competitiveness of American business. Some even point to such gains as evidence of a "short-term" orientation that is said to be destroying American business.

For financial economists, however, theory and evidence suggest that as long as such value increases are not arising from pure transfers from other parties to the corporate "contract," they are reliable predictors of increases in corporate operating efficiency. And, as I discuss later in this chapter, research on LBOs has indeed produced direct evidence of such efficiencies; moreover, macroeconomic data now reveal a dramatic improvement in the health and productivity of American industry during the 1980s.

The Present

In the past two years, restructuring transactions have come to a virtual standstill, and there are few signs today of a well-functioning corporate control market. Total M&A transactions fell 56 percent from a peak of $247 billion in 1988 to $108 billion in 1990; and this decline has accelerated through the first six months of 1991.

Widespread savings and loan (S&L) failures (along with some failures of commercial banks and insurance companies) and a number of highly publicized cases of troubled HLTs have combined with the criminalization of securities law disclosure violations and the high-profile RICO and insider trading prosecutions to create a highly charged political climate.[12] Such political forces have produced a major re-regulation of our financial markets. The political origin of such regulatory initiatives is revealed by the fact that bad real estate loans dwarf junk bond losses and bad HLT loans as contributors to the current weakness of our financial institutions.[13]

With the eclipse of the new issue market for junk bonds, the application of HLT rules to commercial bank lending,[14] and new restrictions on insurance companies,[15] funding for large HLTs has all but disappeared. Even if financing were available, court decisions (including those authorizing the use of poison pills and defensive employee stock ownership plans) and state antitakeover and control shareholder amendments have significantly increased the difficulty of making a successful hostile offer.

As a result, takeovers today are likely to revert to the pattern of the 1960s and the 1970s, when large companies used takeovers of other companies to build corporate "empires." The AT&T acquisition of NCR is an example. And if the past is a reliable guide, many such acquisitions are likely to end up destroying value and reducing corporate efficiency.

Contracting Problems Compounded by Politics

As prices were bid up to more competitive levels in the second half of the 1980s, the markets "overshot." Contracting problems between the promoters of HLTs and the suppliers of capital, as I will argue later, led to too many overpriced deals. In this sense, the financial press is right in attributing *part* of the current conditions in our debt and takeover markets to too many unsound transactions. Such transactions, especially those completed after 1985, were overpriced by their promoters and, as a consequence, overleveraged (and it is important to keep this order of causality in mind).

But it is also clear that intense political pressures to curb the corporate control market have greatly compounded the problems caused by this "contracting failure." However genuine and justified their concern about our deposit insurance funds, the reactions of Congress, the courts, and regulators to losses (which, again, are predominantly the result of real estate, not HLT loans) have had several unfortunate side effects. They have sharply restricted the availability of capital to non-investment grade companies, thereby significantly increasing the rate of corporate defaults. They have also limited the ability of financially troubled companies to reorganize outside of court, thus ensuring that most defaulted companies wind up in bankruptcy. All of this, in my view, has contributed significantly to the current weakness of the economy.

In this chapter, I have seven major aims: First, I review new macroeconomic evidence on changes in productivity in American manufacturing that is dramatically inconsistent with popular claims that corporate control transactions were crippling the industrial economy in the 1980s.

Second, I show how the restructuring movement of the 1980s reflected the re-emergence of active investors in the United States—a group that had been essentially dormant since the 1930s. In so doing, I argue that much of this leveraged restructuring activity addressed a fundamental problem facing many large, mature public companies: the conflict between management and shareholders over control of corporate "free cash flow."

Third, I summarize my conception of "LBO associations" as new organizational forms—structures that overcome the deficiencies of large public conglomerates. I also discuss the similarity between LBO associations and Japanese business financing networks known as "keiretsu."

Fourth, I extend this overseas comparison by summarizing my argument that the highly leveraged financial structures of the 1980s should lead to the "privatization" of bankruptcy (i.e., out-of-court reorganization) that characterizes Japanese practice in reorganizing troubled companies.[16]

Fifth, I present a theory of "boom-bust" cycles in venture markets that explains how private contracting problems combined with the political interference mentioned above to bring about financial distress in many of the leveraged transactions put together in the latter half of the 1980s.

Sixth, I argue that misguided changes in the tax and regulatory codes and in bankruptcy court decisions have blocked the normal economic incentives for creditors to come to agreement outside of Chapter 11, thus almost putting an end to out-of-court reorganizations. The consequence has been an increase in the costs of financial distress and a sharp rise in the number of Chapter 11 filings.

Seventh and last, I propose a set of changes in the Chapter 11 process designed to correct the gross inefficiencies built into the current process. Rather than attempting to preserve the control of current management and extend the life of organizations (in some cases, without economic justification), my proposals reflect the thinking of academic economists and lawyers about how to reduce the costs of financial distress and thus maximize the total value of the firm to all investors.

New Insights from Macroeconomic Data

In addition to the continuing stream of scholarly work documenting efficiency gains by LBO companies, productivity gains are also visible in the aggregate data. As summarized in the top two panels of figure 12.1, the pattern of productivity and unit labor costs in the U.S. manufacturing sector over the period 1950–1989 is inconsistent with popular characterizations of the 1980s as the decade of the dismantling of American industry. Beginning in 1982, there was a dramatic increase in the productivity of the manufacturing sector (see panel A)—a turnaround unmatched in the last forty years. In panel B, we see a sharp acceleration of the steady decline in real unit labor costs since about 1960—a decline that stalled in the 1970s.[17]

Such cost reductions and efficiency gains have not come at the expense of labor generally (although *organized* labor has certainly seen its influence wane). As shown in panels C, D, and E, there has been a rise in total employment and hours worked since the end of the 1981–1982 recession; hourly compensation has continued to rise since 1982 (although at a somewhat slower rate than before); and percentage unemployment has fallen dramatically since 1982.

FIGURE 12.1

Trends in Manufacturing, 1950–1989: Productivity, Unit Labor Costs, Employment, Compensation, and Capital

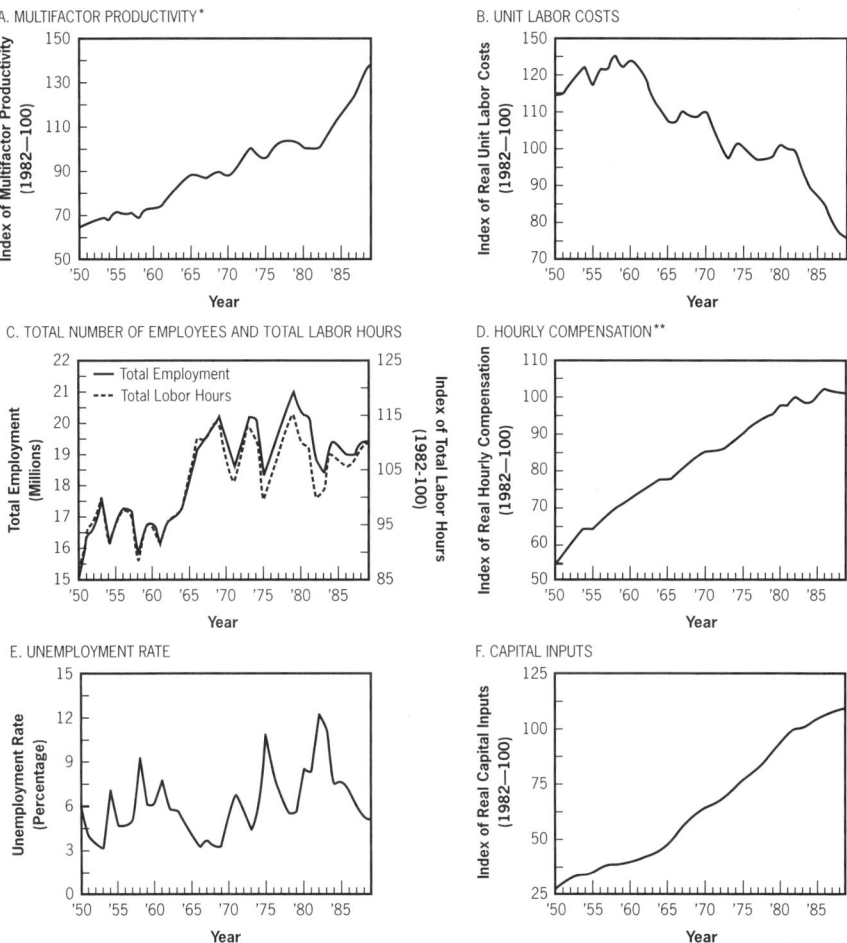

Sources: *Panels A and F*—Bureau of Labor Statistics, "Multifactor Productivity, 1988 and 1989," Table 3. *Panels B and D*—Bureau of Labor Statistics, "International Occupations of Manufacturing Productivity and Labor Cost Trends, 1989" (July 1990), USDL-90-393. *Panel C*—Bureau of Labor Statistics, "Employment and Earnings," supplement obtained from Office of Employment and Unemployment, Bureau of Labor Statistics, "International Comparisons of Manufacturing and Labor Cost Trends, 1989" (July 1990) USDL 90-383, Table 2. *Panel E*— Bureau of Labor Statistics, "Labor Force Statistics Derived from the Population Survey, 1948–1987" (August 1988), Bulletin 2307, Table A.35; Bureau of Labor Statistics, "Unemployment and Earnings, January 1990," Table 11.

*Multifactor Productivity is real output per unit of combined capital and labor.

**Hourly Compensation includes wages and salaries, supplements, employer payments for social security, and other employer-financed benefit plans.

The Effect on Capital Investment

Critics of leveraged restructuring also claim that corporate capital investment was a casualty of the mergers and acquisitions (M&A) activity of the 1980s. But, as shown in panel F, after a pause in 1982, capital growth in the manufacturing sector has continued to rise—although, again, at a slower rate than previously. This pattern is consistent with my "free cash flow" argument that corporate restructuring was a response to excessive capital in many sectors of American industry. The pattern also suggests that, although capital was being squeezed out of the low-growth manufacturing sector by the payouts of cash and substitution of debt for equity, it was being recycled back into the economy. Some of that capital was transferred to smaller companies, including large inflows to the venture capital market. At the same time, the resulting organizational changes and efficiency gains at larger companies have provided the basis for renewed capital spending.[18]

The Effect on Research and Development

Another persistent objection to the control market is that it reduces valuable R&D expenditures. But, as shown in figure 12.2, while M&A activity was rising sharply after the 1982 recession (until plummeting in 1990), real R&D expenditures were reaching new highs in each year of the period from 1975 to 1990. R&D also rose from 1.8 percent to 3.4 percent of sales during this period.[19]

In short, although the macro data do not establish control market activity as a *cause* of the dramatic productivity improvements, they provide no support for the popular outcry against the workings of the corporate control market.[20]

The Costs of Restructuring (and the Alternative to Takeovers)

There is no doubt that the corporate restructuring movement resulted in changes painful to many individuals. With the shrinkage of some companies, there has been loss of jobs among top management and corporate staff, though not among blue collar workers as a group.[21] Much of the contraction resulting from takeovers is fundamentally a reflection of larger economic forces—forces that dictate that changes be made if resources are to be used efficiently and industrial decline is to be halted. Hostile takeovers typically achieve quickly—and thus, I would argue, with considerably lower social costs—the same end brought about in more protracted fashion by intense competition in product markets.[22]

Consider the current plight of our auto industry. Few industries have experienced as severe a retrenchment as the one this industry went through in the 1977–1982 period—and will surely have to experience in the future.[23] It is precisely the auto industry's past immunity to takeover and major restructuring,

FIGURE 12.2

M&A Activity vs. Industry R&D Expenditures (1975–1990)

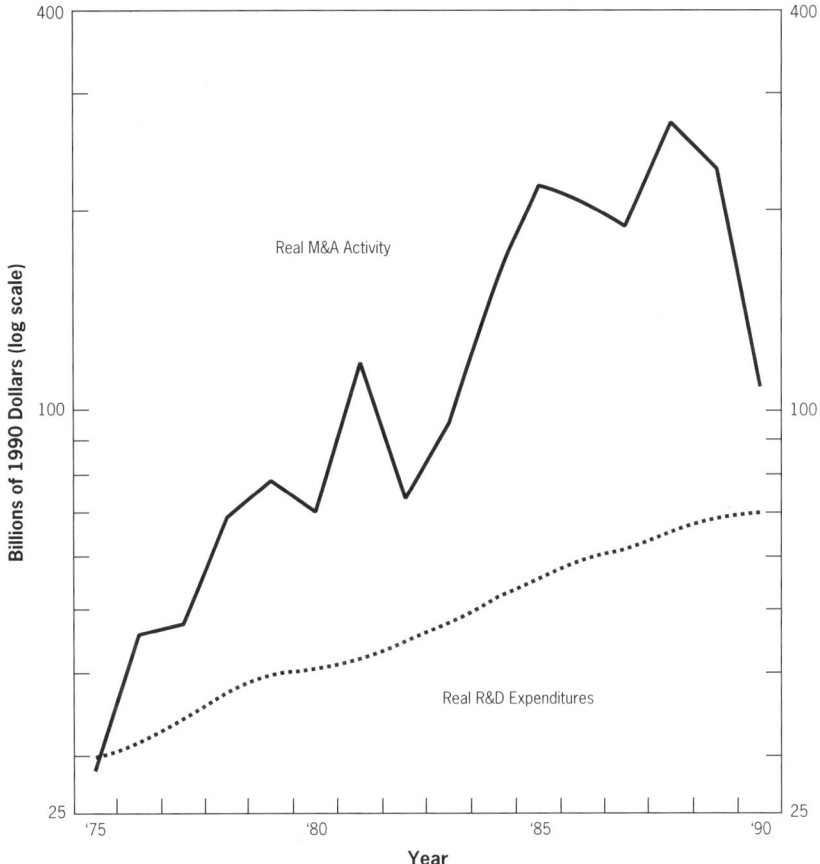

Source: *Business Week,* "R&D Scoreboard," annual; and Merrill Lynch, *Mergerstat Review 1990,* Figure 5.

along with government protection from foreign competitors, that is responsible for the extent of its present requirement to downsize. Had normal economic forces like competition, failure, and takeover been allowed to operate, the massive contraction still required to restore competitiveness to our automobile industry would have been largely behind us today, and the social costs and dislocations would have been far smaller. The devastated economies of Eastern and Central Europe today are vivid examples of what happens when state protection prevents normal economic forces, including failure, from moving resources from lower- to higher-valued uses.

While change imposes costs on some individuals, such costs are outweighed by the benefits to the general economy. At the end of the 1970s, when the Dow Jones average was around 900, Lester Throw complained that one of the principal shortcomings of a "mixed" economy like ours was its inability to "disinvest"—that is, to move capital out of declining industries and into vital ones.[24] But this forced "disinvestment," I would argue, is the primary accomplishment of the wave of restructurings we saw in the 1980s. Such restructuring, as I argue in the next section, reflected the efforts of a new breed of "active" investors to prevent management from wasting resources by reinvesting cash flow in mature, low-return businesses with excess capacity. This is why restructuring activity was concentrated in industries such as oil, tobacco, tires, food processing, retailing, publishing, broadcasting, forest products, commodity chemicals, and financial services.

The Return of Active Investors

Over the last fifty years, institutional investors and financial institutions have been driven out of their former role as active investors. By "active investor" I mean one who holds large equity and/or debt positions and actually monitors management, sits on boards, is sometimes involved in dismissing management, is often closely involved in the strategic direction of the company, and, on occasion, even manages. That description fits people like Warren Buffett; Carl Icahn; Sir James Goldsmith; the Pretzels; and Kohlberg, Craves, and Roberts (KKR).

Before the mid-1930s, investment banks and commercial banks played a much more important role on boards of directors, monitoring management and occasionally engineering changes in management. At the peak of their activities, J. P. Morgan and several of his partners served on boards of directors and played a major role in the strategic direction of many firms.[25]

The diminished role of banks in corporate governance and strategy over the past fifty years is the result of a number of factors. Among the most important are laws passed in the 1930s that increased the costs of being actively involved in the strategic direction of a company while also holding large amounts of its debt or equity.[26] Such regulations, together with today's strongly pro-management and chronically inefficient proxy mechanism,[27] do much to explain why money managers do not serve on boards today and seldom think of getting involved in the strategy of their portfolio companies.

The restrictive laws of the 1930s were passed after an outbreak of populist attacks on the investment banking and financial community. During the formative years of the SEC, then chairman William O. Douglas shocked Wall Street investment bankers with the statement:

[T]he banker [should and will be] restricted to . . . underwriting or selling. Insofar as management [and] formulation of industrial policies [are concerned] . . . the banker will be superseded. The financial power which he has exercised in the past over such processes will pass into other hands.[28]

As Mark Roe interprets Douglas's statement, "Main Street America did not want to be controlled by Wall Street. Congress responded to Main Street, not Wall Street; laws discouraging and prohibiting control resulted."[29]

The consequence of these political forces over the past fifty years has been to leave managers increasingly unmonitored. At present, when the U.S. institutions that own more than 40 percent of all U.S. corporate equity become dissatisfied with management, they have few options other than to sell their shares. Moreover, managers' complaints about the churning of financial institutions' portfolios ring hollow: most prefer churning to a system in which those institutions would actually have direct power to correct a management problem. Few CEOs today like the idea of having institutions with substantial stock ownership sitting on their corporate board. That would bring about the monitoring of managerial activities by people who bear part of the wealth consequences of managerial mistakes and who are not beholden to the CEO for their directorships.

After financial institution monitors left the scene in the post-1940 period, many managers came to believe that their companies belonged to them and that stockholders were merely one of many "stakeholders" the firm had to serve.[30] The growth of this "managerialist" attitude also coincided with a ten-fold reduction in the percentage equity ownership of the CEOs of our largest companies— from roughly 3 percent in 1937 to less than 0.03 percent today.[31] U.S. companies, to be sure, also became much larger (even in inflation-adjusted dollars) over this period; but while management equity ownership was falling by a factor of ten, average company size increased by only about three to four times. The consequence, as Adolph Berle warned us back in the 1930s, is that for almost fifty years we experienced a widening of the divide between ownership and control in our largest public companies.

Why Corporations Should Maximize Value

Financial economists have long understood that the fundamental aim of our corporations ought to be the maximization of their "long-run" value.[32] The critical role of the value-maximizing rule is to provide guidance to decision-makers evaluating tradeoffs of resources at different points in time. (Extended to incorporate the effects of uncertainty, this rule is the essence of modern capital theory.) When Congress and the courts begin to interfere with this primary mandate, they lose sight of what creates value and raises the standard of living in our society. It is precisely by allowing corporations to concentrate on that aim that the long-run interests of all other stakeholders—employees, creditors, suppliers, taxpayers, and so forth—are ultimately best served.[33] Again, the poverty of Eastern and Central Europe today is largely the consequence of eliminating all pressure, or incentive, to maximize the value of business enterprise.

Value-maximizing does not mean that stockholders are an especially deserving group, or that corporate stakeholders other than stockholders should be ignored in management's decision-making. Even the most aggressive maximizer of stockholder wealth must care about other constituencies, such as employees, customers, suppliers, and local communities. Maximizing value, in fact, means allocating corporate resources (to the point where marginal costs equal marginal benefits) among all groups or interests that affect firm value. Value-maximizing decision-making devotes resources to members of each important corporate constituency to improve the terms on which they contract with the company, to maintain the firm's reputation, and to reduce the threat of restrictive regulation. In this sense, there is no conflict between management's service to its stockholders and to other corporate stakeholders.

The Increase in Agency Costs

The banning of financial institutions from fulfilling their critically important monitoring role has resulted in major corporate inefficiencies. The increase in "agency costs"[34] after the 1930s—loosely speaking, the loss in value resulting from the separation between ownership and control in widely held public corporations—appears to have taken a sharp rise in the mid- to late 1960s when a substantial part of corporate America launched diversification programs that led to the assembly of conglomerates. We now know this course was unproductive, and it has been in large part reversed over the past ten years.[35]

It is ironic, moreover, that while most attacks on takeovers have been directed at unaffiliated entrepreneurs such as Icahn and Goldsmith, it is the diversifying acquisitions by our largest corporations such as DuPont, Exxon, R. J. Reynolds, Goodyear, and U.S. Steel that have proven to be the least productive. Given the evidence attesting to the waste caused by corporate diversification, the criticism directed at the KKR buyout of RJR-Nabisco (a transaction that has led to renewed focus) seems misplaced, especially given the lack of controversy surrounding the AT&T takeover of NCR. This misdirected criticism of takeover entrepreneurs ("raiders"), while sparing corporate conglomerators, lays bare the political origins of the opposition.

The fact that takeover and restructuring premiums regularly average about 50 percent indicates that managers have been able to destroy up to a third of the value of the organizations they lead before facing serious threat of displacement.[36] This destruction of value generates large profit opportunities. In response to such opportunities, we have seen the rise of new kinds of institutions whose principal purpose has been to recapture that lost value. Along with the takeover specialists have come others, such as the family funds (owned by the Bass Brothers, the Pritzkers, and the Bronfmans), Warren Buffet's Berkshire Hathaway, and Lazard Frères's Corporate Partners Fund—institutions that have discovered ways to bear the costs associated with insider status while being active in the strategic direction of the firm. These new institutions purchase substantial interests in (or purchase entire) companies and play an active role in them. They often *are* the boards of directors. Because of their significant ownership interest, such institutional directors have far stronger incentives to monitor management than the typical outside directors of our public companies.

The LBO Association: A New Organizational Form

LBO associations such as KKR, Clayton & Dubilier, and Forstmann-Little represent new organizational forms—in effect, a new model of general management. The diversity of the businesses owned by these LBO partnerships makes such organizations look like conventional corporate conglomerates. But such conglomerates, the result of the rush to diversify in the 1960s and 1970s, have generally been overcome by their own internal organizational failures. During the height of the restructuring activity in the 1980s, they were routinely broken up and indirectly replaced by LBO associations that have solved the internal problems of the typical conglomerate.

LBO associations generate large increases in efficiency. They are generally run by partnerships instead of the headquarters office in the typical large, multibusiness diversified corporation. These partnerships perform the monitoring and peak coordination function with a staff numbering in the tens of people and replace the typical corporate headquarters staff of hundreds or thousands.

But while the new LBO associations may look like conventional conglomerates, they have a fundamental affinity with Japanese groups of firms called "keiretsu." LBO partnerships play a dual funding and oversight role that is similar in many ways to that of the main banks in the Japanese keiretsu. Like the main banks, which typically hold significant equity stakes in their corporate borrowers, the leaders of the LBO partnerships hold substantial amounts of equity in their companies and control access to the rest of the capital. Further like the Japanese banks, the LBO partners are actively involved in the monitoring and strategic direction of these firms.

Unlike the typical conglomerate (or the keiretsu, for that matter), the operating heads of the individual business units comprising the typical LBO association also have substantial equity ownership—ownership that gives them a pay-to-performance sensitivity that, on average, is twenty times greater than that experienced by the average corporate CEO.[37] Moreover, the managing partners in the LBO associations—which is really the proper comparison with the CEOs of conglomerates—have an even larger pay-for-performance as a result of their 20 percent override on the value created in the company.

LBO business unit heads also have far less bureaucracy to deal with, and far more decision-making freedom, in running their businesses. In effect, the LBO association substitutes incentives provided by compensation and ownership plans for the direct monitoring and often centralized decision-making in the typical corporate bureaucracy. The compensation and ownership plans make the rewards to managers highly sensitive to the performance of their business units, something that rarely occurs in major corporations.

Also important, the contractual relationship between the partnership headquarters and the suppliers of capital to the buyout funds is very different from that between the corporate headquarters and stockholders in the diversified firm. The buyout funds are organized as limited partnerships in which the managers of the partnership headquarters are the general partners. Unlike the diversified firm, the contract with the limited partners denies partnership headquarters the right to transfer cash or other resources from one LBO business unit to another. Instead, cash payouts from each LBO business unit must be paid out directly to the limited partners of the buyout funds. This reduces the waste of free cash flow that is so prevalent in diversified corporations.[38]

The Evidence on LBOs

Financial economists studying LBOs have produced substantial evidence documenting gains in operating efficiency as well as increases in stockholder value.

Stockholder Gains

As would be expected in a competitive corporate control market, the gains to selling stockholders in LBOs have been roughly comparable to shareholder gains from takeovers. Estimates of the average premium over market two months prior to the buyout range from 40 percent to 50 percent.[39] For buyouts that came back public or were otherwise sold or valued, the total value (adjusted for market movements) increased 96 percent from two months before the buyout to the final sale about three years after the buyout. These gains were divided roughly equally between the pre- and post-buyout investors.[40] The median net-of-market return on the post-buyout equity alone was approximately 785 percent.[41]

Increases in Operating Efficiency

In addition to the studies of value changes, studies examining the operating performance of large samples of LBOs after the buyout have found real increases in productivity. The Kaplan study cited earlier finds average increases in annual operating earnings of 42 percent from the year prior to the buyout to the third year after the buyout, and increases of 25 percent when adjusted for industry and business cycle trends. He also finds 96 percent increases in cash flow in the same period (80 percent increases after adjustment for industry and business cycle trends).

The Bottom Line

In a review paper published in 1990, my Harvard colleague Krishna Palepu summarized the findings of more than two dozen studies of LBOs and their effects as follows:

- Stockholders of firms undergoing LBOs earn substantial returns from the transactions.

- Company productivity and operating performance improve substantially in the years immediately following a buyout. The improvements are a result of the changes in financial and management structure associated with the buyout. There is little evidence of a decline in employment levels or average wage rates of blue-collar workers after a buyout, suggesting that the post-buyout cash-flow improvements are not the result of widespread wealth transfers from workers.

- Although some pre-buyout bondholders suffer losses at the buyout, these losses account for a very small fraction of the total gains to pre-buyout shareholders.

- Buyouts give companies increased depreciation and interest tax shields that account for some of the equity gains from these transactions. Buyouts also increase tax revenues to the U.S. Treasury in several ways, however, and the net effect of LBOs on aggregate tax revenues is likely to be positive.

- LBOs appear to have two opposing effects on firm risk. Although the leverage increase associated with the buyout increases financial risk, the changes in the organizational structure and strategy appear to reduce business risk. The net result is that LBO investors bear significantly lower risk than comparable levered investments in public corporations.[42]

The Privatization of Bankruptcy

The high leverage associated with LBOs and other HLTs—notwithstanding its benefits as a monitoring and incentive device,[43] and the related reductions in business risk just cited—was bound to increase the probability of companies getting into financial trouble. Indeed, when testifying before the House on

LBOs in February 1989, I expressed surprise at how few mistakes we had witnessed in a revolution in business practice as great as that occurring over the last decade.[44] At that time, fewer than thirty of some 1,500 going-private transactions completed since 1979 had gone into formal bankruptcy. Since then, of course, the number of HLTs in default or bankruptcy has risen sharply.

As I also pointed out in my testimony, the costs of dealing with corporate insolvency could be expected—barring unforeseen changes in capital market regulations and the bankruptcy courts—to be much smaller in the new world of high leverage ratios than they have been historically. The reason for my prediction has much to do with the fact that the HLTs that get into trouble today are likely to be fundamentally different from the traditional corporate bankrupts of the past. In contrast to the traditionally low-levered firms that end up eating through their large equity bases and becoming candidates for liquidation, today's troubled HLTs are likely to be fundamentally profitable companies generating large positive (pre-interest) cash flows. And, given our costly and cumbersome court-supervised bankruptcy process (a subject I return to later), it seems clear that far more of this operating value can be preserved by privately resolving conflicts among the firm's claimants rather than filing under Chapter 11.[45]

Because of these stronger incentives to preserve value in the new leverage model, I argued that a different set of institutional arrangements was arising to substitute for the usual bankruptcy process. In short, I predicted that the reorganization process would be "privatized."[46]

Extending the Japanese Parallel

As mentioned above, the funding and governance of companies by LBO associations are strikingly similar to many of the practices of Japanese keiretsu. And this similarity also extends to their practice in reorganizing troubled companies. Japanese companies make intensive use of leverage, far more so than their American counterparts; and Japanese banks appear to allow companies to go into bankruptcy only when it is economic to liquidate them—that is, only when the firm is more valuable dead than alive. As leader of the consortium of banks lending to any firm, the Japanese main bank takes responsibility for evaluating the economic viability of an insolvent firm and for planning its recovery—including the infusion of new capital and top-level managerial manpower (often drawn from the bank itself). Other members of the lending consortium commonly follow the lead of the main bank and contribute additional funding, if required, to the reorganization effort. The main bank bonds its role by making the largest commitment of funds to the effort.[47]

Reorganization in the 1980s

Similar practices appear to be the norm in the American LBO community. (In fact, the restructuring of RJR's balance sheet together with a new equity infusion is a nice illustration of this process.) The combination of debt and equity claims held by Japanese banks had an American analogue in the "strip financing" techniques commonly observed in the early LBOs. The practice of strip financing—wherein roughly proportional "strips" of all securities in the capital structure were held by most of the claimants—reduces the conflicts of interest among classes of claimants that inevitably arise in troubled companies.[48] The intensity of such conflicts—which, as I will argue later, are aggravated by our system—are contributing to the current costs of workouts and bankruptcies.

The stronger incentives created by high leverage to manage the insolvency process more efficiently were also reflected in the extremely low frequency with which LBOs actually entered bankruptcy in the first half of the 1980s, as well as the general experience of troubled companies at that time. For example, ninety-one, or 47 percent, of the 192 NYSE and ASE companies that defaulted during the period 1980–1986 were reorganized privately.[49] Some assert that the early success of LBOs was ensured by the bull market of the middle 1980s. The story was not that simple, however, because during the late 1970s and the first half of the 1980s, major sectors of the economy experienced bad times, and buyouts occurred in many of these sectors.

We now know that LBOs frequently got into trouble in the early 1980s. But instead of entering formal bankruptcy, they were typically reorganized in a short period of time (several months was common), often under new management, and at apparently lower cost than would occur in the courts. Drexel Burnham Lambert, which underwrote much of the high-yield bond offerings throughout the 1980s, also transformed the 3(a)9 exchange offer into a valuable innovation in the workout and reorganization process. The available evidence indicates, moreover, that the direct costs of exchange offers are only about 10 percent of those in the average Chapter 11 of comparable size.[50] Such innovation is to be expected when there are such large efficiency gains to be realized from new reorganization and recontracting procedures.

Moreover, I warned in my House testimony (in February 1989) that serious problems would result among Drexel's clients if regulators hampered its ability to handle reorganizations and workouts. Drexel's position in the high-yield bond market gave it a unique ability to perform this function, and no substitute was likely to emerge soon.

Today, of course, Drexel is gone. And though I seem to have been right about the consequences of Drexel's demise, my predictions about the continuing privatization of bankruptcy could not have been more wrong. What I failed to anticipate were major new regulatory initiatives, a critical change in the tax code, and a misguided bankruptcy court decision that together are forcing many troubled companies into Chapter 11.

Contract Failure in Venture Markets

Judging from press reports, academic case studies of failed transactions,[51] and a study of 119 large LBOs by Steven Kaplan and Jeremy Stein, it now seems clear that more of the transactions completed have been overpriced and, as a result of the overpricing, overleveraged. According to Kaplan and Stein, of the sixty-six large LBOs (greater than $100 million in value) completed during the period 1986-1988, eighteen have defaulted and seven have filed for bankruptcy. In contrast, only four of the fifty-three large LBOs completed during 1980-1985 have defaulted and three filed for bankruptcy.[52] The question troubling economists is this: Are there *systematic* factors that would account for the high concentration of defaults among deals transacted in the latter stages of the leveraged restructuring movement?

I believe there have been two major factors contributing to problems in the market for HLTs. First, the HLT market experienced a "contracting failure"—one that gives rise to the boom-and-bust cycles common in venture markets such as real estate development, oil and gas drilling, and the venture capital market. Second, major changes in the regulatory and legal environment have greatly compounded the problems arising from this contract failure by reducing the ability of companies to refinance their existing debt and, when necessary, to reorganize claims efficiently. Such flexibility is essential to the privatization of bankruptcy I described earlier. By increasing the cost of high leverage, significantly restricting companies' ability to adjust their capital structures, and interfering with the private workout process, regulatory intervention has substantially increased both the frequency and the costs of financial distress and bankruptcy. (In this sense, as I argue later, the regulatory attack on high leverage has become a self-fulfilling prophecy.)

Boom and Bust

My explanation for the boom-and-bust cycles in venture markets—one which applies in particular to the LBO market—centers on a misalignment of incentives between deal-makers and the creditors and investors they bring together. I call this misalignment a *contracting* failure because it can be corrected (without government intervention) by the private parties entering into the arrangements. I call it a *failure* because corrections seem to take too long to appear and the mistakes repeat themselves too often to be consistent with our theory of rational investors.

As explained above, *after* the deal has been completed, the general structure of LBOs provides strong incentives to the relevant parties to maximize value. I refer in particular to the governance structure of the LBO partnership, the 20 percent override received by the LBO general partners as well as their cash investment in the LBO equity, management incentive contracts with high pay-for-performance sensitivity, the control effect of high leverage, constraints on the cross-subsidization of one LBO by another, and the large percentage equity holdings of managers made possible by high leverage.

The contracting failure that concerns me is the tendency for venture markets to evolve in a way that fails to provide incentives for the deal-makers to select and promote *only* deals that are worth more than they cost. Such a misalignment of incentives goes far in explaining not only why LBOs and other HLTs became overpriced, but also why other activities like real estate, venture capital, and oil and gas well drilling go through boom-and-bust cycles.

The Case of LBOs

In the earlier years of the LBO movement, the partnerships that promoted the LBOs put up significantly more equity capital than they did in the latter part of the 1980s. They were forced to do so by the novelty of the transactions and investors' understandable resistance to the unknown. But as the initial deals succeeded and equity returns were reported to be in excess of 100 percent per year, investment capital began to flow into the industry.

In the next stage of this process, both limited partners and suppliers of debt capital demanded and received more of the equity, thus reducing both the deal-maker's commitment of capital and back-end stake in the success of the transaction. Further distorting the incentives of deal-makers, the flood of capital into LBO funds allowed the deal-makers to command "front-end-loaded" fees simply for closing the transactions.[53] Such fees, which often substituted for the actual commitment of equity capital, combined with the convention of the 20 percent override (which amounts in practice to a free warrant on the outcome of the venture), enabled deal-makers both to profit upfront and to hold a residual interest while shifting virtually all downside risk to the creditors and limited partners.[54]

Such an arrangement, whereby deal-makers are effectively being paid for "doing" deals, ensures that too many deals will be done. In such situations, it pays deal-makers who do not value their reputations (or have no reputation to protect) to do deals that they know (or should know) cost more than the value they are expected to produce. Although this arrangement cannot be sustained indefinitely because of the losses it's bound to generate, the several-year information lag revealing the profitability of the deals allows it to continue for some time. During this time, deal-makers can earn fees on bad deals.

As the information on high returns continues to make itself known, and the market continues to mature, the probability of failure also rises because new and inexperienced deal-makers (who thus have less reputational capital at stake) enter the market; the supply of attractive deals thus begins to shrink and prices are bid up to competitive levels. Under these circumstances, the market is likely to overshoot and bidders are more likely to overpay. As a direct consequence, limited partners and creditors—both of whom must rely to some extent on the reputation and assurances of the deal-maker—are more likely to experience losses. In this situation, the "go/no-go" decision effectively falls back on the suppliers of credit, who are generally not able to obtain the necessary information at reasonable cost to make good decisions.[55]

What, then, corrects this contracting failure and restores the market to equilibrium? As losses begin to appear, investors pull back, yields rise sharply—and with them the cost of high leverage. The reputations of many deal-makers are tarnished, and the whole activity becomes tainted. In the meantime, however, some LBO specialist firms—especially well-established deal-makers such as KKR, Clayton & Dubilier, Forstmann Little, and others—continue to have a strong interest in maintaining their reputational capital. Such firms, even if they have fallen to the temptation of front-end-loaded structures, will work hard to salvage troubled deals and to minimize losses to their investment partners.

In contrast, many of the newer players entering the market have considerably less to lose from walking away from a bad deal. The perceived potential reward to breaking into the market with a big success often far outweighs the risk of loss—provided you don't have to commit the firm's capital.

The Revco and Fruehauf failures provide good examples of this problem (see Karen Wruck's 1991 analysis of Revco in the *Journal of Applied Corporate Finance*); and so do the bankruptcies following Interco's leveraged restructuring and Campeau's acquisitions of Allied and Federated.[56] It is interesting that none of these deals was sponsored (or promoted, in the Interco and Campeau cases) by established LBO partnerships; rather, they were all either sponsored or promoted by non-partnership newcomers eager to enter the business.

Incentives to overpay in HLTs were also exaggerated by another set of conflicts of interest. In some of these transactions, the substantial amounts paid to the current managers for their old stock far exceeded their investment in the equity of the newly levered company. Such large upfront distributions almost surely encouraged them—especially if their jobs were also being threatened by a hostile offer—to go along with deals whose expected returns were not commensurate with the risks.

In effect, if not by conscious intent, the investment bankers structured deals that *paid* the managers to abandon their normal caution so that the deals could get done and the fees collected. Again, Revco, Interco, and Campeau provide illustrative examples. In each of these cases, there was no LBO partnership with a long-run reputation to protect. The investment bankers that promoted the deals invested no net money of their own and took out substantial fees. And, in the cases of Revco and Interco, the managers were paid substantial sums to do the deals.[57]

Compounding the Problems by Regulation and New Barriers to Workouts

After almost a decade of progressive deregulation across many sectors of American industry, we are now experiencing "re-regulation" of our financial markets. Much of the S&L industry has effectively been nationalized. Drexel Burnham Lambert, one of the prime movers in the leveraged restructuring movement, has been destroyed. And with the proliferation of poison pills, state antitakeover laws, and growing legal support for the "just say no" defense, the once vigorous market for corporate control is now largely dormant.

As suggested earlier, the regulatory measures designed to purge our credit markets of "speculative excesses" have greatly added to the current difficulties in our HLT markets. When regulators began to step in during the summer of 1989, there were already signs of a normal correction as participants began to realize that the LBO market had overshot the "efficient margin." There was already under way a return to larger equity commitments, less debt, lower prices, lower projected growth rates, and lower bank fees.[58] In the absence of most regulatory intervention, these fundamentally self-correcting processes would have disciplined participants in the venture and credit markets, thereby providing the basis for renewed activity at sustainable prices.

Unfortunately, however, the flurry of legislative and regulatory initiatives provoked by real estate losses overrode such normal market correctives and created a "downward spiral" in prices (and business activity generally). The S&L legislation (FIRREA),[59] HLT regulations, and much tightened oversight by banking regulators depressed high-yield bond prices further, raised the cost of high leverage, and made adjustments to overleveraged capital structures all the more difficult. In so doing, such regulations have caused non-price rationing of credit, along with a sharp constriction of its availability to middle market and small firms.[60] They have also reduced the flexibility of lenders to work with highly leveraged companies who cannot meet lending covenants or current debt service payments. These changes, coming on top of the departure of Drexel, the principal market maker, have caused a sharp increase in defaults. Indeed, nineteen defaults among the Kaplan and Stein sample of 119 large LBOs have occurred since the beginning of 1989; only three in that sample defaulted prior to that time.

Problems with Workouts

Compounding the problem with losses and defaults is surely not what most congressmen and regulators intended when they enacted such policy shifts. In addition to the "political" objections to the control market I've cited earlier, much of the impetus for the new rules and regulations undoubtedly came from legitimate concern about the protection of deposit insurance funds and the soundness of our financial institutions.[61] But I can think of no such charitable explanation to account for the barriers to private workouts thrown up by bankruptcy judges and tax authorities.

As stated earlier, a major means of reorganizing distressed companies in the 1980s was the 3(a)9 exchange offer employed by Drexel during the early 1980s. Such a technique, even in the absence of Drexel, should have been useful for accomplishing out-of-court settlements under current conditions. In January 1990, however, Judge Burton Lifland ruled in the LTV case that bondholders who participate in exchange offers thereby reduce the value of their claim in bankruptcy to the market value of the claim accepted. Because such market values are typically well below face value, bondholders today are not likely to tender their bonds into an offer if there is any serious chance the firm will later file for Chapter 11. This ruling, together with tax penalties imposed in 1990 by Congress on reorganizations outside the bankruptcy court,[62] has caused exchange offers to slow to a trickle and bankruptcies to rise sharply. For example, only two of the 119 LBOs in the Kaplan and Stein study entered bankruptcy prior to 1989. Since then, eight more have followed.

In sum, our political, regulatory, and legal system has produced a set of policy changes that are frustrating instead of encouraging the normal market adjustment process that was under way in 1989. Indeed, from an economist's perspective, such changes seem virtually the opposite of what is necessary to promote the efficient reorganization of troubled companies, an expansion in the availability of debt capital, and a general return to growth. By drying up traditional credit sources, regulation has sharply increased the cost of debt and thus increased the number of defaults. At the same time, other changes have interfered with the private workout process, thus ensuring that many of those defaults will turn into bankruptcies. All this might not be so troubling, except that the rulings and practices of our bankruptcy courts are making the Chapter 11 process seemingly ever more costly, adding to the waste of resources.

A Proposal for Reforming the Bankruptcy Process

The function of the bankruptcy courts is to enforce contracts between the firm and its creditors and to provide a formal process for breaking such contracts when they cannot be fulfilled and when private parties cannot resolve their conflicts outside of court. In addition, bankruptcy courts resolve ambiguities about the size, legitimacy, and priority of claims. Unfortunately, the U.S. bankruptcy system seems to be fundamentally flawed. It is expensive,[63] it exacerbates conflicts among different classes of creditors, and it often takes years to resolve individual cases. As a result of such delays, much of the operating value of businesses can be destroyed.[64]

Much of the problem stems from the following two fundamental premises underlying the revised (1978) U.S. Bankruptcy Code: (1) reorganization is strongly preferred to liquidation (and current management should be given ample opportunity to lead that reorganization); and (2) the restructuring of the firm's contractual claims should, whenever possible, be *completely* voluntary. In practice, a majority in number (representing at least two-thirds of the value) of any class of claimants deemed to be impaired[65] must approve a reorganization. Judges have the power to "cram down" a settlement on a class of creditors without their approval, but they seldom do it. Reflecting the pro-debtor bias in the code, the managers of the firm are effectively given the sole right to propose a plan for 120 days after the filing. Bankruptcy judges also regularly approve multiple extensions of this exclusivity period.[66] As I will argue later, these features of the code give rise to chronic inefficiencies.

Absolute Priority: Theory vs. Practice

In thinking about what we want the bankruptcy system to accomplish and how it might be improved, it is important to distinguish between the different conditions of firms filing for Chapter 11. I find it useful to classify these companies into the following four categories:

1. Companies with profitable operations but the "wrong" capital structures—that is, cases in which the promised time path of payments to claimants does not match the availability of cash flow to make those payments, and a rearrangement of the timing will allow all payments to be made.

2. Companies with profitable operations whose value is being maximized under the current management team, but whose total firm value for reasons now beyond management's control is below the value of total liabilities. In such cases, regardless of how payments on those liabilities are reordered through time, their total face value cannot be covered.

3. Companies with potentially profitable, but poorly managed, operations that could meet their total obligations provided the firm's operating strategy (or the management team) were changed (and perhaps the timing of payments reordered as well).

4. Companies that cannot meet their contractual obligations and whose liquidation value exceeds their going concern value.

In principle (and setting aside for now the problem of investor uncertainty about which of these categories fits a given company), the broad outlines of the bankruptcy process should be very simple.

For companies falling into Case 1—fundamentally profitable firms with the wrong capital structure—the solution is simply to rearrange the timing of the payments through a voluntary financial restructuring in the capital markets. And if such private restructurings are not practicable—because of regulatory constraints on lenders, tax problems, or holdouts—then a simple, low-cost reorganization of the claims in bankruptcy court (using, if possible, the new "pre-packaged bankruptcy" format)[67] should be able to provide complete value to all claimholders.

In Case 2—the well-managed firm in which the maximum total firm value is less than the total claims held by creditors—the company can be reorganized by creating a new capital structure and distributing those claims to each of the claimants, giving value equal to 100 percent of each of the claims until total firm value is exhausted. The last class of claimants to be paid would not in general receive full payment, but would receive mostly equity claims on the new entity. This solution follows what is called *absolute priority*.

Case 3—the case in which the firm's operating strategy is wrong—would involve a change in the operating strategy (and/or management) of the firm together with a new capital structure and a distribution in accordance with absolute priority.

Case 4—in which the firm is worth more dead than alive—calls for the liquidation of the firm's assets and distribution of the proceeds according to the absolute priority rule.

In practice, court-supervised solutions to financial distress seldom bear any relation to these conceptual solutions. A study by Larry Weiss of thirty-seven bankruptcies administered under the 1978 code finds that actual solutions violate the contractually agreed-upon priority rules in almost 80 percent of the cases.[68] Equity holders and lower priority claimants routinely receive partial payment on their claims even though more senior claimants are not fully paid. In two particularly flagrant cases, equity holders retained 100 percent of the equity while unsecured creditors received only 37 percent and 60 percent of their claims.

As suggested earlier, such priority violations are virtually guaranteed when the courts (1) routinely allow the current management team to remain in place, and (2) require reorganization plans to receive the approval of all impaired creditor classes. Through these practices, the courts give management and junior creditors a major lever—in practice, the threat of dragging out the proceedings and thereby adding substantially to the legal and opportunity costs—which they use to expropriate value from more senior claimants.

The Consequences of Failing to Enforce Strict Priority

Current court practices—especially the failure to enforce absolute priority and to limit the period of management's monopoly rights to propose a restructuring to 120 days—are very difficult to justify on efficiency grounds.[69] I can see no argument for violating the contractually agreed-upon priority of valid claims.[70,71] Consistent and widespread violations of absolute priority will generate large inefficiencies in the economy. And they will do it in two principal ways.

First, the larger the deviations from strict priority the system tolerates, the harder the junior creditors will push to expropriate value from the senior claimants. This means more intractable, longer, and more costly conflicts among claimholders. Such conflicts prolong the length and increase the costs of bankruptcy; in so doing, they reduce the value of debtor firms.

But the effect of such violations is not limited to troubled companies in reorganization. Of greater consequence, large and frequent deviations from strict priority will interfere with voluntary contracting and specialization in bearing default risk. This will raise the corporate cost of capital (especially for those smaller and riskier firms that generated much of the economic gains of the 1980s). Senior creditors accustomed to seeing their claims violated will increasingly refuse to allow junior claimants into the capital structure. And when junior claimants are allowed, senior creditors will refuse to lend to all but the highest-rated credits. In the extreme, such a development would reduce all claimants to the same status, which in turn would dictate that the capital structures of all companies with significant default risk would become the equivalent of 100 percent equity.

Given the risk-bearing and control benefits of debt financing, the costs to the economy in the form of increased inefficiencies from thus restricting debt would likely be enormous. As suggested, it would also substantially raise the cost of capital to American firms, especially smaller ones. A significant increase in the "cost of capital" may not sound consequential; but, as demonstrated by the plight of non-investment grade companies during the current "credit crunch," a higher cost of capital means not only fewer leveraged control transactions, but less corporate capital investment, fewer jobs, and reduced growth for the economy as a whole.

The Information Problem (and the Role of Auctions in Solving It)

One of the major, and heretofore unrecognized, reasons for the intractability of intercreditor conflicts is the "information problem" aggravated—if not actually *created*—by our current bankruptcy system.[72] In outlining solutions for the four different classes of bankruptcies listed above, I made the assumption that all claimants have reliable information about the firm's prospects and that their assessments of the value of the reorganized and restructured firm are identical. In practice, of course, there is tremendous uncertainty about the value of the reorganized company. Adding to this uncertainty, there are few, if any, incentives in the current process for interested parties to provide unbiased estimates of the true value of the firm.

To see the issue clearly, let us ignore the optimal capital structure problem and assume the firm's claimants will be paid entirely in common stock in the unlevered reorganized firm.[73] Senior claimants have incentives to underestimate the value of the firm so they will be awarded a larger fraction of the equity. Equity holders have incentives to overestimate the value so they will retain a larger fraction. Junior claimants have more complicated incentives, depending on whether their claim is clearly "in the money" (in which case their incentives are identical to senior creditors') or "out of the money" (in which their position is much like that of the equity holders). Current managers want to retain control, which means they are likely to resist valuable changes in firm strategy (especially if they have no significant equity stake) that would also reduce the probability of their retaining their jobs. The bankruptcy judges—those effectively charged with solving this "information problem"—have neither the information nor the expertise to assess the firm's value.

One way to solve the information and incentive problem would be to allow any party—outsiders as well as current claimants—to make an all-cash bid for the control rights to the company. At the close of the auction, the highest bidder would *immediately* assume control of the company and its operations. The current managers could themselves bid, or they could bid as part of an investor group (including creditors). The investor groups themselves, by bidding for the services of, or deliberately excluding, the current management team, would thus be forced to ascertain whether the managers were valuable to the reorganization of the business or were instead a continuing part of the problem. The firm's new capital structure, moreover, would be in the hands of the bidding groups; and, in determining how they raised the funds, they would be subjected to the market test.

Such an auction process would also do much to reduce the problem of biased information produced by our current system. It would do so by forcing current equity holders attempting to preserve control to back *with their own money* their (otherwise biased) estimates of firm value—or at least to find outside investors willing to back those estimates. The same requirement would apply to creditors, who frequently claim to be able to create more value than the settlement being worked out in the voluntary process.

In such an auction system, the role of the bankruptcy court would be sharply narrowed. After investing the proceeds from the auction of the firm in riskless securities, the court would then proceed with the allocation of that value among claimholders. All claims would accrue interest at the riskless rate, thereby limiting the bias for junior claimants to drag out the proceedings. After determining the legitimacy and priority of claims, the court would then distribute the auction proceeds in *strict accordance with absolute priority*. In contrast to the reality of our Chapter 11 process, the court allocation process (with funds held in a riskless portfolio) could proceed at its own pace without concern that firm value was being eroded by management distractions or uncertainty among employees, customers, or suppliers about the future of the firm.

The auction process would thus have two major advantages over the current system. First, it would separate the task of assessing the firm's value from that of dividing that value among creditors and equity holders, effectively assigning the first to capital markets and the second to the courts. Second, it would shelter the value of the firm's operations from the destructive conflicts among creditors and equity holders over the division of firm value—conflicts that make the current formal bankruptcy process so inefficient.

The auction process would also effectively take the control rights to the firm out of the hands of the court (which effectively delegates them to managers in most bankruptcies) and transfer them to the highest bidder in the market. In so doing, it would also take the court out of the awkward position of having to decide whether current management should be replaced and having to "second guess" the business judgment of professional managers.[74]

Conclusions: Where We Are Headed

Given the current political climate, we are almost certain to see further regulation of our capital markets in the attempt to prevent active investors from playing a major role in corporate governance. Bank and insurance company financing for HLTs is now almost unavailable; and even when it is, it is expensive and available in much smaller amounts than previously.

In emasculating the market for corporate control, regulators will continue to remove the discipline imposed by the new institutional monitors on corporate management. The consequence is likely to be a sharp decline in the productivity and competitiveness of our corporations in the 1990s and beyond. It could well mean a return to the economic stagnation of the 1970s, a period in which corporate returns on capital fell well below investors' cost of capital—and in which inflation-adjusted stockholder returns were thus substantially negative.

In the short run, we are also facing capital shortages for small- to medium-sized companies—those that created most of the growth in the 1980s. Denying credit to such companies has two serious consequences. First, it contributed significantly to the recession of the 1990s and slowed our recovery from it. Second, and perhaps even more important, by removing a major source of competition for large firms, a "credit crunch" will remove another important discipline that acts to limit inefficiencies in our largest companies.

In the absence of a well-functioning control market and vigorous competition from small U.S. firms, the major remaining source of discipline on corporate management is the pressure exerted by international product markets.

Provided we can resist the appeals to shield our companies from global competition by means of quotas and restrictive tariffs—regulations that continue to allow our largest steel and auto companies to remain high-cost producers—the pressure now exerted on corporate management by the globalization of product markets is likely to be the most powerful force for productivity increases. Barring overseas competition, the only other disciplines on corporate management are our current system of internal monitoring by corporate boards of directors and, as a last resort—and the worst of all possible choices—government intervention.

The evidence of the last forty years indicates, to me at least, that the conventional model of internal management control supervised by outside directors has generally failed as an effective control mechanism in our public corporations. As stated earlier, it is not likely to work well in the case of mature companies with large cash flow and few good investment opportunities. There are certainly companies that have reformed without any tangible threat of takeover, or without a crisis in the product markets. For example, the case of General Mills is one that has been well documented by my colleague, Gordon Donaldson;[75] and General Electric's restructuring and reorganization under Jack Welch has been spectacular. But in the vast majority of cases, unless management and the board have a large ownership stake, major *voluntary* reversals in corporate strategy (such as selling or shutting down a major business) are highly unlikely to come about without pressure from capital or product markets.

In the absence of capital market pressure, international competition is most likely to bring about necessary change. But given the incentives and ability of U.S. companies to use the political process to insulate themselves from overseas competitors as well as from the control market, I predict that finding new ways to improve existing internal corporate controls will become an issue of great urgency in the decade ahead of us—one that will attract the attention of politicians, regulators, institutional investors, and management scientists. Coming to a resolution of this issue will be difficult and contentious, but the consequences of failing to restore effective corporate control mean that we must not fail.

Notes

I appreciate the research assistance of Brian Barry, Susan Brumfield, and Steve-Anna Stephens; editorial and substantive comments and help from Don Chew and Karen Wruck; and research support provided by the Division of Research of the Harvard Business School. I bear all responsibility for errors.

1. For supporting evidence, see Sanjai Bhagat, Andre Shleifer, and Robert W. Vishny, "Hostile Takeovers in the 1980s: The Return to Corporate Specialization," *Brookings*

Papers: Microeconomics 1990, pp. 1–84; Steven N. Kaplan, "The Effects of Management Buyouts on Operating Performance and Value," *Journal of Financial Economics*, Vol. 24, No. 2 (October 1989), pp. 217–254; and Robert Comment and Gregg Jarrell, "Corporate Focus and Stock Returns," (Bradley Policy Research Center, Working Paper MR 91–01, May 1991).

2. The equity gains are based on RJR-Nabisco's July 15, 1991, stock and warrant prices of $11.50 each. The original LBO investors contributed about $3.2 billion in equity ($1.5 billion initially on February 9, 1989 and $1.7 billion in the restructuring on July 16, 1990); as of July 15, 1991, the total value of this equity had grown to $7.3 billion. The new public equity purchased for cash or exchanged for debt in March and April of 1991 totaled $2.0 billion; and the total value of this equity had increased to $2.8 billion as of July 15, 1991.
3. Given these conclusive indications of success, it seems ironic that journalist attempts to capitalize on the antagonism to corporate restructuring, e.g., Sarah Bartlett's *The Money Machine* (New York: Warner Books, 1991) should describe the RJR deal as "the deal ... people regard as most symptomatic of the excesses on Wall Street." "RJR Nabisco was not a departure," she goes on to say, "it was the culmination of a process that had gone badly out of control" (p. 237).
4. As revealed in the book, John Greeniaus, head of Johnson's baking unit, told KKR that if "the earnings of this group go up 15 or 20% ... I'd be in trouble." His charter was to spend the excess cash in his Nabisco division to limit earnings in order to produce moderate, but smoothly rising profits—a strategy that would mask the potential profitability of the business. (See Bryan Burrough and John Helyar, *Barbarians at the Gate*, New York, Harper & Row, 1990, pp. 370–371.)

   The Wall Street Journal reported that Greeniaus told them that the company was "looking frantically for ways to spend its tobacco cash," including a $2.8 billion plant modernization program that was expected to produce pre-tax returns of only 5 percent (Peter Waldman, "New RJR Chief Faces a Daunting Challenge at Debt-Heavy Firm, *Wall Street Journal*, March 14, 1989, p. A1:6).
5. Joseph Grundfest, "Just Vote No or Just Don't Vote," Working paper, Stanford Law School (1990).
6. Bill Saporito, "The Tough Cookie at RJR Nabisco," *Fortune* (July 18, 1988).
7. To compound the problem of selection bias, such journalistic accounts often contain inaccurate, or at best misleading, reporting of the facts. Jude Wanniski, editor of the *MediaGuide* (and a former *Wall Street Journal* reporter), calls attention to such reporting in his comments on a *Wall Street Journal* article on the 1986 Safeway LBO that, ironically, was awarded a Pulitzer Prize for "explanatory journalism" (Susan Faludi, "The Reckoning: Safeway LBO Yields Vast Profits but Extracts a Heavy Human Toll," *Wall Street Journal*, May 16, 1990). As Wanniski comments, "This was not business reporting, nor was it a human interest story. This was pure and simple propaganda, the work of an ideologue using the *Journal*'s front page to propagate a specific opinion about how corporate America should conduct its affairs" (Jude Wanniski, *Financial World*, December 11, 1990, p. 13).
8. Measured in 1990 dollars. Measured in nominal dollars, the total value of transactions and total gains were $1,239 billion and $443 billion, respectively.
9. As reported by the Salomon Brothers High Yield Research Group (*Original Issue High-Yield Default Study—1990 Summary*, January 28, 1991), as of the end of 1990, the face value of defaulted publicly placed or registered privately placed high-yield bonds in the period 1978–1990 was roughly $35 billion (about $20 billion of which entered bankruptcy). Given that recovery rates historically average about 40 percent,

actual losses may well be below $20 billion. Not all of these bonds were used to finance control transactions, but I use the total to obtain an upper-bound estimate of losses.
10. More precisely, between February 19, 1991 (before announcing two consecutive declines in quarterly earnings), and July 17, 1991 (the time of this writing).
11. A 1989 study by Laura Stiglin, Steven Kaplan, and myself demonstrates that, contrary to popular assertions, LBO transactions result in increased tax revenues to the U.S. Treasury—increases that average about 60 percent per annum on a permanent basis under the 1986 IRS code (Michael C. Jensen, Steven Kaplan, and Laura Stiglin, "Effects of LBOs on Tax Revenues of the U.S. Treasury," *Tax Notes,* Vol. 42, No. 6 [February 6, 1989], pp. 727–733).

The data presented by a study of pension fund reversions reveal that only about 1 percent of the premiums paid in all takeovers can be explained by reversions of pension plans in the target firms (although the authors of the study do not present this calculation themselves) (Jeffrey Pontiff, Andrei Shleifer, and Michael S. Weisbach, "Reversions of Excess Pension Assets after Takeovers," *Rand Journal of Economics,* Vol. 21, No. 4 [Winter 1990], pp. 600–613).

Joshua Rosett, analyzing over 5,000 union contracts in over 1,000 listed companies in the period 1973–1987, shows that less than 2 percent of the takeover premiums can be explained by reductions in union wages in the first six years after the change in control. Pushing the estimation period out to eighteen years after the change in control increases the percentage to only 5.4 percent of the premium. For hostile takeovers only, union wages *increase* by 3 percent and 6 percent for the two time intervals, respectively (Joshua G. Rosett, "Do Union Wealth Concessions Explain Takeover Premiums? The Evidence on Contract Wages," *Journal of Financial Economics,* Vol. 27, No. 1 [September 1990], pp. 263–282).
12. Many of the most visible of these prosecutions by U.S. Attorney Giuliani have now either been dropped for lack of a case or reversed. The only RICO conviction, Princeton/Newport, has been reversed (although other securities law violations have been upheld), and so too the GAF, Mulheren, and Chestman cases. Only one major conviction of that era remains (Paul Bilzerian), and it is under appeal. The guilty pleas often obtained under threat of RICO prosecution, of course, remain. For a brief discussion of pressures from Congress on the SEC to bring down investment bankers, arbs, and junk bonds, see Glenn Yago, "The Credit Crunch: A Regulatory Squeeze on Growth Capital," (pp. 99–100) in the Spring 1991 issue of *The Journal of Apllied Corporate Finance.*
13. The more fundamental cause of problems among banks is excess capacity caused by regulation and restrictions on takeovers of financial institutions. For elaboration of this point, see note 61.
14. See Creighton Meland, "Clarifying the New Guidelines for Highly-Leveraged Transactions" (Unpublished manuscript, Latham and Watkins, 1990).
15. See "NAIC (National Association of Insurance Companies) Policy Regarding Insurance Companies," Merrill Lynch Fixed-Income Research, June 12, 1990.
16. See the "Middle Market Roundtable" as well as the five articles on the "credit crunch" in the Spring 1991 issue of *The Journal of Applied Corporate Finance.*
17. Interestingly, the Japanese economy experienced similar efficiency increases almost a decade earlier than the United States.
18. Safeway, for example, went through an LBO in 1986 and sold half its stores. It has since come back public and has also launched a record five-year $3.2 billion capital program focused on store remodeling and new store construction.

19. The discrepancy between the data and the impression left by critics turns on a confusion between the level and the rate of increase of R&D spending. While achieving record levels, R&D spending grew more slowly in the late 1980s.

    In a study of 600 acquisitions of U.S. manufacturing firms during the years 1976–1985, Bronwyn Hall found that acquired firms did not have higher R&D expenditures (as a fraction of sales) than did firms in the same industry that were not acquired. Also, she found that "firms involved in mergers showed no difference in their pre- and post-merger R&D performance over those not so involved." See "The Effect of Takeover Activity on Corporate Research and Development," Chapter 3 in *Corporate Takeovers: Cause and Consequences*, ed. Alan Auerbach (Chicago: University of Chicago Press, 1988). In two recent papers, "The Impact of Corporate Restructuring on Industrial Research and Development," *Brookings Papers: Microeconomics 1990*, pp. 85–124, and "Corporate Restructuring and Investment Horizons" (Unpublished manuscript, University of California, Berkeley, December 1990), Hall finds little relation between mergers, control changes, and LBOs and R&D expenditures, but finds a negative effect of leveraged restructurings on R&D. A study by the Office of the Chief Economist at the SEC ("Institutional Ownership, Tender Offers, and Long-Term Investments," April 19, 1985) also concludes that (1) increased institutional stock holdings are not associated with increased takeovers of firms; (2) increased institutional holdings are not associated with decreases in R&D expenditures; (3) firms with high research and development expenditures are not more vulnerable to takeovers; and (4) stock prices respond positively to announcements of increases in R&D expenditures.
20. I have been unable to find references to the sources of data that have formed the bases for the critics' conclusions. Other sectors show somewhat lower rates of growth of productivity than does manufacturing, but I have been unable to find any significant evidence of declines in the aggregate data to support the claims of critics.
21. In their study of 20,000 plants involving control changes, Frank Lichtenberg and Donald Siegel found that changes in control reduce white collar employment in nonproduction facilities, but do not reduce blue collar or R&D employees. They also found significant increases in total factor productivity after both acquisitions and LBOs. For a summary of this work, see Frank Lichtenberg and Donald Siegel, "The Effect of Control Changes on the Productivity of U.S. Manufacturing Plants," *Journal of Applied Corporate Finance* (Summer 1989), pp. 60–67.
22. On rare occasions, the internal control systems manage to accomplish significant change without the threat of product or capital markets. General Mills is an example. In a case study of General Mills, Gordon Donaldson describes the company's decade-long restructuring—a very gradual adjustment process that was finally successful in reversing a disastrous diversification strategy. See Gordon Donaldson, "Voluntary Restructuring: The Case of General Mills," *Journal of Financial Economics*, Vol. 27, No. 1 (September 1990). Donaldson raises the possibility that such a gradual adjustment process has lower social costs than the abrupt change enforced by dramatic restructurings or takeovers. I believe a careful estimate of the social waste associated with keeping people unemployed or underemployed (while still on the payroll) and the wasteful utilization of assets over a decade-long period makes the year-long adjustment following a takeover or LBO a far-lower-cost social strategy.
23. From 1977 to 1982, total employment fell by 336,000 from its high of over 1,000,000 in 1977. From 1982 to 1989, when the industry succeeded in gaining protection by means of import quotas, industry profits increased and employment in the industry rose to almost 840,000 even as U.S. automakers were losing significant market share.
24. Lester Thurow, *The Zero-Sum Society* (New York: Basic Books, 1980), p. 81.

25. See Vincent Carosso, *Investment Banking in America: A History* (Cambridge, MA: Harvard University Press, 1970).
26. For example, the Glass-Steagall Act significantly restricted commercial bank equity holdings as well as bank involvement in investment banking activities. The Chandler Act restricted banks' involvement in the reorganization of companies in which they have substantial debt holdings. In addition, the 1940 Investment Company Act put restrictions on the maximum holdings of investment funds. See Mark Roe, "Political and Legal Restraints on Ownership and Control of Public Companies," *Journal of Financial Economics*, Vol. 27, No. 1 (September 1990), pp. 7–42; and Joseph Grundfest, "Subordination of American Capital," *Journal of Financial Economics*, Vol. 27, No. 1 (September 1990), pp. 89–117.
27. For a historical account of the evolution of our proxy system into its current form, see John Pound, "Proxy Voting and the SEC: Investor Protection Versus Market Efficiency," *Journal of Financial Economics* 29, 2 (1991), pp. 241–284. Bernard Black, formerly on the legal staff of the SEC, concludes his analysis of proxy regulation as follows: "In fact, institutional shareholders are hobbled by a complex web of legal rules that make it difficult, expensive, and legally risky to own large percentage stakes or undertake joint efforts. Legal obstacles are especially great for shareholder efforts to nominate and elect directors, even to a minority of board seats. The proxy rules, in particular, help shareholders in some ways, but mostly hinder shareholder efforts to nominate and elect directors."
28. As cited in Roe (1990), p. 8.
29. Extending Roe's analysis of the influence of politics on finance, former SEC Commissioner Joseph Grundfest analyzes the process through which politicians take advantage of the agency problems between managers and shareholders to transfer wealth to favored constituencies (particularly managers, who are one of the most powerful constituencies in the process) through the securities regulation process. See Grundfest (1990).
30. This view is expressed in the Business Roundtable's March 1990 report, *Corporate Governance and American Competitiveness*. That statement, moreover, is significantly different from a statement it issued twelve years earlier, which emphasized accountability to shareholders alone. For a discussion of this "retreat" from shareholder accountability, see Robert Monks and Nell Minow, *Power and Accountability* (New York: HarperCollins, 1991), pp. 81–84.
31. Michael C. Jensen and Kevin J. Murphy, "CEO Incentives: It's Not How Much You Pay, but How," *Harvard Business Review*, Vol. 90, No. 3 (May/June, 1990), pp. 138–153.
32. I put "long-run" in quotes because financial economists do not distinguish between current and "long-run" values. Virtually all credible evidence that we have suggests that the market is willing to and capable of taking the long view of a corporation's prospects. It does of course make errors, but the evidence indicates that, without inside information, it is almost impossible for investors to tell whether those errors are positive or negative at any given time.
33. Value maximizing is socially optimal assuming there are no externalities or monopoly power. Externalities are the impositions of costs (or conferring of benefits) by one party on others in which the acting party does not bear the costs (or have the opportunity to charge for the benefits). The pollution of air and water, without tax penalties or compensation to those affected, are examples.
34. Agency costs, more generally, reflect management's natural predisposition to growth rather than profitability and the incentives it faces to expand its firms beyond the size that maximizes shareholder wealth. See Gordon Donaldson, *Managing Corporate*

Wealth (New York: Praeger, 1984). Corporate growth is also associated with increases in the level of management compensation. One of the better-documented propositions in compensation theory is that for every 10 percent increase in the size of the company, the CEO's compensation goes up by 3 percent (G. Baker, M. Jensen, and K. Murphy, "Compensation and Incentives," *Journal of Finance* [July 1988], pp. 593–616). Also, the tendency of companies to reward middle managers through promotion rather than year-to-year bonuses also creates an organizational bias toward growth. Only growth can supply the new positions that such promotion-based reward systems require. See George Baker, "Pay-for-Performance for Middle Managers: Causes and Consequences," *Journal of Applied Corporate Finance* (Fall 1990), pp. 50–61.

35. See Comment and Jarrell (1991). See also Michael Porter, "From Competitive Advantage to Corporate Strategy," *Harvard Business Review* (May–June 1987), pp. 43–59.
36. A 50 percent premium that recovers the previous value of the firm means that 33 percent of the previous value was destroyed (50/150=0.33).
37. Kaplan (1989) documents that the median CEO receives $64 per $1,000 change in shareholder wealth from his 6.4 percent equity interest alone. By contrast, Kevin Murphy and I find that the average CEO in the Forbes 1000 receives total pay (including salary, bonus, deferred compensation, stock options, and equity) that changes by only about $3.25 for every $1,000 change in stockholder value (see Jensen and Murphy, 1990).

   In their clinical study of the 1986 OM Scott LBO from ITT, George Baker and Karen Wruck show that after the buyout, in addition to a substantial equity stake, Scott's managers were subject to an annual cash bonus plan that increased the average payouts from three to six times. See "Organizational Changes and Value Creation in Leveraged Buyouts," *Journal of Financial Economics*, Vol. 25 (1989), pp. 163–190.
38. See Michael C. Jensen, "The Agency Costs of Free Cash Flow: Corporate Finance and Takeovers," *American Economic Review*, Vol. 76, No. 2 (May 1986), pp. 323–329. For additional evidence, see also Larry Lang, Rene Stulz, and Ralph Walkling, "A Test of the Free Cash Flow Hypothesis: The Case of Bidder Returns," *Journal of Financial Economics* 29, 2 (1991), pp. 315–335.
39. For a survey of research on the economic effects of LBOs, see Krishna Palepu, "Consequences of Leveraged Buyouts," *Journal of Financial Economics*, Vol. 27 (1990), and the references therein.
40. Kaplan (1989).
41. Average total buyout fees amounted to 5.5 percent of the equity two months prior to the buyout proposal.
42. Krishna Palepu (1990), pp. 260–261.
43. See Jensen (1986). See also Karen Wruck, "Financial Distress, Reorganization, and Organizational Efficiency," *Journal of Financial Economics*, Vol. 27 (1990).
44. Michael C. Jensen, "The Effects of LBOs and Corporate Debt on the Economy," Remarks before the Subcommittee on Telecommunications and Finance, U.S. House of Representatives Hearings on Leveraged Buyouts (Washington, DC, February 22, 1989).
45. Bankruptcy, however, does have special advantages in some cases; for example, in retailing, trade credit is crucial to continuation of the business, and it is difficult to negotiate privately with hundreds or thousands of trade suppliers.
46. See my article, "Active Investors, LBOs, and the Privatization of Bankruptcy," *Journal of Applied Corporate Finance* (Spring 1989), pp. 35–44. My argument was anticipated in part by Robert Haugen and Lemma Senbet in their article, "The Insignificance of Bankruptcy Costs to the Theory of Optimal Capital Structure," *Journal of Finance*, Vol. 33 (1978), pp. 383–393.

47. For a more detailed discussion, see Carl Kester later "Japanese Corporate Governance and the Conservation of Value in Financial Distress," *Journal of Applied Corporate Finance* 4, 2 (1991), pp. 98–104. As I have argued earlier, however, even as our system has begun to look more like the Japanese, the Japanese economy is undergoing changes that are reducing the role of large active investors and thus making their system resemble ours. With the progressive development of U.S.-like capital markets, Japanese managers have been able to loosen the controls once exercised by the banks. So successful have they been in bypassing banks that the top third of Japanese companies are no longer net bank borrowers. As a result of their past success in product market competition, Japanese companies are now "flooded" with free cash flow. Their competitive position today reminds me of the position of American companies in the late 1960s. And like their U.S. counterparts in the 1960s, Japanese companies today appear to be in the process of creating conglomerates. My prediction is that, unless unmonitored Japanese managers prove to be much more capable than American executives of managing large, sprawling organizations, the Japanese economy is likely to produce large numbers of those conglomerates that U.S. capital markets have spent the last ten years trying to pull apart. And if I am right, then Japan is likely to experience its own leveraged restructuring movement. See Michael C. Jensen, "Eclipse of the Public Corporation," *Harvard Business Review*, Vol. 89, No. 5 (September–October 1989), pp. 61–74.
48. For a discussion of strip financing, see Michael C. Jensen, "Takeovers: Their Causes and Consequences," *Journal of Economic Perspectives*, Vol. 2, No. 1 (Winter 1988), pp. 21–48.
49. See Stuart Gilson's article "Managing Default: Some Evidence on How Firms Choose between Workouts and Chapter 11," *Journal of Applied Corporate Finance* 4, 2 (1991), pp. 62–70. Wruck (1990, pp. 425–426), using data obtained privately from Stuart Gilson, reports that only 51 percent of all 381 firms performing in the lowest 5 percent of the NYSE and ASE defaulted in the period 1978–1987. It seems likely that many of these companies avoided default by means of private reorganizations.
50. See Stuart Gilson's article cited above. See also Stuart Gilson, Kose John, and Larry Lang, "Troubled Debt Restructurings: An Empirical Study of Private Reorganization of Companies in Default," *Journal of Financial Economics*, Vol. 27, No. 2 (September 1990), pp. 315–353.
51. See Karen Hopper Wruck, "What Really Went Wrong at Revco?", *Journal of Applied Corporate Finance* 4, 2 (1991), pp. 79–92. See also Steven N. Kaplan, "Campeau's Acquisition of Federated: Value Destroyed or Value Added," *Journal of Financial Economics*, Vol. 25, No.2 (December 1989), pp. 191–212.
52. See Steven N. Kaplan and Jeremy Stein, "The Evolution of Buyout Pricing and Financial Structure in the 1980s" (Unpublished manuscript, University of Chicago, April 1991).
53. Kaplan and Stein (1991) find that, in the fifty-three large LBOs done prior to 1986, total fees amounted to 2.7 percent of the purchase price of the equity. By contrast, in the sixty-six large LBOs completed between 1986 and 1988, total fees rose to 4.9 percent of the purchase price of the equity.
54. Venture capital organizations are structured similarly. See William Sahlman, "The Structure and Governance of Venture Capital Organizations, *Journal of Financial Economics*, Vol. 27, No. 2 (September 1990), pp. 473–521. Some contracts with limited partners help reduce these incentives by making the sharing rule cumulative on all deals funded by the partnership. Under these contracts the deal-maker can't avoid the losses as easily.
55. The decision-making by suppliers of credit may also be distorted by their own "agency problems." Commercial lenders, for example, were often rewarded principally for

loan and fee generation, which in turn arose from the efforts of banks to retain market share by underpricing loans in an industry troubled by chronic excess capacity. High-yield bond mutual fund managers, to the extent they are paid on the basis of funds under management, also have some incentive to gamble on uneconomic deals rather than return funds to subscribers. For an exposition of such "agency problems," see Martin S. Fridson, "Agency Costs: Past and Future," Merrill Lynch *Extra Credit* (June 1991). For a related theory of cycles founded on information lags, not incentives, see Bradford, DeLong, Andrei Shleifer, Lawrence H. Summers, and Robert J. Waldmann, "Positive Feedback Investment Strategies and Destabilizing Rational Speculations," *Journal of Finance* (June 1990), pp. 379–395.

56. Interestingly, the Campeau acquisitions of Allied and Federated and the leveraged restructuring of Interco were all promoted by the same non-LBO partnership investment bank. See Kaplan (1989).

57. See Wruck, "What Really Went Wrong at Revco?" In the case of the Interco restructuring, Interco's managers owned $12.3 million in equity prior to the deal (1.15 percent). They were paid $15.8 million in cash, $13.3 million in debt in the restructured company, and ended up with 4.14 percent of the equity (a trivial amount relative to normal standards) with only a $7.9 million total value (source: Interco May 1989 proxy statement). For a critical review of the price-setting process, see George Anders and Francine Schwadel, "Costly Advice: Wall Streeters Helped Interco Defeat Raiders But at a Heavy Price," *Wall Street Journal,* July 11, 1990.

58. See Kaplan and Stein (1991).

59. The Financial Institutions Reform, Recovery and Enforcement Act, passed in the summer of 1989, which banned the purchase and effectively banned the holding of high-yield bonds by thrifts.

60. See the "Middle Market Roundtable" as well as the Spring 1991 issue of the *Journal of Applied Corporate Finance.*

61. There are admittedly complex economic and political forces at work today that make it difficult for regulators to formulate policy. But in their obsession with protecting the deposit insurance funds, regulators are responding to symptoms while ignoring the fundamental cause of the problems in our S&L and banking systems. With over 12,000 commercial banks, the banking system has substantial excess capacity and is inefficiently organized. It seems unlikely that the new bank reforms now being entertained by Congress will allow for the orderly exit and radical restructuring of the industry that is needed to restore profitability. An active market for corporate control has not been allowed to function in this industry; and it seems doubtful that it will be allowed to do so in the future. In the absence of takeovers, the most likely exit route will be through bankruptcies, forced mergers, and liquidations in response to losses caused by the intense competition in the financial products markets. Without the capital markets to aid in the exit of resources, we can expect individual banks to struggle to add to their capital base to ensure that, when the music stops, they will be one of the survivors. This process, by increasing capacity in an industry that already has to shrink, has led and will continue to lead to substantial waste of scarce resources.

62. Under the Revenue Reconciliation Act of 1990, when new bonds issued in an exchange offer have lower interest rates, the firm must realize taxable income on the exchange. Such exchanges, tax-exempt prior to the Act, are now tax-exempt only if issued in bankruptcy.

63. Frank Easterbrook, however, has pointed out that the direct costs of bankruptcy are lower than the direct costs of taking a company public. See "Is Corporate Bankruptcy

Efficient," *Journal of Financial Economics,* Vol. 27, No. 2 (September 1990), pp. 411–417. No one has as yet obtained a good estimate of the indirect costs of bankruptcy; but, as illustrated in the Eastern Airlines case, they can be substantial.

64. Judge Lifland of the New York bankruptcy court wasted at least hundreds of millions of dollars of creditors' and society's resources by allowing Eastern Airlines to continue to operate in an industry flooded with excess capacity in which exit had to occur and in the face of extremely hostile unions (who prevented a potential sale of the airline and were rumored to want to destroy it). According to Eastern's 10K filed in April 1989 (p. 3), the company had sufficient assets ($4.8 billion) to repay fully its $3.8 billion in liabilities at the time of its bankruptcy filing in 1989. In March of 1990, a year later, management proposed a plan to pay creditors 48 cents on the dollar (or about $1.7 billion), but then backed out of it. It appears $1.2 billion in secured claims has been paid and that little will be paid on the remaining pre-bankruptcy liabilities. Thus, projected losses appear to be in the billions of dollars. Much of the reduction in the value of Eastern's assets while in Chapter 11 illustrates the cost of our current bankruptcy process.

65. In the sense that the plan doesn't promise to pay them what they would get in a straight liquidation under Chapter 7 of the code.

66. This is what Judge Lifland did in the Eastern case. Consistent with these policies, he approved (in June 1991) the *eighth* extension of Lomas Financial Corporation's manager's sole right to propose a plan for reorganization. Such extensions are especially problematic in cases where the managers' strategy has been responsible for the firm's financial difficulties. But it is very difficult, of course, for a judge to make this judgment when he or she has little or no prior knowledge of, or experience with, the company or the industry.

67. For a discussion of this technique—which amounts to a hybrid between private workout and bankruptcy—see the article by John McConnell and Henri Servaes, "The Economics of Pre-Packaged Bankruptcy," *Journal of Applied Corporate Finance* 4, 2 (1991), pp. 93–98.

68. Assuming the courts determine impairment correctly. See the article by Lawrence Weiss, "The Bankruptcy Code and Violations of Absolute Priority," *Journal of Applied Corporate Finance* 4, 2 (1991), pp. 71–78, which is based in turn on Lawrence A. Weiss, "Bankruptcy Resolution: Direct Costs and Violation of Priority of Claims," *Journal of Financial Economics,* Vol. 27, No. 2 (September 1990), pp. 285–314.

69. For a sophisticated attempt to justify the efficiency of the current system, see Easterbrook (1990).

70. As Leonard Rosen (noted bankruptcy counsel and senior partner of Wachtell, Lipton, Rosen & Katz) comments in the Roundtable "Bankruptcies, Workouts, and Turnarounds," *Journal of Applied Corporate Finance* 4, 2 (1991), pp. 34–62, subordinated claimants have shown considerable ingenuity in devising new theories to justify the violation of the priority of the contracts they signed. One that is now popular, and is apparently used frequently as a bargaining threat, is "fraudulent conveyance." Under this theory, which has yet to be widely accepted by the courts, the argument goes that the banks' secured claims should be subordinated to all others because they loaned money to an LBO or other levered transaction in which they earned fees—all the while knowing that the new entity was insolvent. This argument makes little economic sense, for two reasons: (1) the banks are putting large amounts of their own capital at risk in the deal (unlike the investment bankers who receive large fees and frequently play a large role in promoting the deal); and (2) the subordinated debt holders are put in the position of denying that they had information in the prospectus

revealing that the transaction was highly levered and risky, and that they were being paid a risk premium for accepting this risk. While there can be legitimate cases of fraud in which assets are bled from a firm in a leveraged transaction and the new owners end up owning only a shell, the beneficiaries of such fraud are those old shareholders and bondholders who collected the proceeds, not the banks or others who put large amounts of money into the new entity. The theory seems designed to transfer wealth from the banks simply because they are on the scene at the time of the bankruptcy litigation. Widespread acceptance of the theory of fraudulent conveyance would be another important and unwise step in forbidding banks, bondholders, insurance companies, and individuals from engaging in the specialization of bearing default risk in transactions that had any positive probability of ending up in bankruptcy court.

71. Another argument used to justify deviations from strict priority is based on "equitable subordination." The principle of equitable subordination in American law seriously hinders the efficient resolution of financial distress. It does so by prohibiting banks from working closely with financially distressed companies to whom they have loaned money. The Japanese system works in exactly the opposite way. Indeed, it is considered a moral obligation of the company's main bank to play a major role in working with the managers of a financially distressed client to resolve the problem. And this historically has frequently involved placing bank personnel in positions of major responsibility in the client firm. Nissan, for example, was run for years by an alumnus of the Industrial Bank of Japan after IBJ helped it get out of its financial difficulties.

72. Karen Wruck analyzes this generally unrecognized problem in her *Journal of Financial Economics* paper (see Wruck, 1990) and in her clinical study of the Revco LBO, "What Really Went Wrong at Revco?"

73. Or that the claimants will all receive a proportionate strip of all claims in the new capital structure.

74. In fact, the beneficial effects of an auction are sometimes obtained even in our current system. Some companies—Fruehauf, for example—have resolved financial distress privately by sale of all or a major part of the assets to others. And some firms have been purchased out of bankruptcy: A. H. Robins was purchased by American Home Products. But current procedures give managers significant veto power over such offers. The $925 million bid by the Bass Group for Revco in bankruptcy was reportedly blocked, in part, by resistance from management. For additional analysis of an auction system, see Douglas G. Baird, "The Uneasy Case for Corporate Reorganizations," *Journal of Legal Studies* (January 1986), pp. 127–147. For a useful discussion of the current legal maze facing acquirers of bankrupt companies, see Mark D. Brodsky and Joel B. Zwiebel, "Chapter 11 Acquisitions: Payoffs for Patience," *Mergers & Acquisitions* (September–October, 1990), pp. 47–53.

75. See Donaldson (1990).

CHAPTER 13

Where M&A Pays and Where It Strays

Survey of the Research

ROBERT BRUNER

How you assess a particular M&A deal or even the whole flow of M&A activity depends on your frame of reference, on beliefs that help you decide whether specific deals represent the average outcome or instead lie in what statisticians call the "tail of the distribution." This frame of reference is a powerful filter for decision-makers and their advisers, and it typically arises from a blend of personal experience, anecdotes, conventional wisdom, and facts. The aim of this chapter is to enrich your frame of reference about success and failure in M&A with the findings of scientific research.

I have two basic criticisms of the way most people think about M&A.

First, the conventional wisdom is poorly grounded in the scientific evidence on the subject. The fashionable view seems to be that M&A is a loser's game. Yet an objective reading of over 100 studies supports the conclusion that M&A *does* pay.[1] These studies show that the shareholders of the selling firms earn large returns from M&A, that the shareholders of the buyers and sellers *combined* earn significant positive returns, and that the shareholders of buyers generally earn about the required rate of return on investment.

Second, conventional wisdom seems to hold that failure is the average outcome of all classes and varieties of M&A and that, in this sense, M&A is regrettably "homogeneous." Yet the research reveals wide dispersion of returns both within and across studies. And such variation suggests that, like turbulence under the smooth surface of a river, *something* is going on in the world of M&A that differentiates deals and predisposes them to success or failure—and that, like the varying river conditions below the surface, the world of M&A is not homogeneous. In this chapter, I argue that to see the varying states of this world is to build a "view" that better reflects the circumstances and approaches that give rise to success or failure in M&A.

Tip O'Neill, the Boston pol who rose to be Speaker of the U.S. House of Representatives, explained that in trying to understand the workings of Congress, it made no sense to focus on lofty national issues or policy debates within the Washington beltway. Instead, he said, "all politics is local." The mind-set of the successful politician begins with his or her constituency and the hopes and fears in town halls, school boards, and police precincts. It is the same in M&A: the best foundation for pursuing success and avoiding failure in M&A lies in seeing the important ways in which individual deals differ from one another. In other words, *all M&A is local.*

Conventional Wisdom on M&A Failure: Still Hazy after All These Years

The popular view is that M&A is a loser's game. The following excerpts from a recent book are representative:

> The sobering reality is that only about 20% of all mergers really succeed.... [M]ost mergers typically erode shareholder wealth.... [T]he cold, hard reality [is] that most mergers fail to achieve any real financial returns... very high rate of merger failure... rampant merger failure.[2]

I have lost count of the references—in newspaper columns, magazines, and consultants' reports—to this 20 percent success rate.[3] Yet there is no body of empirical research that documents the reputed *high failure rate* of M&A activity with a consistency and level of care equal to the gravity of the assertion. What is missing in the popular discussion is a rigorous definition of what the conventional wisdom means by "failure" in M&A. Here, too, the writers tend to refer vaguely to a shortfall between the goals of a merger and its outcome, without any consideration of the appropriateness of the goals or the general conditions in which the merger took place.

Here's an example of how the conventional wisdom on merger failure takes shape. In December 2002, a columnist wrote in the *Wall Street Journal*, "Most mergers don't work.... A mountain of academic research shows most acquisitions end up costing shareholders."[4] Later, in correspondence with me, this columnist cited as proof a *Business Week* article entitled "Why Most Big Deals Don't Pay Off," which reported that "61% of buyers destroyed shareholder wealth."[5] That article studied 302 large mergers of public companies from 1995 to 2001 and looked at the changes in the buyer's share price in the year following the bid adjusted for changes in the share prices of peer firms or an industry average. On the basis of this evidence, *Business Week* concluded:

> There has been no improvement in CEOs' dealmaking skills since 1995, when *Business Week*'s major survey of mergers in the early 1990s found that half were failures. Since then, an army of consultants and

bankers has tried to help CEOs improve their success rate. But they've failed.

This example reveals a number of problems in making inferences about the profitability of M&A. First, the conventional wisdom generalizes too readily from the findings of a single study (note the columnist's use of "*most* mergers" and "a *mountain* of academic studies"). Second, there is a tendency to exaggerate the extent of failure. By the terms of the *Business Week* study, a share price decline of just a penny would constitute a "failure." But recognizing that most share price movements are subject to a certain amount of noise, a more sensible approach would focus on *significant* failure and exclude the noise. What's more, the study's period of observation was a once-in-a-lifetime outlier in capital market performance—and it requires a truly heroic leap to generalize from that period to other time periods. Especially interesting during this time period was the feverish M&A activity in certain industry segments. For instance, a number of the large deals in the sample involved high-tech or Internet-related companies. And this raises the question: To what extent was the general finding of the study affected by the price collapse of the technology–media–telecommunications sector that started in 2000? Most of the deals in the sample were stock-for-stock exchanges, which, as past research has shown, tend to be worse for buyers than cash deals. The deals in the sample were also big deals, which by their nature have more integration and regulatory problems. And the study focused on deals between two public companies, while acquisitions of private companies—which are far more common than public deals—tend to be much more profitable for buyers.

So was *Business Week*'s sample representative of all M&A? No. It simply gives us insight into the profitability of big public-company deals in a "hot market"—and to vault from there to the assertion that "*most* mergers don't work" is clearly unjustified.[6]

Two recent studies (both by the same authors) offer a cautionary counterpoint to the *WSJ/BW* articles. In the first of the two, the authors examined the two-day abnormal (that is, adjusted for market movements) stock market returns to buyers using a large sample of deals announced from 1980 to 2001.[7] They found that the adjusted returns to buyers measured in dollars (not percentage returns) over this period were significantly negative (–$25.2 million), on average, consistent with the argument that "most mergers don't work." But the authors also reported three other important details. First, the average adjusted return to buyers was a significantly positive 1.1 percent—and their research showed that the inconsistency between the dollar and percentage returns is due to the extreme unprofitability of a few large deals. Second, the authors reported in their follow-up study that most of the losses from 1980 to 2001 were concentrated in just eighty-seven deals, out of a total sample of 12,023; without these deals, the whole sample would have showed a significantly positive dollar return. Third, the eighty-seven culprits were concentrated in the hot M&A market of 1998–2001. Thus, but for a relatively small number of deals in a limited market episode, one would reach a very different conclusion about the profitability of M&A.

The conventional wisdom on M&A thus tends to be either hazy on the evidence or, where solid evidence is offered, too ready to generalize from the findings based on localized conditions. There is more to the story of M&A success and failure. An informed "view" depends on mastering the scientific findings on the profitability of M&A and on understanding how profitability varies by types of deals and companies.

Measurement of M&A Profitability: Better Than What?

Before looking at the findings, we need to define the tests. The benchmark for measuring performance is investors' required returns, commonly defined as the return investors could have earned on other investment opportunities of similar risk. Against this benchmark, we can see three possible outcomes:

1. Value is destroyed. In this case, investment returns are less than those required by investors. Investors are justifiably unhappy because they could have done better investing in another opportunity of similar risk.

2. Value is created. The investment earns a rate of return higher than required. Investors should be happy.

3. Value is preserved. The investment just earns its required rate of return. Economically speaking, investors earn "normal" returns. They should be satisfied.

Judgments about the success or failure of M&A transactions should be linked to these measurable economic outcomes. In economic terms, an investment is "successful" if it does anything other than destroy value.

Why do we focus so narrowly on economics? After all, many managers describe a complex set of motives for acquisitions—shouldn't the benefit of M&A activity be benchmarked against *all* of them? In an ideal world, it would be nice to draw on a range of concerns, much as corporations do today with the balanced scorecard. But managers' motives may have little to do with shareholder returns or with building capabilities that might help achieve strong returns over the longer run. One often hears of M&A deals that are undertaken for vague strategic benefits, the creation of special capabilities, the achievement of competitive scale, or simply because two organizations or their CEOs are especially friendly. The only way one can prove that such benefits add value is by measuring the economic outcomes rigorously, using a common metric across all deals. What's more, special deal-specific definitions of success limit our ability to generalize from the research findings. Increasing shareholder wealth is a fundamental objective of all firms; indeed, in the United States, corporate directors are required to implement policies consistent with shareholders' interests, which is generally synonymous with creating value.[8] Fortunately, benchmarking against value creation does allow us to make generalizations. In what follows, I focus on economic outcomes in the hopes of saying something meaningful grounded in scientific research.

One of the basic conclusions of economics is that when markets are reasonably competitive, players will earn a "fair" rate of return; that is, you get paid for the risk you take, but no more. The intuition for this is simple: when information is free-flowing and entry is easy, a firm earning very high returns will draw competitors as surely as honey draws flies. The entry of these other firms will drive returns down to the point where the marginal investor earns just a fair rate of return. This idea, which has been tested extensively in financial markets, leads directly to the concept of market efficiency, which says that prices incorporate all publicly available information quickly and without bias. Whether a free lunch exists in M&A hinges on returns to investors, and as with tests of capital market efficiency, that hypothesis can be tested using one of three classes of measures:

- Weak form. Did the share price rise? Are the shareholders better off after the deal than they were before? Most simply, was the buyer's stock price higher after the deal than before? Such a before-and-after comparison is widespread, especially in the writings of journalists and securities analysts. But it is a weak test in the sense that it fails to control for factors unrelated to the deal that might have triggered a price change.

- Semi-strong form. Did the firm's returns exceed a benchmark? Are shareholders better off compared with the return on a comparable investment? Introducing a benchmark like the return on the S&P 500 index, or the return on a matched sample of peers that did not merge, strengthens the analysis. This kind of test, which is commonly used in academic research, is more reliable than the weak-form tests because it controls for the possibility that the observed returns were actually driven by factors in the industry or the entire economy, rather than by the merger. But this kind of test is at best *semi*-strong because benchmarks are imperfect.

- Strong form. Are shareholders better off after the deal *than they would have been if the deal had not occurred?* This is the true test of the cost of lost opportunity, the economists' "gold standard" of comparison. And it is what most people *think* they are finding when they look at weak and semi-strong test results. But the true strong-form test could tell a very different story. Consider the case of AOL's acquisition of Time Warner in January 2000. The weak and semi-strong tests would reveal the very large losses to AOL's shareholders in the years following the deal. But in fact, AOL Time Warner outperformed a benchmark portfolio of pure Internet stocks, despite underperforming the S&P 500 index and media and entertainment indexes. And given the implosion of the Internet industry after 2000, it seems likely that AOL's shareholders would have been much *worse* off without the merger. It would appear that AOL's acquisition of Time Warner was shrewd and successful for the buyer, despite what the weak and semi-strong results show (though Time Warner's shareholders appear to have cushioned the collapse of the Internet bubble for AOL's shareholders). The problem, of course, is that strong-form results are unobservable because there is no way to know for certain what would have happened in the absence of the deal.

The distinction among these three kinds of tests is important to bear in mind. The studies summarized in this chapter are, at best, semi-strong. Therefore, we must exercise humility in drawing conclusions about performance in the context of economic opportunity. We are looking through a glass darkly.

Two main research approaches offer findings that can help us in forming a view of M&A profitability. The first are so-called event studies, which examine the abnormal returns to shareholders in the period surrounding the announcement of a transaction. The "raw" return for one day is simply the change in share price plus any dividends paid, divided by the closing share price the day before. The *abnormal return* is the raw return less a benchmark of what investors required that day—typically, the benchmark is the return specified by the capital asset pricing model (CAPM) or, more simply, the return on a large market index like the S&P 500. These studies are based on the assumption that stock markets are *forward-looking* and that share prices are simply the present value of expected future cash flows to shareholders. Since the 1970s, these studies have dominated the field.

By contrast, so-called accounting studies examine the reported financial results (that is, the accounting statements) of acquirers before and after acquisitions to see how financial performance changes. The focus of these studies is on variables such as net income, return on equity or assets, earnings per share, leverage, and liquidity. The best of these studies are structured as matched-sample comparisons in which acquirers' performance is set against that of non-acquirers of similar size that operate in the same industry. In these studies, the question is whether the acquirers outperformed their non-acquiring peers.

If "scientific inquiry" means anything, it is to frame a hypothesis and test it rigorously against the possibility that the result is due merely to chance. Researchers accordingly test for the statistical significance of a result. But statistical significance is not the same as economic materiality. To say that M&A transactions create or destroy value *on average* requires not only the proof of significance (that is, the result is not due to chance) but also some compelling evidence of materiality—namely, that the wealth effects of M&A transactions are large enough for shareholders or society to take notice. Many of the *significant* abnormal returns reported in event studies are as small as 1 or 2 percent. But since these returns occur over just a few days, they are large enough, when viewed on an annualized basis, to cause concern or elation among institutions or other sophisticated investors whose performance can be greatly affected by such events.

The Broad Finding: M&A Pays

Event studies yield insights about market-based returns to target firm shareholders, buyers, and the combined entity.

Abnormal Returns to Target Firms' Shareholders

The findings of twenty-five studies show that target firm shareholders earn returns that are significantly and materially positive, despite variations in time period, type of deal (merger or tender offer), and observation period. In short, the M&A transaction delivers a premium return to target firm shareholders.

Abnormal Returns to Buyer Firms' Shareholders

The pattern of findings about market-based returns to buyer firms' shareholders is more problematic. About 40 percent of roughly fifty studies report negative announcement returns to buyers; 60 percent report positive returns. When statistical significance is taken into account, the studies of returns to buyer firm shareholders show an even stronger positive bias: 26 percent (fourteen studies) show value destruction (significantly negative returns); 31 percent (seventeen studies) show value preservation (insignificantly different from zero); and 46 percent (twenty-three studies) show value creation (significantly positive returns).

A much less buoyant conclusion is offered by sixteen studies of the returns to buyers over a multiyear period *after* the consummation of the transaction. Eleven of these studies report negative and significant returns. One possible interpretation of these results is that the buyers' shareholders have "second thoughts," perhaps based on new information (generally of a negative character) that emerges about the deal. But a thoughtful consumer of these studies might discount these results somewhat because of confounding events that have little or nothing to do with the transaction. Consider three specific cases:

- Two Swiss banks, UBS and SBC, merged in June 1998. The following month Russia defaulted on its international debt. This in turn triggered the collapse of Long Term Capital Management, in which the new Swiss bank, UBS A.G., had a sizeable investment. UBS announced a $900 million write-off of its investment, cashiered its CEO, and shook up management. To the uninformed observer of stock price trends, the breathtaking decline in UBS's share price in the months following its merger might appear to confirm the conventional wisdom that M&A does not pay. But a closer examination suggests that the decline had little to do with the merger and everything to do with external factors.

- AOL announced the deal to acquire Time Warner just at the peak of AOL's share price. With the benefit of hindsight, we know that AOL's shares were overvalued in the stock market. Thus, the deal was a terrible swap for Time Warner's shareholders, but great for AOL's. As discussed later, the massive evaporation in value was due in part to the market's correction of this overvaluation, a correction that was bound to occur whether or not AOL acquired Time Warner. Several studies have presented findings consistent with the notion that acquiring firms tend to pay with stock when they believe their shares are overvalued.[9]

- Advanced Micro Devices acquired NextGen in 1995 and then underperformed its peer group of semiconductor manufacturers in the following year. But the acquisition gave AMD a new future, enabling the firm to introduce its Athlon chip and remain a competitor to Intel. This is a story of an inevitable industry shock produced by rapid technological innovation. We cannot know how AMD would have performed without the NextGen acquisition, but the consensus appears to be that AMD would not be alive today without it. And suggesting that AMD's case is a representative one, a 1996 study supported the idea that the poor performance of companies following acquisitions is often the result of economic turbulence in the industry rather than the acquisition itself.[10] In other words, when managers see trouble approaching in the form of deregulation, technological change, demographic shifts, or other forms of turbulence, they take action (such as an acquisition) to mitigate the trouble. And in such cases, the subsequent problems have more to do with the foreseen turbulence than with the acquisitions themselves.

In short, contaminating events, overvalued stock, and industry shocks could all easily mislead thoughtful practitioners into believing that M&A is fundamentally unprofitable even though these effects may have nothing to do with the transactions themselves. Even more important, buyers are typically much larger than targets, which means that the impact of smaller deals is difficult to measure with any precision. For example, a 1983 study reported that in mergers where the target's market value was equal to 10 percent or more of the buyer's market value, the return to the buyer was a positive (and highly significant) 4.1 percent; but in cases where the target's value was less than 10 percent, the return to the buyer was only 1.7 percent.[11] In other words, what we know about M&A profitability is a blend of noise and large deals. Nonetheless, a reasonable conclusion from these event studies is that buyers essentially break even—which means that acquisitions tend to earn about their required rates of return.

Abnormal Returns to Buyer and Target Firms Combined

Findings of positive abnormal returns to the seller and break-even returns to the buyer raise the question of the *net economic gain* from M&A deals. Perhaps the biggest challenge here stems from the size difference between buyer and target. Because buyers are typically much larger than the sellers, the dollar value of a large percentage gain to the target shareholders could be more than offset by a small percentage loss to the buyer's shareholders.

A number of studies have examined this possibility by forming a portfolio of the buyer and target firms and examining either their weighted average returns (weighted by the relative sizes of the two firms) or the absolute dollar value of returns. Almost all of a group of twenty-four studies on combined returns report positive returns, with fourteen of the twenty-four being significantly positive. These findings suggest that M&A activity does create net gains for the investors in the combined buyer and target firms and thus, presumably, for the economy as a whole.

Reported Financial Performance of Buyers

Another important stream of research on M&A returns is found in a group of fifteen studies of profit margins, growth rates, and returns on assets, capital, and equity. Two of these studies reported significantly negative post-acquisition performance, four reported significantly positive performance, and the rest were in the nonsignificant middle ground.

Three of these studies based their comparisons on pre- and post-merger reported financial performance. An early collection of studies of M&A profitability in seven countries concluded that mergers have "modest effects" on firm profitability in the three to five years after the merger.[12] A 1987 study of 471 acquirers between 1950 and 1977 concluded that the buyers' profitability was one to two percentage points lower than that for a group of control firms—these differences are statistically significant.[13] Another group of five studies found that the performance of buyers is not much different from that of nonbuyers.

But the authors of a more recent—and arguably more meaningful—study of the post-acquisition operating performance of the fifty largest U.S. mergers between 1979 and mid-1984 concluded that the asset productivity of the acquiring firms improved significantly after the deals, as measured by higher operating cash flow returns relative to their non-acquiring peers.[14] The study also reported that acquirers maintained their rates of capital expenditure and R&D spending relative to their industries, suggesting that the improved performance did not come at the expense of fundamental investment in the business. Perhaps most important, however, was the study's finding that the announcement returns to the stocks for the merging firms were significantly associated with the improvement in post-merger operating performance. That is, the market's reaction to the announcement of a given deal tended to be a reasonably reliable predictor of future operating improvements, with more positive reactions correctly anticipating larger increases in operating cash flow.

Surveys of Executives

The findings of scholars in large-sample surveys have been supplemented by studies of smaller samples that often draw some or all of their findings through direct questioning of managers. A 1992 survey of the CEOs of 146 large U.K. companies reported that 77 percent said they believed that profitability increased in the short run after mergers—and 68 percent said that the improvement in profitability lasted for the long run.[15]

Surveys conducted by practitioners are often rather casually reported, limiting our ability to replicate the studies and understand their methodological strengths and weaknesses. Still, the similarity between their findings and those of the scholarly surveys is striking. Six of twelve studies by practitioners reported negative results, with the other six neutral or positive. And both the practitioner and scholarly studies seem consistent with the view that although M&A does not produce abnormal returns, investments in acquisitions tend at least to cover their cost of capital.

Conclusion about the Profitability of M&A

Drawing on the findings from many studies using large samples of observations, the only tenable conclusion is that M&A *does pay* on average. M&A clearly pays for the shareholders of target firms. And most studies of targets and buyers *combined* indicate that these transactions create net value. Finally, for bidders alone, two-thirds of the studies conclude that value is at least preserved if not created. The reality appears to be that most M&A transactions are associated with financial performance that at least compensates investors for their opportunity cost; buyers tend to earn an adequate return, if no more. Thus, the average, benchmark-adjusted return to corporate investment in M&A is close to zero, as we would expect in any form of corporate investment in competitive markets. But if the average is zero, the distribution of corporate returns is wide—which means that many buyers in M&A transactions should prepare to be disappointed.

All M&A Is Local

The broad findings invite careful scrutiny of the returns to buyers. Given an average that is close to zero with considerable variation, one wants to know what might tip the profitability of a deal into the black or the red. If you handicap likely M&A returns like a bettor at the track, you will probably fail. You must have a view about the underlying drivers of M&A profitability to make intelligent guesses. Scholars have studied the drivers for years and by now have produced some key insights that can help the handicapper.

Anecdotes support a range of behavioral explanations focusing on corporate "egos" or other forms of "irrationality," but these don't furnish much of a basis for prescribing solutions. We are likely to get more traction by viewing M&A as a strategic response to the turbulent environment that surrounds the firm. Joseph Schumpeter observed that firms endure relentless change driven by turbulence in their business environment. He argued that canny entrepreneurs and managers seize opportunities created by this turbulence to make a profit. And M&A is one way of capitalizing on turbulence.

A number of scholars have provided evidence consistent with the view that economic turbulence is an important driver of M&A activity. For example, a 1985 study examined the M&A wave of 1894–1904 when more than 1,800 firms disappeared via the formation of ninety-three "trusts."[16] The author found that most M&A activity occurred in industries characterized by capital-intensive, mass-production manufacturing processes in which new firms had recently entered with new and devastating technologies. The M&A of this period benefited the broad economy by removing older and less efficient excess capacity from these industries. Similarly, a 2001 study reported that mergers during the period 1890–1930 were significantly associated with the diffusion of electricity and the internal combustion engine, and that much merger activity from 1971 to 2001 involved the diffusion of information technology.[17]

Michael Jensen, in his 1993 presidential address to the American Finance Association, argued that the restructuring in the 1980s was stimulated not only by advances in information technology, but also by innovations in organizational design, such as the rise of Wal-Mart and the wholesale clubs that introduced a new retailing model. Jensen pointed also to the creation of new markets (such as the high-yield debt market) that stimulated the wave of hostile takeovers and leveraged buyouts.

Consistent with Jensen's argument, a 1996 study found that during the merger wave of the 1980s, industries with the most takeover activity were those that experienced fundamental economic shocks like deregulation, technological innovation, demographic shifts, and input price shocks.[18] The study pointed to M&A activity in banking and broadcasting driven by deregulation, in textiles in response to liberalized trade policies, in the energy industry in response to petroleum price changes, and in food processing due to the demographic shift to low population growth.

These academic studies received confirmation of sorts from a 1998 book by well-known M&A adviser Bruce Wasserstein that cited five main forces driving the merger process: regulatory and political reform, technological change, fluctuations in financial markets, the role of leadership, and the tension between scale and focus.[19]

If industry and general economic turbulence drive M&A, then success or failure is likely to be determined in significant part by the context of the deal. In this sense, as suggested earlier, *all M&A is local*. This view encourages examination of the forces at work in a particular business setting. Key drivers will vary from one setting to the next. Global generalizations about M&A success won't have much practical content. Useful insights about the drivers of M&A profitability are to be found on a more local basis.

Where M&A Pays and Where It Strays

If all M&A is local, then success and failure will depend on the local story. Like Mr. Rogers, we need to put on our cardigans and visit some neighborhoods of profit and loss in M&A, while still wearing the mind-set of the scientific studies. A familiarity with these neighborhoods can help the business practitioner tilt the odds in favor of an economically successful deal. In the survey that follows, I take the perspective of the buyer and survey the neighborhoods in four different cross-sections: strategy, market segments, deal design, and governance.

Neighborhood 1: Strategy

One of the oldest lines of research on the determinants of M&A profitability has concentrated on strategic choices, including attempts to focus or diversify the firm, grow the firm, build market share, exploit strategic synergies, use excess cash, and initiate an acquisition program.

Focus versus Diversification. Whether strategic focus or diversification affects the profitability of the buyer has been the subject of considerable research. The conventional view is that a strategy of acquiring companies in related fields (so-called focusing acquisitions) is the most likely path to the discovery and exploitation of synergies. Executives intuitively understand that acquiring peer competitors offers opportunities for cost savings, asset reductions, and other efficiencies. Some of the early research suggested that an M&A strategy of focus or *relatedness* pays better than diversification.[20]

On the other hand, the classic motive for diversification is to create a portfolio of businesses whose cash flows are imperfectly correlated with each other and which therefore might improve the company's ability to weather adversity. But since portfolio diversification is something shareholders can do on their own, why should they pay managers to do this for them?

A number of scholars have suggested that diversification might pay when the combination of unrelated businesses within a single entity facilitates knowledge transfer among different business divisions, reduces financing costs, creates a critical mass for competition, and exploits better transparency and monitoring through internal capital markets.[21] One study examined twenty-one companies with conglomerate-like structures and found that they produced returns of 18–35 percent per year by making non-synergistic acquisitions.[22] Diversification could also pay in cases where the local capital market is less effective or product markets are experiencing deregulation or other sources of instability.[23] There is evidence that diversification pays when the buyer and target are in information-intensive industries.[24] In general, the research studies are mixed on whether strategic relatedness explains returns to buyers: eight studies find that relatedness is a significant factor in returns to buyers; four studies find no significance. Looking at the research in this area, it seems reasonable to conclude that the degree of relatedness does matter, though perhaps in ways more complicated than even a variety of studies can capture.

But working against this logic, event studies of acquisitions, joint ventures, divestitures, spin-offs, and carve-outs generally suggest that focus pays more than diversification.[25] Moreover, several studies have found that diversified companies tend to have lower relative market values than more focused firms, though the source and nature of the discount remains the subject of debate. Eight studies have documented a "diversification discount" ranging from 8 to 15 percent.[26] On the other hand, nine studies that use finer data and better controls have found that diversification has a neutral or even positive effect on value; the authors of these studies argue that corporate data have a natural bias in favor of the diversification discount and that the units acquired by diversified firms were selling at a discount *before* the acquisition. Studies of postmerger operating performance and productivity have also generated conflicting findings.

In sum, this diverse research suggests some key ideas about the strategy "neighborhood" of M&A. First, focus and relatedness probably pay better as an acquisition strategy than does unrelated diversification, all else being equal. Quite simply, merger benefits are more easily discovered and readily exploited when you stick closer to your knitting. In other words, *strategic linkage pays in M&A*. Second, the qualifier "all else being equal" admits the possibility that a strategy of unrelated diversification can pay when there are unusual skills such as running an LBO association (KKR) or value investing (Berkshire Hathaway). In short, *special managerial skill could trump the need for strategic linkage*—though it's important to keep in mind that most of the lofty claims of managerial skill will not stand up to scrutiny. Large diversified conglomerates (such as ITT, Westinghouse, Gulf & Western, and LTV) were built on the presumption of such skill and then went on to the dinosaur-bone yard. Third, an acquisition strategy of relatedness and focus warrants critical scrutiny, too. Industries are dynamic; their attractiveness as investments changes over time, making a strategy of diversifying acquisitions a potentially valuable mechanism for industrial exit and reentry elsewhere. Just as companies can destroy value by diversifying, they might also destroy value by staying focused. In short, a mindless strategy of focused and related acquisitions is no guarantee of success. In some cases, *the fundamental bet on industry attractiveness trumps the need for strategic linkage.*

Strategic Restructuring Pays. Reinforcing the point about industry attractiveness is the mass of research showing that the sale or redeployment of underperforming businesses is greeted positively by investors. Studies of announcement returns have found that divestitures uniformly create value for shareholders of sellers, on the order of significant abnormal returns of 1–3 percent (although the results for buyers are mixed). Generally, the studies of restructurings suggest that the redeployment of assets seems to be what matters, not merely the sale. In particular, there is evidence that the market rewards divestitures that focus the firm. Carve-outs, spin-offs, and tracking stock have neutral to beneficial effects for shareholders, with generally consistent abnormal returns: spin-offs return roughly 2–4 percent, as compared with 2–3 percent for carve-outs and 3 percent for tracking stocks. As with divestitures, the use of the funds raised in these transactions makes a difference.[27]

Hypotheses about the sources of gains from restructuring center mainly on two possibilities: (1) increased focus improves efficiency and operating returns on capital, and (2) market transactions correct the undervaluation of conglomerates by the market. These possibilities are not mutually exclusive. And the research provides support for both, giving perhaps more weight to the conglomerate inefficiency argument on the grounds of the number of studies confirming the value of corporate focus. But either way, the lesson of such studies is that *continually reshaping the business to respond to changes in the competitive environment pays.*

The Initiation of M&A Programs. When companies announce that they are undertaking a series of acquisitions in pursuit of a particular strategic objective, their share prices rise significantly. The market's systematically positive response to such announcements suggests that most corporate M&A programs tend to create value over the long haul. Investor response to the initiation of M&A programs is consistent with the investor response to restructuring; both encourage a nimble corporate response to evolving conditions.

Strategic Synergies. The buyer's strategy is based heavily on the synergies to be exploited in the transaction. Synergies come in different flavors and include cost savings, revenue enhancements, and financial synergies. These benefits tend to have different degrees of credibility in the eyes of investors, with several studies showing cost savings discounted the least and the others somewhat more. As a 1996 study of bank mergers concluded, "the market is readily persuaded by the cost-cutting motive for mergers, while subjecting other rationales to considerable skepticism."[28] In short, *M&A will pay when synergies are credible.*

Grabs for Market Power. The positive relationship between market share and investor returns is an article of faith among economists and is supported by empirical research. It should follow, then, that acquisitions that increase a company's market share are associated with increased returns to shareholders. And in fact, bidders' returns increase with increases in market share.[29] But as demonstrated in a 1992 study, the stockholder gains from such deals were attributable to increases in efficiency rather than in product prices.[30] Horizontal mergers (the type of deals that increase market share) are typically motivated by the prospect of cost savings and other synergies mentioned earlier. In other words, the shareholder benefits of larger market share may not be a compelling motive for a deal. Bigger is not necessarily better; more efficient is better.

Value Acquiring Pays; Glamour Acquiring Does Not. A 1998 study reported post-acquisition underperformance by "glamour" acquirers (companies with high market-to-book value ratios) and superior performance by value-oriented buyers (low market-to-book ratios).[31] Value acquirers earn significant abnormal returns of 8 percent in mergers and 16 percent in tender offers, while glamour acquirers earn a significant −17 percent in mergers and an insignificant 4 percent in tender offers.

M&A to Use Excess Cash Generally Destroys Value Except When Redeployed Profitably. Cash-rich companies have a choice of returning the cash to investors through dividends or stock buybacks or reinvesting it through such activities as M&A. A number of studies have reported value destruction associated with the announcement of M&A transactions by firms with excess cash. However, my own 1988 study of this question found that transactions pairing "slack-poor" and "slack-rich" companies tend to be value increasing.[32] As my study also showed, before a merger, acquirers tend to have more cash and lower debt ratios than non-acquirers. And the returns to the buyer's shareholders are positively correlated with changes in the buyer's debt ratios that accompany the merger.

Neighborhood 2: Investment Opportunity

A second class of studies suggests that market conditions and the nature of the acquired companies affect the profitability of M&A for buyers. This perspective highlights the segmented nature of the M&A market. Segments that tend to be profitable for buyers are privately owned targets and underperforming targets. More costly to buyers are foreign targets and deals consummated during "hot" market conditions.

Targets That Can Be Restructured. The opportunity to redirect the target company toward more profitable operation would seem to suggest greater opportunity for a profitable merger. Hostile tender offers are the classic arena for this. Some research suggests that targets of hostile tender offers are underperformers with relatively low share prices—in which cases, bidders expect to earn profits from improving the target's performance. But other studies are consistent with the view that targets are healthy but happen to fit very well with the buyer's strategy. Thus, the evidence is mixed on the question of whether takeover targets tend to be inefficient firms. They seem not to be basket cases, but neither are they stellar performers. The bulk of these firms have middling-to-mediocre performance in which the bidder sees a profitable opportunity.

One thread that runs through many of these studies has less to do with efficiency than with a key aspect of governance—namely, the entrenchment of target management. Bidders tend to take more forceful measures mainly after target managers reject friendly entreaties.

Privately Owned Assets. Comparing acquisitions of public and private companies matched by size, industry, and time period, researchers found an average discount of 20–28 percent in the prices paid for private U.S. firms relative to those paid for their publicly traded counterparts—and discounts of as much as 44–54 percent for foreign private targets. Consistent with this finding, several other studies have reported a sizeable positive announcement-day return to bidders when they buy private firms as opposed to public firms. Explanations by researchers point to a lack of information on private companies, a discount for the lack of marketability of private firm securities, bargaining advantages for public buyers of private firms, the absence of competitive bidding that creates favorable purchase prices, and the creation of new power groups in the buyer company that could motivate the buyer to improve performance.

Crossing Borders. Cross-border M&A pays in a fashion consistent with the findings for U.S. domestic M&A. That is, target shareholders earn large returns; buyers essentially break even; and on a combined basis, shareholders gain. The chief difference in crossing borders is that foreign bidders appear to pay more than domestic bidders. Two studies reported that U.S. targets earn materially higher returns than foreign targets.[33] According to five studies, the returns to U.S. targets are higher in cases involving foreign rather than domestic buyers. Some researchers have argued that this premium represents payment for the special local knowledge and market access that the target provides the foreign buyer.[34] Also, acquisition offers foreign companies entry into the U.S. legal regime, which itself can serve to increase value. A stream of studies in the 1990s showed that the legal regime in foreign countries has a significant influence on valuation.

Hot and Cold M&A Markets: Misvaluation of Buyer Firms. Market "windows of opportunity" open and close over time, which creates a very different kind of market segmentation. Two classic sources of this variation are changes in regulation and the appearance of market bubbles. Research shows a slight tendency for bidder returns to decline over time. Returns appear to have been more positive in the 1960s and 1970s than in the 1980s and 1990s, except for deals in technology and banking, where returns to bidders increased in the 1990s. Changing government regulations affect the temperature of M&A markets. These changes take the form of antitrust actions, court decisions, and legislation (such as the Williams Act of 1968).

M&A waves peak during buoyant equity markets, the "hot" markets when security prices are relatively high. The recent equity market peak during the period 1998–2001 was associated with the most M&A activity in U.S. history. Perhaps buyers overpay in hot M&A markets—this might reflect market mania or a private recognition by buyers that their shares are overvalued. As mentioned earlier, a 2003 study suggested that the massive wealth destruction in eighty-seven large deals from 1998 to 2001 reflected the reassessment of buyers' stand-alone valuations.[35] Another study published in the same year reported that the more highly valued (or "overvalued," as indicated by a high price-to-book ratio) is the buyer, the more negative is the investor response to the acquisition announcement.[36] The hot M&A market poses a major dilemma to the CEO of an overvalued company: if you acquire, your shares will drop; if you don't acquire, your shares are also likely to drop. In this can't-win setting, M&A may offer a chance to transfer part of the prospective losses to target company shareholders rather than have your own shareholders absorb them.

Neighborhood 3: Deal Design

A third category of research suggests that the terms of the transaction have a significant influence on M&A profitability for the buyer. Important terms include the form of payment, financing, use of earn-outs and collars, tax treatment, and social issues.

Form of Payment: Cash Versus Stock. Several studies report that stock-based deals are associated with negative returns to the buyer's shareholders at deal announcements, whereas cash deals are neutral or slightly positive. This finding is consistent with the idea that managers time the issuance of shares of stock to occur at the high point in the cycle of the company's fortunes, or in the stock market cycle. Thus, the announcement of payment by shares, like the announcement of an offering of seasoned stock, could be taken as a sign that managers believe the firm's shares are overpriced.

This consistent result across these studies can be summarized as follows: First, although target shareholders earn large positive announcement returns, these returns differ materially with the form of payment. In cases where payment is in cash, target shareholder returns are considerably *higher*. When payment is in stock, target shareholder returns are significantly positive, but materially lower than those for the cash deals. Second, although buyer shareholders basically break even, on average, at announcement, the form of payment produces an important difference in returns that complements the returns to targets. That is, when payment is in cash, estimates of average buyer shareholder returns range from zero to positive, in some cases significantly positive. But when payment is in stock, buyer returns are significantly negative. Tender offers amplify the cash-versus-stock effect; in cases of tender offers paid in cash, the returns to buyers are even higher, and the returns from offers paid in stock are even lower. Also, larger cash deals have more positive returns, and larger equity deals have more negative returns. The studies also reveal that stock tends to be used when a deal is friendly, the buyer's stock price is relatively high, ownership in the buyer is not concentrated, deals are larger in size, and the buyer has less cash.[37]

LBOs. Shareholders of target companies in LBOs earn large abnormal returns, roughly in line with the target returns found in the general studies of all M&A transactions. The large returns to target and buyer shareholders, as we saw earlier, are reliable predictors of significant improvements in operating efficiency. LBO transactions are followed by large increases of operating cash flow relative to sales and by large decreases in capital expenditures. Contrary to the belief of some critics, who argued that LBOs were primarily motivated by tax considerations and would transfer wealth from the public sector to the private sector, studies have also found that on net, tax revenues actually increased as a result of LBOs due to several factors: increased capital gains taxes paid by target firm shareholders; taxes on increased operating earnings; taxes on added interest income earned by creditors; taxes on the capital gains from asset sales; and additional taxes arising from more efficient use of capital.[38]

Use of Earn-Outs. Two studies have reported that the returns to buyers are higher when the payment is structured to be contingent on meeting future performance benchmarks. These returns are greater than returns in straight cash or straight stock deals and are larger when the target's management stays. In this sense, earn-outs and other contingent payment structures can be viewed as providing stronger performance incentives for selling managers as well as a risk management device for the buyer.

Use of Collars. A collar is another risk management device, used in stock-for-stock transactions to hedge uncertainty about the value of the buyer. It changes the payment if the buyer's price falls or rises beyond predetermined triggers and often grants either or both of the merging firms the right to renegotiate the deal if the collar is triggered. In this sense, a collar is effectively an option to cancel a merger.

A 2003 study found that the announcement returns to the buyer's shareholders were not significantly affected by the use of collars.[39] At the same time, the announcement returns were lower, and the targets' returns higher, in transactions involving floating rather than fixed collars.[40] Stock offers with collars were significantly more likely to succeed (that is, to close) than either straight stock or cash offers.

Social Issues: The Merger of Equals. A great deal of anecdotal evidence suggests that "social" (or "managerial") issues, such as selection of the CEO, board, senior management, headquarters location, and compensation, can have a huge influence on deal pricing and profitability to the buyer. Recent research on the "merger of equals" deal structure illustrates this influence. These mergers combine partners of roughly equal influence without the payment of a premium by one party to the other. They are typically mergers effected by an exchange of shares with a low or zero implied acquisition premium.

The studies show that, despite variation over time, premiums in mergers of equals are typically much smaller than those in other deals. Also, target shareholders earn positive abnormal returns that, although significantly positive, are also smaller than those in other deals. A 2004 study concluded that, in mergers of equals, "CEOs trade 'power for premium.' Specifically, they negotiate control rights in the merged firm (both board and management) in exchange for a lower premium for their shareholders."[41] Others note that the mergers-of-equals structure, by signaling an absence of dominance of one side over the other, helps reduce resistance in the target company, thereby increasing the probability that the deal is consummated and building a general sense of teamwork that can pay off in faster post-merger integration.

Tax Exposure. Tax planning considerations are, of course, the focus of considerable professional time and talent in M&A. A 1989 study found that about half of all acquisitions are designed to be "tax-free" or only partly taxable.[42] The form of reorganization is strongly related to the abnormal return at the merger announcement. In taxable deals, the acquisition premium is more than twice as high. Two effects might explain this (though neither explanation is entirely satisfying): (1) in taxable deals, target company shareholders' taxes are due immediately rather than deferred, thus creating a demand for higher payment stimulated by the time value of money; (2) in taxable deals, the buyer is allowed to "step up" the tax basis of the acquired assets, thus affording a larger depreciation tax shield and raising the ceiling on what the buyer can afford to pay. Net operating loss (NOL) carry-forwards and debt tax shields can have a similar effect.

Perhaps because of the target's bargaining power, then, or because of a "winner's curse" effect, buyers *do* pay more in taxable deals. The evidence suggests that an even greater percentage of acquisitions of privately held companies tend to be structured to defer tax payments as a means of estate or investment planning for individual controlling shareholders or family groups. But if taxes clearly affect the form of certain transactions, researchers continue to actively debate whether tax considerations *cause* acquisitions.

Neighborhood 4: Governance

As a general rule, research shows that firms with stronger governance practices are more highly valued. Thus, in the M&A map of returns to buyers, we should observe higher returns associated with shareholder-oriented management and protections for shareholder rights and the rights of minority investors. This extends to governance structures, board independence, the use of antitakeover defenses, and activism by investors.

Activism by Institutional Investors. In 1993, institutional investors blocked a merger between AB Volvo and Renault, and the net effect of this action was to restore and then create value for Volvo's shareholders. Institutions such as pension funds and life insurance companies can be distinguished from individual investors by their large size, strong performance orientation, close proximity to markets, ability to bear transaction costs, and, in many cases, degree of sophistication. Research shows that most transactions in which these investors become active (in the sense of seeking to influence the board of directors and management) tend to be associated with the creation of shareholder value. Studies of LBOs, replacement of executives of underperforming firms, and corporate restructurings reveal significant gains in equity value following realignment and improved governance.

What Managers Have at Stake. Studies suggest that returns to buyer firm shareholders are associated with larger equity interests by managers and employees.[43] In assessing the pattern of performance associated with deal characteristics, a 1997 study concluded that "while takeovers were usually break-even investments, the profitability of individual transactions varied widely . . . [and] the transaction characteristics *that were under management control* substantially influenced the ultimate payoffs from takeovers."[44] Such characteristics include the degree of relatedness of the target and buyer, the form of payment, and whether the transaction was friendly or hostile.

By far the most compelling evidence of the effect of corporate governance on performance is the remarkable increases in value achieved by buyers in LBOs. In LBOs, managers tend to commit a significant portion of their own net worth to the success of the transaction. As reported by Michael Jensen in testimony to Congress in 1989, the average LBO doubled its enterprise value in its four years as a private company—and with debt-to-total capital leverage ratios that averaged 85 percent, the median equity return to the LBO buyers was a remarkable 785 percent.[45] Although part of these returns arose from tax savings due to debt and depreciation shields, economists have concluded that the largest portion of the gains came from efficiencies and greater operational improvements implemented after the LBO.

Approaching the Target: Friendly Versus Hostile. The buyer's approach to the target is influenced by the degree of entrenchment of the target's management. Mergers are typically friendly affairs, negotiated between the top managements of buyer and target firms. Hostile bids, on the other hand, are structured as take-it-or-leave-it proposals made directly to the target firm's shareholders and are often viewed by the target management as coercive. Several studies report larger announcement returns to bidders in tender offers than in friendly negotiated transactions, with successful bidders in hostile takeovers estimated to earn positive abnormal returns of 2 to 4 percent. The higher returns from tender offers may reflect bargain prices as well as the expected economic benefits from replacing management and redirecting the strategy of the firm.

Target shareholders also win in that they receive higher acquisition premiums in hostile deals than in friendly deals. When a target successfully rejects a bidder, the target's share price falls, but typically to a price level higher than prevailed before—in part because unsuccessful takeover attempts often lead to restructurings that unlock value for shareholders. And when a hostile bidder offers cash, the returns are more positive still, which could be explained by the poor health and/or investment attractiveness of the target. As noted earlier, the targets of hostile bids tend to be mediocre performers at best. The larger lesson in this case has to do with ineffective governance and the removal of entrenched and inefficient management.

Use of Antitakeover Defenses. Defenses can help shareholders of well-governed companies by enhancing the bargaining power of management, enabling them to extract high prices from bidders. But defenses can also harm shareholders of poorly run firms by entrenching managers who disregard their duty to shareholders. To make sense of market responses to announcements about takeover defenses, one must have a view about the efficiency and governance of the target company. One gauge of the economic impact of defenses is the reaction of investors to the announcement of takeover defense placements. Several studies suggest that the strength of the target's governance mechanisms is a strong determinant of the market reaction to takeover defenses. When the board of directors is strong and independent, and when the CEO's interests are strongly aligned with shareholder returns, the reaction tends to be positive; when governance is poor or the CEO's rewards are misaligned, the reaction is negative.

Conclusion: What the "Hoods" Tell Us

All M&A is local. The practical value of M&A research lies in the insights it offers into the local conditions associated with the creation or destruction of value. For this reason, blanket assertions about M&A, like the popular claim of general merger failure, are not very useful to practitioners or, for that matter, to scholars. Conventional wisdom tends to be hazy about the evidence of success and failure and tends to take findings that apply in one neighborhood as representative of the whole. Critical thinking about M&A steps well beyond the conventional wisdom to focus on patterns of local profit and loss. Table 13.1 summarizes the range of research insights from the articles surveyed here.

The neighborhoods of profit and loss offer a number of warnings to the CEO. You are *more likely* to fail in M&A when:

1. *Your organization enters a fundamentally unprofitable industry, or refuses to exit from one.* A sound industry bet based on expected returns—thinking like an investor—is a necessary precondition for M&A success. Restructurings and the launch of M&A programs reveal continuous thought and effort to position the firm strategically for the highest profit. On the other hand, some M&A programs that are cloaked in the language of strategic profitability often harbor serious logical traps, such as momentum and glamour acquiring that should be viewed with skepticism. The CEO needs a sensitive

TABLE 13.1

Where M&A Pays and Where It Strays: Adjusted Returns to Buyers by "Neighborhood"

Returns to buyers likely will be higher:	Returns to buyers likely will be lower:
1. Strategic motivation	1. Opportunistic motivation
2. Value acquiring	2. Momentum growth/glamour acquiring
3. Focused/related acquiring	3. Lack of focus/unrelated diversification
4. Credible synergies	4. Incredible synergies
5. To use excess cash profitably	5. Just to use excess cash
6. Negotiated purchases of private firms	6. Auctions of public firms
7. Cross borders for special advantage	7. Cross borders naively
8. Go hostile	8. Negotiate with resistant target
9. Buy during cold M&A markets	9. Buy during hot M&A markets
10. Pay with cash	10. Pay with stock
11. High tax benefits to buyer	11. Low tax benefits to buyer
12. Finance with debt judiciously	12. Over-lever
13. Stage the payments (earn-outs)	13. Pay fully up front
14. Mergers of equals	14. Not a merger of equals
15. Managers have significant stake	15. Managers have low or no stake
16. Shareholder-oriented management	16. Entrenched management
17. Active investors	17. Passive investors
18. Big good deals	18. Big bad deals

humbug detector when listening to assertions about the "strategic" value of an M&A transaction.

2. *Your organization steps far away from what it knows.* Generally, focus and relatedness pay better than unrelated diversification. The discovery and exploitation of merger synergies is more likely when dealing with familiar territory. However, a firm's core competency could be in managing a portfolio of unrelated businesses. Thus, the key strategic driver of profitability has less to do with focus and relatedness and more to do with knowledge, mastery, and competencies. What does your company know? What is it good at doing?

3. *The economic benefits of the deal are improbable or not incremental to the deal.* The capital market judges merger synergies skeptically. At the core of best M&A practice is the impulse to do good things for your shareholders that they cannot do for themselves. But what counts for "synergies" within some buyer firms is a host of projects that would have gotten done eventually with or without the acquisition. This is a failure to think "at the margin" by asking what *new* flows of cash an acquisition will trigger. Just as bad is the tendency to imagine benefits that are highly improbable and to treat them as likely. Revenue-

enhancement synergies from cross-selling, for instance, are notoriously hard to capture—and research shows that they are discounted rather heavily by investors.

4. *You fail to seek some economic advantage.* Competition drives returns to their minimum. As a buyer, you face competitors in auctions, in the purchase of public firms, and generally whenever you move with the crowd. In settings like these, you will pay top dollar. Positive abnormal returns are more likely to be found in less competitive segments of the market—notably, those involving private firms and assets. And making unsolicited offers to the board and its shareholders can preempt interlopers and create bargaining power in negotiations with entrenched managers. In other circumstances, however, bargaining power may reside with the target. A prime example is the target in a foreign country where, because of entry barriers, knowledge of local markets and customs, and market power, the buyer will likely pay a premium.

5. *Your organization is not very creative in deal structuring.* The returns on even a mediocre deal can be enhanced for the buyer through artful deal design. The use of cash, debt financing, tax shields, staged payments, merger-of-equals terms, and earn-out incentive structures are all associated with higher buyer returns.

6. *Your organization has poor checks, balances, and incentives.* This begins at the top, with the composition and processes of the board of directors and their willingness to listen to the shareholders whom they represent. And it extends to your oversight of the firm and the manner in which you have delegated decision authority to others in your firm. Throughout the organization, from operating managers to the front line of deal-doers, your people must *think like investors.* The principle is simple: do you and they have some "skin in the game"?

The survey of scientific research tells us that executives have choices in M&A that, when made thoughtfully, can tilt the odds of success in their favor. This is a very different perspective than conventional thinking might suggest.

Notes

This chapter draws on material from a chapter in my 2005 book, *Deals from Hell: M&A Lessons That Rise above the Ashes* (Hoboken, NJ: Wiley), which is used here with permission of the publisher. The book provides a complete list of references, which is not reproduced here but is available upon request. In the interest of space and readability, in-text references to individual studies and particularly to groups of studies are not all cited in the notes in this chapter, but are available in a reference supplement upon request.

1. See Chapter 3 ("Does M&A Pay?") of my 2004 book, *Applied Mergers and Acquisitions* (Hoboken, NJ: Wiley).
2. T. Grubb and R. Lamb, *Capitalize on Merger Chaos* (New York: Free Press, 2000), pp. 9, 10, 12, 14.

3. Even if this failure rate *were* true, it would be matched or dwarfed by other risks commonly assumed in business and which society generally wants decision-makers to take, including new business start-ups, new product introductions, expansions to new markets, and investments in R&D and new technology. All business is risky. Our purpose in studying failure should be to manage risk better, not to eliminate it.
4. Gregory Zuckerman, "Ahead of the Tape," *Wall Street Journal*, December 30, 2002, p. C1.
5. *Business Week*, October 14, 2002, p. 60.
6. Beyond wishing for more discussion of the sample and research methodology in the *Business Week* article, I offer no criticism about the execution of the research. As far as I can tell, the researchers used an approach that is conventional in academic work.
7. See S. Moeller, F. Schlingemann, and R. Stulz, "Wealth Destruction on a Massive Scale? A Study of Acquiring-Firm Returns in the Recent Merger Wave," Working paper, Ohio State University (August 2003); and "Firm Size and the Gains from Acquisition," *Journal of Financial Economics*, Vol. 73 (2004), pp. 201–228.
8. For brevity, I will follow the lead of most academic researchers and focus on the economic consequences for the shareholders of the acquirer and the target, although the impact on other stakeholders is certainly of interest. This is also consistent with the fact that the primary fiduciary responsibility of directors is to their shareholders.
9. A. Schleifer and R. Vishny, "Stock Market Driven Acquisitions," Working paper, University of Chicago (2001), downloadable from http://papers.ssrn.com/so13/papers.cfm?abstract_id=278563; Moeller, Schlingemann, and Stulz (2003); and M. Dong, D. Hirschleifer, S. Richardson, and S. Teoh, "Does Investor Misvaluation Drive the Takeover Market?," Working paper, Ohio State University (2003).
10. M. Mitchell and J. H. Mulherin, "The Impact of Industry Shocks on Takeover and Restructuring Activity," *Journal of Financial Economics*, Vol. 41 (1996), pp. 193–229.
11. P. Asquith, R. Bruner, and D. Mullins, Jr., "The Gains to Bidding Firms from Merger," *Journal of Financial Economics*, Vol. 11 (1983), pp. 121–139.
12. D. Mueller, *The Determinants and Effects of Mergers: An International Comparison* (Cambridge, MA: Oelgeschlager, Gunn & Hain, 1980).
13. D. Ravenscraft and F. M. Scherer, "Life after Takeovers," *Journal of Industrial Economics*, Vol. 36 (1987), pp. 147–156.
14. P. Healy, K. Palepu, and R. Ruback, "Does Corporate Performance Improve after Mergers?," *Journal of Financial Economics*, Vol. 31 (1992), pp. 135–175.
15. H. Ingham, I. Kran, and A. Lovestam, "Mergers and Profitability: A Managerial Success Story?," *Journal of Management Studies*, Vol. 29 (1992), pp. 195–209.
16. N. R. Lamoreaux, *The Great Merger Movement in American Business, 1895–1904* (Cambridge: Cambridge University Press, 1985).
17. B. Jovanovic and P. Rousseau, "Mergers as Reallocation," NBER Working Paper No. 9279 (October 2002).
18. Mitchell and Mulherin (1996).
19. B. Wasserstein, *Big Deal* (New York: Warner Books, 1998).
20. See, for example, work by Richard Rumelt, who found higher equity returns for strategies of related diversification; his work prompted a critical reappraisal of the conglomerate diversification movement of the 1960s and early 1970s. R. Rumelt, *Strategy, Structure, and Economic Performance* (Boston: Harvard Business School Press, 1974); and "Diversification Strategy and Profitability," *Strategic Management Journal*, Vol. 3 (1982), pp. 359–369.
21. See, for example, M. Salter and W. Weinhold, *Diversification Through Acquisition: Strategies for Maximizing Economic Value* (New York: Free Press, 1979). But the evi-

dence about the effectiveness of internal capital markets is mixed. For instance, a study of the behavior of oil companies during the oil price collapse of the mid-1980s found evidence that "large diversified companies overinvest in and subsidize underperforming segments"; see O. Lamont, "Cash Flow and Investment: Evidence from Internal Capital Markets," *Journal of Finance,* Vol. 52 (1997), p. 106.
22. See P. Anslinger and T. Copeland, "Growth Through Acquisitions: A Fresh Look," *Harvard Business Review,* Vol. 74 (1996) pp. 126–135. They explained the superior performance of these firms as due to seven principles: "Insist on innovative operating strategies. Don't do the deal if you can't find the leader. Offer big incentives to top-level executives. Link compensation to changes in cash flow. Push the pace of change. Foster dynamic relationships among owners, managers, and the board. Hire the best acquirers" (p. 127).
23. The distinction between developed and developing countries is also interesting as a possible focus for diversification strategies. See the reference supplement (available upon request) for some examples.
24. R. Morck and B. Yeung, "Why Investors Sometimes Value Size and Diversification: The Internalization Theory of Synergy," Working paper, University of Alberta, Institute for Financial Research, No. 5-97 (1997).
25. See the reference supplement, available upon request, for these studies.
26. The "diversification discount" is computed as the market value of a company's equity plus the book value of liabilities divided by the company's "imputed" value—measured as the sum of its segment values estimated by the product of a valuation multiple for single-business peers (total capital divided by assets, sales, or operating earnings) times the accounting value for the segment; see P. Berger and E. Ofek, "Diversification's Effect on Firm Value," *Journal of Financial Economics,* Vol. 37 (1995), pp. 39–65.
27. Research has found that investors reacted positively to carve-outs that would generate cash to be paid to creditors, but were neutral in instances where the funds were to be reinvested in the business; see J. Allen and J. McConnell, "Equity Carve-Outs and Managerial Discretion," *Journal of Finance,* Vol. 53 (1998), pp. 163–186.
28. J. Houston and M. Ryngaert, "The Value Added by Bank Acquisitions: Lessons from Wells Fargo's Acquisition of First Interstate," *Journal of Applied Corporate Finance,* Vol. 9, No. 2 (Summer 1996), p. 76.
29. A. Ghosh, "Increasing Market Share as a Rationale for Corporate Acquisitions," Working paper, Baruch College (May 2002).
30. B. Eckbo, "Mergers and the Value of Antitrust Deterrence," *Journal of Finance,* Vol. 47 (1992), pp. 1005–1030.
31. R. P. Rau and T. Vermaelen, "Glamour, Value and the Post-Acquisition Performance of Acquiring Firms," *Journal of Financial Economics,* Vol. 49 (1998), pp. 223–253.
32. R. Bruner, "The Use of Excess Cash and Debt Capacity as a Motive for Merger," *Journal of Financial and Quantitative Analysis,* Vol. 23 (1988), pp. 199–217.
33. J. Wansley, W. Lane, and H. Yang, "Abnormal Returns to Acquired Firms by Type of Acquisition and Method of Payment," *Financial Management,* Vol. 12 (1983), pp. 16–22; and M. W. Marr, Jr., S. Mohta, and M. Spivey, "An Analysis of Foreign Takeovers in the United States," *Managerial and Decision Economics,* Vol. 14 (1993), pp. 285–294.
34. N. Kohers and T. Kohers, "The Value Creation Potential of High-Tech Mergers," *Financial Analysts Journal,* Vol. 53 (2000), pp. 40–48.
35. Moeller, Schlingemann, and Stulz (2003).
36. Dong, Hirschleifer, Richardson, and Teoh (2003).
37. See the reference supplement, available upon request, for all of these studies.

38. M. Jensen, S. Kaplan, and L. Stiglin, "Effects of LBOs on Tax Revenues of the U.S. Treasury," *Tax Notes,* Vol. 42, No. 6 (1989), pp. 727–733.
39. K. Fuller, "Why Some Firms Use Collars in Mergers," *The Financial Review,* Vol. 38 (February 2003), pp. 127–150.
40. A floating collar allows the buyer's share price a range within which to vary but imposes a ceiling and floor on the value to be delivered to target shareholders. A fixed collar establishes a fixed value for the target's shares as long as the buyer's share price remains within the predetermined range; outside that range, the exchange ratio is adjusted. For a detailed discussion of collars, see R. Bruner, *Applied Mergers and Acquisitions.*
41. J. Wulf, "Do CEOs in Mergers Trade Power for Premium?," *Journal of Law, Economics, and Organization,* Vol. 20 (2004), p. 60.
42. C. Hayn, "Tax Attributes as Determinants of Shareholder Gains in Corporate Acquisitions," *Journal of Financial Economics,* Vol. 23 (1989), pp. 121–153.
43. See Sudip Datta, Mai Iskandar-Datta, and Kartik Raman, "In Defense of Incentive Compensation: Its Effect on Corporate Acquisition Policy," *Journal of Applied Corporate Finance,* Vol. 16, No. 4 (2004), pp. 82–88.
44. P. Healy, K. Palepu, and R. Ruback, "Which Takeovers Are Profitable: Strategic or Financial?," *Sloan Management Review,* Vol. 38 (1997), p. 55 (emphasis added).
45. M. Jensen, "Active Investors, LBOs, and the Privatization of Bankruptcy," *Journal of Applied Corporate Finance,* Vol. 2, No. 1 (Spring 1989), p. 39.

CHAPTER 14

Private Equity, Corporate Governance, and the Reinvention of the Market for Corporate Control

KAREN H. WRUCK

THE SECOND HALF OF 2007 saw the end of the second wave of U.S. private equity and the beginning of a credit crunch that continues to work its way through the system. The volume of private equity transactions has dropped dramatically. In the first half of 2007, global buyout volume totaled $527.7 billion. Through mid-June of 2008, total buyouts were down to $124.7 billion, less than a quarter of the prior year's volume. Buyouts over $1 billion in the first half of 2007 numbered 93; in the first half of 2008 there were 32. And the buyouts that are getting done are using notably less leverage, with debt averaging 4.9 times EBITDA in the first half of 2008 as compared to 6.3 times in the first half of 2007.

Another telling indicator of the change in the private equity market is the rate at which agreed-upon buyouts are now being "terminated"—that is, renegotiated or abandoned. Over 20% of the deals struck in 2007 are either rejected or reworked. (By comparison, the percentage of buyouts thus terminated in previous years was 8.3% in 2006, 12.0% in 2005, and 13.1% in 2004.[1]) Some terminated transactions, such as the $6.5 billion Hexion/Huntsman/Apollo deal, are being litigated.[2] Others have avoided litigation, such as the $6.1 billion Penn National Deal in which the banks have agreed to contribute $550 million in cash toward a $1.25 billion out-of-court settlement.[3] And still other deals have been salvaged at lower prices and/or with less generous borrowing terms, including Clear Channel, Home Depot's Supply Division, and the $52 billion buyout of Bell Canada.[4]

All this amounts to a sea change in the industry outlook. As late as mid-2007, Henry Kravis of KKR and others were celebrating what they identified as the "golden age" of private equity. But just six months later, at the World Economic Forum, David Rubenstein of the Carlyle Group stated that the golden age of private equity was over, and that the industry had entered a "purgatory age" in which it would be made to atone for its sins.[5]

As we now know from almost three decades of experience, private equity markets are prone to boom-bust cycles. Several factors have been identified as contributing to these cycles, including relaxed credit market conditions, aggressive deal pricing (reflecting intense competition for deals), and the incentives of many deal-makers to do overpriced deals.[6] Viewed in this light, the sudden fall of private equity does not come as a complete surprise. Even before the end of the second wave in 2007, the performance of private equity firms was being subjected to increased scrutiny and skepticism. In fact, while the funds put together by the top private equity firms have produced persistently strong returns over the years, one widely cited study reported that the *average* returns (net of fees) produced by a large sample of private equity funds established between 1983 and 1997 failed even to match the return to the S&P 500.[7]

At the same time their average returns were being called into question, private equity firms also began to come under attack for taking advantage of the provision of the U.S. tax code that allows partnership earnings from carried interest to be taxed at capital gains rates rather than as ordinary income.[8] This tax controversy was fueled by detailed and much-publicized reports of the personal wealth being amassed by principals in private equity firms.[9]

Without understating the importance of the issues raised above, I'd like to set them aside until the end of this paper. My primary goal in these pages is not to explore the causes of boom-bust cycles or other major controversies that now surround private equity. Nor do I claim any special ability to predict specific industry trends. Rather, my purpose is to show how the private equity market, for all its problems and cycles, has helped reinvent what economists refer to as the "market for corporate control"—particularly in the U.S., which is home to the world's largest such market. And by reinvigorating the U.S. corporate control market, private equity has had profoundly positive effects on the governance and performance of U.S. public companies. Indeed, these effects are important enough to warrant a new definition of the market for corporate control—one that, as presented below, emphasizes corporate governance and the benefits of the competition for deals between private equity firms and public acquirers or, in industry parlance, between "financial" and "strategic" buyers.

Along with improvements in governance, the early buyout firms also pioneered a distinctive approach to reorganizing companies. Scholars and practitioners alike have recognized the combination of high leverage, strong governance, and increased management equity ownership as a key contributor to the success of LBOs.[10] Less appreciated, however, is the ability of early buyout firms such as Berkshire Partners, Clayton & Dubilier, Forstman Little, Hicks Muse, and KKR to develop what might be described as a new approach to reorganizing businesses for efficiency and value.

My own research on private equity—which includes multiple case studies, interviews with buyout specialists and managers of firms acquired in buyouts, and large-sample research on private equity markets and highly leveraged transactions—has led me to identify four principles of reorganization that help explain the success of the top buyout firms. When applied effectively, these principles required changes not only in corporate governance, but in day-to-day management decision-making and operating practices, in the measures used internally to evaluate performance, and in the incentive-and-reward structures used to motivate managers at all levels of the firm. (Leverage, on the other hand, plays a secondary role; the main role of debt in private equity transactions, as I argue below, is to make possible the concentration of ownership that is critical to effective governance and strong incentives.)

In addition to providing a source of competitive advantage for the top buyout firms, the management practices that derive from these four principles of reorganization have been adopted by many *public* companies in their pursuit of shareholder value. In this sense, the impact of private equity extends well beyond the thousands of companies worldwide that have had direct dealings with private equity firms. As I suggest in this paper, private equity's most important and lasting consequence for the global economy may well be its effects on the world's public corporations—those companies that will continue to carry out the lion's share of the world's growth opportunities.

Development of the U.S. Market for Corporate Control

With the rise of unsolicited (or "hostile") takeovers in the late 1970s and early 1980s, finance scholars, corporate managers, and the press turned their attention to the effects on the economy of mergers, acquisitions, and other "corporate control" transactions. At this time, hostile deals were typically decried by the press and corporate executives as driven by greed and damaging to U.S. competitiveness, employees, and local communities. And the creation of a high-yield debt market for new issues and the emergence of private equity in the early 1980s meant that, for the first time, even very large firms were vulnerable to "attacks" by "corporate raiders" like Boone Pickens and Irwin Jacobs.

But financial economists took a very different view of these new developments. A small but growing body of papers was reporting consistent evidence of shareholder gains in M&A transactions, particularly in hostile deals.[11] And in a much-cited 1983 article that surveyed this new literature, finance professors Michael Jensen and Richard Ruback cut through the controversy and rhetoric by reintroducing Henry Manne's concept of a *market* for corporate control. After defining it as "the market in which alternative management teams compete for the right to manage corporate resources," Jensen and Ruback went on to call it "an important component of the managerial labor market." In other words, by acquiring another firm (generally at a significant premium over its current market price), and then making improvements in its performance sufficient to justify the purchase premium, an acquirer's managers were demonstrating their superiority to the managers of not only the acquired firm, but of all actual or potential competitors for the same assets.

Viewing the market for corporate control as an extension of the managerial labor market was a new and powerful idea. If the management team of a large public company was clearly failing to make the most of the investor capital and other corporate resources at its disposal, the corporate control market provided a means by which a more efficient and effective team—whether from another public company or backed by unaffiliated investors—could buy the right to manage those resources, thereby creating value for shareholders and the economy in general. The price for that right was the amount necessary to gain control of the underperforming firm.

A primary contribution of the scholarly research and the new definition of the market for corporate control was thus to change the tone of the debate, shifting the focus away from the greed of financiers and the unfortunate effects of some deals on employees and local communities, and toward the importance of improving the efficiency of resource allocation and use in public corporations. As a consequence, while ethical questions of greed and fairness will always be with us, efficiency and value are now widely accepted as the most important social criterion in transactions involving changes in corporate control.

Viewed in the context of a well-functioning market for corporate control, underperforming public companies represent profit opportunities—opportunities that in turn provide strong incentives to mobilize capital, acquire underused assets, and find ways to capture value by reversing underperformance. Such profit opportunities, and the resulting incentives, gave rise to the first major wave of U.S. private equity transactions in the early 1980s. And this first wave of leveraged buyouts, when viewed together with hostile takeovers (also typically leveraged), can be seen as the beginning of the development of an effective U.S. market for corporate control.

But it was only the beginning. At that time, the ability of potential acquirers—particularly unaffiliated raiders and private equity firms—to profit from corporate underperformance was limited by the relatively small size of the high-yield and private debt markets, and by the size of the private equity market. Another critical constraint was the limited number of private equity shops then capable of reorganizing underperforming firms. As a result, the U.S. market for corporate control was *under*developed—and its lack of development was a major contributor to a governance system notably lacking in either internal or external constraints on management.[12]

Inside U.S. public companies, corporate managers with minimal stock ownership or other equity incentives were focused mainly on growth and diversification, often at the expense of profitability and value. Take the case of

General Mills in the late 1970s. The company's stated mission was to become "the all-weather growth company," which it aimed to carry out by using the flood of cash flow from its core cereal businesses to diversify into toys and games, specialty retail, travel services, and rare coins and stamps. The eventual outcome of this diversification was a serious decline in profitability and stock price—and it required a series of voluntary divestitures and spin-offs spanning more than a decade to undo the damage. After studying this situation, Gordon Donaldson of the Harvard Business School concluded that it "was a minor miracle that it [the voluntary restructuring] happened at all . . . [and it] cost ten years of opportunity to reap the benefits."[13]

In the case of another conglomerate, Beatrice Foods, it took an LBO (completed in the face of a hostile takeover offer) to bring about the needed restructuring. But unlike the case of General Mills, the changes at Beatrice were made quickly. The company's $8.1 billion LBO, which was sponsored by KKR, closed in late 1985. By the end of 1987, just two years later, the company had spun off or divested $6.55 billion in assets, retaining only the domestic food operations. The net effect was significant value added for KKR and its investors, as well as a recovery of lost value by Beatrice shareholders in the form of the large purchase premium paid by KKR to gain control of the firm.[14]

The diversification strategies of General Mills and Beatrice Foods, while reflecting management's preference for growth over value, were at least tacitly supported by their boards of directors. Although nominally representatives of the shareholder interest, corporate directors were generally hand-picked and dominated by the CEO (who also often chaired the board). And the underdeveloped state of the corporate control market at that time meant that dissatisfied shareholders had little recourse *outside* the firm. With hostile takeovers still politically and socially unacceptable, and limited funding for the few investors willing to bear the stigma of being a "corporate raider," the *external* sources of control needed to curb corporate managers' pursuit of growth at all costs were as yet in a formative stage. As a result, tales of diversification followed by major "restructuring" were repeated countless times in the 1970s and 1980s.[15]

But, as the history of the U.S. market for corporate control also makes clear, if the abysmal performance of U.S. companies in the late 1970s was the reflection of failed governance, it also became the catalyst for major governance reform.

A Closer Look at the Corporate Governance Problem

Most business journalists, and many finance scholars, tend to write about capital markets and corporate governance as if they were two distinct subjects. But the connection between capital markets and governance is fundamental: how a company chooses to raise its capital effectively determines the kind of governance system it will be subjected to.

The objective of a governance system is to ensure that the interests of a company's managers are consistent with those of its shareholders. This raises the basic question of why, in most large enterprises, the top managers are not the dominant shareholders. The answer has to do with comparative advantage in risk-bearing.

From economists' vantage point, the principal advantage of the public corporation is its efficiency in spreading risk among well-diversified investors, thereby providing the firm with a low-cost source of equity capital. In fact, the public corporation can be thought of as an ingenious risk management device—a form of organization that allows equity investors to specialize in bearing the residual risk of the firm without having to manage it, while at the same time allowing managers to run the firm without supplying the capital and bearing the entire residual risk of the business. Consider the case of General Electric. At the end of 2007, the firm's market cap stood at $374 billion[16]—an amount that had fluctuated by an average of $3.7 billion per day during that year. It is hard to imagine an individual, or small group of individuals, having both the expertise to run GE and the capital and risk tolerance to bear the residual risk of such a huge enterprise.

But this separation of management and risk-bearing has a downside: the need for corporate governance and incentive compensation to help ensure that the managers serve the interests of the residual risk-bearing shareholders. In their pathbreaking 1976 paper on "agency costs," Jensen and his colleague Bill Meckling identified and analyzed potential conflicts of interest between management and shareholders as a "principal-agent" problem. As we saw earlier in the cases of General Mills and Beatrice Foods, managers place a higher value on growth, size, and diversification than shareholders (who, of course, can diversify their own portfolios). And as this managerial preference for size and diversification suggests, investors also have greater tolerance for risk-taking, provided the anticipated returns are high enough to justify the risks. When the expected returns fall below the cost of capital, investors would prefer that the firm's excess capital be paid out in the form of dividends and stock repurchases—while risk-averse managers, all else equal, would prefer to keep the cash inside the firm.

Corporate managers, then, when viewed as self-interested and risk-averse agents for their shareholders, tend to prefer more than the value-maximizing amount of growth and assets, and less than the optimal amount of risk-taking and payouts to investors. "Agency costs" consist partly of the direct costs incurred in trying to manage these conflicts—say, in the form of auditing fees, and the costs associated with executive contracts and incentive comp plans.

And, given the impossibility of *eliminating* these conflicts through contracts alone, agency costs also include the "residual loss in firm value" that results from having limited governance and board oversight over managers without significant equity stakes. For our purposes, what's important to keep in mind is that such agency costs are recognized, and reflected in the stock prices of public companies, by outside investors who understand the limits of their information and control.

The role of governance, then, is to give the shareholders some degree of control over managers whose interests are not fully consistent with their own. To put this in more formal terms, in companies where managerial decision-making and residual risk-bearing have been separated, the residual risk bearers must possess and be able to exercise what I will later call "governance rights." Moreover, they must be able to exercise such rights not only after things have clearly gone wrong, but at critical points when companies are contemplating new strategies or major organizational changes. When residual risk bearers have no governance rights—a condition that many finance scholars view as an accurate characterization of corporate America up through the early 1980s—agency problems lead predictably to widespread underperformance and value destruction.[17]

Effective Corporate Governance: The Private Equity Model

The governance structure used by top private equity firms has been the subject of considerable study by finance academics, and its main features are now well documented.[18] The typical board of a private-equity-controlled company has relatively few (generally five to eight) members, a non-management chair, and only one management director. Among the non-management directors are financiers and individuals with strong management experience or industry expertise. Finally, and perhaps most important, the board of directors has significant equity-based incentives, either through direct share ownership or an incentive structure whose payoffs are tightly linked to appreciation in share value (including carried interest).

A good example is the post-buyout governance structure of O.M. Scott, a lawn and plant care company that in 1986 was bought from its conglomerate parent ITT by the buyout firm Clayton & Dubilier (C&D). Upon taking control of the company, C&D established a five-person board of directors, with one management director, three C&D partners, and one outside director with extensive operating experience. One C&D director served as Scott's operating partner, working with managers to develop an effective strategy for improving performance. The C&D partners represented a 61.4% equity position—a position that, when combined with management's and employees' equity stake of

17.5%, is representative of the highly concentrated ownership structure associated with buyouts.[19]

A comparison of Scott's governance under C&D to its pre-buyout "governance" as part of ITT illustrates how private equity addresses the agency problems endemic to large, and especially diversified, public corporations. Prior to the buyout, Scott's top executive was one of many division managers in ITT's consumer products group. He reported a few times a year to ITT headquarters and what "equity" he had consisted of stock options in ITT. ITT was itself governed by an 11-member board whose equity ownership totaled 0.6% of the shares outstanding. After the buyout, Scott's top manager was the CEO and 10% equity holder of a stand-alone company, reporting on a weekly (if not daily) basis to a five-person board that included three partners of C&D, the 60% owner of his company's stock.

As the features of the Scott deal are meant to suggest, private equity firms combine significant and concentrated share ownership with effective board oversight, thereby reuniting the corporate risk-bearing and governance functions that are separated when companies go public. And the results of such changes in ownership and governance have been impressive. Within two years of being acquired by C&D, for example, Scott had increased its sales by 25% and its earnings before interest and taxes (EBIT) by over 50%. And these earnings increases, which were achieved while *raising* spending on R&D and marketing and distribution, are consistent with those reported for large samples of private equity buyouts. For example, two separate studies of large samples of LBOs in the 1980s both reported 40% average increases in operating income during a two-year period following the buyouts.[20] Another study of LBO companies that eventually went public through IPOs (known as "reverse LBOs") showed that these firms not only became more profitable after going private, but continued to be more profitable than their industry peers during the first two years *after their IPOs*.[21]

Costs of Going Private

But, as the decision by some LBO companies to return to public ownership suggests, there is also a major cost to concentrating ownership: at bottom, the decision to go private means forgoing the risk-bearing economies and the resulting lower cost of equity capital provided by equity public markets. In other words, the benefits of better corporate governance and stronger incentives that are made possible by concentrating equity ownership come at the cost of restricting shareholders' access to liquidity and their ability to diversify risk. In this sense, going private represents a decision to trade off efficiencies in risk-bearing and lower-cost equity for the gains associated with concentrated equity ownership and the stronger governance and incentives that come with it.[22]

And it is these costs of going private that ensure that the governance structures implemented by private equity firms in most of their individual portfolio companies are not "permanent." At some point, private equity deals seek a major "liquidity event" that allows investors to sell all or part of their investment. Indeed, the finite life of the limited partnership structure underlying private equity, typically seven to ten years, eventually *forces* the occurrence of such an event.[23]

One possible liquidity event is that the portfolio company is sold to another private equity group (or, alternatively, pays a liquidating dividend to its current owners and is recapitalized, with some changes in ownership). In such cases, although the cast of characters may change, the company stays private and the basic governance and equity ownership structure likely remains the same. Another common outcome is sale of the firm to another corporation, public or private, in which case the firm becomes subject to the governance system of the buyer. A third possibility—limited mainly to larger buyouts by the most reputable buyout private equity firms—is public ownership through an IPO. In the case of such reverse LBOs, the firm's managers and investors sell part of their equity stake, thereby diluting ownership concentration; and the infusion of new equity has the effect of reducing leverage. And after the IPOs, the debt of reverse LBO firms continues to fall, and the structure of their boards and their management incentive plans begin to look more like those of "typical" public companies.

But somewhat surprisingly, in light of these post-IPO changes in ownership and capital structure, a recent study by Jerry Cao and Josh Lerner of more than 500 reverse LBOs that went private during the period 1983-2001 reports that such companies outperformed both the broad stock market and other IPOs for several years *after* their return to public ownership.[24] This performance suggests that, having experienced the benefits of private equity-style governance and management, public companies do not completely revert to their pre-buyout ways. In other words, we may have evidence of "permanent" organizational change and learning (a point I will come back to).

A New Approach to Reorganizing for Value

In addition to a superior governance model, private equity can be credited with a second major contribution: the development of a systematic approach to reorganizing companies for efficiency and value. Perennially successful buyout firms have used this approach to increase the productivity of many portfolio companies, in most cases without changing top management or the firm's core assets. In the process, they have developed specific knowledge and skills that allow them to tackle the challenges posed by the next portfolio firm quickly and effectively. In other words, the reorganization process becomes sufficiently routine to the point where it can be thought of as a reorganizing "technology," a source of competitive advantage and value in itself.

In any reorganization effort, there are two primary questions that must be addressed. One is which assets should remain with the organization—and which should be sold or shut down? The second is what is the best "organizational structure" for a given enterprise? Private equity firms decide which assets should remain based on their contribution to firm value; assets that cannot earn their required rate of return on capital under private equity's ownership are sold or shut down.

In discussing the approach of private equity to reorganization, I find it useful to begin with a corporate "coordination and control" framework that was developed by Jensen and Meckling to address the dual problem of managing information and incentives in large organizations.[25] The framework identifies three critical elements of organizational structure:

1. The allocation of decision rights—that is, who gets to make what decisions?

2. Internal performance measurement—how is success defined for the firm, for business units, and for individuals?

3. Reward and punishment systems, including promotion and compensation systems.

Note that although compensation gets a lot of attention, it is only part of the story. And because of the difficulty of getting information—particularly in private firms—about internal decision-making structures and performance measurement systems, these first two elements of organizational design are often overlooked. But, as documented by a body of case studies and other "field" research, buyouts by private equity firms tend to be followed by dramatic changes in both decision-making authority and performance measures.[26]

To offer one example, while visiting Sterling Chemicals over a several-year period after its 1986 buyout by Gordon Cain, I found clear evidence of the potential value from decentralizing decision-making. In the case of Sterling, decentralization was the outcome of a firm-wide quality management program that aimed to exploit the "specific knowledge" of managers and employees throughout the firm by expanding their decision rights. And this "empowering" of employees was accompanied by major changes in the firm's performance measurement and reward systems. Especially notable among such changes was the adoption of profit-sharing and employee stock ownership plans for Sterling's highly unionized workforce. This combination of changes provided employees with both the decision-making autonomy and the incentives to put their accumulated specific knowledge to work in ways that improved performance. And, as I reported in my study, the result was a significant increase in value.[27]

Another reorganization I observed at close quarters was Safeway. In 1985, Safeway was the largest public grocery store chain in the U.S. Faced with a number of challenges, including an inability to compete with strong regional chains that used non-union labor, the company became the target of a hostile takeover offer. In response, management took the company private in a $4.3 billion LBO sponsored by KKR.

As part of its reorganization under KKR, Safeway made a simple but important change in its performance measurement systems. Before the buyout, Safeway's key performance measures were based on sales and net income benchmarked against those of other national grocery chains—which, it turns out, were not its fiercest competitors. After the LBO, Safeway developed a performance measure called *return on market value*, or ROMV. ROMV was the ratio of annual operating cash flow to the estimated market value of assets (and hence the amount that could be realized by selling those assets). The market value of assets was determined primarily through the appraisal of Safeway's real estate holdings, which were then "marked to market." ROMV was calculated at both the divisional and corporate level, and management bonuses were tied to achieving a 20% target ROMV.

With the help of ROMV, Safeway's managers identified stores and divisions with substandard performance. If they could not be made competitive, they were marked for sale or closure. And the fact that, after the buyout, Safeway's managers owned 10% of the company's common stock ensured that they had strong incentives to make such difficult decisions. (Before the LBO, Safeway's managers and directors as a group owned just 0.6% of its common stock.)

Following these changes in performance measurement and compensation, the company sold $1.8 billion in assets. In the process, they were able to renegotiate about half of their 1,300 labor union contracts. Management's focus then turned to improving the performance of the stores that remained. And improve it did: After running for five years under its revamped performance measurement and compensation systems, the company had increased its enterprise value by $1.6 billion—an increase that came after, and on top of, KKR's payment of a $1.8 billion takeover premium to buy the company from Safeway's public shareholders.

Four Principles and a Question of Competitive Advantage

To sum up, then, my synthesis of a large and growing body of research points to a set of four principles that can be viewed as the foundation of the reorganizing approach taken by the best private equity firms:

1. Governance by a small board of directors with significant equity ownership;

2. Decentralization of decision-making;

3. Adoption of new performance measures that emphasize cash flow and long-run value; and

4. Adoption of a new management compensation system that includes:

   a. Higher levels of compensation, with more pay at risk,

   b. Bonuses based on cash flow and/or value metrics, and

   c. Significant percentage management equity ownership.

The bottom line here is that a major part of the long-run success of private equity can be attributed to its ability to reorganize companies in a way that makes the most of their existing knowledge, managerial expertise, and assets. This is crucial when it comes to day-to-day decision-making, detailed problem-solving, and issues of implementation. In other words, I would argue that, although the best buyout firms have the ability to *govern* their operating companies, they do not generally have the ability to *manage* them. And while it's true that many buyout firms have added "operating" capability in the form of experienced corporate managers (many of them former CEOs) to their own staffs, this capability is not a substitute for effective management and reorganization at the portfolio firm level. This makes reorganization based on effective decentralization and performance measurement-and-reward systems a critical part of the private equity success story. A schematic of the process is presented in Figure 14.1

An important question, then, is the extent to which these four reorganizing principles constitute a source of sustainable competitive advantage. The answer is not obvious; after all, the principles identified above are not "rocket science." But they may be hard to put into practice. As one example, there is no shortage of public information documenting Southwest Airline's business strategy, organization structure, and management practices, yet no other airline seems to be willing and able to replicate its success.

The Secondary Role of Debt Also worth noting here is that substantial debt or high leverage is not one of the four principles. This is not because debt is unimportant in buyout transactions, but rather because, in an organizational and management sense, its role is a secondary one. Set aside for a moment the tax benefits of debt, and the higher returns associated with leveraged equity. From an organizational perspective, the primary role of debt financing is *to make possible the creation of the concentrated equity ownership structure that is fundamental to the effective governance and strong incentives* associated with buyouts. Leverage accomplishes this concentration of ownership by "shrinking" the dollar amount of equity required to buy the portfolio firm to the point where managers can own a significant percentage equity interest and private equity investors can own the rest.

FIGURE 14.1

Reorganizing the Firm for Value

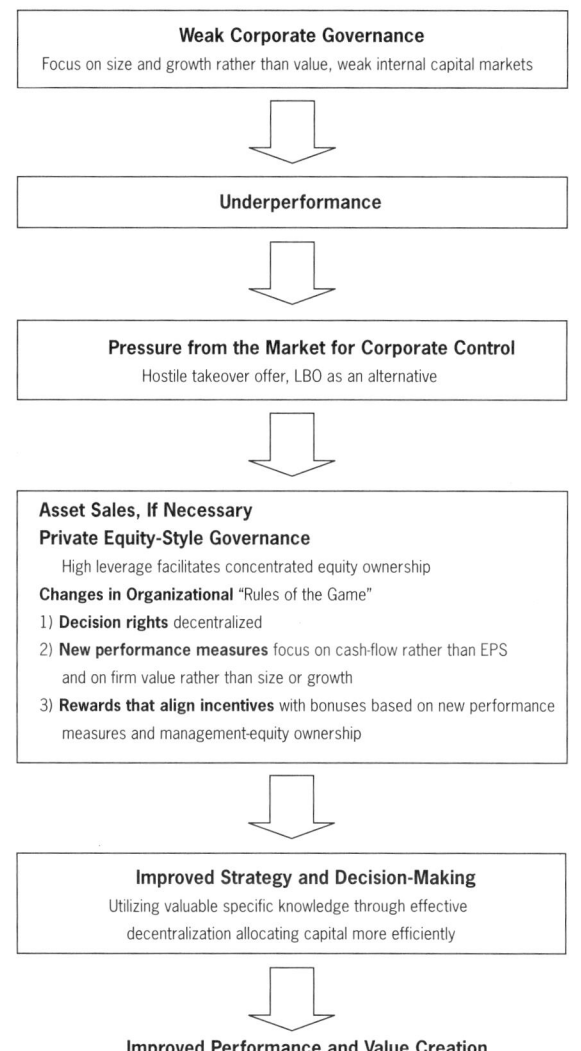

In tight credit market conditions like today's, private equity transactions will be done with less leverage, and hence produce fewer tax benefits and less leveraged (and thus lower) equity returns. Even so, today's credit market conditions should not prevent private equity firms from effectively reorganizing those portfolio firms they do manage to acquire. Indeed, tight credit markets and a soft economy are likely to make reorganizing capabilities even more important since there are fewer alternative sources of value to exploit. Finally, to the extent that easy credit encouraged the entry of private equity firms that were less skilled at governance and reorganization, current conditions will expose their limitations, identify them as "marginal" players, and force them to shrink or exit.

Private Equity Markets and the Contest for "Governance Rights"

The last 20 years have seen the evolution of a more competitive and dynamic market for corporate control, not only in the U.S., but in the U.K. and increasingly in continental Europe and Asia. And one predictable effect of this development has been to strengthen the governance systems and improve the performance of public companies, even those that have not been parties to private equity or any kind of control transactions.[28]

To illustrate these "indirect" benefits of a well-functioning corporate control market, one common response by public companies to the potential threat posed by hostile takeovers and LBOs in the 1980s (as we saw in the case of General Mills) was to sell "non-core" businesses worth more in the hands of other companies or investors. Another response, often combined with such asset sales, was to borrow (or use the proceeds from the sales) to buy back shares in what became known as "leveraged recaps."[29] As these examples are meant to suggest, many companies recognized that the best way to protect themselves from the threat of takeover was to anticipate the acquirers' action and do it themselves. But a more fundamental solution, as many companies also learned, was to adopt at least some aspects of the more effective governance and management processes of their would-be acquirers—those processes that were leading companies to *volunteer* to sell underused assets and to distribute excess capital.[30]

Much of this restructuring activity came to a halt in the early 1990s when the market for leveraged (and hence most hostile) transactions was essentially shut down, in large part through regulatory overreaction.[31] At that point, large institutional investors responded to the resulting governance "vacuum" by using their new clout to become more active in confronting the boards of underperforming companies, taking advantage of relaxed restrictions on proxy fights, and encouraging companies to provide top executives with more generous equity incentives, mainly in the form of stock options.[32]

But when leveraged financing markets began to recover in the mid-1990s, the U.S. private equity markets made a dramatic comeback. The volume of U.S. private equity deals soared from $35 billion in 1996 to $782 billion in 2007. And private equity played a growing role in M&A transactions, participating in over 20% of total deals in 2007's $4.4 trillion M&A market (as compared to just

3.1% in 1996).³³ Private equity also became a global phenomenon, with substantial growth in the U.K., continental Europe, and other parts of the world. Between 2001 and 2007, 12% of all global LBO transactions were done outside North America and Western Europe.³⁴

A New Definition of the Market for Control

In light of private equity's increased share of the global M&A market—and of its positive effects on control markets and corporate governance generally—I propose the following variation on Jensen and Ruback's definition of the market for corporate control:

> The market for corporate control is the market in which providers of capital, or their representatives, compete for the right to govern the corporation. Governance rights include the right to establish governance structures and processes, to hire, fire and set the compensation of top managers, to veto or ratify major strategic initiatives, and to serve as "internal consultants" to managers.³⁵

By "providers of capital" I mean not only investors and investment firms, but also corporations seeking to invest in or buy the operations of other companies. While this definition does not mention the managerial labor market, it has strong implications for how that market functions. For example, through the exercise of its "governance rights" (as just defined), a buyer can retain or fire incumbent managers, or change the structure of its executive compensation contracts.

When the corporate control market is redefined in this way, the importance of private equity, both for the control market and the governance of public companies, becomes more clear. Think about what happens when a private equity firm and public company bid for the same business. Corporate bidders bring to the table the risk-bearing benefits of diffuse ownership along with the value of any operational or other synergies between the bidder and target. But set against the value of those advantages are the costs of the companies' less effective governance and incentives. Even if they adopt some of the governance and incentive characteristics of private equity, corporate bidders cannot perfectly replicate the structure because of their inability (or unwillingness) to concentrate ownership. Private equity firms, on the other hand, bring the benefits of strong governance and incentives while lacking the benefits of efficient risk-bearing and the possibility of synergies.

Now, if we assume that all bidders are "rational" (in the sense of being unwilling to overpay), a public company suitor will win the contest for control whenever the benefits of public-market risk-bearing and the synergies associated with the specific business combination outweigh the expected value of the stronger governance and incentives associated with private equity. As a general rule, this is likely to be true in riskier industries with significant economies of scale and growth opportunities requiring large, ongoing investment and infusions of equity. Private equity firms are likely to win the contest under the opposite circumstances—that is, relatively stable cash flows and limited growth opportunities (though buyout firms have placed increased emphasis on growth in recent years) and modest ongoing investment and capital-raising requirements.

But having offered this generalization, with public companies adopting stronger governance practices, and private equity firms gaining access to increasingly large pools of capital and acquiring management and operating expertise in particular industries, the distinctions between the two types of bidders have begun to blur. This "convergence" of public and private equity practices has at least three important implications: First, private equity will increasingly be viewed as mainstream, as opposed to an "alternative," source of capital. Second, the returns to private equity are likely to become more pedestrian, with lower expectations on the part of investors and lower actual returns. Third, stronger governance in public companies implies that we will see fewer cases of the excessive bidding and overpayment by public acquirers—as in the case of Time Warner's purchase of AOL and the Daimler-Chrysler merger—that resulted in massive shareholder losses during the late 1990s and early 2000s.

The Import of PIPEs and Other Private Placements

One of the most visible and striking forms of the convergence of private and public equity markets is the recent growth of private placements of equity, and of a more liquid kind of private placement known as a PIPE (short for "private investment in public equity"). A private placement is the sale of a block of newly issued stock in a publicly traded company to a single or small group of sophisticated (or at least "qualified") investors. The shares are often unregistered at the time of issuance; and unless the issuer files a registration statement, they cannot be traded until held for two years. PIPEs, by contrast, are registered with the SEC within 30 days of issuance and can be publicly traded as soon as the registration becomes effective. Between 1995 and 2007, the number of private placements of equity increased from 127 to 2,430, with aggregate proceeds soaring from less than $2 billion to almost $145 billion. And of the $145 billion raised in 2007, $50 billion, or over a third, took the form of PIPEs.[36]

A simple or traditional PIPE involves the issuance of common stock at a fixed price, or convertible preferred stock at a fixed price with a fixed conversion ration. More complex or structured PIPEs involve "contingent" (or option-like) pricing arrangements, variable conversion ratios, and a variety of other contractual provisions.

One recent study of PIPEs reported that they tend to be issued by poorly performing companies, and that contingent pricing provisions tend to be used in cases of "extreme uncertainty" to allow investors to earn appropriate risk-adjusted returns.[37] Consistent with and adding to this picture, another study found that among PIPE investors, hedge funds tend to be attracted to weaker issuers and to protect their returns by using contingent contracting terms.[38]

But this leaves a number of important questions unanswered. For example, are PIPEs and private placements generally best characterized as "partial buyouts," but without the access to governance and reorganization rights provided by a typical private equity purchase of an entire firm? Do private placement and PIPE investors become actively involved in the affairs of the issuer? If so, what role do they play and what is the effect of these relationships on performance?

In a recent study,[39] Yilin Wu and I put together a sample of 1,976 private placements of common stock spanning the ten-year period from 1989 to 1999 (ending just before the burst of the NASDAQ bubble, when the number of such transactions fell off sharply) and then "hand-collected" data on placement terms and investor identity. Although our primary source of data was the private placement contracts, we also used other sources to help identify "relationships" between issuers and investors, and to classify such relationships as either "pre-existing" or "new." Our study showed, first of all, that almost two-thirds (64%) of the issuers in our sample placed at least some shares with investors with whom they had a pre-placement relationship—that is, with current managers, key business partners, current 5% or greater block-holders, or current directors. In addition, in many private placements, new relationships, mainly in the form of new directorships, were created as part of the placement agreement. Taking both pre-existing and new relationships into account, we found that only 8% of placements were issued entirely to complete "outsiders" with no current or previous ties to the firm.

Our study also furnished evidence that "relationship investors" (as defined above) provide issuers with access to larger amounts of capital and gain greater governance influence than outside investors. But our most powerful and persistent finding was a strong, positive association between *new relationships formed as part of the placement agreement and the issuer's stock returns and operating profitability over the following two to three years. And given that the vast majority of new relationships are governance-related, involving board seats and/or new 5% or greater blocks, this finding constitutes persuasive evidence that the increased monitoring and better governance facilitated by some private placements can create significant value for all investors, passive as well as active.*

To test the extent to which non-participating public investors benefit from the relationships between private placement investors and issuing firms, we also estimated the "alphas" (or excess returns) from a variety of simulated trading strategies that were all based on the use of only publicly available information. Depending on the type of relationship involved in the private placement, the issuer's stock was either purchased or sold short on the day after announcement and held for two (or three) years. For example, one of our trading strategies was to *buy* the stock of issuers selling stock to investors with whom they already have a relationship and to *short* the issuers selling stock only to outsiders. After controlling for market movements, the firm size and book-to-market factors, and momentum, this strategy yielded a two-year excess return of almost 17%—striking evidence of the value of relationships to non-participating public investors.[40]

In sum, our findings suggest that PIPEs and private placements provide an opportunity for productive collaboration between private and public equity. But to make it work, investors must have a relationship that provides them with governance rights or some other means of exerting influence on the issuing firm. In such situations, the private placement can create a partnership in which active investors supply governance expertise while public investors continue to furnish most of the equity capital and bear most of the residual risk. (What's more, the governance benefits of PIPES can be realized without debt financing, an attractive feature in today's environment.)

Bumps in the Road

While we have clearly passed the peak of the second major wave of U.S. leveraged buyouts, it seems equally clear that private equity has established itself as a permanent and significant feature of capital markets and the market for corporate control. As discussed earlier, private equity has been a major force in reinvigorating the U.S. corporate control market and strengthening the governance of U.S. public companies. In addition, the principles of reorganization that govern the practice of the top buyout firms have also clearly influenced management practices in a broad range of companies, public as well as private. But there are nevertheless a number of important and controversial issues that have raised bumps in the road.

Tax Angles. One policy area of particular concern is the tax code. While some have objected that buyout firms benefit from the tax deductibility of interest, this benefit accrues to all companies, public as well as private, that use debt financing—and thus interest deductibility is unlikely to be a target of policy change. But the same cannot be said about the preferential tax treatment of partnership profits. More specifically, earnings received in the form of "carried interest" are taxed at the capital gains rate rather than at the higher ordinary income rate. And a number of scholars, politicians, and others view this as a loophole that is being aggressively and unfairly exploited by private equity partners.[41]

The threat of a change to the tax code that more than doubles the effective tax rate on partnership carried interest is very real. With the subprime crisis, the weak economy, and an upcoming presidential election, it has received less attention recently, but will likely come up again.

Entry, Exit, and Shifting Markets. Because high profits attract entry, new private equity firms enter the industry during boom times. Other than the ability to raise funds for investment, which is relatively easy during booms, there are few real barriers to entry in private equity. Indeed in 2006, a record 2,700 private equity firms raised over $220 billion for investment, and over 170 funds had over $1 billion in assets under management. But, at the end of a boom cycle, such ease of entry creates potential problems.

One problem is that, following a period of rampant entry, many private equity firms lack the experience and expertise in governing and reorganizing portfolio firms required to manage their investments effectively through boom and bust. To the extent active engagement in governance and organizational redesign are fundamental parts of private equity's value proposition, "passive" approaches to private equity are unlikely to yield adequate returns for the risk borne. When the market contracts, investors in the funds of many of the private equity firms that were able to make money in easier times will experience poor returns. And as a result, the firms themselves will become marginal players, unable to raise new funds. A substantial number of such failures could tarnish the reputation of the industry.

Moreover, deals-in-progress that are caught in shifting market conditions will either fall apart or require renegotiating. As mentioned earlier, an unusually high percentage of buyout agreements have been "terminated" in 2008, with a number of such deals being re-struck at lower prices and/or with tighter credit terms. The fallout from such terminations may be increased reluctance on the part of target managers to enter into friendly deals with private equity, which could reduce the opportunity set of viable private equity transactions.

Incentive Dilution. A potential agency problem that has received little emphasis to date results from conflicts of interest between general partners (GPs) and limited partners (LPs). It is critical that their incentives are aligned if the private equity market is to function effectively.

Under the typical "2 and 20" payout structure, GPs receive a fee of 2% of assets under management annually and 20% of the profit (the "carried interest") from the fund. GPs often invest in the fund alongside LPs, typically contributing

1% to 5% of the total. The carried interest, along with the GPs' investment in the fund, work to align the incentives of GPs and LPs. But because management fees are paid regardless of performance, they do nothing to align incentives. In addition to management fees, GPs often receive upfront deal fees and monitoring fees, which are also independent of performance.

As deals get larger, the management fee, which is effectively a percentage of deal size, becomes substantial. And when the bulk of the rewards from a deal come from "non-contingent" payouts rather than those based on profitability or share value, GPs have an incentive to close the deal even when the expected returns are inadequate from a risk-return standpoint. This is a clear prescription for too many deals—or, more precisely, deals transacted at prices that are likely to turn out to be too high.[42]

There are also potential incentive problems when private equity firms tap public equity markets. Raising funds through a limited partnership structure imposes a time constraint (the limited life of the partnership) and discipline with respect to how the money can be deployed. In contrast, money raised in public equity markets is permanent capital and imposes far fewer constraints on the issuing firm. Thus, when a private equity firm goes public, the strength of the alignment between partner and investor interests is diminished.

The Politics of Finance. The private equity industry would be well served by considering the potential damage that can be imposed on a sector by what financial economists now refer to as the "politics of finance."[43] Unusually high profitability attracts not only attention in the press, but also scrutiny by politicians and regulators. The attack on "windfall profits" when oil prices rise dramatically is one good example. Another is the press and regulatory attack on the high yield market in the early 1990s. In short, there is abundant historical precedent for political and regulatory responses to situations perceived to be "unfair" and profits and earnings that are viewed as "excessive."

But, as those who have been on the receiving end of such responses are aware, there is no requirement that the political or regulatory responses be based on scientific evidence—that is, on the "central tendencies," or representative cases, that research helps us to identify. Instead, they are likely to be a reaction to a relatively small number of sensational and highly politicized examples. For example, many legal and finance scholars view at least parts of Sarbanes–Oxley as an overreaching and costly regulatory response to a very small number of highly visible and egregious breakdowns in governance.[44]

The highly publicized payouts that followed Blackstone's IPO, and similarly detailed reports of payouts to other private equity players, have the potential to damage the entire sector. Given the negative fallout that can result from this type of media attention, it probably makes sense to award substantial payouts with as little publicity as possible.

From Avant Garde to Mainstream?

Private equity has evolved from an *avant garde*, boutique business to an important force in capital markets and in the economy. But if private equity is to be fully accepted, Main Street must be given a better understanding of its role in facilitating economic growth and creating or sustaining jobs. This will not happen unless the industry communicates its message.

People know that General Motors and General Electric are large and important companies. They do not know that the same is true of Blackstone, KKR, TPG, and others. In 2006, taken as a whole, Blackstone's 35 to 40 portfolio companies generated over $50 billion in revenues and employed over 300,000 people, making it the equivalent of a top 20 company in the Fortune 500. TPG's portfolio companies generated $41 billion in revenues and employed 255,000. And Carlyle's portfolio companies generated $31 billion in revenues and employed 150,000. People know that their welfare in retirement depends on the performance of the stock market, but most do not understand that it also depends on the performance of private equity investments—and that this dependence is likely to grow.

Leaders in the private equity arena are more like successful entrepreneurs than successful investment bankers or traders—more like Bill Gates, the founder of software giant Microsoft, than like Bill Gross, founder of asset management titan Pacific Investment Management. They are the owners and leaders of major businesses, with all the attendant challenges and responsibilities. Addressing these challenges publicly and proactively could make a big difference for both the industry and the economy.

Notes

This chapter is based on a presentation given at the American Enterprise Institute, Conference on The History, Impact and Future of Private Equity: Ownership, Governance and Firm Performance, November 27, 2007, Washington D.C. I would like to thank John Chapman, Michael Jensen, Steve Kaplan, Josh Lerner, and Annette Poulson, and especially Don Chew for helpful discussion, questions, comments, and suggestions. Research support from the Dice Center for Financial Research, the Fisher College of Business, and The Ohio State University is gratefully acknowledged.

1. The source of these statistics is *Deal Journal, The Wall Street Journal,* July 3, 2008, July 7, 2008, which relies on data from Dealogic, Private Equity Analyst, Standard & Poors, Moody's Investor Services, and FactSet MergeMetrics.
2. See, for example, Peter Lattman, "Hunstman Sues Apollo in Texas over Buyout Battle," *The Wall Street Journal,* June 24, 2008.
3. Peter Lattman and Tamara Audi, "Wachovia, Deutsche Bank Bring End to Penn National Deal," *The Wall Street Journal,* July 4, 2008.
4. Heidi Moore, "Private Equity Wins Again: BCE Buyout Proves the Customer is Always Right," *The Wall Street Journal,* July 7, 2008.

5. Allan Sloan and Katie Benner, "The Year of Vulture," *CNNMoney.com*, May 15, 2008.
6. The incentives of deal-makers are a function of the payoffs they receive from fees, carried interest, and so forth. As discussed at the end of this chapter, high levels of fees in relation to equity commitments are a prescription for overpriced (and thus too many) deals. For a discussion of the factors leading to boom-bust cycles in LBOs, see Jensen (1991), Kaplan and Stein (1993), Kaplan and Schoar (2005), Axelson, Jenkinson, Strömberg, and Weisbach (2007). Full citations of all academic papers cited in this chapter can be found in the References at the end.
7. Kaplan and Schoar (2005) run an experiment for each buyout fund in their sample. They assess the value returned to investors by the buyout fund and compare it to the value that would have been returned to investors had they instead made the same investment in the S&P 500. They find that the S&P investment strategy would have been worth 25% more on average. Moreover, to the extent the beta of private equity is greater than one, the return to the S&P 500 understates the correct performance benchmark.
8. See Fleischer (2008).
9. Henry Sender, "How Blackstone will Divvy up its Riches," *The Wall Street Journal*, June 12, 2007.
10. See for example, Kaplan (1997) and Kaplan and Holmstrom (2001, 2003).
11. The evidence showed that most of the value gains accrue to target shareholders, with bidder shareholders experiencing no gain or a small decline. The decline was attributed to a tendency by bidders to overpay in friendly deals. For example, in a study of 47 hostile takeovers (larger than $100 million) attempted in 1985 and 1986, Bhide (1989) reported that the targets of hostile deals tended to be low-growth, poorly performing, diversified companies with little management ownership. By contrast, the targets of the 30 larger friendly deals transacted in the same period tended to be single-industry firms with strong performance and high insider ownership.
12. As Jensen summarized the situation, the managements of U.S. public companies in the early 1980s could preside over the destruction of "up to a third of the value" of their organizations before "facing a serious threat of displacement" by either their boards or outside investors. Michael Jensen, "Corporate Control and the Politics of Finance," *Journal of Applied Corporate Finance*, Vol. 4 No. 2 (Summer 1991), p. 22.
13. Donaldson (1990), p. 139.
14. In 1990, the remaining operations were sold to ConAgra. And, according to calculations made by George Baker, Beatrice's shareholders recovered most if not all of the value lost through its poor diversification strategy in the $1 billion purchase premium paid by KKR; and when this premium is added to the $1.2 billion ultimately realized by KKR and its investors, the net gains to all shareholders (buying as well as selling) from Beatrice's LBO were estimated at $2.2 billion. See Baker (1992). Today, perhaps the most notable remnant of Beatrice is the successor to Borden Chemicals, Hexion, a private specially chemical firm controlled by Leon Black's Apollo.
15. In his study of 28 successful hostile takeovers completed in 1985 and 1986 (cited earlier in note 11), Bhide (1989) notes that, after the 28 deals closed, 81 businesses were soon divested; and of the 81, as many as 78 had been previously acquired rather than developed from within.
16. According to the CIA Worldfact book, this is slightly greater than the 2007 official exchange rate GPD of Sweden ($371.5 billion) and slightly less than the official exchange rate GDP of Switzerland ($386.8 billion).
17. A defective governance structure is analogous to the non-surviving organizational form identified by Fama and Jensen (1983 (a) and (b)). Adopting their terminology more precisely, a firm in which decision management rights are co-located with deci-

sion control rights and at the same time separated from residual risk bearing cannot survive. Moreover, Jensen and his colleague Bill Meckling were sufficiently pessimistic about the U.S. governance system in the early 1980s that they published an article called "Can the Public Corporation Survive?" There they argued that U.S. policymakers and managers of U.S. companies had so lost sight of their primary obligation to efficiency and shareholder value that their future as competitive enterprises was in doubt. In other words, managers of public companies were failing to serve stockholders; and given the state of the stock and IPO markets, which reflected such poor performance, competent owners of private companies intent on maximizing value would simply choose to remain private.

18. See, for example, Jensen (1989) and Baker and Wruck (1990).
19. Over the next few years, three new directors were added. One was an academic turf expert, one was a consumer products expert, and one was the president of a company Scott acquired after its buyout. Each of these directors received significant compensation in the form of stock options.
20. Kaplan (1989), Smith (1990).
21. Cao (2008), Cao and Lerner (2007).
22. To see the tradeoff more clearly, recall that the main advantage of diffuse ownership is the relatively low cost of equity that results from providing investors with liquidity and the opportunity to diversify away firm-specific risk. In a private equity structure, managers are exposed to firm-specific risk through their human capital and share ownership, but have strong incentives to maximize value. General partners are less exposed to firm-specific risk since they invest in a number of portfolio companies and may have well-diversified personal portfolios. Nevertheless they bear more firm-specific risk than well-diversified, passive equity investors because of the illiquidity of their investments and the potentially large effects of deal outcomes on their reputations and human capital. Limited partners, by contrast, have the greatest opportunity to hold well-diversified portfolios. They are generally, although not always, large institutional investors with only a portion of their assets allocated to alternative investments such as private equity.
23. According to a study by Steve Kaplan of 183 LBOs larger than $100 million that were closed during the period 1979–1986, 62% of the LBO firms remained privately owned four or more years after their buyout, another 24% were owned by public companies, and 14% were independent publicly traded firms. Of the LBO firms that remained private, some continued to be owned by the original buyout firm, but others had been purchased by other private firms.
24. Cao and Lerner also found that the buyout sponsors owned an average of about 55% of the equity in their portfolio firms just before the IPOs. After the IPOs, their average ownership stake dropped to about 38%. Leslie and Oyer (2008) find that differences in debt and in management compensation between LBO and public companies lend to narrow (and then disappear) during the two years following the IPO.
25. See Jensen and Meckling (1995).
26. See, for example, Baker and Wruck (1990), and Wruck (1991, 1994, 1997a and 1997b).
27. Between 1987 and 1988, Sterling's sales increased from $413.2 million to $699.0 million, and EBITDA increased from $129.0 million to $340.1 million. The outstanding performance in 1988 was in part due to increases in operational efficiency and in part due to a substantial increase in the world price of styrene monomer, which increased Sterling's margins because styrene was a major product. By the end of 1988, the company had reduced its debt to $90.8 million from $200.5 million at the time of the buyout, and paid $190.3 million in dividends. The dividend payout was almost 28

times the $6.8 million equity investment made at the time of the buyout. For more detail see Wruck and Jensen (1994).
28. In addition to the "private" market-based solutions discussed below, some of the more recent improvements have been attributed to the regulatory response to highly publicized governance failures such as Enron and WorldCom. The Sarbanes-Oxley (SOX) Act, passed in 2002, and the adoption of governance rules and guidelines by stock exchanges, made certain governance practices mandatory. SOX places restrictions on insider trading and emphasizes the independence of the audit committee, focusing on internal controls and transparency in reporting. NYSE rules and guidelines, adopted in late 2003, require that the majority of directors be independent, that the compensation and nominating committees be comprised of independent directors, that non-management directors meet regularly without managers present, that shareholders vote on the adoption of new equity compensation plans and on material revisions to existing plans, and that companies make their corporate governance guidelines available.
29. See Wruck (1991) for a discussion of the governance, organizational and value changes associated with Sealed Air Corporations' leveraged recapitalization. See also Palepu and Wruck (1992), who show that companies undertaking recapitalizations as a defensive measure underperform other recap firms following the transactions.
30. A recent example of a very large public company taking such steps is IBM, which, after increasing its quarterly dividend by 50% in April 2006, sold its printer division into a joint venture arrangement in January 2007, and announced a $15 billion share repurchase plan in April 2007. It's also interesting to note that, at around the same time, a number of technology firms became private equity targets and IBM's former chairman Lou Gerstner became Chairman of the private equity firm The Carlyle Group, prompting rumors of IBM as a possible target.
31. See Jensen (1991), "Corporate Control and the Politics of Finance."
32. Holmstrom and Kaplan (2001, 2003) identify a number of important causal factors that helped bring about improved governance. Among them are the dramatic increase in the fraction of shares held by institutional investors and 1992 changes to SEC rules reducing the cost of mounting a proxy fight; these combined to increase shareholder activism. Consistent with increased activism is evidence of an increase equity-based compensation for executives and directors, some evidence of a reduction in the size of boards, and an increase of the sensitivity of CEO turnover to performance (Kaplan and Minton (2008)). While there have been improvements, long-standing governance critics like Michael Jensen and Robert Monks argue that there are still major problems in need of reform. (*JACF* Roundtable Discussion on Corporate Governance (Winter 2008)).
33. Between 2001 and 2007, 12% of all global LBO transactions were done outside North America and Western Europe. For an overview of the Global Impact of Private Equity, see the Executive Summary of the World Economic Forum (2008) Report. It provides references to more detailed research done as part of the forum.
34. Sources: Thompson Financial and Dealogic.
35. What I call governance rights include the top-level control rights that Fama and Jensen (1983a and b) and Fuller and Jensen (2002) identify as rights that must be allocated to the board of the directors for governance to be effective.
36. The source is Sagient Research (http://www.sagientresearch.com). Private placements include private investments in public equity (PIPE), 144-A placements and Regulation S transactions.
37. Chaplinsky and Haushalter (2007).
38. Brophy, Ouimet, and Sialm (2007).

39. Wruck and Wu (2008).
40. One finding that came as a bit of a surprise was the poor performance of companies making private placements to key business partners where no new relationships were formed as part of the placement agreement. This is confirmed by the estimated excess returns to the trading strategy of *shorting* the stock of all issuers selling to "key business partners" in which no new relationships are formed, and going long in the rest. The returns of this strategy ranged from 17.2% to 29.0%. Our explanation of this finding is that key business partners tend to have pre-placement relationships with the firm that involve some kind of firm-specific investment (consider, for example, an OEM that has invested to become a primary supplier to a specific automobile company). Such investors often find themselves hostage to the fortunes of the issuer, forced to share the pain by virtue of their relationships.
41. For example, Fleischer (2008), a legal scholar, states: "Partnership profit interests are treated more favorably than other economically similar methods of compensation, such as partnership capital interests, restricted stock, or at-the-money non-qualified stock options (the corporate equivalent of a partnership profit interest). The tax treatment of carry is roughly equivalent to that of Incentive Stock Options or ISOs. Congress has limited ISO treatment to relatively modest amounts: the tax subsidy for partnership profits interests is not similarly limited. A partnership profit interest is, under current law, the single most tax-efficient form of compensation available without limitation to highly-paid executives." Fleischer (2008), p. 2.
42. In my case study of Revco's failed buyout in the late 1980s (see Wruck (1991)), I found that, with the exception of one outside investor, all the parties to the transaction received more in fees than they invested in equity, meaning that, even if the equity turned out to be worthless, they still made money. And there is some new evidence that suggests that this could be a problem. Metrick and Yasuda (2007) finds that 60% of the typical partner compensation in their sample of private equity firms comes from fees, with the remainder coming from carried interest.
43. Jensen (1991) coined this phrase in describing the fall of the junk bond market in the late 1990s.
44. See, for example, Romano (2004).

References

Axelson, Ulf, Tim Jenkinson, Michael S. Weisbach, and Per Johan Strömberg, 2007, "Leverage and Pricing in Buyouts: An Empirical Analysis," Working Paper, Swedish Institute for Financial Research. Available at SSRN: http://ssrn.com/abstract=1027127.

Baker, George P., and Karen H. Wruck, 1989, Organizational Changes and Value Creation in Leveraged Buyouts: The Case of O.M. Scott & Sons Company, *Journal of Financial Economics,* Vol. 25, pp. 163–190.

Barry, Brian K., Willy Burkhardt, and Michael C. Jensen, 2001a, Wisconsin Central Ltd. Railroad and Berkshire Partners (A): Leveraged Buyouts and Financial Distress, HBS Case No: 9-190-062 and teaching note 5-899-050.

Barry, Brian K., Willy Burkhardt, and Michael C. Jensen, 2001b, Wisconsin Central Ltd. Railroad and Berkshire Partners (B): LBO Associations and Corporate Governance, HBS Case No: 9-190-070 and teaching note 5-899-050.

Berle, Adolf A., and Gardiner C. Means, 1932, *The Modern Corporation and Private Property*, New York, Macmillan Publishing Co.

Bhide, Amar, 1989, "The Causes and Consequences of Hostile Takeovers," *Journal of Applied Corporate Finance*, Vol. 2, pp. 36–59.

Brophy, David J., Paige Parker Ouimet, and Clemens Sialm, 2008, "Hedge Funds as Investors of Last Resort?" forthcoming in *Review of Financial Studies*. Available at SSRN: http://ssrn.com/abstract=782791.

Cao, Jerry X., and Josh Lerner, 2007, "The Performance of Reverse Leveraged Buyouts," forthcoming in *Journal of Financial Economics*. Available at SSRN: http://ssrn.com/abstract=938952.

Chaplinsky, Susan J., and David Haushalter, 2007, "Financing Under Extreme Uncertainty: Contract Terms and Returns to Private Investments in Public Equity," Working paper, University of Virginia. Available at SSRN: http://ssrn.com/abstract=907676.

DeAngelo, Harry, and Linda DeAngelo, 1989, "Proxy Contests and the Governance of Publicly Held Corporations," *Journal of Financial Economics*, Vol. 23, pp. 29–59.

Dodd, Peter, and Jerold B. Warner, 1983, "On Corporate Governance: A Study of Proxy Contests," *Journal of Financial Economics*, Vol. 11, pp. 401–438.

Donaldson, Gordon, 1990, "Voluntary Restructuring: The Case of General Mills" *Journal of Financial Economics*, Vol. 27, pp. 117–141.

Fama, Eugene F., and Michael C. Jensen, 1983a, "Separation of Ownership and Control," Michael C. Jensen, *Foundations of Organizational Strategy*, Harvard University Press, 1998, and *Journal of Law and Economics*, Vol. 26, pp. 301–325. Available at SSRN: http://ssrn.com/abstract=94034.

Fama, Eugene F., and Michael C. Jensen, 1983b, "Agency Problems and Residual Claims," Michael C. Jensen, *Foundations of Organizational Strategy*, Harvard University Press, 1998, and *Journal of Law and Economics*, Vol. 26, pp. 327–349. Available at SSRN: http://ssrn.com/abstract=94032.

Fleischer, Victor, 2008, "Two and Twenty: Taxing Partnership Profits in Private Equity Funds," forthcoming in *New York University Law Review*. Available at SSRN: http://ssrn.com/abstract=892440.

Fuller, Joseph, and Michael C. Jensen, 2002, "What's A Director To Do?," *Best Practices; Ideas and Insights from the World's Foremost Business Thinkers*, Cambridge, MA: Perseus Publishing and London, Bloomsbury Publishing, 2003. Available at SSRN: http://ssrn.com/abstract=357722.

Holmstrom, Bengt, and Steven N. Kaplan, 2001, "Corporate Governance and Merger Activity in the U.S.: Making Sense of the 1980s and 1990s," *Journal of Economic Perspectives*, Vol. 15, pp. 121–144.

Holmstrom, Bengt, and Steven N. Kaplan, 2003, "The State of U.S. Corporate Governance: What's Right and What's Wrong?" ECGI Finance Working Paper 23-2003. Available at SSRN: http//ssrn.com/abstract=441100.

Jensen, Michael C., 1989, "Eclipse of the Public Corporation," *Harvard Business Review,* Vol. 67, pp. 61–74, revised 1997. Available at SSRN: http://ssrn.com/abstract=146149.

Jensen, Michael C., 1991, "Corporate Control and the Politics of Finance," *Journal of Applied Corporate Finance,* Vol. 4, pp. 13–33. Available at SSRN: http://ssrn.com/abstract=350421.

Jensen, Michael C., and William H. Meckling, 1976, "Theory of the Firm: Managerial Behavior, Agency Costs and Ownership Structure." Michael C. Jensen, *A Theory of the Firm: Governance, Residual Claims and Organizational Forms,* Harvard University Press, Dec. 2000, and *Journal of Financial Economics,* Vol. 3, pp. 305–360. Available at SSRN: http://ssrn.com/abstract=94043.

Jensen, Michael C., and William H. Meckling, 1995, "Specific and General Knowledge and Organizational Structure," Michael C. Jensen, *Foundations of Organizational Strategy,* Harvard University Press, 1998; *Journal of Applied Corporate Finance,* Vol. 8, pp. 4–18. Available at SSRN: http://ssrn.com/abstract=6658.

Jensen, Michael C., and Richard S. Ruback, 1983, "The Market for Corporate Control: The Scientific Evidence," *Journal of Financial Economics,* Vol. 11, pp. 5–50. Available at SSRN: http://ssrn.com/abstract=244158.

Kaplan, Steven N., 1989, "The Effects of Management Buyouts on Operating Performance and Value," *Journal of Financial Economics,* Vol. 24, pp. 217–254.

Kaplan, Steven N., 1991, "The Staying Power of Leveraged Buyouts," *Journal of Financial Economics,* Vol. 29, pp. 287–314.

Kaplan, Steven N., 1997, "The Evolution of U.S. Corporate Governance: We Are All Henry Kravis Now," *Journal of Private Equity,* Vol. 1, pp. 7–14.

Kaplan, Steven N., and Bernadette A. Minton, 2008, "How has CEO Turnover Changed? Increasingly Performance Sensitive Boards and Increasingly Uneasy CEOs," NBER Working Paper No. W12465. Available at SSRN: http://ssrn.com/abstract=924751

Kaplan, Steven N., and Antoinette Schoar, 2005, "Private Equity Performance: Returns, Persistence and Capital Flows," *Journal of Finance,* Vol. 60, pp. 1791–1823. Available at SSRN: http://ssrn.com/abstract=473341.

Kaplan, Steven N., and Jeremy C. Stein, 1993, "The Evolution of Buyout Pricing and Financial Structure," *Quarterly Journal of Economics,* Vol. 108, pp. 313–357. Available at SSRN: http://ssrn.com/abstract=396682.

Lerner, Josh, and Anurand Gurung, editors, 2008, Global Impact of Alternative Investments Report and Working Paper Series. Available at: http://www.weforum.org/pdf/cgi/pe/Executive_Summary.pdf, http://www.weforum.org/pdf/cgi/pe/Full_Report.pdf.

Leslie, Phillip, and Paul Oyer, 2008, Managerial Incentives and Strategic Change: Evidence from Private Equity, Working Paper, Stanford Business School.

Manne, Henry G., 1965, "Mergers and the Market for Corporate Control," *Journal of Political Economy,* Vol. 73, pp. 110–120.

Metrick, Andrew, and Ayako Yasuda, 2007, "The Economics of Private Equity Funds," Working paper, Swedish Institute for Financial Research. Available at SSRN: http://ssrn.com/abstract=996334.

Moeller, Sara B., Frederik P. Schlingemann, and René M. Stulz, 2004, "Wealth Destruction on a Massive Scale? A Study of Acquiring-Firm Returns in the Recent Merger Wave," *Journal of Finance,* Vol. 60, pp. 757–782. Available at SSRN: http://ssrn.com/abstract=571064.

Mulherin, Harold S., and Annette B. Poulson, 1998, "Proxy Contests and Corporate Change: Implications for Shareholder Wealth," *Journal of Financial Economics,* Vol. 47, pp. 279–314.

Palepu, Krishna G., and Karen H. Wruck, 1992, Consequences of Leveraged Shareholder Payouts: Defensive versus Voluntary Recapitalizations, Working paper, Harvard Business School.

Romano, Roberta, 2004, "The Sarbanes-Oxley Act and the Making of Quack Corporate Governance" NYU, Law and Econ Research Paper 04-032; Yale Law & Econ Research Paper 297; Yale ICF Working Paper 04-37; ECGI — Finance Working Paper 52/2004. Available at SSRN: http://ssrn.com/abstract=596101.

Smith, Abbie J., 1990, "Corporate Ownership Structure and Performance: The Case of Management Buyouts," *Journal of Financial Economics,* Vol. 27, pp. 143–64.

Smith, Adam, 1904, first published in 1776, *The Wealth of Nations.* Edited by Edwin Cannan, Reprint edition 1937. New York, Modern Library.

Stewart, G. Bennett, 1990, "Remaking the Public Corporation from Within," *Harvard Business Review,* Vol. 68, pp. 126–137.

U.S. Corporate Governance: Accomplishments and Failings: A Discussion with Michael Jensen and Robert Monks, Moderated by Ralph Walkling, *Journal of Applied Corporate Finance,* Vol. 20, pp. 28–46.

Wruck, Karen Hopper, 1991, "What Really Went Wrong at Revco?" *Journal of Applied Corporate Finance,* Vol. 4, pp. 79–92.

Wruck, Karen Hopper, 1994, Financial Policy, Internal Control, and Performance: Sealed Air Corporation's Leveraged Special Dividend, *Journal of Financial Economics,* Vol. 36, pp. 157–192.

Wruck, Karen Hopper, and Michael C. Jensen, 1994, "Science, Specific Knowledge and Total Quality Management," *Journal of Accounting and Economics,* Vol. 18, pp. 247–287.

Wruck, Karen Hopper, and A. Scott Keating, 1997a, Sterling Chemicals Inc. Quality and Process Improvement, Harvard Business School Case 9-493-026 and teaching note 5-897-160.

Wruck, Karen Hopper, and Sherry P. Roper, 1997b, American Cyanamid Case Series 9-897-048, 9-897-178, 9-897-064 and teaching note 5-897-161.

Wruck, Karen Hopper, and Steve-Anna Stephens, 1997c, Safeway, Inc.'s Leveraged Buyout Inc. Harvard Business School Case Series 9-294-139, 9-294-14, 9-294-141 and teaching note 5-897-184.

Wruck, Karen Hopper, and Yilin Wu, 2008, "Relationships, Corporate Governance, and Performance: Evidence from Private Placements of Common Stock," forthcoming, *Journal of Corporate Finance,* Charles A. Dice Center Working Paper No. 2007-18; Fisher College of Business Working Paper No. 2008-03-019. Available at SSRN: http://ssrn.com/abstract=998530.

About the Contributors

LUCIAN A. BEBCHUK is the William J. Friedman and Alicia Townsend Friedman Professor of Law, Economics, and Finance and Director of the Program on Corporate Governance at Harvard Law School.

ROBERT BRUNER is Dean and Charles C. Abbott Professor of Business Administration and Distinguished Professor of Business Administration at the Darden Graduate School of Business Administration, University of Virginia.

BRIAN BUSHEE is Associate Professor of Accounting at the University of Pennsylvania's Wharton School.

JOHN E. CORE is the Ira A. Lipman Professor of Accounting at the University of Pennsylvania's Wharton School.

JASON DRAHO is Associate Editor of Morgan Stanley's *Journal of Applied Corporate Finance*.

JESSE M. FRIED is a Professor of Law at the University of California Berkeley–Berkeley and Faculty Co-Director of the Berkeley Center for Law, Business and the Economy.

JOSEPH FULLER is a co-founder and Chief Executive Officer of Monitor Group, a leading global consultancy.

STUART L. GILLAN is Associate and Jerry S. Rawls Professor of Finance at Texas Tech University.

WAYNE R. GUAY is Associate Professor at the University of Pennsylvania's Wharton School.

BENGT HOLMSTROM is the Paul A. Samuelson Professor of Economics at Massachusetts Institute of Technology. He holds a joint appointment with MIT's Sloan School of Management.

MICHAEL C. JENSEN is Jesse Isidor Straus Professor of Business Administration, Emeritus, of the Harvard Business School and a Senior Advisor to the Monitor Company.

STEVEN N. KAPLAN is Neubauer Family Professor of Entrepreneurship and Finance at the University of Chicago's Booth School of Business.

HENRY MCVEY is Managing Director at Fortress Investment Group LLC and former Managing Director and Chief U.S. Investment Strategist at Morgan Stanley & Co.

NELL MINOW is co-founder and Editor of The Corporate Library and former President of Institutional Shareholder Services, Inc.

ROBERT MONKS is a longtime proponent of corporate governance reforms and the founder of Lens Governance Advisors, Institutional Shareholder Services, and the investment fund known as LENS.

ANIL SHIVDASANI is a Managing Director at the Citi Financial Strategy Group.

LAURA T. STARKS holds the Charles E. and Sarah M. Seay Regents Chair of Finance and is Chairman of the Department of Finance and Director of the AIM Investment Center in the McCombs School of Business at the University of Texas at Austin.

RANDALL S. THOMAS is John S. Beasley II Professor of Law and Business at the Vanderbilt University Law School.

KAREN H. WRUCK is Associate Dean for MBA Programs, Dean's Distinguished Professor and Professor of Finance at the Fisher College of Business at the Ohio State University.

MARC ZENNER is Managing Director in Capital Structure Advisory & Solutions at J. P. Morgan and formerly global head of the Financial Strategies team at Citigroup.

Index

Italicized page numbers denote tables or illustrations.

abnormal returns, 285; to buyer firm shareholders, 286–288; to combined buyer/target firms, 288; in M&A, 286–288; to target firm shareholders, 286, 288
absolute priority, 265, 266
academic economists, 245
accountability: management, 56, 79–80, 81, 88n3. *See also* corporate accountability
active investors, 252–253, 274nn26–27, 274nn29–30
Adelphia, 184
Advanced Micro Devices (AMD), 287
AFLAC, 197
agency conflicts, 185, 187, 198, 200nn4–5; boards of directors and, 207; U.S. shareholder activism and, 207
agency costs, 254–255, 274n34, 274n36, 312
AIMR. *See* Association for Investment Management and Research
Allied and Federated, 262, 277n57
AMD. *See* Advanced Micro Devices
American Express, 207
American Finance Association, 290

Amos, Dan, 197
analysts: celebrity, 163; compensation, 163; earnings and, 161; earnings game and, 161, 162, 163, 164, 165, 166, 167, 168, 169n3; executives and, 161, 167; expectations and companies, 162, 165; managers and, 167, 168; shareholders and, 161
Anderson, Ronald, 184, 186, 188, 192, 193
Anheuser-Busch, 188, 195
antitakeover measures: corporate governance research on, 90, 101–102; defenses use in M&A profit/loss neighborhood of governance, 301; executive compensation and, 126; shareholders and, 101–102
AOL, 287, 322
Apache Corporation, 195, 196
Apollo Group Inc., 197
arm's-length contracting: boards of directors and, 120–124; directors and, 120; executive compensation and, 113, 120–125, 127, 132, 141n4; limits of, 120–124; manager compensation and, 120; shareholders and, 120
Armstrong World Industries, 53–54, 58

Association for Investment Management and Research (AIMR), 178, 180
AT&T, 170, 247
auctions, 264–269, 279nn73–74

Balanced Scorecard, xii, xiii; corporate objective and, 4–5; multiple objectives and, 18; performance measure and, 19, 21–22; stakeholder theory and, 17. *See also* stakeholder theory
Ballmer, Steven, 147–148, *149*
bankruptcy, 277n62; court decisions, 248; LBOs and, 264; retailing and, 275n45. *See also* Chapter 11
bankruptcy privatization, 248, 257; company reorganization and, 258–260, 276n49; Japanese parallel to, 258, 276n47
bankruptcy reform proposal, 264, 277n63, 278nn64–66; absolute priority and, 265, 266; company categories/solutions in, 265, 266; information problem/auction solution in, 264–269, 279nn73–74; strict priority enforcement in, 266–267, 278n70, 279n71
banks: HLTs and, 246; regulation and, 272n13, 277n61; takeovers and, 272n13
Barbarians at the Gate (Burrough and Helyar), 79, 80, 82, 88n1, 244, 272n4
Bartlett, Sarah, 272n3
Bear Stearns, xi
Beatrice Foods, 311, 328n14
Berkshire Hathaway, 67, 161, 173, *174*
"Best Practices for Research," 168
Blackstone, 327
board committees, 90, 91, 92, 94–95
boards of directors: 2000s regulatory changes and, 43; accountability improvements for, 138–140; agency conflicts and, 207; arm's-length contracting and, 120–124; CEO pay and, xvi; CEOs and, 53, 54, 59, 87–88, 89n22; corporate governance research on, 90, 91, 92, 93–97, 108n2; executive compensation and, 114, 120–124, 125, 127, 138–140; executive firings and, 124; independent, 90, 91, 92, 93; internal corporate governance and, xiv–xv; nominations, 54–55; private equity firm reorganization principles and, 317; purpose of, 53; remedies for inadequate, 207–208, 230n21; shareholders and, 51, 54, 55, 81, 82, 88, 207; SOX impact on, 39; stakeholder theory and, 11–12; stock market and, 207–208, 230n21; U.K. corporate governance and, 57–58; uninvited candidates for, 52; U.S. corporate governance and, 36–37, 46n27, 59; U.S. family-run companies and, 192, *193*; U.S. shareholder activism and, 212. *See also* corporate boards of directors; directors
bonuses: executive compensation and, 136, 137, 146, 147, 156n4; incentives and, 147; windfalls in, 136
boom-bust cycles: in private equity markets, 308, 328nn6–7; in venture markets, 248, 260–261
Boston Scientific, 200n8
Brin, Sergey, 170
Buffet, Warren, 67, 113, 161, 174
Bush, George W., 69
Business Council, 84
Business Roundtable, 83, 84; CEOs and, 87; corporate accountability and, 85–87, 89n22; corporate governance and, 85–88, 89n22; corporate restructuring and, 244; directors and, 87–88, 89n29; managers and, 244; shareholders and, 87–88
Business Week, 184, 188, 281–282, 304n6
buyer competition, in corporate control market, 308

buyer firms: abnormal returns to combined target and, 288; abnormal returns to shareholders of, 286–288; corporate governance and, 308; financial performance of, 288–289; M&A and, 286–289; misvaluation in M&A profit/loss neighborhood of investment opportunity, 296
buyout firms: company reorganization and, 308, 309. *See also* private equity firms
buyouts: 2007, 307; private equity market and, 307; termination, 307. *See also* leveraged buyouts

Cain, Gordon, 316
California Public Employees' Retirement System (CalPERS), *103, 174,* 175, 206, 209, 212, 213, 221, 225, 226; corporate governance guidelines (2002), 107–108
California State Teachers Retirement System (CalSTRS), 206
Campeau, 262, 277*n*57
capital: investment and manufacturing productivity research, 250, 272*n*18; markets and corporate governance, 311
Carlyle, 327
C&D. *See* Clayton & Dubilier
CEO. *See* chief executive officer
CEO pay: boards of directors and, xvi; criticism of, 113–114; incentives/portfolio value and, *150. See also* executive compensation; U.S. CEO pay; U.S. executive compensation
CFO. *See* chief financial officer
chairman: CEOs and, 94; corporate governance research on, 94
Chambers, John, 163
Chapter 11, 248, 264. *See also* bankruptcy
charitable foundations, 208

chief executive officer (CEO): boards of directors and, 53, 54, 59, 87–88, 89*n*22; Business Roundtable and, 87; chairman and, 94; corporate governance research on, 93–95; descendent, 197, 198, 201*nn*14–15; directors and, 82, 87, 89*n*10, 89*n*22; earnings game and, 162; founders, 197; money managers and, 207; shareholders and, 83; SOX impact on, 38, 39, 46*n*32; stock and, 147, 156*n*5; turnover in 1980s/1990s, 36, 46*n*27; of U.K. companies, 289; of U.S. family-run companies, 197, 198; variables of, xvi; Wall Street problems with, xvi–xvii. *See also* CEO pay; executives; U.S. CEO pay
chief financial officer (CFO), xvi, 201*n*10; SOX impact on, 38, 39, 46*n*32
Cisco, 162, 163
Clayton & Dubilier (C&D), 313, 314, 329*n*19
Coca-Cola, 170
Code of Best Practices (1992), 40
collars, 298, 306*n*40
Comcast, 191
Commission on Public Trust and Private Enterprise, 41, 46*n*35
companies: analysts expectations and, 162, 165; investors and, 171; joint stock, ix; numbers game and, 170, 182*n*5; overvalued stock damage to, 162–164; targets of U.S. shareholder activism, 209, 226–227, 232*n*67. *See also* family-run companies; insurance companies; public companies; U.K. companies; U.S. companies
company reorganization: bankruptcy privatization and, 258–260, 276*n*49; buyout firms and, 308, 309; Japan troubled, 248; private equity firms and, 310, 315–317, *318,* 329*n*27. *See also* private equity firm reorganization principles

compensation: analysts, 163; corporate governance research on directors, 90, 99–100; internal corporate governance, xv; issues of U.S. companies, xv–xvi; U.S. corporate governance, xv. *See also* equity compensation; executive compensation; manager compensation

competition: corporate control market buyer, 308; private equity firm reorganization principles and, 318

Conference Board, 2002 recommendations, 41–42, 46n35

Congress, 51, 69, 85, 277n61

contract: failure in venture markets and LBOs, 260–263, 276nn53–55, 277nn56–57; problems and politics, 247–248. *See also* arm's-length contracting

control, corporate. *See* corporate control

control systems, stakeholder theory and internal, 12

Coors, 195

corporate accountability, 79, 88n3; Business Roundtable and, 85–87, 89n22; myth of, 80–88

corporate boards of directors: management and, xiv–xv, 79–80, 88n3, 207; role of, xiv; shareholders and, xiv, xv; structure, xv. *See also* boards of directors; directors

corporate control: academic economists and, 245; corporate restructuring and, 245; internal, 270; investors and, 243; managers and, 243, 310; media and, 244, 245, 246, 271n7; owners and, 81; politics of finance and, 243; popular beliefs about, 245; U.S. family-run companies and, 188, 193–196, 198–199, 200, 201n17

corporate control market, 59; 1980s, 243–245; buyer competition in, 308; corporate governance and, 308; corporate restructuring and, 246;

external corporate governance and, xix–xxi; hostile takeovers and, 309, 328n11; LBOs and, xix, xx, 243; M&A and, 243; new definition of, 321–322, 330n35; politics and, 247–248; private equity and, xx; private equity firms and, 308, 321–322; private equity markets and, 308, 324; public companies and, 310, 320, 321–322, 330nn29–30; regulation and, 263, 269–270, 277n59, 277nn61–62; reinvention/corporate governance and private equity, 307; research, 310; takeovers and, 243; workouts and, 263–264. *See also* U.S. corporate control market

corporate control transactions: 1976–1990 value of, 245, 271n8; 1980s, 247; gains, 246, 272n11; industrial economy and, 247; losses, 245–246, 271n9, 272n10; manufacturing productivity research and, 247; research, 247; shareholders and, 245, 246

corporate efficiency: LBOs and, 246. *See also* corporate inefficiency

corporate finance, 49

corporate goal. *See* corporate objective

corporate governance: broad perspectives on, xii–xiv; Business Roundtable and, 85–88, 89n22; buyer firms and, 308; CalPERS guidelines (2002), 107–108; capital markets and, 311; corporate control market and, 308; corporate control market reinvention/private equity and, 307; debates over, xii, 3; effective, 313–314; failures and regulation, 330n28; family-run companies, 185, 191–192, 193; ISS scorecard (2002), 103–104; M&A profit/loss neighborhood of, 299–301; management and, 312; managers and, 312–313; NYSE new/former rules (2002), 105–107; performance measuring in, 3–4;

private equity firm reorganization principles and, 309, 317; private equity firms and, xx, 61, 313–314, 315, 329n19; problem, 311–313, 328nn16–17; rights and private equity markets, 320–321, 330n28, 330n33; shareholders and, 313. *See also* external corporate governance; foreign corporate governance; internal corporate governance; U.K. corporate governance; U.S. corporate governance

corporate governance proposals: NASDAQ 2002, 40; NYSE 2002, 40; studies, *210*, *211*, *212*, 213, *214–220*, 221–222, 223, 224–229, 231n35, 231n38, 231n40, 231n42, 232n45, 232n48, 232n51

corporate governance research, 102, 104–108; on antitakeover measures, 90, 101–102; on board committees, 90, 94–95; on boards of directors, 90, 91, 92, 93–97, 108n2; on CEOs, 93–95; on chairman, 94; on corporate governance principles, *103*; on director compensation, 90, 99–100; on directors, 90, 91, 92, 93–97, 99–100, 108n2; on executive compensation, 90, 97–98, *99*, 100, 108n4; on executive stock options, 97, 98–99; on executive stock ownership, 97–98, *99*; on ownership, 97–98, *99*, 108n4; on private equity firms, 313; on shareholders, 98–99, 100–102

corporate inefficiency: LBOs and, 245; media and, 245; takeovers and, 245. *See also* corporate efficiency

corporate law, 69, 70

corporate management. *See* management

corporate objective: Balanced Scorecard and, 4–5; single-valued vs. multiple, 5, 7, 23n3; stakeholder theory and, 4, 5, 8–9; value maximization and, 4, 5, 7, 8; value seeking and, 7. *See also* multiple objectives; single-valued objective; stakeholder theory; value maximization

corporate pension funds, 207, 230n17; institutional investors and, 208

corporate raiders, x, 62, 243, 244

corporate reorganization. *See* company reorganization

corporate restructuring: 1980s, 245, 247; academic economists and, 245; corporate control and, 245; corporate control market and, 246; in M&A profit/loss neighborhood of strategy, 293, 306n27; manufacturing productivity research and, 250–252, 273nn21–23; media and, 245, 246, 271n7; opposition to, 243–244, 272n3; of targets in M&A profit/loss neighborhood of investment opportunity, 295; transactions in the present, 246–247

corporations: publicly traded, ix; purpose of, xii, 3; value maximization and, 253–254, 274nn32–33

Council of Institutional Investors, 205, 206, 213, 232n60

credit: crunch (2007), 307; private equity firm reorganization principles and, 318–319

Daimler-Chrysler, 322

deal design, in M&A, 297–299, 306n40

debt: private equity firm reorganization principles and, 318; U.S. family-run companies and, 198

dedicated holders, xvii, xviii

dedicated institutions, 172, 173, *174*, *175*, 176, 177, 178, 179, *180*, 181. *See also* institutional investors

Del Guercio, Diane, 226

Dell, 185, 189

Department of Labor, 207; Interpretative Bulletin 94-2, 230n17

Diller, Barry, 162, 167

directors: arm's-length contracting and, 120; Business Roundtable and, 87–88, 89n29; CEOs and, 82, 87, 89n10, 89n22; corporate governance research on, 90, 91, 92, 93–97, 99–100, 108n2; corporate governance research on compensation of, 90, 99–100; independent, 90, 91, 92, 93, 212; management and, 82–83; myth of duty of, 80–82; shareholders and, 80–81, 82, 87–88, 89n29; stock options and, 99–100; U.S. shareholder activism and, 212. See also boards of directors

disclosure: earnings game and, 161, 166, 167; executive compensation, 100; institutional investors and, 178–179, 180, 181; investor base and, xviii, 171, 181; numbers game and, 181; stock price volatility and, 179, 180, 181, 183n23; U.S. family-run companies and, 194

dividend neutrality, 137–138

Dow Jones & Company, 61

Drexel, 264

earnings: analysts and, 161; executive compensation and corporate, 116, 117

earnings before interest and taxes (EBIT), 314

earnings game: analysts and, 161, 162, 163, 164, 165, 166, 167, 168, 169n3; CEOs and, 162; disclosure and, 161, 166, 167; earnings guidance as, 161; Enron and, 163–164; executive compensation and, 162–163; executives and, 162, 163, 164, 169n3; investors and, 167, 169n3; management and, 161, 164, 166, 167; managers and, 164, 166, 167, 168; Nortel and, 165–166, 169n6; press and, 166; restarting conversation on, 166–168; stockholders and, 166; Wall Street and, 161, 162, 164, 165, 168. See also numbers game

earnings guidance, 196; criticism, xvi; as earnings game, 161

earnings management: criticism of, xvi; public companies and, 64–68

earn-outs, 298

Eastern Airlines, 278n64, 278n66

Eastman Kodak, 207

EBIT. See earnings before interest and taxes

Economic Value Added (EVA), performance measure and, 20

economists: academic, 245; financial, 246

EGM. See extraordinary general meeting

Eisenberg, Melvin, 80

Eli Lilly, 189, 200n7

Employment Retirement Income Security Act (ERISA), 207, 230n17

English companies. See U.K. companies

Enron, xv, xvii, 44, 162, 226, 330n28; earnings game and, 163–164

equity: pay plans, xi. See also private equity

equity compensation, xv, 43–44; executive compensation and, 131–132, 135–136; executive compensation and non-, 130–131; manager compensation and, 131–132; manager compensation and non-, 130–131; U.S. corporate governance and, 26, 27; windfalls in, 131–132, 135–136

equity incentives, xi; executive compensation and, 152–153, 157n12; windfalls and, 152–153

ERISA. See Employment Retirement Income Security Act

Eubanks, Gordon, 170

EVA. See Economic Value Added

executive(s): analysts and, 161, 167; corporate governance research on stock ownership of, 97–98, 99; earnings game and, 162, 163, 164, 169n3; firings and boards of directors,

124; M&A and, 289; stock sales and executive stock options, 153–154, 157nn13–15. *See also* chief executive officers

executive compensation: antitakeover measures and, 126; arm's-length contracting and, 113, 120–125, 127, 132, 141n4; boards of directors and, 114, 120–124, 125, 127, 138–140; bonuses and, 136, 137, 146, 147, 156n4; camouflage/stealth in, 127–129; corporate governance research on, 90, 97–98, 99, 100, 108n4; disclosure, 100; dividend neutrality and, 137–138; earnings game and, 162–163; equity compensation and, 131–132, 135–136; equity incentives and, 152–153, 157n12; gratuitous goodbye payments in, 129; improving pay arrangements in, 135–138; incentives vs., 155n3, 156n8; internal corporate governance and, xv–xvi; management and, 113, 125, 127; non-equity compensation and, 130–131; pay and performance and, 135; pay and power in, 125–129; pay without performance and, 130–133; pensions and, 138; problems/criticisms with, 113–116; severance pay and, 132–133; shareholders and, 55, 68–69, 70, 125, 126, 127, 130; stakes of, 116, *117*, 118; transparency and, 133–135; U.K. corporate governance and, 70; windfalls and, 131–132, 135–136. *See also* CEO pay; manager compensation; U.S. CEO pay; U.S. executive compensation

executive stock options: corporate governance research on, 97, 98–99; executive stock sales and, 153–154, 157nn13–15; indexation and, 72–73, 157n12

external corporate governance: corporate control market and, xix–xxi; criticism of U.S., x; mechanism criticism, x; mechanism types, x; ownership structure, xvi–xix

externality problems, and value maximization, 8, 15

extraordinary general meeting (EGM), xiii–xiv, 55, 56

Fama, Eugene, 230n21, 328n17

families, vs. markets and stakeholder theory, 12–14

"Family Portrait, A" (McVey), 200

family-run companies: agency conflict and, 185, 200nn4–5; corporate governance, 185, 191–192, *193*; management and, 185, 193, 195, 197–198, 200; performance, 184, 185, 200n3; research on, 184–185, 200n1, 200nn3–5; shareholders and, 185. *See also* U.S. family-run companies

Fannie Mae, 132

Fidelity, 207

fiduciary standard, 80

finance: corporate, 49; corporate control and politics of, 243; private equity controversies and politics of, 326

Financial Institutions Reform, Recovery and Enforcement Act (FIRREA), 263, 277n59

firings, executive, 124

firm: value maximization of total, 7–8. *See also* buyer firms; buyout firms; companies; corporations; LBO firms; private equity firms; target firms

firm value, 4; insider stock ownership and, 98, *99*; single-valued objective and, 8; stakeholder theory and, 11. *See also* value maximization

FIRREA. *See* Financial Institutions Reform, Recovery and Enforcement Act

Forbes, 186

Ford, Henry, 184

Ford Motor Company, 188

foreign corporate governance: 1990s changes in, 37–38; problems of, 28; shareholder activism and, 37; U.S. corporate governance and, 28, 29, 37–38
Fortune, 244
Fortune 500, 327
foundations, charitable, 208
founders: CEOs, 197; of U.S. family-run companies, 189, 192, 193, 197
Freeman, Edward, 23n1
funds: index, 87, 89n24; mutual, 207; U.S. shareholder activism and private equity, 203; U.S. shareholder activism and union, 206. *See also* hedge funds; pension funds

gadfly investors, 204, 230n9
Galvin, Chris, 195
Gates, Bill, 327
GE. *See* General Electric
General Electric (GE), 164, 270, 312, 327, 328n16
General Mills, 270, 311, 320
General Motors (GM), 83, 327
Georgeson Shareholders' 2005 Annual Corporate Governance Review, 210, 231n35
Gillette, 162, 165, 170
Glass-Steagall Act, 202
GM. *See* General Motors
Goldberg, Arthur, 83
Google Inc., 170
governance: M&A profit/loss neighborhood of, 299–301. *See also* corporate governance
Grass, Martin, 197
Greeniaus, John, 272n4
Gross, Bill, 327
gross domestic product (GDP): foreign corporate governance and, 29, 44n2; U.S. corporate governance and, 29, 44n2
Grubman, Jack, 163
Grundfest, Joseph, 244

Hall, Brian, 149, 156n8
Hawkins, Jennifer, 226
Hayek, Friedrich von, 12–14
hedge funds: relationship investing and, 227, 233n72; U.S. companies and, 59; U.S. shareholder activism and, 203, 206, 209, 227–229, 230n3, 233n72
highly leveraged transactions (HLTs): banks and, 246; shareholders and, 245; takeovers and, 246; troubled, 246
HLTs. *See* highly leveraged transactions (HLTs)
Hodges, Luther, 84
Holmstrom, Bengt, 144–145, 208, 330n32
Home Depot, 227, 228
hostile takeovers, 85; corporate control market and, 309, 328n11
Huson, Mark, 226

IB 94-2. *See* Interpretative Bulletin 94-2
IBM, 245, 246, 272n10
incentives: bonuses and, 147; CEO pay/portfolio value and, *150*; dilution in private equity controversies, 325–326, 331n42; executive compensation vs., 155n3, 156n8; U.S. executive compensation and, 144–147, *148*, *149*, *150*, 151–155, 155n3, 156n8, 156nn4–6, 157n10, 157nn12–15; U.S. executive compensation and performance, 144–147, *148*, *149*, *150*, 155n3, 156n8, 156nn4–6. *See also* equity incentives; pay incentives; portfolio incentives
index fund, 87, 89n24
indexation: Conference Board recommendations for, 41–42; executive stock options and, 72–73, 157n12
insider trading prosecutions, 246
institutional investors: activism in M&A profit/loss neighborhood of governance, 299–300; attracting, 176–178; classification of, 171–173, *174*,

175, 176, 182*n*13; conflicts of interests, 208; corporate pension funds and, 208; disclosure and, 178–179, *180*, 181; foreign, 171; insurance companies and, 208; legal types, *175*; management and, xvii, xviii; portfolio characteristics of, *174*; research on, xvii, 170, 171–173, *174*, *175*, 176–179, *180*, 181, 182*n*13, 183*n*18; stock price volatility and, 179, *180*, 181, 183*n*23; types of, xvii–xviii; U.S. corporate governance and, xviii–xix, *205*; U.S. shareholder activism and, *205*, 206–207, 208, 209, 212–213, *214–220*, 229; U.S. stock market and, *205*. *See also* dedicated holders; dedicated institutions; investors; quasi-indexers; transient investors

Institutional Shareholder Services (ISS), 48, 60; corporate governance scorecard (2002), 103–104

insurance companies: institutional investors and, 208; restrictions on, 246

Interco, 262, 277*nn*56–57

internal corporate governance, ix; aspects, xiv–xvi; boards of directors and, xiv–xv; compensation structures, xv; criticism of U.S., x; executive compensation and, xv–xvi; mechanism criticism, x; mechanism types, x

International Flavors & Fragrances, 200*n*8

Interpretative Bulletin 94-2 (IB 94-2), 230*n*17

investing, relationship, 227, 233*n*72

investment: managers, 208; manufacturing productivity research and capital, 250, 272*n*18; opportunity in M&A profit/loss neighborhood, 295–296; PIPE, 322–324, 330*n*36, 331*n*40; U.S. company over, 245; U.S. company under, 245

investor(s): active, 252–253, 274*nn*26–27, 274*nn*29–30; companies and, 171; corporate control and, 243; earnings game and, 167, 169*n*3; gadfly, 204, 230*n*9; identifying/attracting right, 170–171, 176–178; individual, 171, 176; managers and, 171, 172, 175–176, 177, 181; numbers game and, 170, 181; retail, 171; transient, xvii–xviii, 172, 173, *174*, *175*, 176, 177, 178, 179, *180*, 181. *See also* institutional investors

investor base, xvii; disclosure and, xviii, 171, 181

Investor Relations (IR), 171, 178

Investor Responsibility Research Center (IRRC), 208

Investors for Director Accountability, 205

Investors' Rights Association of America (IRAA), 205

IR. *See* Investor Relations

IRAA. *See* Investors' Rights Association of America

IRRC. *See* Investor Responsibility Research Center

ISS. *See* Institutional Shareholder Services

ITT, 313, 314

Japan: parallel to bankruptcy privatization, 258, 276*n*47; troubled company reorganization in, 248

Japanese business financing networks. *See* keiretsu

Jensen, Michael, 198, 230*n*21, 290, 309, 316, 321, 328*n*12, 328*n*17

Johnson, Ross, 244

Journal of Applied Corporate Finance, 144

junk bonds, 246

Kaplan, Robert, 17–19, 21

Kaplan, Steve, 144–145, 260, 261, 264, 276*n*53, 329*n*23, 330*n*32

Ke, Bin, 176
keiretsu, 247, 258
Kilts, Jim, 162, 165
KKR, 62, 63, 243, 244, 272n4, 307, 311, 327, 328n14
Kodak, 245
Korn Ferry survey (2002), 37
Kravis, Henry, 311

labor, and corporate restructuring, 244
law, corporate, 69, 70
LBO. *See* leveraged buyout
LBO associations, 247, 255–257, 275n37
LBO firms, 62, 63; public companies and, 314. *See also* private equity firms
Lehman Brothers, xi
LENS, 48, 61
leveraged buyouts (LBOs), x, xi, 49, 62, 271n7; bankruptcy and, 264; bottom line on, 257; corporate control market and, xix, xx, 243; corporate efficiency and, 246; corporate inefficiency and, 245; evidence on, 256; in M&A profit/loss neighborhood of deal design, 297–298; operating efficiency increases and, 256–257; stockholder gains and, 256, 275n41; study (1980s), 260; transactions, 272n11; venture market contract failure and, 260–263, 276nn53–55, 277nn56–57
Lewis, Peter, 196
Liebman, Jeff, 149, 156n8
Lilly Foundation, 189, 200n7
Lipton, Martin, 49, 50, 60, 66
London Stock Exchange (LSE), 40
Long Term Capital Management, 287
Lorsch, Jay, 36
LSE. *See* London Stock Exchange

M&A. *See* mergers and acquisitions
M&A profit/loss neighborhoods, 291–301, 302, 303
M&A profit/loss neighborhood, of deal design: collars use in, 298, 306n40; earn-outs use in, 298; LBOs in, 297–298; payment form/cash vs. stock in, 297; social issues/merger of equals in, 298–299; tax exposure in, 299
M&A profit/loss neighborhood, of governance: antitakeover defenses use in, 301; friendly vs. hostile target approaching in, 300–301; institutional investors' activism in, 299–300; managers' stakes in, 300
M&A profit/loss neighborhood, of investment opportunity: border crossing in, 296; hot/cold M&A markets/buyer firm misvaluation in, 296; privately owned assets in, 295; restructuring targets in, 295
M&A profit/loss neighborhood, of strategy: excess cash use/value/redeployed profitability in, 294–295; focus vs. diversification in, 291–293, 304nn20–21, 305n26, 305nn22–23; M&A programs initiation in, 293–294; market power grabs in, 294; strategic restructuring in, 293, 306n27; strategic synergies in, 294; value acquiring/glamour acquiring in, 294
MacIver, Elizabeth, 36
Main Street, vs. Wall Street, 244
management: accountability, 56, 79–80, 81, 88n3; corporate boards of directors and, xiv–xv, 79–80, 88n3, 207; corporate governance and, 312; directors and, 82–83; earnings, xvi, 64–68; earnings game and, 161, 164, 166, 167; executive compensation and, 113, 125, 127; family-run companies and, 185, 193, 195, 197–198, 200; fiduciary standard and, 80; institutional investors and, xvii, xviii; owners and, 80, 81; private equity firm reorganization principles and, 309, 318, 324; private pension funds and, 208; proposals and voting, 224, 232n55; public companies and, 310;

public pension funds and, 208; shareholders and, 79, 81, 82; U.K. companies and, 58; Wall Street problems with, xvi–xvii

manager(s): analysts and, 167, 168; Business Roundtable and, 244; corporate control and, 243, 310; corporate governance and, 312–313; earnings game and, 164, 166, 167, 168; investors and, 171, 172, 175–176, 177, 181; markets and shortsightedness of, 170; numbers game and, 170; overvalued stock and, 167; remedies for inadequate, 208; shareholders and, 207; stakeholder theory and, 11–12; stakes in M&A profit/loss neighborhood of governance, 300; stock market and, 208. *See also* money managers

manager compensation, 116; arm's-length contracting and, 120; equity compensation and, 131–132; non-equity compensation and, 130–131; in private equity firm reorganization principles, 318. *See also* executive compensation

Manne, Henry, 309

manufacturing productivity research, 247, 248, 249, 272n17; capital investment and, 250, 272n18; corporate control transactions and, 247; corporate restructuring/takeovers and, 250–252, 273nn21–23; R&D and, 250, 251, 273nn19–20

market(s): corporate governance and capital, 311; vs. families and stakeholder theory, 12–14; long-term value and enlightened stakeholder theory, 16; manager shortsightedness and, 170; power grabs in M&A profit/loss neighborhood of strategy, 294; private equity controversies of entry/exit/shifting, 325; regulation of financial, 246, 263; share and profit tradeoff, 6. *See also* corporate control market; private equity markets; stock market; venture market; Wall Street

market for corporate control. *See* corporate control market

Marx, Karl, 81

McVey, Henry, 200

Meckling, W., 198

media: corporate control and, 244, 245, 246, 271n7; corporate inefficiency and, 245; corporate restructuring and, 245, 246, 271n7; hostility towards Wall Street, 244; selection bias, 245, 271n7

MediaGuide, 271n7

Meeker, Mary, 163

mergers and acquisitions (M&A), xi; abnormal returns in, 286–288; buyer firms and, 286–289; conventional wisdom on failure of, 280, 281–283, 304n3, 304n6; corporate control market and, 243; criticisms of conventional wisdom about, 280; executives and, 289; failure in, 280, 281–283, 304n3, 304n6; frame of reference on, 280; as local, 281, 290–291, 301; profit conclusions about, 289–290; profitability measurement, 283–286, 304n8; research surveys, 280, 282, 283–301, 302, 303, 304n8; success in, 280, 281, 283, 286–290; target firms and, 286, 288, 295, 300–301; transactions, 246; value destruction of, xx, 286; value increasing of, xx, 286–290, 294–295. *See also* M&A profit/loss neighborhoods

Merrill Lynch, xvii

Microsoft, 147–148, *149*, 164, 185, 189

Minow, Bob, 48

Minow, Nell, 48, 60

Money Machine, The (Bartlett), 272n3

money managers: CEOs and, 207; private pension funds and, 208; U.S. shareholder activism and, 207

monopoly, and value maximization, 8, 15, 24*n*6
Morgan, J. P., 202
Morgan Stanley, 184, 189, 200
Motorola, 195
multiple objectives: Balanced Scorecard and, 18; handicap of, 7, 23*n*3; as no objective, 7; single-valued objective vs., 5, 7, 23*n*3
Murdoch, Rupert, 61
mutual funds, and U.S. shareholder activism, 207

Nacchio, Joe, 163
NASDAQ corporate governance proposals (2002), 40
net present value (NPV), 65, 66, 201*n*10
New York Stock Exchange (NYSE), 102, *103;* corporate governance proposals (2002), 40; new/former corporate governance rules (2002), 105–107
NextGen, 287
Noe, Christopher, 178
Nortel, xvii, 162; earnings game and, 165–166, 169*n*6
Norton, David, 17–19, 21
NPV. *See* net present value
numbers game: companies and, 170, 182*n*5; disclosure and, 181; investors and, 170, 181; managers and, 170. *See also* earnings game
Numeric Investors L.P., 173, *174*
NYSE. *See* New York Stock Exchange

O. M. Scott, 313, 314
Obama, Barack, 68
O'Neill, Tip, 280
Oracle, 189
organizational structure, 316
overpayment, and U.S. executive compensation, 151–152, 154–155, 157*n*10
overregulation, and U.S. corporate governance, 27

overvalued stock: company damage by, 162–164; managers and, 167
owners: corporate control and, 81; management and, 80, 81; public companies with absentee, 207
ownership: corporate governance research on, 97–98, *99*, 108*n*4; corporate governance research on executive stock, 97–98, *99;* firm value and insider stock, 98, *99;* optimal, 187; performance and, 187; U.S. family-run companies and, 186, 187, 188, 192, 193, 195, 199

Paccar, Inc., 196
Pacific Investment Management, 327
Page, Larry, 170
Palepu, Krishna, 257
Parmalat, 184
pay: executive compensation and improving arrangements for, 135–138; executive compensation and severance, 132–133; and power in executive compensation, 125–129; U.S. executive compensation overpayment, 151–152, 154–155, 157*n*10. *See also* CEO pay; Say on Pay
pay and performance, xvi; executive compensation and, 135; pay and power vs., 125
pay incentives, 146; portfolio incentives vs., 147, *148,* 149, 156*n*6
pay without performance, 113; executive compensation and, 130–133
pension funds: reversions, 272*n*11; U.S. survey (1993), 208–209. *See also* corporate pension funds; private pension funds; public pension funds
pensions, and executive compensation, 138
Pensions and Investments, 207
PepsiCo, 170
performance: buyer firms financial, 288–289; family-run companies, 184,

185, 200n3; incentives and U.S. executive compensation, 144–147, *148, 149, 150,* 155n3, 156n8, 156nn4–6; ownership and, 187; U.S. family-run companies, 184, 185, 190, *191,* 192, *193,* 194, 195, 196, 197, 198, 199, 200n3; U.S. shareholder activism and, 209, 224–225, 232n60. *See also* pay and performance; pay without performance

performance measures: Balanced Scorecard and, 19, 21–22; divisional, 20–21; EVA and, 20; performance drivers and, 20–21, 25n23; in private equity firm reorganization principles, 309, 318; value creation and, 20

Perot, Ross, 83

Petroni, Kathy, 176

Pickens, T. Boone, 204, 205

PIPE. *See* private investment in public equity

politicians: corporate restructuring and, 244; prosecutions and, 246, 272n12

politics: contract problems and, 247–248; corporate control market and, 247–248; of finance in corporate control, 243; of finance in private equity controversies, 326; regulation and, 246

Porter, Michael, 173, 175

portfolio: characteristics of institutional investors, *174;* value and CEO pay/incentives, *150*

portfolio incentives, 146, 153; pay incentives vs., 147, *148,* 149, 156n6

press, and earnings game, 166

private equity: 2007 2nd wave end of, 307, 308; avant garde to mainstream evolution of, 327; corporate control market and, xx; corporate governance/corporate control market reinvention and, 307; funds and U.S. shareholder activism, 203; model, 61–64; research, 308–309, 313; transaction drop-off, 307; U.S. companies and, 59; U.S. corporate governance and, 49, 50

private equity controversies: entry/exit/shifting markets in, 325; incentive dilution in, 325–326, 331n42; politics of finance in, 326; tax code in, 308, 324–325, 331n41

private equity firm(s), xiv; company reorganization and, 310, 315–317, *318,* 329n27; corporate control market and, 308, 321–322; corporate governance and, xx, 61, 313–314, 315, 329n19; corporate governance research on, 313; cost of becoming, 314–315, 329nn22–24; public companies and, xx, xxi, 61, 62–63, 64; reorganization principles of, xx–xxi; U.S. M&A and, xx, 320–321, 330n33. *See also* buyout firms

private equity firm reorganization principles, *318;* boards of directors and, 317; competition and, 318; corporate governance and, 309, 317; credit and, 318–319; debt and, 318; decision-making decentralization in, 318; management and, 309, 318, 324; manager compensation in, 318; performance measures in, 309, 318; public company adoption of, 309

private equity markets: boom-bust cycles in, 308, 328nn6–7; buyouts and, 307; contest for corporate governance rights and, 320–321, 330n28, 330n33; corporate control market and, 308, 324; U.S. corporate control market and, 308, 324

private investment in public equity (PIPE), 322–324, 330n36, 331n40

private pension funds: management and, 208; money managers and, 208; public pension funds and, 209; U.S. shareholder activism and, 207, 209

private placements, 322–324, 330n36, 331n40
privatization, bankruptcy. *See* bankruptcy privatization
profit: conclusions about M&A, 289–290; in M&A profit/loss neighborhood of strategy, 294–295; tradeoff between market share and, 6
profit maximization: social welfare and, 8, 9–10, 24nn6–7, 24nn9–10; value maximization and, 9
Progressive Insurance, 67, 182n5, 183n18, 183n23, 196
proposals: voting on management, 224, 232n55. *See also* bankruptcy reform proposal; corporate governance proposals; shareholder proposals
prosecutions: insider trading, 246; politicians and, 246, 272n12; RICO, 246, 272n12
public companies: with absentee owners, 207; adoption of private equity firm reorganization principles, 309; corporate control market and, 310, 320, 321–322, 330nn29–30; earnings management and, 64–68; LBO firms and, 314; management and, 310; private equity firms and, xx, xxi, 61, 62–63, 64; shareholders and, 61–62; underperforming, 310; U.S. family-run companies and, 184, 199, 200n1. *See also* private investment in public equity
public pension funds: management and, 208; private pension funds and, 209; U.S. shareholder activism and, 206, 207, 208, 209
publicly traded corporations: business activity domination by, ix; U.S., ix

quasi-indexers, xvii, xviii, 172, 173, *174, 175,* 176, 177, 178, 179, *180,* 181. *See also* institutional investors
Qwest, 163

raiders, corporate, x, 62, 243, 244
Raines, Franklin, 132
R&D. *See* research and development (R&D)
Reeb, David, 184, 186, 188, 192, 193
regulation: banks and, 272n13, 277n61; codes, 248; corporate control market and, 263, 269–270, 277n59, 277nn61–62; corporate governance failures and, 330n28; of financial markets, 246, 263; politics and, 246; U.S. corporate governance and over, 27
Relational Investors, 227, 228
relationship investing, 227, 233n72
reorganization, company. *See* company reorganization
research: corporate control transaction, 247; on family-run companies, 184–185, 200n1, 200nn3–5; on institutional investors, xvii, 170, 171–173, *174, 175,* 176–179, *180,* 181, 182n13, 183n18; on M&A, 280, 282, 283–301, *302, 303,* 304n8; private equity, 308–309, 313; on U.S. family-run companies, 184, 185–189, *190, 191, 192, 193,* 194–200, 200n8, 201n17, 201nn14–15. *See also* corporate governance research; manufacturing productivity research
research and development (R&D), manufacturing productivity research and, 250, *251,* 273nn19–20
restructuring, corporate. *See* corporate restructuring
retailing, and bankruptcy, 275n45
return on assets (ROA), 91, 184
return on market value (ROMV), 317
returns: executive compensation and stock, 28; market-based, 286; raw, 285. *See also* abnormal returns
Revco, 262, 331n42
Revenue Reconciliation Act of 1990, 277n62
RICO prosecutions, 246, 272n12

Rite Aid, 197
RJR-Nabisco, 243, 244, 272nn2–4
ROA. *See* return on assets
Robinson, James D., 207
Romano, Roberta, 208
ROMV. *See* return on market value
Rosett, Joshua, 272n11
Roth, John, 165, 166
Ruback, Richard, 309, 321
Russia, 287

Safeway, 271n7, 317
Salomon Brothers, 271n9
Sarbanes-Oxley Act (SOX) (2002), 26, 38–40, 46n32, 51, 70, 330n28
savings and loan (S&L), 246
Say on Pay, 55, 68–69, 70
SBC, 287
Schwab, Stuart, 206
Sears, 52, 58, 225
SEC. *See* Securities and Exchange Commission
Securities and Exchange Commission (SEC), xv, 161, 166, 194, 203, 204; Rule 14a-8 (1943), 229
Securities Industry Association, 168
securities law violations, 246, 272n12
selection bias, 245, 271n7
severance pay, and executive compensation, 132–133
shareholder(s): abnormal returns to buyer firm, 286–288; abnormal returns to target firm, 286, 288; agency conflict and, 185, 200nn4–5; analysts and, 161; antitakeover measures and, 101–102; arm's-length contracting and, 120; boards of directors and, 51, 54, 55, 81, 82, 88, 207; Business Roundtable and, 87–88; CEOs and, 83; corporate boards of directors and, xiv, xv; corporate control transactions and, 245, 246; corporate governance and, 313; corporate governance research on, 98–99, 100–102; directors and, 80–81, 82, 87–88, 89n29; executive compensation and, 55, 68–69, 70, 125, 126, 127, 130; family-run companies and, 185; HLTs and, 245; management and, 79, 81, 82; managers and, 207; public companies and, 61–62; SOX impact on, 38–39; stock market and, 208; stockholders vs., 5; U.S. corporate governance and, 26, 35; U.S. executive compensation and, 55, 68–69
shareholder activism: foreign corporate governance and, 37; U.S. corporate governance and, xviii–xix, 35, 49, 50, 330n32. *See also* U.S. shareholder activism
shareholder democracy, 60; expansion, xiii, 51–53; U.K. model of, 55
shareholder proposals: studies, *210, 211, 212, 213, 214–220,* 221–222, *223,* 224–229, 231n35, 231n38, 231n40, 231n42, 232n45, 232n48, 232n51; U.S. shareholder activism and, 229; voting outcomes of, 222, 223, 224, 232n45, 232n48, 232n51
shares: tradeoff between profit and market, 6; U.S. family-run companies and dual-class, 198–199
Simon Property Group, 196
single-valued objective: better and worse in, 7–8; firm value and, 8; multiple objectives vs., 5, 7, 23n3; scorecard vs., 5; stakeholder theory vs., 6
S&L. *See* savings and loan
Smith, Adam, ix, 81
Smith, Michael, 226
social value, 8
social welfare: profit maximization and, 8, 9–10, 24nn6–7, 24nn9–10; stakeholder theory and, 11; value maximization and, 8–9, 10, 24n6, 24n12

Southwest Airline, 318
SOX. *See* Sarbanes-Oxley Act (2002)
S&P 500, U.S. family-run companies in, 185, 188, 189, *190*, *191*, 192, *193*, 200*n*8
Sperling, John, 197
stakeholder, 4, 23*n*1
stakeholder theory, 22–23, 24*n*17; Balanced Scorecard and, 17; boards of directors and, 11–12; corporate objective and, 4, 5, 8–9; families vs. markets and, 12–14; firm value and, 11; internal control systems and, 12; managers and, 11–12; roots of, 12–14; single-valued objective vs., 6; social welfare and, 11; tradeoffs specification and, 11, 24*n*13; value maximization and, xii, xiii, 4, 5, 10, 11, 12. *See also* Balanced Scorecard
stakeholder theory, enlightened, 5, 15; enlightened value maximization and, 14; long-term market value and, 16; value measurability/imperfect knowledge and, 16–17
"State of U.S. Corporate Governance, The" (Holmstrom and Kaplan), 144
Stein, Jeremy, 260, 261, 264, 276*n*53
Sterling Chemicals, 316, 329*n*27
stock: CEOs and, 147, 156*n*5; price volatility/institutional investors and disclosure, 179, *180*, 181, 183*n*23; restricted, 42, 47*n*36; returns and executive compensation, 28. *See also* overvalued stock
stock exchange. *See* London Stock Exchange; New York Stock Exchange
stock market: boards of directors and, 207–208, 230*n*21; forward looking, 285; managers and, 208; shareholders and, 208; U.S. shareholder activism and short-term reactions of, 213, 221–222, 231*n*40, 231*n*42
stock market, foreign, U.S. stock market and, 28

stock market, U.S.: foreign stock market and, 28; institutional investors and, *205*; U.S. corporate governance and, *27*, 28
stock option grants, 44; executive, xi
stock options: directors and, 99–100; expensing, 43, 47*n*37. *See also* executive stock options
stock ownership: corporate governance research on executive, 97–98, *99*; firm value and insider, 98, *99*
stockholders: earnings game and, 166; shareholders vs., 5
studies: corporate governance proposal, *210*, *211*, 212, 213, *214*–*220*, 221–222, 223, 224–229, 231*n*35, 231*n*38, 231*n*40, 231*n*42, 232*n*45, 232*n*48, 232*n*51; event, 286; LBOs (1980s), 260; shareholder proposal, *210*, *211*, 212, 213, *214*–*220*, 221–222, 223, 224–229, 231*n*35, 231*n*38, 231*n*40, 231*n*42, 232*n*45, 232*n*48, 232*n*51; U.S. shareholder activism (1993), 208–209
Summers, Larry, 54
surveys: Korn Ferry (2002), 37; M&A research, 280, 282, 283–301, *302*, *303*, 304*n*8; U.S. pension funds (1993), 208–209
Symantec Corporation, 170

takeovers, 272*n*11; banks and, 272*n*13; corporate control market and, 243; corporate inefficiency and, 245; HLTs and, 246; manufacturing productivity research and, 250–252, 273*nn*21–23; in the present, 246–247; union wages and, 272*n*11; unsound transactions and, 247. *See also* antitakeover measures; hostile takeovers
target firms: abnormal returns to combined buyer and, 288; abnormal returns to shareholders of, 286, 288; M&A and, 286, 288, 295, 300–301
tax: code in private equity controversies, 308, 324–325, 331*n*41; codes, 248;

exposure in M&A profit/loss neighborhood of deal design, 299
Teachers Insurance and Annuity Association, College Retirement Equities Fund (TIAA-CREF), 209, 212, 221
Texaco, 206, 212
Thomas, Randall, 206
TIAA-CREF. *See* Teachers Insurance and Annuity Association, College Retirement Equities Fund
Time Warner, 287, 322
Tirole, Jean, 208
TPG, 327
tradeoffs: market share and profit, 6; specification and stakeholder theory, 11, 24*n*13; through time and value, 10, 24*nn*11–12
trading, insider. *See* insider trading
transactions: LBO, 272*n*11; M&A, 246; takeovers and unsound, 247. *See also* corporate control transactions; highly leveraged transactions
transient investors, xvii–xviii, 172, 173, *174, 175*, 176, 177, 178, 179, *180*, 181. *See also* institutional investors
transparency, and executive compensation, 133–135
turnkey operations, ix

UBS, 287
UBS A.G., 287
U.K. *See* United Kingdom
U.K. companies: CEOs of, 289; management and, 58; U.S. companies vs., xiv, 56–57, 58
U.K. corporate governance: boards of directors and, 57–58; executive compensation and, 70; U.S. corporate governance vs., 56–57, 58
union: funds and U.S. shareholder activism, 206; wages and takeovers, 272*n*11

United Kingdom (U.K.), xiv; shareholder democracy model of, 55–60
United Shareholders Association (USA), 204
United States (U.S.): criticism of, x–xi; M&A and private equity firms, xx, 320–321, 330*n*33; publicly traded corporations, ix. *See also* stock market, U.S.
Unruh, Jesse, 205, 206
U.S. *See* United States
U.S. Bankruptcy Code (1978), 265
U.S. CEO pay: problems with, xiii, xiv, xvi, 113–114. *See also* CEO pay; executive compensation; U.S. executive compensation
U.S. companies: compensation issues, xv–xvi; hedge funds and, 59; overinvestment, 245; private equity and, 59; U.K. companies vs., xiv, 56–57, 58; underinvestment, 245. *See also* U.S. family-run companies
U.S. corporate control market: development of, 309–311, 328*nn*11–12, 328*nn*14–15; private equity markets and, 308, 324. *See also* corporate control market
U.S. corporate governance: 1980s/1990s changes in, xi, xiii, 27, 29–38, 45*n*11, 45*n*13, 46*n*19, 46*n*27, 49; 2000s regulatory changes, 38–43, 46*n*32, 46*n*35, 47*n*36; boards of directors and, 36–37, 46*n*27, 59; compensation structures, xv; controversies surrounding, xiii–xiv, 44; criticism of external, x; criticism of internal, x; criticism/problems with, x–xii, xvi, 27, 44, 49, 114; current state of, xiii, 26–28; equity-based compensation and, 26, 27; failures/scandals of, 26, 27, 28, 44, 48; foreign corporate governance and, 28, 29, 37–38; GDP and, 29, 44*n*2; institutional investors

U.S. corporate governance (*continued*) and, xviii–xix, *205*; overregulation and, 27; private equity and, 49, 50; reform, 48, 50; shareholder activism and, xviii–xix, 35, 49, 50; shareholders and, 26, 35; U.K. corporate governance vs., 56–57, 58; U.S. executive compensation and, 26, 28, 32–35, 45*n*11, 45*n*13, 46*n*19, 50, 68–76, 114–116; U.S. shareholder activism and, 202, 209, *210, 211,* 212, 213, *214–220,* 221–222, *223,* 224–227, 230*n*6, 231*n*35, 231*n*38, 231*n*40, 231*n*42, 232*n*45, 232*n*48, 232*n*51, 330*n*32; U.S. stock market and, *27,* 28. *See also* corporate governance

U.S. executive compensation: 1980s/1990s changes in, 32–35, 45*n*11, 46*n*19; 2000s regulatory changes and, 38, 41, 42, 43, 46*n*32, 46*n*35; aggregate top-five (1993-2003), 116, *117;* Conference Board recommendations for, 41, 42, 46*n*35; corporate earnings and, 116, *117;* criticism of, 144; incentives and, 144–147, *148, 149, 150,* 151–155, 155*n*3, 156*n*8, 156*nn*4–6, 157*n*10, 157*nn*12–15; overpayment concerns about, 151–152, 154–155, 157*n*10; performance incentives and, 144–147, *148, 149, 150,* 155*n*3, 156*n*8, 156*nn*4–6; shareholders and, 55, 68–69; SOX impact on, 38, 46*n*32; stock returns and, 28; support for, 144–145; U.S. corporate governance and, 26, 28, 32–35, 45*n*11, 45*n*13, 46*n*19, 50, 68–76, 114–116. *See also* CEO pay; executive compensation; U.S. executive compensation

U.S. family-run companies: active family members in, 192, *193;* benefits of, xviii, 186, 193, 200; boards of directors and, 192, *193;* CEOs of, 197, 198; corporate control and, 188, 193–196, 198–199, 200, 201*n*17; costs of, 186, 193, 198–199; debt and, 198; disclosure and, 194; downside of, 186–188; dual-class shares and, 198–199; founders of, 189, 192, 193, 197; long-term focus of, 196; ownership and, 186, 187, 188, 192, 193, 195, 199; performance, 184, 185, 190, *191,* 192, *193,* 194, 195, 196, 197, 198, 199, 200*n*3; in practice, 193–195; public companies and, 184, 199, 200*n*1; recognizing, 188–189, *190;* research on, 184, 185–189, *190, 191,* 192, *193,* 194–200, 200*n*8, 201*n*17, 201*nn*14–15; in S&P 500, 185, 188, 189, *190, 191,* 192, *193,* 200*n*8; value creation and, 196. *See also* family-run companies

U.S. shareholder activism: agency conflicts and, 207; boards of directors and, 212; company targets of, 209, 226–227, 232*n*67; corporate governance proposals studies on, *210, 211,* 212, 213, *214–220,* 221–222, *223,* 224–229, 231*n*35, 231*n*38, 231*n*40, 231*n*42, 232*n*45, 232*n*48, 232*n*51; costs/benefits of, 209; directors and, 212; effectiveness of, 212–213, *214–220,* 224–225; evolution of, 202–203, 330*n*32; hedge funds and, 203, 206, 209, 227–229, 230*n*3, 233*n*72; institutional investors and, 205, 206–207, 208, 209, 212–213, *214–220,* 229; money managers and, 207; motives for, 207–209; mutual funds and, 207; performance and, 209, 224–225, 232*n*60; private equity funds and, 203; private pension funds and, 207, 209; public pension funds and, 206, 207, 208, 209; shareholder proposals and, 229; short history of, 204–205; short-term stock market reactions and, 213, 221–222, 231*n*40, 231*n*42; study (1993), 208–209; union funds and, 206; U.S. corporate governance and, 202, 209, *210, 211,*

212, 213, *214–220*, 221–222, 223, 224–227, 230n6, 231n35, 231n38, 231n40, 231n42, 232n45, 232n48, 232n51; varieties of, 203–204. *See also* shareholder activism
USA. *See* United Shareholders Association

valuation multiples, 91, 108n1
value: acquiring in M&A profit/loss neighborhoods, 294–295; CEO pay/incentives and portfolio, *150;* of corporate control transactions (1976-1990), 245, 271n8; enlightened stakeholder theory and long-term market, 16; net present, 65, 66, 201n10; return on market, 317; seeking and corporate objective, 7; as social value, 8; tradeoffs through time and, 10, 24nn11–12. *See also* Economic Value Added; firm value; overvalued stock; single-valued objective
value creation: performance measure and, 20; U.S. family-run companies and, 196
Value Line, 177
value maximization, xviii, 21; corporate objective and, 4, 5, 7, 8; corporations and, 253–254, 274nn32–33; externality problems and, 8, 15; monopoly and, 8, 15, 24n6; profit maximization and, 9; social welfare and, 8–9, 10, 24n6, 24n12; stakeholder theory and, xii, xiii, 4, 5, 10, 11, 12; total firm, 7–8

value maximization, enlightened, xiii, 5, 15; enlightened stakeholder theory and, 14; value measurability/imperfect knowledge and, 16–17
venture market: boom-bust cycles in, 248, 260–261; contract failure and LBOs, 260–263, 276nn53–55, 277nn56–57
Viacom, 191

Wall Street: CEO problems with, xvi–xvii; earnings game and, 161, 162, 164, 165, 168; Main Street vs., 244; management problems with, xvi–xvii; media hostility towards, 244; walk, 203. *See also* market
Wall Street Journal, 197, 221, 271n7, 272n4, 281
Wal-Mart, 188, 189, 290
Wang Laboratories, 199
Wanniski, Jude, 271n7
Wasserstein, Bruce, 291
Wealth of Nations, The (Smith), ix
Whitmore, Kay, 207
windfalls: in bonuses, 136; equity incentives and, 152–153; in equity-based compensation, 131–132, 135–136; executive compensation and, 131–132, 135–136
workouts, and corporate control market, 263–264
WorldCom, xv, 330n28
W. W. Grainger, 195

Xerox, 245